ISRAEL'S IMPACT, 1950-51

A Personal Record

Allen Lesser

UNIVERSITY
PRESS OF
AMERICA

LANHAM • NEW YORK • LONDON

All University Press of America books are produced on acid-free
paper which exceeds the minimum standards set by the National
Historical Publications and Records Commission.

For My Children

LARRY, HOWARD, SUSAN and HANNA

And My Grandchildren

LAUREN and ADAM

To Whom All This Is History

CONTENTS

v

THE **JEWISH NEWSLETTER**
AHEAD OF   THE NEWS

Cross-Section U.S.A.

PRIVATELY CIRCULATED
**NOT FOR PUBLICATION
WITHOUT PERMISSION**
Editor & Publisher
ALLEN LESSER
1133 BROADWAY, NEW YORK 10, N.Y.
Subscription $10. per year

VOL. IV, NO. 19   (Whole Number 97)   NOVEMBER 8, 1951

** ACCORDING TO PLAN: Four top executives of the New York Association
for New Americans have received notice that their jobs will end by February 1, 1952, and that NYANA itself will probably close shop by July 1,
an exclusive report from very reliable sources revealed this week. At
least one of the executives has left as of Oct. 31. Head of NYANA is
Louis Bennett, who took the job in 1949 on a 3-year contract. NYANA was
set up by United Service for New Americans on July 5, 1949, to take care
of immigrants--mostly DPs--who settled in N.Y. area. Hard-core cases
will be taken over either by other agencies or placed on the public relief rolls.
        Similar procedure is being urged on local communities elsewhere by
USNA, which will received considerably less money from UJA in 1952 than
it did this year.
        Last week, spokesmen for NYANA, USNA and CJFWF all denied knowledge
of any "impending changes" in answer to CROSS-SECTION's queries.

                        The Newsletter

                             vi

INTRODUCTION

This is a personal record based on one man's on-the-spot report of events, personalities and organizations in the American Jewish community during the years 1950 and 1951, showing how they were affected by the new state of Israel and what changes took place after an uneasy armistice was imposed in 1948 by the United Nations on Israel and her Arab neighbors.

In 1950, I began to publish **Cross-Section, U.S.A.**, a national weekly newsletter, out of New York in order to report the new directions and other developments affecting American Jews and their institutions. At about the same time, I was carrying on a weekly exchange of correspondence with Joseph Leftwich, an English journalist and writer, whom I had met earlier in New York through mutual friends. My letters to him were concerned largely with the problems I faced in covering the news and the rumors about Jewish leaders and their organizations. Although the newsletter was public and my correspondence private, they were generally complimentary, one often supplementing the other. Together they provide an insight into many of the changes that took place in reaction to the miraculous revival of the state of Israel after two thousand years of Jewish dispersion.

New York was the center of Jewish communal activity, and my newsletter was able to report many details about decisions, developments and personnel changes that were not recorded in the contemporary press. **Cross-Section, U.S.A.** was completely independent, and it appeared weekly. It was mimeographed on four sides of a folded foolscap-sized sheet and was distributed by first-class mail. Although it never achieved a circulation of more than a thousand subscribers, it enjoyed considerable influence and was often quoted in the English Jewish press. It ceased publication as an independent newsletter at the close of 1951, when I ran out of funds, but continued for another year and a half as a syndicated column in the English Jewish press.

During the terms of President Harry Truman and President Dwight D. Eisenhower, the Middle East and Israel in particular became the center of increasing

vii

American attention, highlighted by the Jewish refugee
problem in the wake of World War II, and the opposition
of the British and the French to the resettlement of
the refugees in Israel. The extent of American interest
was manifested when the United Nations proposal for the
internationalization of Jerusalem became a political
issue in the 1949 New York Senatorial campaign that
pitted the Democratic incumbent, Herbert H. Lehman,
against the Republican candidate, John Foster Dulles.
Later, in the decade of the cold war, the United States
became a Mediterranean power and signified its involve-
ment in the Middle East by President Eisenhower's order
dispatching the Marines to Lebanon in order to scotch
a threatened civil war. In the context of the increasing American role in the Middle East, the impact of a
sovereign Israel on American Jews and their communal
agencies, in particular, was staggering.

For American Jews, the emergence of Israel as a
nation meant that new relationships had to be established, organizational ideologies defined and traditional programs reevaluated, objectives had to be
changed or dropped altogether, and methods of operation
reexamined. It was a soul-searching period. After 1948,
what were to be the new directions and goals of the
powerful Zionist Organization of America (ZOA), the
largest Jewish organization in the world? What was its
relationship to the new government of Israel, and how
were their responsibilities to be divided? What should
be the limits on the functions of the formerly all-
inclusive Jewish Agency, and how were its activities
in Israel to be separated from the Israel government's
functions? Which goals should Hadassah, the Jewish
National Fund (JNF), the religious and other American
Zionist organizations pursue now that their major task
of establishing the state of Israel had been achieved?

Some major decisions made immediately after the
state was declared gave an indication of the direction
future actions would take. For example, it became imperative to reorganize the World Zionist Organization
(WZO) and its operating arm, the Jewish Agency, because
they had served as a kind of government-in-exile for
the Jewish people. Obviously, Israeli government leaders could not at the same time conduct or be responsible for the activities of a voluntary international
agency such as the World Zionist Organization. To avoid
any conflict of interest, Prime Minister David Ben-
Gurion, who had been chairman of the Jewish Agency,
and other officers of the WZO who became officers of
Israel's government therefore had to resign. Before

1948, the Jewish Agency had full responsibility for the transportation, resettlement and education of Jewish refugees in mandated Israel; after independence was declared, it found itself so completely overwhelmed by the flood of European immigrants that it had to call upon the Israel government for help. In the process, it necessarily had to agree to a limitation of its authority.

Prior to 1948, coordination of fundraising for Israel had been a major task of the ZOA. All funds for Israel went to the United Palestine Appeal (UPA), which was a constituent organization of the United Jewish Appeal (UJA). But by 1950, Ben-Gurion, fearful of the power that the ZOA might exert through its fundraising potential and mindful of earlier internal Zionist fights for control, moved to transfer authority over UPA from the ZOA to an ad hoc group in the UJA headed by Henry Montor, Rudolf G. Sonneborn and Abraham Feinberg. This move also had the approval of the major Jewish welfare funds and Hadassah as well as some smaller Zionist parties, who were not unhappy to see the grip of the ZOA on fundraising weakened.

As far as the Israelis were concerned, Zionism by 1950 was no longer a functioning ideology. From their point of view, the sole remaining major function of Zionism in the Diaspora was to encourage **aliya**, that is, emigration to Israel--and to provide the funds for it. American Zionists, on the other hand, insisted on the continuing mission of Herzlian Zionism but literally did not know what to do to keep the mission going. To begin with, they agreed on a program of establishing projects in Israel that would help in building up the state. Hadassah assumed responsibilities for health care; the Labor Zionists, though numerically weak in the United States, were the governing party in Israel and they therefore concentrated their Israel efforts on social welfare projects. The ZOA, composed of general Zionists, after considerable groping and fumbling, decided on such special projects as schools, recreation camps, and a ZOA cultural house in Tel Aviv. None of these efforts was entirely responsive, however, and the question of the role of Zionism in America after the establishment of the state of Israel remained unresolved.

At least one American Jewish leader was bold enough to say that Zionism and the ZOA had fulfilled their mission with the establishment of the state of Israel and now should be dissolved. Writing in the **Congress Weekly** in December 1948, David Petegorsky, the

executive director of the American Jewish Congress, ob-
served--a little too hastily--that "the Zionist movement evokes the disciplined loyalty of a proportion-
ately decreasing section of American Jewry. The full
and effective mobilization of political action for
Israel in this country can be achieved today only by a
much more inclusive and all-embracing body than the
Zionist Organization of America."

American defense agencies faced no less a dilemma
than the Zionists. For years their fundraising appeal
had enjoyed top priority in the American Jewish community; now Israel's needs preempted that position.
Was the fight against anti-Semitism to remain the major
activity of the American Jewish Committee, the Anti-
Defamation League of the B'nai B'rith (ADL), the American Jewish Congress and the Jewish Labor Committee
notwithstanding the sharp decline in anti-Jewish mani-
festations in the wake of the new state of Israel? How
should the infiltration of communists be handled? Of
equal concern to the community were the questions about
the way in which the annual fundraising drives in each
locality were to be managed, especially who was to make
the decisions on the distribution of funds. How much
was to go Israel; how much was to remain here for domestic local and national philanthropies?

It was all very confusing, and questions of ever-
increasing complexities continued to be raised. Additionally, the Federal government's policy toward Israel
and the Arab countries served to compound Jewish organizational difficulties.

Against this background, **Cross-Section, U.S.A.**
(hereinafter referred to as the Newsletter) dutifully
recorded the interplay of issues and personalities, and
the rise of new leadership in American Jewish ranks. At
the same time, much that was not hard news but was only
rumor or speculation, gossip or suspicion, found its
way into the letters I wrote to Leftwich. I had made it
a principle to print only hard news in the Newsletter
and to label any other reports that were not, but what
I wrote in my private correspondence was never tidy
enough to be regarded as history. In any case, I was
not consciously writing a history in either medium; I
was simply reporting the day-to-day events that took
place in a lively community as well as the things I
heard in passing but could not always verify. Complete
files of the Newsletter may be found in the libraries
of the American Jewish Committee and the American Jewish Archives.

It was an advantage that I was born and grew up in

New York City and was educated in its public schools. In Boys High School, I majored in Latin and history, studies that I continued at New York University. I took little part in school activities, however, and scored only average grades. The year after I was graduated, the country was plunged into the deepest economic depression in its history, and the scars left on me by that experience have never fully healed. In the early 1930s, after I had earned a Master of Arts degree in education, teaching jobs in the New York schools were highly valued, but the competition for each position was fierce and the examiners ruthless. I managed somehow to complete the difficult written and oral English examinations successfully but I was nevertheless denied a teaching license because of a slight speech impediment. Eventually, I landed a job with the English Jewish weekly edited by the famous Rabbi Stephen S. Wise and his son James at the munificent salary of $15 a week. It served as my introduction to the Jewish communal world and confirmed my career as a journalist, the taste for which I had acquired in my high school days when I briefly covered some sports events for the **Brooklyn Daily Eagle.**

Some years later, I was fortunate enough to become the assistant editor of the prestigious **The Menorah Journal,** a quarterly of Jewish cultural and humanistic writing. It had once been the monthly organ of the Intercollegiate Menorah Society under the leadership of the brilliant Henry Hurwitz, but it had fallen upon difficult days during the depression following the dissolution of the college clubs. Though my tenure at **The Menorah Journal** in the late 1930s was short, my friendship with Henry Hurwitz continued to the end of his life many years later. He not only encouraged me to write, but he also taught me how to be a good editor. He was a wonderful teacher and an inspiration to many famous American writers as well as artists in other fields, who owe their initial opportunity and encouragement to Henry Hurwitz.

In those pre-World War II days, anti-Semitism in the United States had reached an all-time peak of intensity. The rantings of Father Charles E. Coughlin on nationwide radio, his nationally circulated paper, **Social Justice,** and the flood of anti-Semitic materials he inspired provided American Jews with a frightening background to accompany the rise of Nazism in Europe. The agitation brought American Jews close to a state of panic and intensified their demands upon the small and ineffectual community agencies for action.

At that time, the ADL and the American Jewish Committee were just beginning to recruit staff and develop programs to meet the challenge of the bigots. In 1937 I joined the staff of the American Jewish Committee as a writer and remained there for almost six years. During most of that time, I was the managing editor of the **Contemporary Jewish Record,** a monthly magazine, which was the American Jewish Committee's first venture into the periodical field. It provided among its many features a graphic record of the Nazi decrees against Jews and the way they were implemented. It contained the first details of the Holocaust. I had no editor but was responsible to an editorial board, and the experience sharpened and enlarged my knowledge of organizational management as well as the American Jewish community. As editor, it was also possible for me to give many emigre writers, among them Thomas Mann and Hannah Arendt, their earliest opportunity to be published in this country after their escape from Nazi Germany. Another writer who was sent to me for an assignment, a young journalist just returned from Europe, was Alan Cranston; and he provided the magazine with an article on "Congress and the Alien Act."

Two years after I left the American Jewish Committee, the **Contemporary Jewish Record** was revamped under a new editor and renamed **Commentary.**

The United States was at war with Germany and Japan when I left, and I had hoped to serve in the armed forces. When I was rejected for physical reasons, however, I went to work for the Office of War Information. There I became editor of the **European Intelligence Digest,** a daily publication of news about people and conditions inside Nazi-occupied Europe; it was the forerunner of the present **Foreign Broadcast Information Service,** currently distributed by the U.S. Department of Commerce.

After the war, I was appointed editor of the **Jewish News,** a weekly newspaper published by the Essex County Jewish Community Council, in Newark, N.J. This became an intensive first-hand experience in dealing with an active local community. It also gave me an opportunity to experiment with a tabloid newspaper which would reflect the excitement as well as the limitations of local news reporting.

Two years later, my old friend Henry Hurwitz invited me to come back to **The Menorah Journal** as its managing editor. Somehow he had kept the quarterly going during the war years, although at times he was unable to print more than one issue a year, a situation which kept him in perennial hot water with the post office, whose officials bureaucratically insisted that he had to publish four times a year in order to keep his second-class mailing permit. While fending off the post office with one hand and bankruptcy with the other, Henry nevertheless managed to find new friends who were willing to help him continue the magazine. With this renewed financial strength, Henry declared himself ready to launch a new crusading effort to reform the American Jewish community.

Stirred by the establishment of the state of Israel, Henry had developed a plan for community reform which I was asked to implement. It was an extraordinarily ambitious undertaking, calling for an in-depth investigation into the activities, fundraising and accounting methods of the American Jewish Committee, the ADL, the American Jewish Congress and the Jewish Telegraphic Agency (JTA). Despite our limited resources, however, the investigations were brought to a successful conclusion and the resulting reports published in successive issues of **The Menorah Journal**, where they attracted nationwide attention. The conditions I exposed in these articles shook up the powerful communal agencies and led to a much-needed housecleaning. Although their budgets and financial reports had previously been kept secret, **The Menorah Journal's** expose impelled the defense agencies to submit them to the Council of Jewish Federations and Welfare Funds, which released them for publication in the **American Jewish Year Book**. Regrettably, however, none of these reports was audited, as **The Menorah Journal** had insisted was essential for the moral health of the community, but their publication was a long overdue step forward.

In order to continue the objectives of community reform and the elimination of agency secrecy where public funds were concerned, I decided to publish the Newsletter. I had to resign from **The Menorah Journal** in order to do it, but I had managed to accumulate enough money to support my family for at least two years. I gambled that in that time the Newsletter would become self-supporting. To maintain the independence of the Newsletter, I was resolved not to seek any sponsors, or to launch any fundraising appeals. The Newsletter had to survive on the basis of subscriptions alone, and I learned too late that in the Jewish field at $10 a year that was not possible.

To attract attention, I began the new publication with an analysis of the complex way the Jewish community funds its organizations. It was the first time

anyone had attempted to trace the connecting and inter-
connecting trails by which funds raised primarily for
Israel were actually disbursed, with consequences which
are related in some detail in the first two chapters of
this book. As subsequent pages illustrate, fundraising
for Israel left its mark on every facet of community
organizational life.

I owe much for advice and encouragement to Dr.
Howard M. Sachar, professor of history at George Washington University, who read critically many early chapters of this book. His criticisms and suggestions have
proved invaluable.

A.L.

1

THE UNITED FUNDRAISING EFFORT

Jewish philanthropy is a phenomenon on American soil. Charity on a nationwide scale at the million dollar level was entirely unknown before the rise of the United Jewish Appeal (UJA). To make fundraising on this large scale possible, the Jewish community had to develop a discipline which is outstanding. It is all the more remarkable because it is voluntary, self-imposed as part of a community responsibility. There are no enforceable sanctions to compel acceptance of that responsibility or to enforce that discipline, nothing save community recognition, yet each year Jews raise hundreds of millions of dollars for a wide variety of Jewish institutions and causes both domestic and overseas. The need to help Israel, especially in the rescue of persecuted Jews and the resettlement of homeless refugees, is the priority appeal.

Unlike Jewish communities in other countries, the American Jewish community of the 20th century is united by its philanthropy rather than by its religion. Out of a traditional religious concern for poor and needy Jews, and the religious teaching that each Jew is personally responsible for the welfare of his brothers, American Jewish philanthropy has grown to its present level. Every community conducts its own fundraising drive annually at a time of the year convenient to its leading citizens, usually in the spring or the autumn. The proceeds are then distributed among local institutions and national agencies. The success of this arrangement has set the fundraising pattern for most other secular American social services, a distinct Jewish contribution to the American scene.

Much of the success of the fundraising drives can be attributed to the fact that donations are tax exempt, with the one notable exception of the sale of Israel bonds. Guidance and direction are provided by the Council of Jewish Federations and Welfare Funds (CJFWF), a national umbrella organization of the local community welfare funds. While the actual fundraising is directed

1

by professionals, the leaders of the appeal and the members of the committee which determines the distribution
of funds are prominent local citizens. The largest proportion of the funds they raise is turned over to the
UJA, a national fundraising and coordinating agency.
UJA in turn divides the funds among its three constituent agencies, the United Palestine Appeal (UPA), the
Joint Distribution Committee (JDC), and the United Service for New Americans (USNA). This was the arrangement
in 1950.

Under the leadership of UJA director Henry Montor,
this evolutionary philanthropic Jewish structure had
grown to such enormous and complex proportions by January 1950 that the Newsletter, in an attempt to describe
the web of cross-fertilizing beneficiaries of that philanthropy, was able to draw the following picture:

> Apart from the national UJA, at least 19
> organizations who requested funds from the
> community Combined Appeals, Federations and
> Welfare Funds in 1949 based their appeal in
> whole or part on the grounds of rendering aid
> to Israel. Among them are such diverse agen-
> cies as the Jewish Labor Committee, the Na-
> tional Council of Jewish Women, JTA, HIAS
> (Hebrew Immigrant Aid Society) and the Pales-
> tine Symphonic Choir.
>
> The following maze indicates the need-
> lessly wasteful manner of obtaining and dis-
> tributing funds raised in local communities:
>
> (1) Despite UJA "crisis" appeals for aid
> to Israel, the UPA still receives about
> $10,000,000 less than JDC-USNA as its share of
> the campaign. UPA grants funds to the Jewish
> National Fund (JNF) and the Palestine Founda-
> tion Fund; also to the Zionist Organization of
> America (ZOA) and other American Zionist
> groups. Thus, the actual amount reaching
> Israel is considerably less than UPA's share
> ($49,796,000 in 1948).
>
> (2) Hadassah makes grants to JNF, which
> also receives funds from UPA; and to the Jew-
> ish Agency for Youth Aliya, which also re-
> ceives funds from UPA, from the Pioneer
> Women's Organization, and from the Mizrachi
> Women's Organization. Hadassah also makes
> grants to the Hebrew University Medical
> School, which also receives funds from the
> American Friends of the Hebrew University.

(3) The American Friends of the Hebrew University, which appeals to the community federations and welfare funds, also receives funds from the National Council of Jewish Women, JDC, JNF, UPA and the Jewish Agency.

(4) JDC, which received funds from UJA, makes grants to Palestine institutions which are included in the appeal of the American Fund for Palestine Institutions, which receives funds from local federations and welfare funds.

(5) The Labor Zionist Committee, the fundraising body of the Pioneer Women's Organization (which makes grants to the Jewish Agency for Youth Aliya), the Poale-Zion Organization and the Jewish National Workers' Alliance, appeals to local federations and welfare funds in order to provide relief to Labor Zionists in Europe and Israel. JDC claims that this relief duplicates its own work in these areas.

(6) Histadruth (General Federation of Jewish Labor), which runs an independent campaign in the United States, makes grants to the Weizmann Institute, which appeals directly to local federations and welfare funds.

(7) The Jewish Agency, whose recent advertisements in the general and Jewish press warned contributors against campaigns which it had not "authorized," looks the other way when certain Zionist agencies launch drives in direct competition with community federations and welfare fund campaigns, most of whose funds go the UJA, which raises funds for Israel.

The Newsletter analysis, dated January 4, concludes in some exasperation with the following rhetorical question:

Will some wizard--mathematical or otherwise--please come forward and tell us (1) Why this chaotic fundraising jungle can't be replaced by one drive for Israel only, without tacked-on national agencies, and (2) How much money raised in our communities actually does arrive in Israel?

This competition in fundraising for Israel was accompanied by appeals from national Zionist and non-Zionist organizations for specific projects which they had sponsored and were conducting in Israel. The potential dangers inherent in such competition were pointed out by the Newsletter in the following report:

> While the Israel government, fearful of offending American Jewish sensibilities, nods tolerantly, American Jewish organizations are having a field day in Israel with their pet projects designed for maximum fundraising appeal in the United States. Among recent instances are:
>
> **Example 1:** "Information" centers have been opened by B'nai B'rith (District Grand Lodge Office in Jerusalem) to serve Ben B'rith tourists;
>
> ZOA House in Tel Aviv (now under construction);
>
> YM-YWHA in Jerusalem (affiliated with National Jewish Welfare Board);
>
> American Jewish Committee plans, which included expansion of services at its offices at 4 Shapiro Street, Tel Aviv, have been held up pending results of the 1950 Joint Defense Appeal (JDA) campaign.
>
> **Example 2:** Most Americans regard Hadassah's contribution to Israel in terms of Youth Aliya and medical care; ORT (Organization for Rehabilitation through Training) in terms of vocational training. Last week, Rabbi M.C. Weiler, honorary president of the South African ORT, told a luncheon meeting of the ORT board of directors in New York City: "ORT in Israel is necessary because of the influx of new immigrants who have no trades."
>
> Nevertheless, a Jewish Agency report discloses that Hadassah has just opened a Hotel Management Institute in Jerusalem to train candidates in hotel management and "technology"--preferably young Americans--in anticipation of the expected tourist rush. A fashion institute to train designers and mass production pattern makers was also opened recently as part of Hadassah's Brandeis Vocational Center in Jerusalem. The $400,000 "expansion program" for vocational education was begun lsat year.

Also in the competition for training refugee girls is the vocational program of the newly revived Women's League for Israel.

The danger for Israel lies in the unchecked introduction of the vicious American practice of fragmentation and the implied insult to the Israeli government, which is treated like a poor relation rather than a sovereign government. Proper corrective would be an American Joint Palestine Appeal which would bypass all splinter groups and turn funds over directly to the Jewish Agency.

Given the emergency created in these early years by the rush of immigrants to Israel, most of whom were penniless and in need of all kinds of assistance, and the desperate appeals of the Israel government for financial help in resettling these refugees as well as in providing for their defense against Arab terrorist attacks, it is small wonder that American Jewish organizations improvised various methods of assistance while at the same time taking advantage of the situation to expand the scope of their operations. Local federations and welfare funds, however, faced with a multiplicity of appeals for more and more money began to insist upon consolidation of the fundraising drives. This effort had the support of the national leaders and the UJA, and as a result achieved some successes. On a national level, the Jewish Agency spearheaded an effort to eliminate some campaigns and was able to persuade a number of groups, such as the Poale Agudath Israel and the Agudath Israel of America, a branch of the world union of Orthodox Jews, to give up their campaigns in exchange for a fixed allocation from the 1950 UJA appeal. The Jewish Agency was able to justify the consolidation agreement because the funds received by these organizations were to be used for their coreligionists in Israel.

As part of their campaign, UJA leaders made a special effort to publicize the fact that there was a broad community representation in their planning and budgeting. The Atlantic City conference, which set the 1950 UJA "minimum" goal at $272,455,888--a staggering sum for that time--was ostensibly a community decision; in fact, however, all the goals and procedures had been set well in advance by the professional fundraising staff headed by Henry Montor. Born in Nova Scotia in 1905, this extraordinary and complex man won recognition not only as a genius in the field of fundraising but he was also acclaimed in 1960 by Prime Minister David Ben-

Gurion as one of the "10 individuals most responsible
for the creation of the State of Israel." Montor was
brought to Pittsburgh when he was two years old, but his
parents moved again to Steubenville, Ohio, where he grew
up. Apparently he intended to become a rabbi because he
transferred from the University of Cincinnati to the
Hebrew Union College in that city.

In 1925, Montor suddenly left Cincinnati for New
York accompanied by rumors of a scandal involving the
wife of a professor at the Hebrew Union College. He
changed his name from Henry Goldberg to its French
equivalent, Henry Montor, and landed a job as assistant
editor of the **New Palestine,** the magazine published by
the ZOA. His initial training in fundraising came on the
job when he advanced from publicity director of the
United Palestine Appeal to its executive director. In
1937, when the United Jewish Appeal for Refugees and
Overseas Needs was launched as the combined appeal of
the UPA and the JDC, he was named executive vice president. The UJA goal that year was $20 million. Montor
counted among his friends most large contributors to
Jewish causes, but his closest friends were the American
philanthropist Rudolf G. Sonneborn and Israel's Finance
Minister Eliezer Kaplan.

Prior to the establishment of Israel, Montor had
been the most trusted UJA staff professional of Rabbi
Abba Hillel Silver, one of the most outstanding Zionist
leaders of the day. Other veteran Zionists, however, did
not have the same confidence in Montor as Silver did.
For example, former ZOA president Emanuel Neumann, a
very close associate of Rabbi Silver, in his autobiographical memoir, entitled **In the Arena**, describes Montor as "an able and dynamic organizer and director,
though at times as later became apparent, rather erratic
in his doings." Golda Meir, later Israel's Prime Minister, also knew Montor and characteristically minced no
words in her description of the man. She had met him
for the first time in 1948, and in her autobiography,
entitled **My Life,** she describes Montor as "brusque,
gifted and deeply concerned with Israel, a slave driver
who mercilessly drove himself as well as others in the
attempt to raise ever larger sums of money."

It was this insatiable ambition rather than any
ideological differences that led to Montor's break with
Rabbi Silver and the Zionists. It occurred at a meeting
of the executive committee of the American Zionist
Emergency Council as early as 1944. Stressing his support for the official Zionist policy that establishment
of an independent state was a primary goal of the move-

ment, Montor nevertheless argued that more funds could be raised if the emphasis on the establishment of a Jewish state were reduced and priority be given to a clear drive for "free immigration" into Palestine. Thereby, he explained, the American Jewish community could be united more easily. He was probably correct in his assumption that non-Zionists were more likely to contribute and that more money could be raised in this way, but he should have realized that his recommendation was reopening the wounds of an earlier Zionist ideological fight on the same issue. The members of the committee were outraged and Rabbi Silver immediately rejected Montor's proposal. When Montor persisted in his argument and threatened to resign if his recommendation was voted down, Rabbi Silver promptly accepted his resignation from the committee.

Montor's break with Rabbi Silver apparently was a calculated first step in a strategy designed to wrest control of fundraising for Israel from the leadership of the ZOA. Information pieced together from various sources indicates that in 1945, when David Ben-Gurion came to New York seeking financial help for the Jewish settlements in Palestine, the Yishuv, he was given a very cool reception by Rabbi Silver and other ZOA officials, and his appeal for funds was treated with considerably less urgency than he felt it deserved. Angered, he was directed to Henry Montor, and in a meeting between the two men held on June 25, 1945, he spelled out exactly what he needed.

Montor promptly called on his wealthy friend Rudolf G. Sonneborn. Without hesitation they agreed to help Ben-Gurion, and together they got on the telephone and began calling a select group of friends. They gave as few details as possible and invited their friends to a secret meeting to be held in Sonneborn's duplex bachelor apartment on East 57th Street. July 1, 1945, was a blistering hot day and the apartment was not air conditioned. Nevertheless, the meeting which began at 9:30 in the morning lasted 11 hours and no one left. Ben-Gurion, flanked by Eliezer Kaplan, Reuven Shiloah, Ya'acov Dori and Meyer Weisgal, outlined his plan for the establishment of the independent state of Israel and spelled out in detail the Yishuv's need for guns, tanks, and all the military necessities for a Jewish army. No one was allowed to take notes on what was said and no names of those present were recorded. It was all very secretive, very conspiratorial, and when the meeting was over, the Yishuv was more than a million dollars richer.

From that day on, Sonneborn became a staunch backer
of Henry Montor. As a young man fresh out of the U.S.
Naval Air Force, Sonneborn had been persuaded in 1919 to
visit Palestine by Supreme Court Justice Louis D.
Brandeis. Accompanying him on the trip were Robert Szold
and Dr. Harry Friedenwald, and these veteran Zionists
left a lasting impression on the young millionaire.
Afterward he became the youngest member of the first
American Zionist Commission, an experience which confirmed his enthusiasm for Zionism and his love for
Israel.

Montor's break with the Zionists was complete after
the state was established. He had charged the ZOA with
using funds obtained from the UPA for political ends in
Israel; ZOA in turn opposed the renomination of Montor
as director of UJA in January 1949. In this fight he had
the support of Henry Morgenthau, Jr., who insisted that
he would not accept the new position of chairman of the
UJA unless Montor was retained as the executive vice-
chairman. Morgenthau had been Secretary of the Treasury
under President Franklin Delano Roosevelt and had
brought considerable prestige to the UJA. The issue was
put up to Prime Minister Ben-Gurion, who naturally up-
held the Morgenthau-Montor position. Thereupon, Rabbi
Abba Hillel Silver and Dr. Emanuel Neumann promptly
resigned from the Jewish Agency, leaving Montor the victor and free to solidify his position as director of all
fundraising for Israel.

Montor not only had the backing of the leaders of
Israel, he also had the support of the Jewish community
leaders in thirty of the largest welfare funds in the
United States. These community representatives had
called for the overhauling of the UPA, and in accordance
with their recommendations, it was reorganized as an
independent agency with authority to disburse funds in
the United States as well as Israel, a change which, in
effect, gave Montor enormous power. He had dealt the ZOA
a crippling blow by stripping it of its leadership in
fundraising for Israel while he, Montor, was now in a
position to consolidate all Zionist fundraising. Hadassah and the Mizrachi had supported Montor and were
not unhappy to see the ZOA's power reduced.

From this new towering position of authority, the
"Fund Raiser," as the Israelis now called Montor, was
able to institute his plan for raising more funds than
ever before from the American Jewish community. Beginning in 1950, he put before the communities what was
then regarded as the most daring and radical proposal
in fundraising history: a demand upon each community

to guarantee in advance of its campaign that it would allocate a specific percentage of its funds to UJA. Since Montor's advance allocation demand, especially on some of the larger communities, ran as high as 75 percent, the result was an almost immediate cry of shock followed by an outburst of indignation. Outraged local community leaders threatened to break away from the UJA and run their own campaigns. Local organizations also saw in the pre-campaign percentage allocation a threat to their very existence and warned that they would be forced to undertake independent fund drives, a consequence no one wanted.

On January 18, the Newsletter reported that the following communities were actually in open revolt against the Montor plan:

> Not only Chicago but also Baltimore, Hartford (Conn.) and several other communities are up in arms against the UJA demand for a guaranteed percentage allocation in advance of the 1950 campaign. The Chicago dispute may be settled by a compromise giving UJA about 55 percent of the campaign receipts--a sharp defeat for UJA and Henry Montor, its chief negotiator--but so far a complete break is indicated only in Hartford. In Los Angeles, UJA adherents won an allocation of 70 percent, an increase of 8 percent over 1949, but only after bitter opposition from the local Federation of Jewish Welfare Organizations, which threatened to "secede" and run its own campaign.
>
> Those who suspected the rubber-stamp character of the much-publicized community representation at the UJA Atlantic City conference, which set the $272,455,888 "minimum" goal, are now saying: "I told you so!"

Montor apparently had anticipated resistance to his demands and was prepared to negotiate with community leaders. In Chicago, after several weeks of hard bargaining, he was able to reach an agreement much more to to his liking than the earlier reports had indicated. In February, the Newsletter reported that a settlement had been reached in Chicago along the following lines:

> The current issue of **New Palestine**, ZOA organ, editorializes on the conflict between Chicago and the UJA over the percentage of campaign proceeds to be allocated as follows:

"The die is cast. The United Jewish Appeal seems destined to have its own distinct campaign for Chicago apart from drives for funds for local needs. Last week an agreement giving UJA 64 percent of campaign proceeds up to $6,500,000, less percentage for shrinking, was announced in Chicago."

In Seattle, the chairman of the Federated Jewish Fund Budget Committee, Melville Monheimer, bluntly outlined the problem facing communities as he saw it. In his annual report to the Fund, he said: "The trouble nationally seems to be that each agency believes that it is not getting enough to carry on its self-assumed responsibility in the ever-recurring emergencies they say we now face. Like the man in the fable who constantly cried 'wolf,' we have had so many emergencies that emergencies have become chronic....Some agencies spend as much as 40 percent to collect their money, and there are one or two which spend as high as 80 percent ....Our local wants have been submerged or completely disregarded....Last year it was planned to retain some of the money raised for the Federated Jewish Fund for Seattle requirements but the trustees yielded to the pressure from Over Seas and from Palestine....It is the hope of your chairman that this year will see a balancing of the needs and demands."

Monheimer's complaint was shared by other communities throughout the country, but despite harsh words and growing bitterness, local communities recognized Israel's needs and grudgingly yielded to Montor's demand for pre-campaign percentage allocation of total receipts. He could be a tough bargainer as Indianapolis discovered. It had put off making a decision until the very last minute, yielding only in the face of a threat by Henry Montor to run a separate, competing campaign. Louisville, after a stiff bargaining session over Montor's insistence on a 75 percent pre-campaign allocation, offered 54 percent and like Chicago finally settled for 65 percent. Commenting on the UJA campaign in its early stages, the Newsletter reported:

Noticeable lack of enthusiasm and insistence of local funds upon priority for local institutions indicate sharp drop in total receipts. No tears will be shed over sharp curtailment of defense agency activities, which face long overdue deflation of swollen budgets. But chief sufferers will be smaller national educational and cultural agencies, many of whom already face closing.

The Newsletter then warned that the community bitterness over what was generally regarded as Montor's high-handed practices could very well spell the end of a united campaign and its replacement by a separate "United Israel Campaign" the following year. The report went on to add that despite a genuine crisis situation in Israel, "it is highly probable that the 1950 UJA campaign for $273 million will not raise more than about $100 million. All indications point to the fact that the charity boom of 1948 and 1949 is definitely over." The Newsletter echoed Melville Monheimer's warning about excessive use of the "emergency" appeal, and went on to assert, with added emphasis, that **"an emergency situation does exist now** in Israel where an immigration crisis is a lot closer than most people realize, and in the United States over the drop in fundraising. Hard realistic thinking and decisive slashing of allocations for pet projects, fringe activities, luxury boondoggling and everything else that diverts money from immediate needs are essential if the emergency is to be overcome."

In a later series of reports, the Newsletter spelled out details of the immigration crisis in Israel and offered specific recommendations about places where cuts could be made in UJA allocations in order to provide additional funds for Israel. Most contributors to UJA, for example, did not know that the largest percentage of UJA allocations went, not to Israel, but to the JDC for overseas relief and to its associated organization, the USNA, for the resettlement of European refugees in the United States. In 1948, a peak year for UJA collections, the UPA received only $49,796,000 as its share of the campaign. The beneficiaries of UPA in that year were the Palestine Foundation Fund (Keren Hayesod) and the JNF (Keren Kayemeth). Subsequently, other Zionist organizations were added as beneficiaries after being persuaded to give up their separate campaigns in exchange for specific sums from the UPA funds.

A blunt description of the critical situation in Israel was reported at the end of March by Cyrus L. Sulzberger, the chief foreign correspondent of the **New York Times.** In a series of dispatches from the Middle East, he warned that in the event of a depression in the United States, it would be "difficult to see what Israel could do for outside funds....The state faces a period of great fiscal stress. Its dreams of organizing vast fishing and farming industries will take years to realize.... (The United States) is going to have to grant sufficient financial support to the present Israeli regime to avoid seeing the country go bust and perhaps swing into Communist hands."

Sulzberger's pessimism was exaggerated but the situation was genuinely serious. The critical immigration statistics were reported by the Newsletter in the following detail:

> The Jewish Agency, which handles immigration to Israel, is in the red for 1949 by IL 11.3 million (about $17 million), with more than 90,000 newcomers still living in the unsatisfactory transit camps. Its total income for 1949 was only IL 25 million. For the fiscal year October 1949 to September 1950, the Agency has budgeted IL 40 million (about $60 million) for an immigration of 150,000 persons. This figure does **not** take into account an expected additional immigration of 90,000 Iraqi Jews recently granted permission to leave by the Iraqi regent.
>
> The **Israel Economist,** leading independent Jerusalem monthly, discussing this problem, states: "No special economic insight is needed to realize that this state of affairs cannot go on indefinitely. The **borrowing capacity of the Agency is approaching the point of exhaustion, and there are unfortunately few signs that the situation can be relieved in the near future by an appreciable rise in donations.**"

The Newsletter then proceeded to offer a six-point program to meet the emergency although it was under no illusions about the fact that its recommendations would fall on deaf ears as far as the organizations were concerned. Its appeal called on Jewish community leaders to take the following radical steps:

> 1. Give full support to your local campaigns.
> 2. All UPA funds (about $60 million in 1948) should be turned over to the Jewish Agency. This would involve suspension (for this year at least) of allocations to the Jewish National Fund, Mizrachi Palestine Fund, Constructive Fund of World Confederation of General Zionists, Agudath Israel

World Organization, and World Union of Poale
Agudath Israel--all of which now share in UPA
funds.

3. Temporary cessation of the JDC-promoted North African emigration and from other
non-emergency areas; and reduction of JDC's
allocation of $44 million from this year's
UJA to about $25 million, with the difference
going to the Jewish Agency.

4. Elimination of the USNA from the UJA
campaign, funds for its subsidiary, NYANA
(New York Association for New Americans), to
come solely from the New York UJA campaign.

5. A six-months halt of all duplicating
campaigns for special Israel projects, such
as those conducted by Hadassah, Women's League
for Israel, Pioneer Women, Palestine Light-
house, and other competing funds.

6. And for next year, a United Israel
Campaign!

We are aware of legal contracts, agreements and other arrangements that govern the
allocation of UJA funds. Nevertheless, the
emergency is real enough to call for prompt
elimination of these complications.

These recommendations were not entirely original. In
March, the New York Board of Rabbis, conscious of the
critical situation, voted a resolution urging that top
priority be given to the UJA over all other drives.
Previously, the Board of Rabbis had unanimously called
on the New York UJA to dissociate itself from all non-
relief agency beneficiaries and to distribute its collections exclusively to the UPA, the JDC and the USNA.
In reporting this action, the Newsletter added that
"the New York UJA ignored the request, and the Rabbis
never pressed for a satisfactory reply."

Not only were the recommendations for the emergency
ignored by the UJA leadership, but they also refused to
issue audited reports of its income and expenditures
as a matter of policy. The Newsletter was able to report, however, that UJA did send to "UJA contributors,
spurred by disclosures in **The Menorah Journal** two years
ago, on request an 8-page brochure which purports to
give exact receipts, expenses and disbursements for
campaigns from 1938-1948." The Newsletter cautioned
readers that the statistics in the brochure were not
audited and did not add up, pointing out that for each
campaign there existed "an unaccounted-for gap ranging

from several hundred thousand dollars to over $2 million between 'Cash Allotments Received' minus 'Expenses' and the 'Total Allocation Payments to Beneficiaries.'" Until recently, similar unaudited statistics were "reported" each year, but publication in the **American Jewish Year Book** has been discontinued.

From a source described by the Newsletter as authentic, it was able to provide its readers with the following report of the 1949 campaign cash receipts of the UJA:

> From January 1, 1949 through March 1950, UJA received $85,975,897. This is all the cash raised by the 1949 drive!
> An additional $29,184,674 was received by the UJA during this period on account of the 1948 and earlier campaigns.
> Grand total from all campaigns: $115,160,571.

UJA's refusal to release audited reports of its income and expenditures despite the fact that its funds are tax-exempt makes it impossible to explain why the UJA reported to the **American Jewish Year Book** (vol.53, 1952, p.227) that it had raised a total of $103,000,000 in 1949, a figure substantially different from the total cited in the Newsletter. There is no other amount in the **Year Book** for UJA, no account of expenses incurred for fundraising, administration and other "fancy blotter" costs. The Newsletter reflected some of the criticism aroused by the failure of UJA to account responsibly to the community for the manner in which it spent public funds. Describing the agreement governing the distribution of the 1950 campaign funds, the Newsletter offered the following observation:

> UJA appeals for contributions primarily on the basis of need for aid for Israel. But under the terms of the 1950 agreement between the UPA and the JDC, the UPA will get only about half of the cash receipts of the 1950 campaign if the drive raises $75 million this year.
> This is how the distribution percentages work out:
> Of the first $50 million collected, JDC will get 40 percent.
> Of the next $25 million collected, JDC will get 30 percent.

This means that out of $75 million, JDC
will get $27,500,000.

Of the remaining $47,500,000, USNA and
NYANA are to receive a sum as yet undeter-
mined but which may run as high as
$15,000,000. Smaller lump sum grants will go
to the Agudath Israel and the Poale Agudath
Israel, and probably several other organizations, under special agreements with UJA.

Next week, **Cross-Section, U.S.A.** expects
to bring you the actual amounts distributed
during the first three months of 1950 to the
three constituent agencies of UJA and to the
new member NYANA. Contributors who believe
that the largest share of their donations is
going to Israel in view of the urgent need
there should prepare themselves for a rude
shock!

It was obvious that under this arrangement UPA
could not hope to get more than between $25 and $50
million. This business-as-usual distribution of funds
contrasted sharply with the desperate note of urgency in
the UJA appeals for aid to meet the very real emergency
in Israel, and it led the Newsletter to express an
indignation which unfortunately was not matched by the
community. For some contributors, a donation to the UJA
was a form of affiliation with the Jewish community in
place of religious observances; for others, apathy or
community pressure was probably responsible for their
willingness to go along without protest. The Newsletter's appeals for reform, therefore, fell on deaf ears
for the most part, but it nevertheless continued to call
for community pressure on the UJA for change. If any
contributors experienced the "rude shock" predicted by
the Newsletter in anticipation of the following disclosure, it never reached our editorial desk:

While advertisements of the UJA repeatedly emphasize the urgent need for aid to
Israel, UJA itself is giving less to the UPA
than it is to its other agencies. At no time
since 1938 has UPA received more than JDC/
USNA. This year, out of $21,593,333 received
in cash from January 1 to March 20, UPA got
only 46 percent!

As we promised last week, we present
exclusively UJA's actual **secret** cash disbursements for the period mentioned above:

```
JDC......................$7,556,866
USNA.....................$1,023,167
NYANA....................$3,050,000
UPA......................$9,963,300
```
Thus, while Israel's need grows more des-
perate each day, UPA gets only $9,963,300
while JDC/USNA and NYANA walk away with
$11,630,033.
**Communities which have mortgaged them-
selves to local banks in order to advance immediate cash for Israel, please take note!**

Another one of UJA's reprehensible practices was the
release of exaggerated reports of campaign successes in
order to create an optimistic climate. One illustration
was the statement by Dr. Israel Goldstein, a distinguished American rabbi and a member of the Jewish
Agency, on his arrival in Israel on April 12. At a
press conference, Rabbi Goldstein told Tel Aviv newspapermen that the UJA would probably raise $150,000,000
in 1950 (there was no mention of the initial UJA goal of
$273,000,000). Out of that amount, he said, the JNF and
the Palestine Foundation Fund would get $90,000,000, and
the remaining $60,000,000 would go the JDC and the USNA.
Obviously, the well-meaning rabbi was not aware of the
true fundraising picture but was simply repeating what
he had been told by Henry Montor or another UJA official. Additional reports indicate that responsible community leaders were fed similarly overoptimistic and
exaggerated accounts of campaign results.
A sharper description of the economic situation was
contained in my letter to Joseph Leftwich, in which I
said: "Smaller organizations are being driven to the
wall, while the bigger ones will have to curtail
sharply. Everyone is worried, but UJA goes on with its
blackmail unperturbed. The pay-off may come at the end
of the year. The trouble is not enough people realize
that they're going through a revolution, and worse yet,
don't want to face it. What Shaftesley [John Shaftesley,
editor of the London **Jewish Chronicle**] calls my 'de-
bunking' is really Lesser's Cassandra-like warnings,
but they're not falling on enough ears yet. He's wrong
when he says it's easy to criticize--it's much easier
and far more lucrative to be a good boy and play ball--
particularly when your friends begin to preface everything they say to you by, 'This is not for publication.' Believe me, there's nothing tougher than being
the opposition in a hostile milieu."
By the middle of June, it became obvious to Montor
and the lay UJA leaders that the campaign was falling

far short of its "goal," and something like panic began to hit the ranks of the fundraisers. Concerning the emergency conference that the UJA called in Chicago, the Newsletter reported:

> With UJA drives in most large communities in their closing weeks, consternation greeted the announcement that only $53,762,000 in cash had been received thus far by UJA. This sum includes several millions collected this year from campaigns as far back as 1947. Despite renewed pleas by leaders at the Chicago conference of UJA, whose goal was set at the fantastic figure of $273 million, it now seems likely that no more than $10 to $12 million additional will be collected before the end of the year. Pessimistic predictions by **Cross-Section, U.S.A.** and other observers early this year are now shown to have been overoptimistic. Barring a miracle, the 1950 campaign will produce **less** by 16 percent, or about $15 to $20 million, than last year's drive, and the smallest amount since the end of the war.
>
> Threats by JDC spokesmen at the conference that immigration to Israel will be stopped by October unless more money is forthcoming were an insult to the 500 attending delegates and their communities. Substantial reductions in the allocations agreed upon for JDC/USNA/NYANA will leave sufficient money for Israel's needs; and at JDC's own figure of $100 per person for transportation costs, enough to move all "now or never" immigrants to Israel. JDC has already received over $21 million from UJA this year, while USNA/NYANA have been given about $8 million.
>
> Panicky cries from UJA and JDC spokesmen at this time reflect their own lack of foresight and selfish refusal to modify arrangements made during the flush months of 1949 in the face of numerous danger signals. The community is fed up with UJA blackmail tactics, wildly exaggerated "budgets" and propaganda stunts. It is time our leaders and their professional fundraisers presented the community with honest facts, audited financial statements and a decent approach to contributors as intelligent mature adults!
>
> Communities can help by sending delegates to UJA meetings who will act for the community rather than as rubber stamps for UJA leaders!

Reports from communities that had completed their drives showed substantial declines and added further to the desperation of UJA measures. In New York, where the goal was $90 million, only $25 million--and most of that in pledges--had been raised by the end of June. "Actual cash collections," said the Newsletter, "will be even lower (allow at least 10 percent for 'shrinkage'), and some pledges will not be taken up until next year." In Newark, N.J., Community Council President Alan V. Lowenstein reported: "Our local UJA will raise substantially less in 1950 as compared with 1949." Detroit reported that it had raised only $4,515,000 compared with $5,300,000 in 1949 and $5,750,000 in 1948. Louisville, Kentucky, which raised $616,000 in 1949, showed a decline to $515,297 in 1950. And in Los Angeles, where less than $6 million had been raised toward a goal of $11,620,000, the drive was extended into the summer.

The Newsletter reported that national UJA officials were trying to persuade communities with fall campaigns to undertake two drives, one of them to be exclusively for the UJA. The first to feel the pressure was Boston, where much bad feeling and sharp division resulted from this latest UJA effort to reduce or sidetrack allocations for local agencies. Boston rejected the recommendation and held its combined appeal, as usual, but the bitterness that was created over the decision caused considerable damage to the campaign.

More details about the effect of the failure of the campaign were contained in my letter to my friend Leftwich on June 16. I wrote him that most national organizations were in a panic and had begun to slash their budgets even further than they had previously been cut. Programs were being curtailed and personnel fired in the effort to live within their budgets. The UJA had actually raised only about $40 million, I said, adding that "the released figure of $53 million includes about $15 million from last year's campaign and the 1947 campaign." UJA's problems were compounded by "a general tightening up of business conditions," but this was only partly responsible for the failure of the appeal. I added:

"The real reason in my biased opinion is that people have got fed up with UJA tactics. Considerable resentment exists in local communities over UJA's demand for pre-campaign allocations and bludgeoning tactics in getting communities to agree to their demands. Also responsible are meaningless budgets and goals set so high that they obviously had to be padded. You can't fool the people all the time. And this apparently is the year of reckoning. Look for radical realignments among the organizations as the going gets tough this fall and winter."

The failure of the UJA campaign left Israel in a desperate situation. The slow pace of UJA cash collections during the summer months meant that Israel would be without funds and would have to curtail immigration. UJA, therefore, appealed to the communities once more, this time with a request to obtain more bank loans in advance of next year's collections--another Montor innovation--although most communities had already borrowed to the hilt. The appeal was made against the advice of the CJFWF.

More trouble seemed to be in store for the UJA, the Newsletter reported, over future arrangements between the UJA and the Joint Defense Appeal (JDA), the fundraising body for the American Jewish Committee and the ADL, which were threatened by the poor results of the campaign. "Radical developments" could be expected, said the Newsletter, when contracts come up for renewal. The Orthodox rabbinate also took this critical moment to voice dissatisfaction over their fundraising arrangements. At a meeting in Chicago, the Orthodox Rabbinical Council resolved to negotiate with the UJA and the Jewish Agency for an exception that would allow them to conduct independent fundraising drives, charging that smaller Orthodox institutions were being hurt by the Jewish Agency's ban on unauthorized community campaigns. The rabbis also voted to ask for an allocation from the New York UJA notwithstanding their dissatisfaction with existing campaign arrangements.

Warnings of impending financial collapse in Israel came repeatedly from the **Israel Economist**, one of the best informed monthly publications. In its April issue, it carried the following warning, which the Newsletter quoted:

> In the battle for economic survival, Israel has still achieved no decisive victory. Reserves of foreign currency are being rapidly exhausted....To expect anything else but a falling off in gift dollar receipts from America within the next few years is to display an optimism for which there appears to be no possible justification.

By midsummer the Israel government arrived at a decision. It decided to continue immigration and to meet the money crisis by changing the fundraising structure.

This is the way the Newsletter broke the news on August 10 of the Israel government's dramatic move:

> Meeting in Jerusalem last week with Premier David Ben-Gurion were American section Jewish Agency members Baruch Zuckerman of the Labor Zionists, Hadassah's Mrs. Rose Halprin, and the chairman Dr. Nahum Goldmann. Also present were Dr. Joseph Schwartz of the JDC, and Henry Montor of the UJA. Subject of the discussions was the feasibility of an Israel bond issue to be sold in the United States as a substitute for or supplement to the UJA, whose failure this year has left Israel in a bad financial hole. Director of the Israel bond campaign would be Henry Montor, and the sponsor of the campaign would be the Palestine Economic Corporation. Montor would receive a much higher remuneration than his present salary.

The report was sensational; it concluded with the observation: "Conspicuous by its absence at and in the discussion is the Zionist Organization of America, which apparently is still in the Israeli doghouse." Along with this news scoop, the Newsletter added to this revelation the equally shocking report that Henry Montor had submitted his resignation as director of the UJA. Its efforts to confirm the report by reaching Montor were unsuccessful, and in answer to its repeated inquiries on Montor's whereabouts, UJA headquarters said that he was out of town and that they had no information about his resignation.

Over a period of more than a week, UJA spokesmen told the Newsletter on different occasions: "Mr. Montor is away on part vacation, part business trip"; "Mr. Montor will be back in ten days to two weeks"; "No, we don't know where to reach him; we don't know where he is"; and "No, we know nothing about his resignation, and no one but Mr. Montor can confirm or deny the report." Attempts to reach Montor at his home in Bayside, Long Island, were likewise unsuccessful.

I wrote to Leftwich that Montor's resignation was the biggest news of the week but that from Zionist sources I had learned the following:

"This was actually only a maneuver connected with the prospective bond issue. Montor avoided me like the plague when I tried to reach him for confirmation, but Rudolf Sonneborn admitted to me that he too had heard the same 'stories' about Montor and the bond issue but

indicated that they were not yet fact; they were still
in the discussion stage....Sonneborn, of course,
wouldn't let me quote him, though I must say he was extremely friendly and urged me to call him whenever I had
any questions on important matters. Quite a difference
in attitude from the time I called him on his resignation from the Jewish Telegraphic Agency. He's also one
of my subscribers.

"Montor is top man in all Israeli fundraising plans,
and the Israel government will give him almost anything
he wants. If the bond issue goes through, as seems
likely, Montor will not only be the top-salaried man in
the history of Jewish communal activity--he's probably
that now, with his $40,000 plus $15,000 for expenses in
a year--but will practically double his present income
through bond-selling commissions. Not bad for the former
Mr. Henry Goldberg ('Mont-or'). He's powerful enough,
apparently, to kick the whole ZOA into the background.
Ben-Gurion seems to have written them off completely,
and permits men like Montor and Nahum Goldmann to run
the show here. I dread the reaction when Israel wakes
up, as eventually it must. The slick Americans are
taking those yokels for an awful ride. It's a great
life, and if at times I sound slightly bitter, blame it
on my **cheder** notions of Jewish honor and **tzedaka**."

From its usual reliable sources, the Newsletter
learned that earlier in the year Prime Minister Ben-
Gurion had considered Montor's suggestions for an Israel
bond issue but had hesitated to approve it for fear of
weakening the UJA campaign. Audited but secret UJA reports, unofficially leaked to the Newsletter, showed
that the UJA had raised a total of $97,530,027 in 1948,
but in the next year the drive had raised only
$77,769,343, or 20.3 percent less. These audited re-
ports, which have never been released, also showed that
in 1948, community funds had given the UJA 72 percent of
their total allocations, but that this had dropped in
1949 to only 61 percent. Larger communities gave pro-
portionately less to the UJA, more of their funds going
to serve local institutions. In 1950, campaign results
were running 16 to 20 percent less than the previous
year, and this apparently impelled Ben-Gurion to decide
to go ahead with the Israel bond issue.

To Leftwich I boasted at the time that "I've started
my own little sensation with the UJA revelations last
week and the promise of more to come this week. My
figures are authentic, based on some confidential
reports I managed to lay my hands on."

In August, the UPA announced that its agencies in
Israel had spent over $55.5 million from January through

May 1950. This sum, UPA explained, exceeded its income by about $16 million. Queried by the Newsletter, a UPA spokesman refused to reveal how much the agency had received from the UJA for the same period. However, Israel's Finance Minister Eliezer Kaplan disclosed that from January through August the Israel government's income from the UPA and other unspecified national funds had totaled IL 16 million (about $44,800,000 at the normal rate of exchange). In November, the Newsletter, after persistent inquiries, learned that the UPA had remitted through its beneficiary agencies about $40 million since January 1, a figure that approximated the Israeli Minister's disclosure. The UPA, as well as the UJA, continued to refuse the Newsletter's request for audited figures.

A dispatch from Jerusalem to the **Jewish Chronicle** (London) by its correspondent Jon Kimche confirmed the report of the Israel government's decision to launch a bond drive. Prime Minister David Ben-Gurion was said to have told American members of the Jewish Agency that the UJA could no longer raise enough funds to help Israel meet its immigration and defense needs. The Newsletter disclosed the following details of the Prime Minister's statement:

> Prime Minister Ben-Gurion is reported to have said that Israel needed a capital of $1 billion to get on a sound financial basis, and that no large-scale charity could provide it. To replenish Israel's empty foreign currency coffers, the meeting discussed floating a bond issue in the United States, redeemable at fixed rates and bearing a guaranteed interest. Informed circles here said there is no likelihood that Ben-Gurion will come to the United States in the fall to inaugurate the bond campaign.
>
> The **Jewish Chronicle's** report on Prime Minister Ben-Gurion's statement--of vital interest to every active American Jew--appeared in its issue of August 4, three weeks ago. It has not appeared in a single American English Jewish paper to date!

News about Israel's financial plight and the failure of the UJA drive to raise at least as much as it had in 1949, however, did circulate, and proposals were put forward in some community circles for a separate campaign for Israel and other overseas purposes. Community executives, at a meeting early in September under the auspices of the CJFWF, expressed their concern over the threat to the existence of the UJA as a unified drive from Zionist groups on the one hand, and from dissatisfied local community organizations, who warned that they might run their own campaigns, on the other hand. The community leaders urged that, in any case, the Israel bond campaign should be conducted separately from the annual UJA drive.

A year-end review of events in the **Rosh Hashana** issue of the Newsletter made the following points:

During the year 5711, developments on three major "fronts" of the American Jewish community will prove critical. These are: (1) United Jewish Appeal, (2) Zionism, and (3) the interrelation of Israel and American Jewry.

(1) UJA for 1951 presents a fuzzy, confused picture which should be clarified in October, when discussions and negotiations for 1951 agreements must be concluded.

Informed circles, however, expect that UJA will continue as a major U.S. fundraising arm. The much-discussed Israel bond drive will probably be conducted by another agency in cooperation with UJA and as a supplement to it.

Changes in the top leadership of UJA will involve Henry Morgenthau Jr., who has long wanted to be relieved on the responsibility. The name of Eddie Cantor has been put forth seriously as a possible successor. Secrecy still surrounds the position and plans of top fundraiser Henry Montor.

Although the economic plight of Israel will get worse in coming months and may be further complicated by governmental changes, the financial arrangements between UPA and JDC for distribution of the UJA receipts are not expected to differ materially from the 1950 percentages.

Despite some pressure, particularly from the Zionists, there is no likelihood of a United Israel drive in place of UJA for next year. Resistance of communities to mobilize for two separate drives in one year will also pigeonhole suggestions for separate overseas and local campaigns.

Korean war and higher U.S. taxes have improved the outlook for tax-exempt UJA campaign

in 1951, but few leaders honestly expect
American Jewry to raise anything approaching
the $300-odd million a year for three years (in
donations, bonds and investments) that Prime
Minister Ben-Gurion has been asking for. Ef-
forts to extract as much as possible from
American Jewry for Israel's needs will be
fought bitterly by many communities and by many
U.S. agencies, including the American Jewish
Committee.

Fundraising record of American Jewry since
World War II puts Alice-in-Wonderland stamp on
three-year billion dollar goal of Israelis.
UJA, for example, has never raised as much as
$100 million in one year! The high-water mark
was $97,530,027 in 1948. In that year, UPA's
share was only $49,796,000--of which Israel got
even less! Pledges of support for the bond
issue by American leaders are sincere but psy-
chological effect of unattainable dollar goal
will discourage rather than increase giving.

(2) Zionism in the United States will experience a resurgence of strength primarily
because Israel, in need of all the friends and
allies it can get, now thinks the effort is
worthwhile. Leadership and direction will come
from the American section of the Jewish Agency
rather than from any particular American
Zionist organization. Plans are now in the making for a conference on American Zionism late
this fall, sponsored by the Jewish Agency. (The
World Zionist Congress meeting, set for December, has been postponed until Spring, possibly
indefinitely.)

Israeli pressure on American Zionists will
be renewed for a more intensive drive to spread
understanding of Zionist philosophy and to
translate it into appropriate action. This
means chalutziut, with emphasis on so-called
"technical" chalutzim, that is, physicians,
engineers, scientists, social workers, teachers
and mechanics.

War mobilization in the United States, however, now under way, will probably lead to
shelving of chalutziut drive for some time to
come. Nevertheless, as recently as August 22,
Israel Schen, editor of the Jewish Agency's
Zionist Newsletter (Jerusalem), appealed for
American chalutzim. He complained: "The propa-

ganda for **chalutziut** that has been emanating
from Jerusalem during the past year has been on
the whole of a kind which avoided treading on
the corns of American Zionists." Ignoring manpower problem created here by the Korean war,
Schen urges American Zionists to assume responsibility for producing "a far larger number of
pioneers than at present."

In view of the ideological weakness of
American Zionists, particularly since the
establishment of the state of Israel, the following observation by Schen is especially interesting: "Zionism still remains essentially
unchanged by the emergence of the state of
Israel and the appearance of American Jewry as
the dominant force in the Diaspora."

(3) Israel-American Jewish relations will
not be radically changed as the result of
statements by Jacob Blaustein, president of the
American Jewish Committee, from Jerusalem.
"Exile" concept cannot be eliminated by any one
statement as long as it involves the whole complex of religious belief.

On **Rosh Hashana,** for example, Conservative
and Orthodox congregations still pray: "Sound
the great Shofar for our liberation; raise the
banner to assemble our exiled ones; bring nigh
our scattered ones from among the nations; and
our dispersed ones gather from the extremities
of the earth; and lead us into Zion, our city,
in joyous acclamation; and into Jerusalem."

Thus, the "ingathering" of the exiles is
not only a Zionist duty but a religious duty as
well. The problem will not be solved by American Zionist efforts to redefine "exile" or by
American non-Zionist and anti-Zionist efforts
to proclaim the non-existence of "exile."
Nevertheless, the struggle for commanding
influence over American Jewry between the
American Jewish Committee and the American
Zionists on the ideological (as well as fundraising) front will be sharpened as the American Jewish Committee continues to press for
community acceptance of its anti-nationalist
"integrationist" philosophy. In this fight,
religious Zionists may eventually bring up the
heaviest ideological guns.

In succeeding chapters, the several controversial

issues referred to briefly in this summary of annual communal developments will be taken up in detail.

2

BONDS FOR ISRAEL

Regardless of the anxiety of American Jews over the poor results of the 1950 UJA campaign, the Israel government had already made up its mind to change the American fundraising structure and seek to solve its financial problems through the sale of interest bearing Israel bonds rather than through the UJA. This decision was made clearly evident at the national conference of the community leadership, which was called by the UJA and the ZOA on October 24 in Washington, D.C., to plan the fund drives for 1951. The CJFWF was also asked to be a sponsor of the meeting but its leadership decided not to accept the invitation for fear of endangering its tax-exempt status. The American Jewish Committee was not invited, a pointed snub that was not lost upon observers of community action. The Newsletter had the following comment about the meeting:

> Present plans call for a UJA drive begin-
> ning this winter; a bond drive is to follow in
> the spring. Director of both campaigns will be
> Henry Montor, with one of his lieutenants nomi-
> nally in charge of the bond drive.
> Informed quarters say that fear of endan-
> gering the tax-exempt status of community funds
> will keep the CJFWF and many local welfare
> funds from sponsoring the bond drive. They
> will, however, cooperate to the extent of mak-
> ing their lists, etc., available to the bond
> salesmen.
> The JDC leadership is definitely opposed to
> the bond issue; it favors tax-exempt gifts. The
> silence of such top leaders as William Rosen-
> wald may be significant.

Mixed feelings about the proposed Israel bond drive and the effects of its competition for funds upon the UJA campaign led to considerable behind-the-scenes ne-

27

gotiations as well as much press comment. Conflicting
reports about the relations of Israel bonds and the UJA,
and the actions they proposed to take during the year
were often caused by abrupt changes in the plans of the
leadership to meet situations they had not foreseen.
Some projections in the press forecast a drop of as much
as $15 million in the 1951 UJA campaign. Others, how-
ever, optimistically predicted that the anticipated bond
sale would make up for the UJA loss and possibly go far
beyond it. Favorable opinion in Israel was accurately
reflected by the **Israel Economist** (Jerusalem) which,
commenting on the anticipated "substantial" drop in UJA
funds, nevertheless said: "This, however, would not
matter greatly if the loan could be assured of reasonable success. For in that case, contributions to the
campaign proceeds would be used for the actual absorption work."

No doubt, in the euphoria of these early days,
Israelis felt that the proceeds of the bond sale would
also free them from the limitations on the use of UJA
contributions imposed by their tax-exempt status, but
some UJA contributors could have interpreted the **Israel
Economist**'s comment to mean that their donations would
be used to help pay the interest charges on the Israel
bonds--and some did. Their uneasiness was not allayed
when the Israel government officially announced that
Henry Montor would lead the 1951 UJA drive as well as
the Israel bond campaign. This would be done, according
to the official announcement, by insuring that "his resignation will not take effect until May 1951, after the
UJA drive, at which time the bond campaign will begin."
The same news release also confirmed the Newsletter's
earlier report that Henry Morgenthau Jr., would resign
at the same time as the general chairman of the UJA.

At the National Planning Conference in Washington,
Henry Montor optimistically predicted that the 1950 UJA
campaign, despite its slow start, would eventually raise
$90 million. In reporting this prediction the Newsletter
reminded readers that the successful 1949 campaign had
raised a total of only $77,769,343. Just before the
Washington conference, which was held on October 24, I
had written to Leftwich to compliment him on an editorial he had written for the **Jewish Chronicle**. I said:

"Your report on Israel's plight doesn't shock me; I
expect much worse before the situation gets better. Eban
himself put it very diplomatically here the other day
that conditions would get worse. The **New York Times**
quoted him as saying: 'The victory on the economic front
can be achieved only by several years of sustained ef-

fort; and the period of transition is likely to be increasingly critical and austere.'

"It wouldn't surprise me in the least to see the Ben-Gurion government go once things get really bad, say about the turn of the year. If the Mapam takes over, there'll really be hell to pay because I think they're about as close to the communists as any party can be without actually swearing allegiance to Stalin.

"Montor is going to head up both the UJA and the bond drives, and care will be taken that the latter will not interfere with the former. JDC and the American Jewish Committee don't like the idea of a non-tax-exempt fund drive and will fight the bond drive sub rosa wherever they can. I'll have more details about that and the October 24 conference next week."

In the closing weeks of the year, reports on the fall-off in the UJA campaign from the previous year's results continued to reach the Newsletter. The Combined Jewish Appeal of Boston closed its fall campaign with a decline of more than $400,000 under the 1949 drive. Chicago reported a drop of about $1,000,000 under the prevous year's results. In both cities, the likelihood was that the local Jewish agencies would bear the brunt of the shortfall.

The biggest blow to community leaders came early in November when the JDA notified the delegates to its national conference that it was severing all connections with the New York UJA because of the drop in receipts and that it would launch an independent campaign in 1951. The JDA had been a beneficiary of the UJA since 1947, but as early as April 1950, the Newsletter had predicted that the JDA would withdraw from the New York UJA if the percentage of its receipts was not increased over the seven percent it had been receiving. On November 9, the Newsletter reported the following reasons for the JDA's withdrawal:

Break with the UJA came over the latter's refusal to meet the JDA demand for a guaranteed minimum. Spurred by dwindling receipts in New York, JDA's decision is not expected to affect its relations with welfare funds throughout the country at present.

First public indication of JDA's decision came last week at the Harmonie Club luncheon of the American Jewish Committee marking the start of a "trade and industry" program. Realtors at the luncheon heard Gustave M. Berne, American Jewish Committee treasurer, say: "The American

Jewish Committee is now faced with a crisis in funds to support its work. A trade and industry program will help us meet this crisis by winning support from Jewish communities throughout the country."

Three-day ADL meeting last month also discussed drop in funds and necessity for "cutbacks." Said ADL chairman Judge Meier Steinbrink: "The answer is not in ruinous cutbacks--though reductions will be made--but in finding new additional sources of funds that will provide for the minimal needs."

Spokesmen for the National Jewish Welfare Board (JWB) and the American Jewish Congress, who are among the beneficiaries of the New York UJA, told **Cross-Section, U.S.A.** that they are not planning to leave New York UJA or contemplating any other changes in their fundraising programs at the present time. The CJFWF said it had not been asked to mediate the dispute between the JDA and the UJA, and would take no action unless requested to do so by one of these agencies.

Supporters of the UJA had received an earlier shock shortly before the JDA announcement when the JDC, after consultation with the CJFWF, obtained the consent of the UJA to launch a special independent fund drive for $2,500,000 before the end of the year. Ostensibly the drive was aimed at members of the anti-Zionist American Council for Judaism, who refused to recognize the UJA or contribute to it. On this development, the Newsletter brought up a question that Jewish community activists were already asking themselves:

> Coming on the heels of fervent Zionist and non-Zionist promises to build a stronger UJA in 1951 made at the Washington conference, and in the face of UJA's request for $50 million in cash by December 31 (local funds delivered $5 million at the conference itself, of which JDC got about 40 percent), JDC's action followed by JDA's split with the New York UJA has fundraisers asking themselves: Has the breakup of UJA begun? Their reasoning takes the line: if an exception can be made for JDC, why not other organizations? And where does that leave united fundraising?

The JDC's problems were also discussed at the plenary session of the Jewish Agency Executive, which opened in New York later that November. The JDC had decided to drop Youth Aliya from its list of beneficiaries and, as a consequence, Youth Aliya (which also received some of its financial assistance from Hadassah) was now requesting permission from the Jewish Agency to run an independent campaign, thus adding further to the feeling that the UJA was on the verge of a breakup. In my letter to Leftwich at this time, I warned that the financial crisis in Israel brought about in part by the UJA failure might force the resignation of the Ben-Gurion government, and I speculated on what impact this eventuality might have on American Jews. I wrote:

"I imagine it must be very hard for an Englishman to appreciate how jittery American Jews feel about the fall of an Israel government. The association in most minds here is with the sort of thing that happens in France, and all the papers have been carrying assurances that Israel is really quite stable, etc., etc. Also the Silver-Montor fight is out in the open again, while the 'anti-nationalists' are doing everything in their power to keep funds for Israel in their proper proportion and at the same time hypocritically praising Israel to the skies. The double talk of the American Jewish Committee and the CJFWF is enough to drive a sane man crazy.

"Actually, there's enough money for all current needs if the communal structures were streamlined and the duplication and waste eliminated. But everybody is out for as much money as they can collect, and hurrah for UJA--Down with the bond drive! which has them all frightened to death. Meanwhile, the contributing public is getting more and more critical and disgusted. Your editorial said they were tired of giving; that's not quite correct. What's really happened is a slowly growing suspicion that they're being taken as suckers, and while they want to help, they try to be certain that their contributions go where they want them to. If they're not sure, they don't give. Unfortunately, they also don't care enough to express their suspicions publicly."

Despite some hesitation and considerable fear for the future of the UJA, on which they were dependent, most American Jewish organizations readily accepted the Israel decision to launch a bond sale. Their hesitation was reflected most clearly in the English Jewish press, which delayed carrying the news of the decision for several weeks, a delay that has never been satisfactorily explained. The first announcement of Ben-Gur-

ion's proposal for an Israel bond issue was carried by
the **Jewish Chronicle** (London) on August 4, as we have
previously noted, and about a week and a half later, the
Prime Minister elaborated upon his proposal at a convention of the Mapai political party. To the enthusiastic
delegates, he announced that he was confident of raising
a billion dollars in three years from the sale of the
government bonds, and it was promptly reported by the
New York Times and the Yiddish dailies. Only one English
weekly, however, carried the story, the **Jewish Advocate**
(Boston) which frontpaged it but reported it without attribution. All of these papers also reported Ben-Gurion's emphatic confidence in the ability of American
Jews to meet the billion dollar goal. The Newsletter
noted that the **National Jewish Post** (Indianapolis) and
the **Jewish News** (Detroit), both of which receive last-
minute news flashes by direct wire from the JTA, did not
carry the announcement by Ben-Gurion, and added that the
"UJA, Jewish Agency and American Zionist organizations
would not comment on their reactions to the proposed
bond issue when queried by **Cross-Section, U.S.A.**"

An editorial on the proposed bond issue appeared in
the **Canadian Jewish Chronicle** as early as August 11, and
it concluded with the following question: "That it would
be a good thing to abolish charity drives goes without
saying: the question is whether the time for such a
change has yet arrived."

To stimulate interest in the new Israel bond proposal, a conference was hastily arranged in Jerusalem by
the Israel government on September 3 to which fifty
American welfare fund leaders and Zionists were invited.
Officially the conference was sponsored by the Joint Development Authority of the Jewish Agency, and its announced purpose was to consider "a long-range program
for economic development of Israel, and America's relation to that program." The strategy, obviously, was
Montor's but he was staying in the background at this
point.

Some of the leaders who had been invited apparently
had serious doubts about how far they would be able to
commit their organizations. ZOA president Benjamin G.
Browdy, for example, met with his Inner Committee prior
to his departure for Israel and heard a number of opinions concerning the projected Israel bond issue and
what its relation to the UJA and the UPA should be. According to the Newsletter report of the meeting,
national committeeman Morris Margulies urged Browdy to
exercise considerable caution before committing the ZOA
to any responsibility for the bond campaign; he believed

that there should be two distinct structures, one to conduct the UJA campaign and the other to direct the Israel bond sale. The veteran Zionist officer also recommended that priority be given to what he called a "constructive" UJA campaign which would be free of "atrocity" stories and the unpopular high pressure tactics by Montor.

The Newsletter observed that "at the same meeting, National ZOA Project Funds chairman and vice president Louis Falk pointed out that the UJA had lost the confidence of the rank and file, scored its failure to issue audited reports, and quoted facts and figures from **Cross-Section, U.S.A.**" Falk was a subscriber to the Newsletter and obviously had been influenced by its reports.

Among those attending the Jerusalem conference called by the Israel government was a delegation from the American Jewish Committee, headed by its president Jacob Blaustein. The support of the non-Zionist American Jewish Committee was especially sought after by Ben-Gurion because he believed that among its members were many of the wealthiest Jews in America. This view was reflected in an editorial in the **National Jewish Post** (Indianapolis) which conceded that the Israel bond drive would hurt the UJA, but insisted that American Jews would succeed in both campaigns. The editorial then said: "If Mr. Blaustein and the American Jewish Committee were to get behind the bond sale with full and complete support, its success might not be assured, but there would be at least the feeling that all the resources of American Jewry would be supporting the effort."

The only editorial in a Jewish newspaper to come to grips realistically with the problem involved in fundraising for Israel appeared on August 18 in the **Jewish Chronicle** (London). It was entitled, "Are We Tired of Giving?," and the Newsletter summarized it in the following comment:

> It explored the causes of the downward trend of funds during the past three years, cited "warning voices" at the beginning of the 1950 UJA drive which said the goal was "fantastic," blamed UJA leaders' "lack of foresight" and failure to modify plans made "during the flush months of 1949, ignoring the numerous danger signals."
>
> Pointing to statements by JDC leaders promising "one-time" campaigns since 1946, the

Chronicle concludes: (1) "Jews feel that what they strove for has now been fulfilled and they can sit back for a time and breathe freely again"; (2) "Philanthropic collections will not now suffice for Israel"; and (3) "The present critical decline...is largely due to the general dissatisfaction with the whole purpose of continued overseas fundraising."

The editorial seemed to be echoing many of the points which the Newsletter had been making, but it was not until several weeks later that I learned that my suspicion that it had been inspired by the Newsletter's disclosures was correct. In my letter to Leftwich of September 7, I wrote:

"So you were the one who wrote the JC editorial....I thought the editorial said many things that needed saying out loud, and pointedly called attention to it in the Newsletter. You may have noticed that Louis A. Falk, of the ZOA, also used my material in a much sharper attack on the UJA than I had indicated in the story. He has been a very enthusiastic subscriber--I've never met him--and has got me several subscriptions among leading Zionists.

"I was particularly impressed by your point about JDC spokesmen repeatedly promising a one-time all-out campaign. That has been a very sore point among communities here and has been thrown up at the UJA many times. Now, I see, we are to have another one-time three-year drive for sums so fantastically large that the campaign will defeat itself. American Jewry has never raised that kind of money ($333 million a year) for **all** purposes, much less for one cause. But no one has yet expressed publicly anything but the most optimistic belief in the ability of American Jews to shell out such a vast amount of money. The war and inflation, which has already begun, may help increase contributions next year, but even in the peak year of 1948, the UJA did not raise more than $85 million.

"I don't know; sometimes I doubt my own sense of values and judgment when I read apparently considered statements by men in responsible posts on the ability of a comparatively handful of people to raise staggering sums of money. Of course, it means everybody else will be squeezed, and already the American Jewish Committee has begun a counterattack."

The leaders of Israel had faith in the ability of American Jews to meet this extraordinary challenge despite the doubts and pessimism of many Americans. In one session of the Jerusalem conference, American Jewish representatives were told about Israel's immediate need for more manpower and how the plan submitted by Dr. Arie Grunbaum, director of the economic research department in Prime Minister Ben-Gurion's office, would implement it. Grunbaum called for an annual immigration of 200,000 persons in order to bring Israel's total population in 1953 to about 1,800,000. About 20 percent of these immigrants would be engaged in agriculture, according to the plan. The cost of absorbing them was estimated to be only IL 600 per person, a little more than half the actual cost at the time. To Israelis, who expected a more detailed blueprint based on fact rather than assumptions and estimates, the plan was a disappointment. The Newsletter had the following comment in its report:

> American Jewish leaders were called to a three-day conference in Jerusalem to be "sold" on this plan rather than to be consulted on Israel's present economic difficulties. (The Israel pound was reported to be selling for $1 on the Tel Aviv black market, $1.50 in New York City.) A few American voices were raised to advocate a temporary curtailment of immigration but were quickly silenced. Premier Ben-Gurion told delegates that more Israel manpower was essential even if continued immigration was "politically irrational or economically unfeasible." The basis for this manpower demand is the fear of an Arab "second round."
>
> The question was left open whether one billion dollars is to be raised by the bond issue alone or by a combination of other methods. Several American delegates called for the separation of the UJA overseas drive from domestic campaigns. Stanley Myers, president of CJFWF, and Harold Linder, of the JDC, urged caution and careful investigation before making a decision on the bond issue.

An editorial in the **Intermountain Jewish News** (Denver) early in October reflected much of the uneasiness in the community over the impending change in fundraising for Israel. The editorial observed that reaction to the news about the proposed Israel bonds issue "here and elsewhere is not unanimous. The success of any bond undertaking ... will depend on grassroots cooperation and enthusiasm in the communities of America."

At the CJFWF regional conferences in New Orleans
and in Pittsburg, president Stanley C. Myers assured
delegates that the UJA effort would be strengthened and
"if possible, enlarged." He emphasized the fact that
Israel bond sales "must be over and above maximum funds
contributed to welfare funds; and they must not be a
diversion from or in any way a substitute for philanthropic funds." Moreover, he went on, the primacy that
should be given to domestic agency requirements in 1951
would be greatly enouraged if a central fund were created for Israeli needs exclusively. This was one of the
earliest recommendations to be made by a leading communal official for a separate Israel fund, a proposal initiated by the Newsletter as early as January 4. His optimism, however, was not reflected by the director of
the CJFWF in Detroit, Isidore Sobeloff, who told the
CJFWF West Central Regional Conference that "Jews of
America are giving less this year for overseas needs
because it has not been possible to maintain the high
level of excitement."

How high that level could be was soon to be demonstrated by Henry Montor. To introduce the Israel bond
sale formally, Henry Montor called for a "National
Planning Conference for Israel and Jewish Reconstruction" to be held in Washington, D.C., on October 27 to
29. The call was issued in the names of 50 communal
leaders who had attended the Jerusalem conference the
previous month. According to the Newsletter, the decision of the CJFWF not to be a sponsor of the meeting was
the reason why individual sponsors were named instead of
the organizations originally proposed. The CJFWF was
fearful that participation in the bond sale might be endangering its tax-exempt status. "The bid to JDC's
[European] director-general Dr. Joseph J. Schwartz to
replace Mr. Montor as director of UJA in 1952 is an attempt to appease JDC, which is opposed to the bond issue
and fears its effects on the 1951 UJA drive," the
Newsletter concluded.

To clear the way for a Washington conference, all
other major Jewish events scheduled for that week were
called off. A scheduled National Conference on Jewish
Education, for example, the first of its kind, was postponed until January of the following year. The fact that
Jewish educators had been preparing for it for more than
six months and had cleared the date for their conference
for the same weekend long before the Israel bond meeting
was even thought of was held to be of no consequence.
With scarcely concealed bitterness, Dr. Judah Pilch, the
executive director of the American Association for Jew-

ish Education, yielded to Montor's pressure and announced the postponement of its conference. He pointed out that the association had been given only one week's notice to call off the conference. "A week ago we learned that the American delegation ... had found it necessary to call an emergency conference on aid to Israel," Dr. Pilch explained. Only brief mention of the postponement was made by the **American Jewish Year Book** in its summary of Jewish education activities.

The Washington conference proved to be no more of an emergency than the overdone one-time "all-out" JDC campaigns. The Newsletter carried the following description of the conference, which opened on November 2:

> Delegates to the National Planning Conference in Washington, D.C., last weekend heard what one observer called "an avalanche of oratory" of mixed quality; came away with few facts they had not had before. Most important were details of the proposed Israel bond issue, disclosed by Henry Montor last Thursday when he stressed that the purpose of the conference was to consider not only the bond issue but how to meet the total economic needs of Israel. Most facts about bonds had been disclosed early last month by the **New York Times;** it confirmed the **Cross-Section, U.S.A.** report that the bonds would carry 4 percent interest and mature in 20 years. Mr. Montor also insisted that it was a mistake to speak of the goal of the bond drive as $1 billion; this sum included investments, proposed U.S. government grants-in-aid and other forms of economic help.
>
> Delegates heard the UJA director give repeated assurances that there was no "substitute for UJA free American dollars," that "UJA would be the best way of helping Israel" if all the money needed could be raised that way; and that the bond issue would not be competitive; but they came away unconvinced and fearful of bond competition.

Once more the suspicion grew that the so-called "historic" Washington conference, despite all the talk about emergency and unity, was little more than a publicity stunt to promote the introduction of the Israel bond campaign. It was obvious to some delegates, at least, that all the necessary plans for the campaign,

including the schedule which called for the UJA drive to
begin in December 1950 and come to a close officially
before the start of the Israel bond campaign in May
1951, had been decided upon long before the conference,
probably in Jerusalem the previous July. The Newsletter
added the following information:

> Not revealed [at the conference] was the
> plan to introduce a special bill in the
> Congress for a grant-in-aid to Israel under the
> Point Four program in order not to commit
> Israel to the Marshall Plan, which the Ben-Gur-
> ion government does not want to join. State De-
> partment opposition to the bill is expected.
> Incidentally, the Israeli press continues to
> speak of and to expect a billion dollar drive,
> not a "loan," to consist of the bond sale, in-
> vestments and government grants, as Henry Mon-
> tor, UJA director, told community delegates in
> Washington.

Some reputable publications, such as the **Israel
Economist,** however, cautioned against too much optimism
about Israel's ability to raise a billion dollars in the
United States. A veteran Israel journalist, Robert
Weltsch, was also critical of the statements at the
Washington conference and called instead for the enlist-
ment of "real economic and financial experts (and not
propagandists)" to examine Israel's economic policy and
structure in the light of that nation's economic reali-
ties. In an article in the **Jewish Chronicle** (London) on
November 10, Weltsch noted that Israel would probably
need foreign aid even if all immigration were to be
halted. He concluded "Diaspora Jewry may still have to
play an important role for Israel by helping to pave the
way for economic sanity. This cannot be done by 'conferences.' The Washington conference may give the UJA drive
in America a new impulse, but what is needed is not hol-
low public speeches but a brains trust of some authority, and the application to Israel of the capacities of
men who have proved their qualifications elsewhere."
Weltsch's words proved to be more prophetic than he
may have realized at the time, but they were nevertheless swept aside by the torrent of highly optimistic releases that Israeli officials continued to issue. Kol
Yisrael, the official Israel radio, quoted Israel's
Finance Minister Eliezer Kaplan on November 19 as saying
that preparations for the Israel bond issue were fully
under way and that all Jewish organizations in the

United States had pledged their wholehearted support. Moreover, he added, the ZOA alone had promised to sell over $100 million worth of Israel bonds to its members and friends. He further encouraged troubled Israelis by announcing that Israel had obtained a $25 million loan from the Export-Import Bank for agricultural development. On the subject of business investments, Kaplan conceded that he had not done as much as he would have liked but that he had nevertheless succeeded in interesting two large American chemical companies in Israel's potentials. He did not disclose their names.

In the American Jewish community, however, grumbling about the Israel bond drive continued to be heard. Some of it found expression in **Commentary** magazine for December, in an article entitled "A Billion Dollars for Israel." Author of the feature was Hal Lehrman, a controversial journalist who had made his reputation as head of the U.S. Office of War Information branch office in Turkey during the war. The Newsletter described the article as

> a smartly disguised attack on the Israeli 4-point plan, containing just enough valid criticism and "inside" information to win the confidence of an unsuspecting reader; arouses suspicion only when the former OWI propagandist quotes a casual conversation between "one large and one medium-sized UJA leader" with the accuracy of a court reporter. Lehrman pleads for more funds for domestic charities, seems to speak from the point of view held by the New York Federation leaders rather than the American Jewish Committee.

Later that month, Kaplan announced the official details about the Israel bond sale. Contrary to early reports, Israel bonds, he said, as well as savings certificates would be issued for a 15-year term and would bear interest of $3\frac{1}{2}$ to 4 percent beginning on May 11, 1951, the date of Israel's Independence Day. The actual Israel bond campaign itself would be launched in April and its goal would be $500 million. The Israel bond issue would be underwritten by a new American Jewish group especially created for this purpose called "Friends of Israel."

Other aspects of the Israel bond campaign were worked out with equal thoroughness. It was decided, for example, to approach individuals through the organizations in which they were members and that the organization's chapters would be encouraged to compete with one another in order to stimulate sales. Among other suggestions given consideration were proposals for a payroll deduction scheme and a campaign for "bond-a-month" pledges. But at the annual UJA meeting in Atlantic City in December, the impact of the projected Israel bond drive as well as the problems that might be anticipated because of the war in Korea and President Harry Truman's proclamation of a national emergency were much more on the minds of the delegates than the announcement of the change in UJA leadership from Henry Montor to Joseph J. Schwartz. However, when some delegates tried to bring up the fact that a United States war bond drive was scheduled to begin in late March or April and that national attention would be centered on that drive rather than the Israel bond sale, which was also scheduled to begin at the same time, they were quickly silenced.

The delegates also were not told about a separate $5 million bond issue which had been quietly registered with the Securities and Exchange Commission by AMPAL, the American Palestine Trading Corporation. These securities were to be 15-year, 4 percent sinking fund bonds, and the proceeds of the sale were to be used for the expansion of agriculture, industry and commerce in Israel. As I wrote to my friend Leftwich in December, any resemblance to the projected Israel bonds was purely accidental. I then added:

"The bad news from Korea has thrown businessmen and people here generally into the depths of gloom, ruined the Christmas holiday business season, and generally given people a great deal to worry about....Most people are quite serious about the world situation and very much worried over the changes in living that are inevitable for the next year. The memory of wartime rationing, scarcities and black markets is still very fresh.

"Worst of all is the general feeling of uncertainty, of not knowing where we're going and what's going to happen to us. The fumbling hand of our top leadership, its failure to decide whether we're in war or not, its lack of anything beyond a day-to-day policy and the growing disillusion with the **idea** of a United Nations, inter alia--all add up to a very dangerous frame of mind, to a failure of nerve possibly; but more likely to a mounting demand for a 'quick' war and let's get it over with. The youngsters still look forward to going into the army, even many of those who were veterans of the last war, and while a few Cassandras continue to remind us of the devastation of an atomic war, most

people apparently are going to refuse to think about it
until it happens, blindly hoping meanwhile that our
bombs will get there first and wreak such havoc as to
end things at once. All of which is utter nonsense,
of course.

"Against this background, our own problems shrink to
insignificance."

Even without reference to the general situation,
there were sufficient grounds for uneasiness within the
American Jewish community in the developments that followed the failure of the 1950 UJA campaign. Welfare fund
representatives began to speak openly about their fears
of a break-up in the united fundraising system that had
prevailed thus far. They pointed not only to the separate campaign announced by the JDA but also to the fight
of the ZOA against the Montor-Israel domination of the
fundraising programs and the increasingly difficult
roles assumed by the CJFWF and the JDC.

Most delegates expected that these and other anxi-
eties would surface at the General Assembly called by
the CJFWF for December 1 in Washington, D.C. At that
meeting the CJFWF stood ready to float a stand-by fundraising plan in the event of a break-up of the UJA. Very
serious consideration was being given to the plan which
called for a "community-sponsored national campaign
organization," and it was to be presented by Julian
Freeman, of Indianapolis, the chairman of the CJFWF Committee on Stable and Unified Fund Raising. A "blueprint"
of the plan was made available to the Newsletter, which
described it in the following terms:

> Details of the plan indicate that the new
> organization would operate much in the manner
> of the national mobilization campaign of the
> community chests. The CJFWF's publicity and
> fundraising services to the communities would
> be expanded to include formulation of a cam-
> paign "theme," providing special personnel
> where needed and requested, establishment of
> standards, and generally assisting communities
> in all ways needed for a successful and unified
> drive.
> Unlike the UJA, the proposed new organiza-
> tion would not budget, allocate, receive or
> distribute funds. It would operate on a budget
> of about one half of one percent of the total
> raised by the Welfare Funds, a sum considerably
> less than current UJA costs.
> **The plan for a national campaign organiza-
> tion will go into effect whenever the communi-**

ties themselves decide by vote that they want
it.
UJA forces are being marshalled to oppose
this revolutionary proposal as well as the
CJFWF recommendations to implement creation of
a central Israeli fund. The likelihood is that
the fight will take place in committees rather
than officially out in the open, for the
present.

To this report, the Newsletter appended a reminder that
at the beginning of the year, in its March 16 issue, it
had warned that "community bitterness [over UJA bargaining tactics] may spell the end of the UJA this year;
United Israel Campaign next year."
    At the American Zionist Council (AZC) meeting in
November, attention was centered on the CJFWF plan to
the exclusion of all Zionist business. A distorted description of the CJFWF plan had been reported by the
Tog, a New York Yiddish daily, and it was also carried
in English throughout the country by the Seven Arts
Feature Service, a subsidiary of the JTA. Because of
that, in a most unusual step, the AZC invited reporters
for the **New York Times** and the **New York Herald Tribune**
to cover the Sunday night meeting. Next morning the
newspapers reported that the American Zionist groups,
led by Hadassah, were at odds over the proposal for a
Central Israel Fund not only with the CJFWF but also
with the Jewish Agency. The latter was included by the
opposition because Harry Lurie, the executive director
of the CJFWF, had disclosed that the Jewish Agency not
only supported the proposed fund but also had contributed several of its features.
    The increasing confusion over who was on which side
was pictured in the following disclosure by the Newsletter of November 22:

    Welfare Fund fears that the UJA was en-
    dangered were encouraged by the UPA blast
    against Mr. Lurie for disclosing the Jewish
    Agency backing for the Central Israel Fund; and
    by the American Zionist Council's resolution
    to "support the UJA wherever it may be forced
    to organize its own campaign after failing to
    reach a satisfactory agreement with the local
    welfare funds with regard to the share of UJA
    in the local campaign."
    Not revealed in the first reports was the
    possibility that veteran Zionist leader and

chairman of the American Zionist Council, Louis Lipsky, will resign as a protest against the refusal of Zionist groups to compromise on their "autonomy" and allow the Council to be their spokesman.

At the time this report was carried, I was negotiating with John Shaftesley, editor of the London **Jewish Chronicle** over a weekly "American Letter" which I had offered to write for that paper. I had sent him a sample copy of the letter but he indicated to Leftwich that he was not satisfied with it. The letter dealt for the most part with the maneuvering of the fundraising leaders over the UJA and the Israel bonds but not with the proposed Central Israel Fund, and Shaftesley had therefore charged that I had pulled punches in my comments about the UJA. According to Leftwich, he was especially put out because I had not included a report of the CJFWF plan for a separate Israel fund even though he had been told that the plan was disclosed only after I had already sent him my observations. In a letter I wrote to Leftwich on November 23, I made my own resentment over Shaftesley's attitude quite clear. I said:

"I frankly feared he [Shaftesley] would have thought I was taking him way out on a limb if I had actually spelled out all the implications of my analysis. Don't forget, that was written more than four weeks ago, when everybody was being too, too brotherly and swearing on ten Bibles that UJA would be stronger than ever. And here I come along saying that the whole fundraising structure was bursting at the seams and likely to blow sky high!

"Naturally I was scared, too, at the conclusions that stared at me. In view of the current blow-up, which caught the CJFWF by surprise, I'd say that Shaftesley still has a good article. I suggested to him that if it wasn't too late, he supplement the piece with the details of the CJFWF plan which I had published last week. Actually the attack is being spearheaded by Hadassah and is being directed at Henry Montor, who originally proposed the Central Israel Fund idea in Jerusalem last July and literally sold it to the Israel government and the Jewish Agency. They apparently think Montor is a genius.

"The CJFWF man Lurie was present at the meeting when the plan was discussed and the recommendations that will be made in Washington by him are entirely in line with the government's suggestions. That's what one of the CJFWF's men told me yesterday and nothing the Zionists

have said contradicts it. Most of them don't even know
what the plan involves, but they have brought enough
pressure to bear to make the Jewish Agency here back
down. The **New York Herald Tribune's** Paul Tobenkin has
done a very fine job in getting more of the facts in
the dispute, much better than the **New York Times**."

Hadassah had, of course, quickly and correctly interpreted the plan for a central Israel fund as another
effort by Henry Montor, with the full cooperation of the
Ben-Gurion government to monopolize control in his hands
and to squeeze out all the Zionist organizations altogether from any voice in fundraising for Israel,
thereby also weakening their hold on their membership.
In short, Montor for his ambitions and Ben-Gurion for
reasons of state together would have liked to see the
Zionist organizations wither and disappear from the
American scene. In this connection, it should be noted
that S.Z. Shragai, a member of the Jewish Agency Executive, told a reporter for the London **Jewish Chronicle**
in blunt terms that "the Israel government is for the
abolition of the World Zionist Organization" and its replacement by a "Friends of Israel Association" throughout the world, whose functions would be limited largely
to fundraising for Israel.

Before the anticipated confrontation could take
place, however, calmer heads prevailed and an agreement
to reconstitute the UJA for 1951 was hastily concluded
between the UPA and JDC. It happened barely a week before the CJFWF general assembly was to meet in Washington, D.C., and under the agreement, the CJFWF for the
first time was permitted to have a voice in the UJA campaign policy. As a mark of the truce between the two
factions, Israel Foreign Minister Moshe Sharett agreed
to be the principal speaker at the CJFWF assembly.
Nevertheless, for the record the following actions, as
reported by the Newsletter, were to take place:

> The CJFWF proposals will be introduced as
> scheduled on Friday, December 1, but no open
> fight is anticipated. Zionist delegates will
> fight the proposals in committee and probably
> defeat them there. Every effort will be made
> before the close of the assembly to assure the
> Jewish public that all groups are solidly be-
> hind the UJA.

Little of this behind-the-scenes negotiating was
evident in the English Jewish press and even less to the
general American Jewish public. The **National Jewish**

Post, the most independent publication of them all and the only one to be circulated nationally, clearly demonstrated its failure to understand the implications of the Central Israel Fund as proposed by the CJFWF when it declared in an editorial that "the **Post** favors that proposal, also, at least in theory....If a Central Israeli Fund [sic] means the crippling of Hadassah and Histadruth fundraising efforts, then the **Post** is opposed. If the Fund means the elimination of many doubtful drives by agencies taking advantage of the lack of any system, then the **Post** is for it."

Delegates to the CJFWF assembly apparently were no better informed than the English Jewish press. Most speeches and discussions centered on the 4-point program of the Israel government, and the closest the assembly came to a controversial statement was a reference to the Central Israel Fund made by president-elect Julian Freeman in his acceptance speech. Few delegates realized that he was actually throwing the Central Israel Fund issue back into the laps of the competitive Zionist groups when he said: "No Central Israel Fund--either partial or complete--can be established unless the Jewish Agency and the Zionist organizations agree. They do not now agree."

At the time he made this pronouncement, Freeman knew that the Jewish Agency had reversed itself because of pressure from the communities and had gone on record as opposing the Central Israel Fund proposal. Nevertheless, he went on to tell the delegates that the Jewish Agency was prepared to start informal steps in the direction of a central Israel budget along the lines recommended by the CJFWF. However, no specific action on the Israel issue was taken by the assembly.

Barely a week after the close of this conference, the UJA announced that its 1951 campaign would be launched at the national conference to be held in Atlantic City, N.J., on December 16 and 17. An agreement reconstituting the 1951 UJA had been arrived at and it called for a major portion of the proceeds this time to go to the UPA. The percentage arrangements as reported by the Newsletter, though tentative and subject to change, gave 67 percent to UPA and 33 percent to JDC of the first $55 million; out of everything raised above that figure, $87\frac{1}{2}$ percent was to go to UPA and $12\frac{1}{2}$ percent to JDC. Since both percentages add up to 100 percent, the obvious question raised by the Newsletter was: where was the money to come from for the USNA share as well as for such substantial costs of the campaign as expenses and salaries?

From the JDC point of view, this arrangement apparently was a small price to pay in exchange for control
of the UJA. The Newsletter had a caustic observation on
the events at the conference and its labored efforts to
provide a show of unity over the transfer of the direction of the UJA from Henry Montor to Dr. Joseph J.
Schwartz, when it reported the following:

> Moving with the precision of an old-guard
> political machine, the 1951 UJA drive opened
> with a get-together in Atlantic City, December
> 16, "unanimously elected" Edward M.M. War-
> burg as general chairman to succeed Henry Mor-
> genthau Jr., and calmly announced "goals" of
> its "three" constituent agencies totaling
> $202,684,577. (Quotes are used to indicate key
> propaganda words employed without relation to
> their dictionary meaning.)
>   Choice of Mr. Warburg, who is chairman of
> the JDC, and Dr. Joseph Schwartz, JDC director
> general, to succeed Henry Montor as UJA direc-
> tor, marks the transfer of UJA control from the
> Israel government to American non-Zionists.
> This is the "reward" offered JDC in return for
> its support of the Israel bond issue, which it
> previously opposed.
>   "Explanations" made to justify UPA's
> $174,046,000 "goal," JDC's $22,350,000 "bud-
> get," and USNA's $7,288,577 "needs" can be
> taken seriously only by the naive and the ig-
> norant. Compare, for example, Dr. Nahum Gold-
> mann's "explanation" that $15 million was
> needed to retransport 200,000 immigrants to
> Israel with JDC's actual cost in 1949 of $24
> million for 240,000 persons. Or the "predic-
> tion" of USNA president William Rosenwald that
> 20,000 refugees would enter the United States
> in 1951 compared with the statement last month
> on the immigration lag caused by the provisions
> of the DP (Displaced Persons) bill made by
> Stanley Myers, former president of CJFWF. As
> for USNA's gall in requesting over $7 million,
> thus confirming our reports last month, it is
> commentary on the meeting that no one rose in
> protest.

Indignant at the inflated sums set forth as goals of
a campaign that was being launched at a time of increasingly severe economic conditions, the Newsletter edi-

torially concluded its report with the following: "We believe that it is high time our communal leaders told us the truth about how much they need and what they need it for; high time they junked the callous cynicism of the Montor regime and the exaggerations that insulted the intelligence of every Jewish contributor."

Some of this anger is also reflected in my regular letter to Leftwich, in which I said:

"These are exciting times in which to be alive and well and working. Our civilization is spinning itself out; most of us have lost our values and soon we shall probably also lose our valuables; and we seem very likely to be entering upon a period of darkness and intolerance, of violence and bloodshed and slavery. But for those few who have not lost their balance, who can still appreciate and fight for standards of honesty and morality--in short for our Judaism--now is not only an opportunity but a duty. I've even come around to saying--when I wonder how I'll make my living next year--like the old Jews, God will worry about it and take care of it. I'm going to continue the Newsletter, but I will have to find other ways to increase my income.

"...You may be having it tough in England, but it's nothing compared to what our organizations here are going to experience next year. They are worried silly now, but they're going to be a lot worse off than they realize. They've grown fat in the fleshpots of New York, but the palmy postwar days are over and the American war mobilization is going to cost fantastic sums before long.

"I fully expect to see a sharp drop in the general standard of living within the year. So, if I am almost broke now--I had put aside enough money for my year's unsuccessful experiment with the Newsletter (unsuccessful only financially, that is)--I won't be much worse off than the rest of my compatriots next year. With the inflationary boom destined to grow worse, money isn't going to have too much meaning anyway and planning for the future something out of the distant past. The bad news from Korea has thrown businessmen and people here into the depths of gloom, ruined the Christmas holiday business season, and generally given people a great deal to worry about."

On this pessimistic note, the Newsletter closed out the first year of its publication. Perhaps the most important development of the year was the introduction of the Israel bond issue which, together with investments, contributions and American government grants-in-aid, was expected to raise the unprecedented sum of $1 billion

for Israel in three years. This plan was the brain child
of Henry Montor, his ambitious response to the sharp decline in UJA receipts at a time when Israel's need for
money had reached critical proportions. As a consequence, the entire community fundraising structure was
jarred when Henry Morgenthau Jr., and Henry Montor, together with most of their professional fundraising
staff, transferred from the UJA to the new Israel bond
organization. This structure was based on the UJA for
many years, and the revolutionary change aroused strong
fears that the days of the UJA were numbered.

Montor was the author also of the proposal for a
standby plan, introduced by the CJFWF, that would
establish a community sponsored national campaign organization to replace the UJA. Announcement of this plan
shortly after the October Israel bond sale conference
was greeted with indignation by American Zionist organizations led by Hadassah, who charged that it was an
attempt to sabotage the UPA, a major constituent of the
UJA, and its affiliated agencies. So strong was the protest that the American section of the Jewish Agency,
which had originally supported the CJFWF proposal for a
Central Israel Fund, reversed itself and voted against
the proposal shortly before it was introduced.

Out of the controversy which was created by the proposal for a central fund came assurances from all sides
of strong support for the UJA, and pledges that the new
Israel bond campaign would be timed so that both appeals
would not conflict with each other and thereby weaken
the communal structure. As partial insurance for these
pledges, it was agreed that leadership of the UJA would
be placed in the hands of the non-Zionist JDC and its
leaders, Edward M.M. Warburg and Joseph J. Schwartz.

3

THE ZIONIST PROGRAM

Before the establishment of the state of Israel, the
ZOA and other American Zionist groups formed the
largest, wealthiest and most influential Jewish force in
the world. The ranks of the ZOA in particular had grown
spectacularly, from less than 150,000 in 1943 to more
than 400,000 men and women in 1945. Hadassah, the
Women's Zionist Organization, experienced a similar extraordinary growth. American Zionists, in their determination to help the remnants of the European Jewish communities destroyed by the Nazis to find a new home in
Palestine, had the unquestioned support not only of all
American Jews but also of a majority of the American
people and their representatives in the Congress.
Zionists controlled all fundraising in the United States
for the rescue of European Jewish refugees and for the
upbuilding of the Yishuv, the Jewish homeland in Palestine, where they were to be resettled. And although
David Ben-Gurion and other leaders of Palestine Jews
controlled the World Zionist Organization (WZO) and its
alter ego, the Jewish Agency, no basic changes could be
made without the approval of the American Zionists, who
were led by Rabbi Abba Hillel Silver, of Cleveland, and
Dr. Emanuel Neumann, the president of the ZOA.

After the establishment of the state of Israel in
May 1948, changes were drastic and widespread. As we
have noted earlier, the WZO was separated immediately
from the Israel government, thus creating two voices--
one for Diaspora Jewry and one for the Israelis--where
previously there had been only one. Questions over the
function and goals of the ZOA in the new post-state era,
now that the basic objective of the Zionist movement,
namely an independent Israel, had been achieved, arose
almost as quickly. Moreover, new and disturbing questions about the relationship between American Zionists
and the people of Israel were not long in surfacing and
calling for answers. Even such mundane arrangements as
the responsibility for the transportation of immigrants
to Israel was shifted from the Jewish Agency to the JDC,

49

and in 1950, back to the Jewish Agency again. At the end of the year, the JDC, which was originally set up decades earlier by American Jews to help persecuted European Jews, was given the responsibility of raising funds through the UJA, but in Israel its responsibility was reduced to only one important function, namely, the maintenance of MALBEN, the homes for the elderly and the infirm.

Among other important changes that took place in 1950 were the admission of the Hebrew Sheltering and Immigrant Aid Society (HIAS)--once concerned almost exclusively with the emigration of European Jews to the United States and their resettlement here--into the management of immigration to Israel; and the expansion of the Organization for Rehabilitation Through Training (ORT) activities in Israel at the behest of the Israel government. At the World Zionist Congress, there was an unsuccessful attempt to streamline its fundraising arms in the United States by combining the UPA, the JNF, and the Palestine Foundation Fund into one organization. Also defeated at the World Zionist Congress was an effort to set up territorial Zionist federations in place of the existing Zionist party organizations.

Long and highly animated discussions took place over proposals for new major objectives for the Zionist movement. Chief among the suggestions that emerged was the recommendation that the ZOA undertake the task of persuading American Jews to make **aliya,** that is, to pick up and resettle in Israel. Prime Minister Ben-Gurion had insisted that this be made the primary goal of the ZOA and most Israelis agreed with him. This also became one of the important decisions reached by the Jewish Agency Executive at its meeting in Jerusalem.

The leaders of the ZOA, however, were somewhat less than enthusiastic about persuading their members to leave their comfortable American homes for a pioneering existence in Israel. Meilech Neustadt, a Tel Aviv journalist, writing in the January issue of **Israel,** the organ of the World Poale-Zion (Labor Zionist organization), castigated the ZOA for refusing to make **aliya** of American Jews a primary objective of the movement and publicly expressing doubts over its advisability. Neustadt called on the ZOA to undertake a vigorous educational program to prepare American Jews for mass emigration to Israel, to establish **hechalutz** (pioneer) groups and training centers throughout the country, and to encourage widespread study of the Hebrew language. American Jews must realize that "being a Zionist means going to Israel!" Neustadt declared emphatically.

On this demand, the Newsletter offered the following comment:

> Dr. Abba Hillel Silver also supports imme-
> diate action on this basic tenet of Herzlian
> philosophy, which all American Zionists--at
> least nominally--support. President Daniel
> Frisch, of ZOA, however, advocates a go-slow
> policy and, fearful of adverse American re-
> action, has publicly hedged on the Israeli de-
> mand and cut off American **chalutziut** support.
> The issue critically affects the future of the
> American Zionist movement and will probably be
> resolved this summer at the World Zionist Con-
> gress meeting. American Zionists will have to
> make up their minds whether to remain advocates
> of Herzlian Zionism or change their movement
> into a sort of philanthropic Friends of Zion,
> which Israelis regard with scorn.

The problem was temporarily resolved when the Jewish Agency settled on a 3-point program, namely, **aliya,** **hechalutz** training centers, and popular study of the Hebrew language. The campaign to implement this program was officially adopted at a conference of the Hechalutz Organization of America in New York on February 15 to 18. The opening speeches of two Israel members of the Jewish Agency, Zvi Lurie and Baruch Zuckerman, set the tone of the meeting when they sharply criticized the ZOA for its failure--in their words--to "provide manpower for Israel's reconstruction."

They were followed by Dr. Nahum Goldmann, chairman of the American section of the Jewish Agency, who strongly emphasized the priority of **aliya** as the basic task of American Zionists. Dr. Goldmann expressed the hope that "American Jews will never be driven to Israel by the bloody anti-Semitism which wrecked European Jewry." His speech echoed a statement he had made at a press conference shortly before the convention, in which he said: "The whole Zionist movement is unanimous in ac-cepting that the encouragement and preparation of large numbers of Jews, especially among the youth, for settle-ment in Israel is one of the vital tasks of Zionism in the coming years."

Another Jewish Agency member, Dr. Israel Goldstein, who was the rabbi of the prestigious Congregation B'nai Jeshurun of New York, in an address before the Young Judea Alumni Reunion one day after the Hechalutz conven-tion, continued to exert pressure for **aliya**. He appealed

to the Young Judea Alumni to identify themselves closely
with the pioneer immigration movement in Israel. But despite his appeal and the optimistic hopes of Dr. Goldmann, resistance to the arguments for **aliya** continued to
be widespread, especially under the leadership of the
rabbis themselves. On February 23, the Newsletter
reported:

> Before the opening of this campaign, Ameri-
> can Zionists and religious leaders indicated
> their resistance to the Israeli demand for mass
> American **aliya.** Basic to the campaign is the
> Herzlian thesis that **Galuth** Jews are imperiled
> by anti-Semitism. Sharp denial of this belief
> came from the Union of Orthodox Hebrew Congre-
> gations and several Conservative rabbis. **Jewish
> Life,** organ of the Orthodox Union, recently
> editorialized: "...To predicate this movement
> upon the supposition of an anti-Semitic
> America, with a demand for the mass transferral
> of American Jewry to Israel, is a disservice to
> all concerned and futile to boot.... Mass immi-
> gration as a practical policy occurs only when
> circumstances compel it. Nor, under any circum-
> stances, can or should American Jewry yield its
> rightful place for reasons of present or poten-
> tial anti-Semitism."
> Similar reaction was voiced by noted Dr.
> Louis M. Levitsky, rabbi of the Conservative
> Oheb Shalom Congregation of Newark, N.J., who
> strongly affirmed his faith in the possibili-
> ties of a "dignified Jewish life" under Ameri-
> can democracy. Scoring "groups of people who
> see no peaceful and secure future for Jews in
> this country," Dr. Levitsky added: "What is
> difficult to understand are the young people
> who have been indoctrinated with the idea that
> what happened in Germany will happen here, and
> therefore they'd better get over to Israel
> before it's too late."

Dr. Levitsky probably reflected the sentiments of
most Americans, who were not eager to give up the
luxuries of American living for the threadbare hardships
of the settlers in Israel. Zionist leaders for the most
part either remained silent on the question of **aliya,** or
at best gave it lip service. It was a difficult and confusing time for them particularly because they had to
resolve the problem of affirming all the principles of

Zionist philosophy while at the same time establishing new objectives and functions for their organizations. At the ZOA, the problem was further compounded when the popular Daniel Frisch, who had succeeded Dr. Neumann as president of ZOA in 1949, fell ill within a few months after his election and died unexpectedly while undergoing surgery early the next year.

Frisch's policies never really had a chance to surface, and his friend and successor, Benjamin G. Browdy, did little to put them into effect. Browdy was a wealthy businessman out of Brooklyn, N.Y., who was probably more ambitious and well-meaning than knowledgeable about Zionism. He held office until 1952 and undoubtedly helped ZOA enormously to survive during some of its darkest days. While his own policies may have been more defensive than creative, they did chart out the direction ZOA was to take in the next decade.

Prime Minister David Ben-Gurion had minced no words in telling American Zionists what he expected their new role to be. At a meeting of the Zionist General Council in Jerusalem on April 24, he told delegates in effect to confine their activities to education and fundraising if they chose not to make **aliya**. He had the full support of the Israel cabinet, he said, in his demand that Israel assume complete control over immigration and resettlement. Furthermore, he insisted, the Jewish Agency, which had been created to represent non-Zionists as well as Zionists, should be absorbed by the World Zionist Organization since it no longer was needed.

The Newsletter did not report the immediate reaction of the American Zionists to these unprecedented demands, but it did say that "the speech by Dr. Nahum Goldmann, head of the American section of the Jewish Agency, in reply to Prime Minister Ben-Gurion revealed that the American delegation was lined up solidly against the Israeli point of view, including also the Israel government's demand that the Palestine Foundation Fund absorb the JNF."

When Dr. Israel Goldstein, at the same session, rose to the defense of the ZOA, the Israel Minister of Labor, Mrs. Golda Myerson (she had not yet Hebraized her last name) sharply retorted that "some of the finest Jews in the United States never paid membership dues in any Zionist organization." What his answer was has not been recorded. A report on the meeting was broadcast by Israel Schen over Kol Yisrael, the Israel shortwave radio, and quoted by the Newsletter as follows:"

"The last item under the headline of Or-

ganizational Questions is whether the Jewish
Agency should continue in existence (if it does
not, it should be merged with the [World]
Zionist Organization). The Jewish Agency, set
up under the provisions of Article 4 of the
Mandate and designed to represent non-Zionists
as well as Zionists, has, it is felt, lost
whatever justification it has ever had and now
constitutes an anomaly.... The Jewish Agency
and the [World] Zionist Organization are now
synonymous."

Also up for discussion is the redefinition
of the aim of Zionists, which Israeli leaders
insist is (1) education for emigration; (2)
establishment of **hechalutz** centers; and (3)
study of Hebrew.

At a press conference held before the ZOA national
convention in Chicago, Browdy vowed to devote the sessions to "action upon issues which will determine the
entire future course of the ZOA." With the pressures of
the Israel government in the background, the convention
opened on June 30 with all the Zionist leaders in attendance. Echoing the decisions taken by the World Zionist General Council, the ZOA resolved to support **chalutziut**, to stimulate the study of the Hebrew language, to
encourage private investments in Israel industry, to
develop tourism to Israel, and to pursue vigorously
political action in the United States. The Newsletter
observed that such veteran Zionists as Louis Lipsky,
Emanuel Neumann and Louis Falk were emphasizing the need
for a new clarified policy and a definition of functions
for the ZOA and the Jewish Agency, then went on to say:

We sincerely hope that the Chicago delegates, on the basis of these broad proposals
get down to brass-tack details. How does one
persuade American businessmen to invest in
Israel when, for example, the Securities and
Exchange Commission reports on Israel shares
offered here have been consistently unfavorable? What can be done to streamline overlapping and duplicating organizations doing Zionist work here, thus eliminating confusion and
waste? The Jewish Agency, for example, is reported spending more than $500,000 a year **in
this country** for fundraising and "education."
No successful program can ignore these
problems.

The Jewish Agency was also sharply criticized for allocating $15,000 a year for five years to help fund the Center of Israeli Studies, which had been set up at Columbia University with Dr. Salo Baron as its head. The Newsletter called this a "fantastic waste of dollars donated to Israel and desperately needed there." The responsibility for underwriting the Center, said the Newsletter, would have been better assumed by the ZOA.

At the ZOA convention, Rabbi Abba Hillel Silver and Louis Lipsky blamed the decline of the organization on the refusal of the Israel government to "empower it as a central Zionist body" in the United States, and on the Israel government's obvious "preference for non-Zionist control over fundraising in the United States." Their remarks constituted one of the sharpest rebukes that American Zionists ever delivered in public to the Ben-Gurion government. The Newsletter drew attention to the issue in the following comment:

> Comparison of the text of the speeches by David Ben-Gurion at the Zionist General Council meeting last April with those by Rabbi Abba Hillel Silver and Emanuel Neumann at the ZOA Chicago convention clarifies the basic issue dividing these leaders on the future of post-Israel Zionism. Differences boil down to one point: Is the Zionist movement **identical** with the State and all its achievements, as the Ben-Gurion school claims; or should the Zionist movement "become essentially and primarily a movement of Diaspora Jewry, oriented toward Israel," and bound by spiritual rather than formal ties, as the Silver-Neumann school argues?
>
> All the rest (**chalutziut**, student exchange, pilgrimages, investments, etc.) is commentary, as the rabbis say.
>
> Ideologically, according to Ben-Gurion, every Zionist is a potential **chalutz**, although he is willing to concede that for the present, a token **chalutziut** from the West is acceptable. Realistic Dr. Neumann warns: "If you attempt to re-define the term 'Zionist,' applying it only to prospective settlers in Israel, the movement will contract to the dimensions of a Chalutz Organization and cease to exist as a great mass movement in the free countries of the West."

The argument was critical and fundamental, and on

the point that Dr. Neumann made, the American Zionists
succeeded in winning. But they suffered defeats on all
other questions. The veteran diplomat, Dr. Nahum Goldmann, tried to put the best possible face on a difficult
situation when, at a press conference following his return from Jerusalem, he told reporters that agreements
which had been reached with the government of Israel
would define "once and for all the functions of Zionism
for the future." Actually, this was Goldmann's diploma-
tic way of softening the blows that American Zionism had
received at the hands of Ben-Gurion.

There was nothing altruistic about the way Goldmann
was reacting to the situation. At the Zionist General
Council meeting, for example, he had actually criticized
the Zionist leadership quite severely for being a
"closed shop" and demanded that it should be opened up
to make room for new faces. In an effort to save as much
as possible of the Jewish Agency's authority and in the
face of the demand by Ben-Gurion that it be eliminated
altogether, Goldmann had also joined the Prime Minister
in his attack on the ZOA request for a charter from the
Israel government and in the recommendation that the JNF
be absorbed by the Palestine Foundation Fund. This recommendation, incidentally, had aroused a storm of protest from American Jews, many of whom recalled with
nostalgia and sympathy the early years of the Zionist
movement when the JNF had placed a little blue tin box
in every Jewish home for contributions to rebuild the
Holy Land. It saved the JNF, but Goldmann's maneuverings
were of no avail, as the Newsletter concluded in the
following report:

> Analysis of decisions made at the Zionist
> General Council's meetings reveals the extent
> of Premier Ben-Gurion's victory; defeat for the
> Jewish Agency and American Zionists. Latter did
> not get the charter they wanted; the Joint Au-
> thority to which Dr. Goldmann was forced to
> agree takes from the Jewish Agency its power to
> decide and execute immigration and settlement
> policy in Israel and places it firmly in gov-
> ernment hands. Minister of Labor Golda Myerson
> termed former separate Agency and government
> budgets for immigration and settlement an "ab-
> surdity"; Premier Ben-Gurion said bluntly:
> "Immigration and settlement are not instruments
> for the use of Zionist organizations; Zionist
> organizations are for the service of immigra-
> tion and settlement."

Surveying the battlefield after this blast, the Newsletter observed: "Hit by the American Council for Judaism at one extreme, and by the Israel government on the other, ZOA faces a doubtful future."

The ZOA managed to maintain a bold front, however, and despite the pessimism of veteran Zionists, its leaders did come up at the Chicago convention with some positive recommendations for future programs. One program called for the establishment of special ZOA projects in Israel, including a ZOA house in Tel Aviv which would serve as a center for cultural and other ZOA activities in Israel. Another proposal, put forward by president-elect Benjamin G. Browdy, called for a greater measure of democratic representation in the leadership of the American Jewish communities. This would be demonstrated by a marked increase of Zionist influence and participation in the raising and allocation of community funds. This obvious attempt to restore Zionist leadership in fundraising proved to be highly controversial and at once drew down on Browdy's head the wrath of the non-Zionists.

The decisive contributions of Zionists to UJA campaigns was detailed by Morris Margulies, a veteran member of the ZOA Executive Committee, in an article in the **New Palestine,** but Browdy's proposal for greater democracy was bitterly attacked by the **Exponent,** the organ of the Philadelphia federation. In an editorial questioning the effectivenss of Zionists in fundraising, the **Exponent** asked: "Do the men now heading the Zionist movement really believe that a better job could be done--would be done--if they were in control?"

The Newsletter also was critical of the results of the ZOA convention in Chicago. The convention turned the spotlight on the weaknesses of the ZOA, the Newsletter said, and it predicted that Browdy would not get anywhere "with his proposal for more democracy in American Jewish life until ZOA demonstrates an ability to clear up the confusion and eliminate duplication in Zionist ranks." It was also critical of the ZOA projects program, saying that it was "neither novel nor new. It will no more attract new members now than it did last year." Despite the Newsletter's pessimistic prediction, the program proved to be vital and permanent. The projects program got away to a strong, fast start and within a month after the convention resolution was adopted, the first shipment was made of materials and equipment to assist Israel army veterans. The ZOA Projects Committee also disclosed its plans for the establishment of trade schools in two Israeli youth villages that had been "adopted" by the ZOA, and eventually these were completed. President Browdy's resolution calling for greater democracy in community fundraising continued to come under heavy fire, this time from the American Jewish Committee. In a highly critical article, published in its magazine **Commentary**, Hal Lehrman, who was not known for any special familiarity with the operations of the American Jewish community, displayed such intimate knowledge of the American fundraising scene as to arouse the suspicion that his criticism was inspired. The Newsletter did not hesitate to point an accusing finger at the article in the following comment:

> Eyebrows will be raised and pointed questions asked about under-surface meaning of Hal Lehrman's article, "Turning Point in Jewish Philanthropy," in September **Commentary**, organ of the American Jewish Committee. Lehrman, a journalist whose reputation is based on his knowledge of European affairs, discusses the American fundraising structure and problems with the assurance of an "insider." He uses "confidential" statistics and financial reports obtainable only from the CJFWF and not available to the press. Unfortunately, the result is a fuzzy rather than a clear picture of the position of the American Jewish Committee and the CJFWF on the Zionist demand for democratization of community funds and their relationship to the UJA.
> Lehrman says: "The truth is that democratic government of funds...cannot exist unless American Jews miraculously shed their variegated diversities...and become a monolithic, uniformly thinking, 'democratic' society...."

Neither the Newsletter's suspicions nor Lehrman's attack appears to have had much impact, but the issue of "democratization" never went very far because it was overtaken by the competition among organizations to sell the most Israel bonds. Israeli newspapers had devoted considerable space to comment on the best way for American Jews to help Israel in the light of the new Israel bond issue. The left-wing newspaper **Al Hamishmar**, for example, sharply criticized the Ben-Gurion government for weakening the Zionist movement by turning to American non-Zionists for help. The paper also warned Israel that the United States government would insist upon acceptance of specific demands before it would consent to the sale of Israel bonds in the country, a reflection, incidentally, of the Soviet propaganda line at that period. The independent newspaper **Ha'aretz** suggested that American contributors and investors in Israel should be given some control over the way their money was to be spent. And a similar view was expressed by the Orthodox newspaper **Hatzofeh**, which emphasized the need for a strong Zionist organizations in the United States that would have the right to confer with the Israel government on the allocation of American funds. More colorful was the criticism of the opposition Irgun newspaper **Herut**, which charged the Ben-Gurion government with treating American Zionists as if they were nothing more than a pump to be used to extract money from other American Jews.

Israel's prime minister, however, had come to the hard-nose conclusion, probably with the aid of Henry Montor, that the important money in the United States was held by the non-Zionist American Jewish Committee membership rather than by the Zionists. At the Jerusalem conference, therefore, Ben-Gurion struck a private deal with Jacob Blaustein, the oil millionaire president of the American Jewish Committee, to enlist non-Zionist support for the proposed Israel bond sale. At a luncheon in Jerusalem for the delegates, Ben-Gurion had attempted to broaden his definition of Zionism in such a way as to make it possible for non-Zionists like the American Jewish Committee to support Israel without reservation or fear of compromising their anti-nationalist policy. Seeking to identify Zionism with Judaism, Ben-Gurion said: "Ours is a Messianic movement....Ours is a movement which seeks the redemption of the nation together with the redemption of the world. We, and not America or Russia, shall redeem the world, and we derive our democracy from neither of those countries. The way to the world's regeneration is the Jewish way; that is why the Jewish people came into existence and struggled. But it will not achieve this by force.... The Jewish people will redeem the world by being an exemplary people and furnishing an example by its way of life."

Jacob Blaustein's reply to Ben-Gurion's exalted definition of Zionism and his "clarification" of the relationship between Israel and American Jews emphasized his anti-nationalist views. He made a special point of saying that American Jews "vigorously repudiate any suggestion that they are in exile." The "clarification" that he went on to present drew the following comment from the Newsletter:

Text of the statement by Jacob Blaustein, president of the American Jewish Committee, at the Jerusalem luncheon (as released by the Israel Office of Information) reveals the intense isolationism of the American Jewish Committee's point of view, going far beyond the question of political affiliation. Replying to Premier Ben-Gurion, American Jewish Committee president Blaustein made a special point of contrasting "my own country" with "your country." He left no doubt that the American Jewish Committee's attitude was that of a stranger to Israel, friendly and philanthropically inclined, but a stranger nevertheless. Problems of discrimination and persecution, said the American Jewish Committee president, "must be dealt with by each Jewish community itself in accordance with its own wishes, traditions, needs and aspirations."

The "isolated" community concept (as well as the claim that American Jews no longer live in exile) follows proposals first set forth at the 1950 annual meeting of the American Jewish Committee last January. It offers the community an issue on which it will have to take sides in the near future. The obvious historical parallel to the American Jewish Committee point of view is the point of view of the Babylonian Jews who refused to return from exile 2,500 years ago.

To the surprise of most of the delegates, Ben-Gurion responded by agreeing that American Jews owe no allegiance to Israel and that the Israel government fully respects the right of Jews in other lands to conduct their internal affairs without interference from Israel. Obviously, these words were intended to allay any fears that American Jews, and particularly the American Jewish Committee, may have entertained about Israel's adherence to the basic tenets of Zionism.

Oddly enough, Blaustein's statement does not appear in the **American Jewish Year Book,** vol. 53, page 182, although that volume is produced by the American Jewish Committee; in spite of its critical importance, it is referred to only as an "exchange of views" with Ben-Gurion, partial text of whose statement does appear on that page. The veteran American Zionist leader Louis Lipsky took sharp issue with Blaustein's pronouncement. In an exclusive statement to the Newsletter, Lipsky em-

phasized the complexity of meanings that are involved in
the Jewish concept of the term "exile," then added: "It
takes an enormous self-assurance on the part of Mr.
Jacob Blaustein, an oil man, to express with such ease
and confidence such a definition of a Jewish traditional
conception."

The American non-Zionist position on the question of
Galuth, or exile, was probably best expressed by Dr.
Sidney Hook, chairman of the department of philsophy at
New York University. In 1946, he had prepared a paper
for the National Council of Jewish Women, an organization with much the same ideological views as the American Jewish Committee, in which he defined the Council's
attitude toward the future state of Israel in the following terms:

"Council stands four square on the proposition that
the American Jewish community--the largest Jewish community in the world--is primarily interested in the survival of the American Jews in a democratic America. This
is its basic orientation. It repudiates any notion that
because it is Jewish, it is less American than any other
group, that its true home is elsewhere, and that it is
in exile from the land of its ancestors. Rooted as it is
in America, the American Jewish community is also
vitally concerned with the welfare of its compatriots--
no matter for what reason it regards them as compa-
triots--in other regions of the world, for as we have
seen, persecution of Jews anywhere is an incipient
threat to the status of Jews everywhere. In this respect
our concern with the Jews in Palestine differs only in
degree from our concern with the Jews in Germany and
other parts of Europe. No one objected to Council's
activities on behalf of persecuted German Jewry on the
ground that they represented a departure from its American orientation. And it is obvious that the life and security of most of what is left of European Jewry are at
present tied up with the continuation and up-building of
Jewish Palestine."

Both the National Council of Jewish Women and the
American Jewish Committee have adhered to this concept
to the present day. This strongly anti-nationalist approach to Israel and to Zionist philosophy led some of
the leading members of these organizations to form the
American Council for Judaism, with its distinctly anti-
state, anti-Israel position. While today the American
Council for Judaism has practically vanished from the
American scene in terms of membership and influence, the
ideological struggle over the American Jewish Commit-
tiee's anti-nationalist policy and negation of the

"exile" concept has continued to plague American communal relations as well as the relation of American Jews
to Israel.
For American Zionists, the realization that Ben-
Gurion's "clarification" was made to secure Jacob Blaustein's pledge to obtain American Jewish Committee support for the proposed Israel bond sale proved to be a
bitter pill to swallow. "Astounding," was the comment of
Dr. Samuel Margoshes in his column in the **Tog**, the New
York Yiddish daily. "By strengthening the American Jewish Committee, Israel's Premier would be weakening a
great many other groups in America, notably the Zionist
groups," he wrote on August 27.
At the Hadassah convention that month, Mrs. Samuel
Halprin, its president, wasted no time in clarifying
where she and her organization stood on the question of
"exile": "The Jewish community is divided into the
Galuth--that part which lives in lands where Jews are in
danger; and the Diaspora--that part which enjoys freedom
and equality in democratic countries. It is in the Diaspora that Jews of the United States belong," she proclaimed.
Mrs. Halprin's attempt at "clarification," which
cannot be regarded as anything more than a play on
words, contributed to the confusion in the minds of many
Americans over the Jewish concept of "exile." Their confusion was further compounded by the views expressed by
Orthodox rabbis, and also by visiting Israelis. In Great
Britain, for example, members of the Israel Knesset attending the Conference of Jewish Communities in the
British Commonwealth and Empire told delegates that the
Galuth must be liquidated, and every Jew must regard
himself as part of Israel, duty bound to settle there at
the earliest opportunity. British Chief Rabbi Israel
Brodie, however, assured the delegates that Israel had
no intention of seeking the dissolution of the Diaspora.
He observed that Israel at some point would have to depend on herself as an independent country while Jews in
the Diaspora could concentrate on developing their own
Jewish life. And when Mapai spokesman Pinhas Lubianiker
warned British Zionists that they had better move to
Israel if they did not want to suffer the same fate as
their European brethren in the next war, he was taken to
task by ZOA spokesman Dr. Samuel Margoshes, who wrote in
his newspaper column: "Mr. Lubianiker has not answered
the question why he believes that in case of a world
armed conflict, Israel would be in a position to afford
Jews the security of life and limb which the democratic
countries would deny them."

The issue continued to come up again and again.
Thirty years later, in 1980, it was raised at the annual
meeting of the World Jewish Congress, and as recently as
1981, it came up again at the annual meeting of the
American Jewish Committee. An editorial on the subject,
entitled "New Zionism," appeared in the Canadian Zionist
and was widely distributed by the ZOA in January 1981.
The author of the editorial, Aryeh Ben-Dov, called for a
"redefinition of Zionism" and cited a number of Jewish
scholars who had expressed a similar opinion. He concluded: "Reformulate the Zionist program and redesign
its structure? By all means. This should and must be
done. The Zionist ideal, however, must remain the core
of the program and the basis of its framework." It is
clear, therefore, that after more than thirty years of
discussion and debate, the issues of Galuth, the role of
Zionism and the relationship of American Jews to Israel
are apparently no nearer a resolution.

Money was the subject of the report by Benjamin G.
Browdy to the National Executive Committee of the ZOA
when he met with them on his return from the Jerusalem
conference. He told the committee that new investments
in Israel during 1949 totaled $220 million and he urged
it to find ways to stimulate and encourage more investments. The Newsletter, in reporting his statement,
added:

> The fact is (as we reported on March 9)
> that of the total 1949 investment, a good part
> came from the $100 million U.S. Export-Import
> Bank loan, while only IL 7,068,000 (about $16
> million) was the total foreign investment, the
> only kind that will help Israel overcome her
> dollar shortage.

In effect, Browdy was signaling the ZOA to make a
last-ditch effort to retain some measure of influence
over fundraising for Israel. A warning to the same
effect to American Zionists was issued by Dr. Nahum
Goldmann when he said: "If the Zionist movement wants to
continue playing its leading role, it will have to 'deliver the goods.'" And Israel's Ambassador Abba Eban
told a New York group in September that the economic
situation in Israel was likely to get worse before it
would show improvement. "The period of transition is
likely to be increasingly critical and austere," he
warned. As if to lend emphasis to his warning, the
Israel pound nosedived on the New York foreign currency
market from $1.40 on September 1 to $1.15 on October 1.

Within the same week, ZOA president Browdy appealed to the United States government to provide Israel with a grant of $500 million over a period of three to four years; a similar plea came from the American Jewish Committee president Blaustein at a Chicago conference. In reporting these appeals, the Newsletter recalled that in March the **New York Times** foreign correspondent Cyrus L. Sulzberger, in the course of his survey of the Middle East, had warned: "[The United States] is going to have to grant sufficient financial support to the present Israeli regime to avoid seeing the country go bust and perhaps swing into Communist hands."

Israel's financial crisis spurred the ZOA to increase its projects program. The Projects Committee, chaired by textile millionaire Fred Monosson of Boston, shipped a cargo of milk powder and prepared to send tons of other foodstuffs. In addition, when the Committee learned that Israel had been forced to halt the importation of American periodicals because of the shortage of dollar exchange funds, it undertook to provide Israeli citizens with a large number of free subscriptions to American newspapers. It also distributed over 100,000 copies of American magazines through Israeli veterans clubs. Funds for these efforts came from the ZOA Projects Fund, headed by Louis A. Falk.

By October, Israel's financial difficulties had worsened to such an extent that it led to the fall of the Ben-Gurion government, an event not entirely unexpected. The Israeli system of proportional representation voting led inevitably to a proliferation of political parties, and as a consequence, no one party was able to achieve a majority in the Knesset without forming a coalition with some of the smaller parties. The Labor government, which Ben-Gurion headed, was itself made up of anti-religious left and right wing Socialist groups but with the smaller non-Socialist and religious parties holding the balance of power. There was no formal opposition party of any substantial size at first, and the ZOA call for the formation of a center party of general Zionists, which could be supported in the United States by the ZOA, was bound to have serious consequences. Initially it aroused considerable opposition within the ZOA itself to any kind of affiliation with an Israeli political party. A strong faction, headed among others by Louis Lipsky, who was then chairman of the American Zionist Council, fought to nullify the recommendation. Lipsky insisted that the ZOA, as an American organization, should keep itself free from political activity in Israel. The fact that the Ben-Gurion government was a

Socialist regime and the ZOA membership was made up
largely of middle class Americans to whom Socialism represented radicalism and Marxism, also entered into the
controversy.
Leaders of the ZOA seized the opportunity presented
by the fall of the Israel government to launch their own
counter-attack against Ben-Gurion. At a National Executive Committee meeting in New York, Rabbi Abba Hillel
Silver, politically a staunch Republican, led off the
attack, which was fully reported in the **New York Herald
Tribune** despite the fact that it was made in a closed
meeting. The Newsletter revealed that the report had
been leaked to the newspaper by Dr. Emanuel Neumann. It
described the proceedings of the meeting in the following terms:

> Formation of a united General Zionist Party
> in Israel, "sufficiently large and influential
> to serve as a stabilizing force between groups
> and classes committed to conflicting ideolo-
> gies" was pledged last week by the National
> Executive Committee of the ZOA in a statement
> of policy issued on the eve of the Washington
> conference. ZOA president Benjamin G. Browdy
> and Rabbi Abba Hillel Silver, in his capacity
> as chairman of the World Zionist Affairs Com-
> mittee, urged the healing of the rift between
> the General Zionists in Israel and the amalga-
> mation of the center parties into a strong
> political party which the ZOA would support.
> Referring to the resignation of the Ben-
> Gurion government, Mr. Browdy said that "the
> political situation in Israel...could be dif-
> ferent today" if there had been a united Gen-
> eral Zionist party in the last elections. (In
> the 1949 elections, General Zionists polled
> 23,000 votes; the splinter Progressives,
> 18,000. Their total would have placed them
> sixth in line behind Mapai's 155,000 total.)
> The statements of Mr. Browdy and Rabbi
> Silver were interpreted by some observers as
> tantamount to a declaration of political war
> against Premier Ben-Gurion. They recalled the
> repeated snubs suffered by American Zionists at
> the hands of the Ben-Gurion government, includ-
> ing its failure to consult with ZOA on the ap-
> pointment of Mr. Henry Montor, director of UJA,
> to head the Israel bond drive; its action in
> repeatedly bypassing the ZOA in fundraising

plans and programs; the bitter attack on the
Ben-Gurion government by Dr. Emanuel Neumann,
former ZOA president and staunch ally of Dr.
Silver in Jerusalem last September; and the
openly expressed charge that the Israel government was working to weaken the Zionist movement
here.

Strong support for the new ZOA policy was voiced the
next week at the Mizrachi convention in Atlantic City.
In Israel, the Mizrachi party was affiliated with the
Religious bloc which had engineered the downfall of the
Ben-Gurion government. It was not surprising, therefore,
to hear the chairman of the American Mizrachi organization, Leon Gellman, accuse the Ben-Gurion government
with attempting to take "all fundraising activities out
of the hands of loyal and stalwart Zionists and transfer
them to non-Zionists and even anti-Zionists."
Other Mizrachi speakers at the convention echoed the
ZOA call for "democratization" of the welfare funds.
They also urged the welfare funds as well as the CJFWF
"to limit new local construction to minimum needs and to
allocate the greatest sum of the monies collected for
the rehabilitation program in Israel." A more political
approach was voiced by the Cleveland **Jewish Review and
Observer** in an editorial which praised the Mizrachi and
offered the following advice: "The convention's chief
task [is] to convince American religious Zionism that
the Religious bloc in Israel is capable of handling
whatever job that is assigned to it in a mandate from
the people." Delegates did not ignore the fact that
Cleveland was the home town of Rabbi Abba Hillel Silver.
Although Ben-Gurion was able to resolve his differences with the Religious party bloc and restore his
coalition government in relatively short order, the
American Zionist attack continued. This time it was
against the Jewish Agency which, by unanimous agreement,
had discontinued making grants for special projects to
Zionist political parties in Israel with the marked exception of the Mizrachi and the General Zionists. The
Jewish Agency paid for these grants out of funds received from the UPA.
Political differences also affected the American
Zionist Council. At an early period, before the controversy over political affiliation with Israeli parties
had surfaced, tensions were already present and they
threatened to reduce the ability of the American Zionist
Council to function. In November, the AZC convened a
conference of 250 "top Zionists" for the purpose of

holding "a full and frank discussion of internal problems affecting the Zionist movement in this country."
The conference agenda approached the actual situation
obliquely by defining the problems as those created by
the overlapping functions of the several Zionist groups.
The discussions quickly became acrimonious, and before
the conference was over, a disgusted Louis Lipsky, the
AZC chairman, had handed in his resignation.

Lipsky's letter of resignation was not released, but
apparently a copy was made available to the **Jewish Daily
Forward,** the labor-oriented Yiddish newspaper. The Newsletter summarized the **Forward's** report as follows:

> True reasons for the resignation of Louis
> Lipsky as chairman of the American Zionist
> Council were contained in his letter of re-
> signation which was not made public, the **For-
> ward,** New York Yiddish daily, claimed last Fri-
> day. According to the newspaper, Mr. Lipsky
> resigned only after his efforts to persuade ZOA
> and Hadassah to coordinate their activities
> through the Zionist Council had failed. Mr.
> Lipsky also charged ZOA president Browdy with
> failure to respect an agreement made with the
> late Daniel Frisch to make coordination ef-
> fective, and pointed to the ZOA missions to
> President Truman as examples of activities
> which often conflicted with Israeli policy and
> the work of Israeli officials here, the **Forward**
> said.

Possibly as a consequence of Lipsky's complaint, the
AZC took united action and sent a strong protest to the
State Department against its approval of a shipment of
steel to Iraq. The steel was intended for the construction of an oil pipeline designed to bypass the Haifa oil
refineries. According to the Newsletter, this was the
first time an American Zionist protest was heard against
the effort by American oil companies and the Arab countries to prevent oil from reaching the Haifa refineries.
As early as February, the Newletter had made the following accusation:

> American oil companies (Standard and
> Aramco), backed by the United States State De-
> partment, have supported the Arab oil boycott
> of Haifa as part of their offensive against
> British sterling oil. Why American Zionist or-
> ganizations have failed to pressure the State

Department for a change in policy on Haifa oil is beyond our comprehension.

The Haifa refineries, which had been closed since the 1948 war, were owned by the British, and after Israel won her independence, negotiations were opened between the Israel representative, David Horowitz, and the head of the Anglo-Iranian Oil Company, Sir William Frazer, with a view to reopening them. Israel planned to take over the refineries if the British were willing to reopen them. American oil companies, however, were preparing to open their own refineries in Lebanon, and their intention to construct a new 30-inch pipeline to carry oil from the Kirkuk field to Banias, a small port on the Syrian coast, was reported by the Newsletter in May. This pipeline would bypass the existing one which terminated in Haifa.

About 200,000 tons of American steel were needed to complete the Kirkuk pipeline in time for its scheduled opening in 1952. Steel, however, was on a wartime priority list because of the Korean war, and special permission from the State Department was needed before it could be shipped abroad. Despite the Newsletter's appeals for Zionist action to forestall such permission, however, no action was taken until the AZC's protest was made at the beginning of November, about six months later. On December 7, the Newsletter disclosed the extent of the American oil companies' operation in the following report:

> Completion of "Tapline," the oil pipeline from Saudi Arabia to Sidon, Lebanon, built by the Arabian-American Oil Company (Aramco), has just been announced. A large part of the cost of over $200 million was incurred as a result of the roundabout route of the pipeline through Jordan and Syria, taken to avoid crossing the borders of Israel. U.S. shipment of steel for the Kirkuk-Banias (Syrian) pipeline, now under construction, was protested last month by the American Zionist Council. A third line, from the South Persian oil fields to Tartus, Syria, is also planned.
>
> When these lines are completed, the American freeze-out of Haifa, with its large pipeline and huge refineries, will be an accomplished fact. A new refinery is also planned for Sidon, and the start of construction has been delayed only because of the threat of war with the U.S.S.R.

My indignation over what I called "this State Department supported outrage" was reflected in my letter to Leftwich, in which, among other matters, I quoted Louis Lipsky when he said: "The Zionists--Louis Lipsky with whom I had lunch yesterday said--off the record-- they were dead but didn't have sense enough to lie down decently. He scoffed at their projects program and the sincere but bumbling Mr. Browdy."

4

ANTI-NATIONALISM AND THE DEFENSE AGENCIES

Long before the state of Israel came into existence, the American Jewish Committee was confronted with the problem of defining its position on Jewish nationalism. In that respect, it had an advantage over the Zionist organizations because as early as 1943, it had to come up with an answer to the question of where it stood on the issue of a Jewish state. While to most Zionists at that time an independent state was a distant objective, years away from realization and therefore requiring little or no thought about the consequences of its establishment, the American Jewish Committee faced an immediate crisis when a number of its members as well as its executive secretary, Sidney Wallach, resigned in order to organize the anti-state American Council for Judaism. The Committee rejected the Council's position, but it was not yet ready to go beyond that rejection.

Again, in September 1943, during World War II, the American Jewish Committee once more was called on to make a decision when it participated in the proceedings of the American Jewish Conference, a one-time assembly which had been called to formulate a unified American Jewish program on foreign political questions, including Palestine and the Yishuv. Over the objections of the American Jewish Committee and several other organizations, the Conference by a large majority adopted a resolution calling for support of the Biltmore Declaration, a Zionist statement urging the establishment of a Jewish state in Palestine. This time, the American Jewish Committee walked out.

The Committee never actually opposed the establishment of a state of Israel, and in 1944, it joined in denouncing the American Council for Judaism when that organization submitted a memorandum to the State Department opposing a Jewish state and questioning the loyalty of American Jews who favored the state. At that time the American Jewish Committee emphasized that it supported an "international trusteeship responsible to the United

71

Nations" for a reasonable period of time before Israel
would become "a self-governing commonwealth." Eight
months after the state of Israel proclaimed its independence, however, the American Jewish Committee spelled
out a much clearer and stronger pledge of support for
the new state in its historic "Statement of Views,"
adopted on January 23, 1949, at its annual meeting. Convinced that it was not abandoning its long-established
non-Zionist and anti-nationalist beliefs, it emphasized
the following position:

"We hold the establishment of the State of Israel to
be an event of historic significance. We applaud its recognition by our own and other governments. We look forward to Israel's assumption of its full place among the
family of nations as a government guaranteeing complete
equality to all its inhabitants, without regard to race,
creed or national origin, and as an advocate of liberty
and peace in the Near East and throughout the world.
Citizens of the United States are Americans and citizens
of Israel are Israelis; this we affirm with all its implications; and just as our government speaks only for
its citizens, so Israel speaks only for its citizens.
Within the framework of American interests, we shall aid
in the upbuilding of Israel as a vital spiritual and
cultural center and in the development of its capacity
to provide a free and dignified life for those who desire to make it their home."

The basic philosophy expressed in this statement is
essentially the same as that prescribed by Dr. Sidney
Hook for the National Council of Jewish Women three
years earlier. A noted philosopher, educator and writer,
Dr. Hook in his statement, by implication denied the
Zionist and the Judaic concept that all Jews outside of
Israel were living in **Galuth**, that is, in exile, and
have the duty and responsibility to return to Israel
when that becomes possible. He also denied that the
religio-nationalistic character of Jews, which is particularly native in origin in the Middle East, still
existed, and asserted in its place that Jews now are
Westernized and exclusively the nationals of the countries in which they enjoy citizenship; they owe allegiance to no other entity. In this respect, he further
rejected the religious as well as the Zionist tenets
that Jews are one people and one nation, responsible for
each other.

Unlike Dr. Hook's unequivocal statement, however,
the position of the American Jewish Committee was awk-
ward and confusing, and its corollaries were never fully
spelled out. During the early decades of its existence

the American Jewish Committee included in its leadership
men like Jacob H. Schiff, Felix M. Warburg and Cyrus
Adler, who were deeply religious and who were pillars of
the Conservative Judaism movement. They helped to found
the Jewish Theological Seminary and remained closely
allied to it. The anti-nationalist philosophy, which the
American Jewish Committee later adopted, placed it
closer to the philosophy and approach of early Reform
Judaism. Nevertheless, it continued to remain more
closely attached to the Seminary than to the Hebrew
Union College. And despite its antipathy toward Jewish
nationalism, the members of the American Jewish Committee provided the fledgling state of Israel with enormous
financial and political support.

In 1949, the newly elected president, Jacob Blaustein of Baltimore, led a delegation to Israel where he
conferred with Prime Minister Ben-Gurion. A founder of
the American Oil Company (AMOCO), a board member of
other oil companies and a multi-millionaire, Blaustein
had long been active in American political affairs as
well as in Jewish organizational matters before becoming
president of the American Jewish Committee. He had also
maintained a long-term interest in the development of
the Yishuv for personal as well as business reasons.
When he met Ben-Gurion again the following year, Blaustein pledged full-hearted support for the projected
Israel bond issue while at the same time making it very
clear to the Prime Minister that the American Jewish
Committee was not accepting the concept of "exile" for
American Jews. A wide-ranging exchange of views between
the two men resulted in the formulation by the American
Jewish Committee of its position toward Israel, which
included the following definitive statement:

"The American Jewish community sees its fortunes
tied to the fate of liberal democracy in the United
States, sustained by its heritage as Americans and as
Jews. We seek to strengthen both of these vital links to
the past and to all humanity by enhancing the American
democratic political system, American cultural diversity
and American well-being.

"As to Israel, the vast majority of American Jewry
recognizes the necessity and desirability of helping to
make it a strong, viable, self-supporting state. This,
for the sake of Israel itself, and the good of the
world. The American Jewish Committee has been active, as
have other Jewish organizations in the United States, in
rendering, within the framework of their American citizenship, every possible support to Israel; and I am sure
this support will continue and that we shall do all we

can to increase further our share in the great historic
task of helping Israel to solve its problems and develop
as a free, independent and flourishing democracy."

This position, with its extreme sensitiveness on the
implied but never stated question of dual loyalty, resulted inevitably in some ambivalence in the attitudes
of American Jewish Committee members, especially for
those with strong anti-nationalist views. One of them
was articulate enough to provide his own formulation of
what he thought the position of the American Jewish Committee ought to be, and in April 1950, the Newsletter
summarized what he said in the following report:

> One interpretation of the American Jewish
> Committee's new policy of fighting Jewish "na-
> tionalism" was offered recently by Fred H.
> Roth, president of the American Jewish Commit-
> tee chapter in Cincinnati. Criticizing the
> American Council for Judaism for its anti-Zion-
> ist publicity tactics, Mr. Roth told the annual
> meeting of the American Jewish Committee chap-
> ter in that city that the American Jewish Com-
> mittee and the Council both "view world Jewish
> nationalism in much the same way."
> Avowing friendship for Israel, Mr. Roth
> continued: "Like the American Council we re-
> main non-Zionist. Unlike the American Council,
> however, we do not believe that world Jewish
> nationalism and Zionism are synonymous. Nor do
> we believe that world Jewish nationalism--
> whether or not basic to Zionism--has ever won
> the support of more than a small minority of
> Zionists."

One significant reaction to this tortured view of
the differences between the American Jewish Committee
and the American Council for Judaism as well as to the
American Jewish Committee's statement itself came from
the American Council for Judaism in the form or a detailed analysis of the differences it perceived between
its attitude toward Jewish nationalism and that of the
American Jewish Committee. In part this analysis was
also designed to help win over sympathetic members of
the American Jewish Committee. The drive was spearheaded by Rabbi Elmer Berger, the executive director of
the American Council, who in numerous speaking engage-
ments rarely failed to criticize Jacob Blaustein for his
"gratuitous" exchange of views with Prime Minister Ben-
Gurion.

The emphasis on American Jews as citizens with a single loyalty to the United States only received its fullest expression at the annual meeting of the American Jewish Committee in New York on January 20-22, 1950. The Newsletter reported that Blaustein and the other leaders left no doubt about their ambition to be the dominent influence in the American Jewish community. The Newsletter carried the following report:

> Keynote development was the change in emphasis from propaganda against anti-Semitism to propaganda directed to Jews. Main Committee propaganda points are: (1) need to strengthen "confidence in permanence and security of Jewish life in America" (Irving M. Engel, executive committee chairman); (2) the challenge to Jews as a special group to "maintain, promote and defend a common American civilization" along with other "ethnic, racial and religious groups" (John Slawson, executive vice president); and (3) to win acceptance of the American Jewish Committee's "developed philosophy of Jewish life" (Alan M. Stroock, vice president).
> This philosophy is the "integrationist philosophy" of the American Jewish Committee expounded by executive vice president John Slawson at the Chicago meeting of the American Jewish Committee last December (see **Committee Reporter** for December 1949). Its purpose is to "immunize them [American Jews] against the influence of those groups whose spiritual assets are not in America but elsewhere." (Note: AJC and NCRAC recently condemned Lessing Rosenwald Jr., and the American Council for Judaism for expressing a similar "philosophy.")
> Jews who adhere to the traditional philosophy of Judaism as expounded by the Reform Hebrew Union College, the Conservative Jewish Theological Seminary, and the Orthodox Yeshivas should find little need for the secular "integrationist philosophy" of the American Jewish Committee to justify their living as good American citizens.

As might be expected, reaction to the publication of these aims was critical and strong. Zionist leaders unanimously charged the American Jewish Committee with waging a campaign to isolate the American Jewish community from the rest of the Jews of the world. Both

sides resorted to publicity in the general press, the
New York Times and the **New York Herald Tribune** in particular, an action which caused considerable distress to
Jews generally, as the controversy intensified. Efforts
to keep controversial Jewish issues out of the general
press were disregarded by Jacob Blaustein of the American Jewish Committee and Judge Meir Steinbrink of the
Anti-Defamation League when they openly declared war
against the recommendation by Zionist groups that all
fundraising appeals for that year be devoted solely to
Israel. Their statements, made at the annual meeting of
the JDA, were fully reported in the New York newspapers.
The NCRAC had previously urged all groups, especially
the American Council for Judaism, to keep controversial
Jewish actions and statements out of the public press,
but its advice was generally ignored. Jerome N. Curtis,
president of the Jewish Community Council of Cleveland,
appealed to all local organizations in that city to submit in advance any statements likely to have a public
relations impact, but his well-intentioned effort was
also promptly rejected on the ground that it was censorship.

Later that year, a minor sensation was caused by the
publication of a letter in the **New York Times** on December 24 recommending the application of the principle of
home rule by the state of Israel as a "juridical device" to help solve the "basic problem" of religious
freedom. The letter was signed by Harold Riegelman, a
vice president of the American Jewish Committee; Jacob
M. Dinnes, a New York attorney; and New York Supreme
Court Justice Samuel H. Hofstadter. They were impelled
to act, they explained, because of the "many practical
questions inherent in applying the principle of a Jew-
ish-patterned state within the guarantee to the adherents of other creeds of freedom of observance. The
problem is complicated by differences in meaning and
importance which sacred values have for Jews of various
shades of orthodoxy--the reform, the non-observant and
the secularist."

The letter, in the form of a memorandum, was sent to
"Israeli government officials" and simultaneously released to the general press. Apart from the impudence of
both actions, no one raised the question of direct
American Jewish Committee complicity in the memorandum-
letter, but few Zionists doubted that its inspiration
had come from that organization. It marked the first of
a number of efforts by the American Jewish Committee, in
its self-appointed role of defender of Jewish rights--
some as recent as 1980--to call attention to the problem

of religious freedom in Israel where the Orthodox rabbinate have the sole and complete authority over matters of marriage, death and inheritance.

From the point of view of the American Jewish Committee, these questions involved the individual rights of Jews in a foreign government, which is the way it regarded the Israel government. In reality, this was an oversimplification of a highly complex problem involving religion and nationality as one unit, a problem inherent in the basic nature of Judaism itself rather than a question of the rights of Jews in a Moslem or Christian state, or a communist state. It had been recognized as such by the British under the Mandate, by the Turkish Empire before that, and currently by the Israel government, all of whom chose to sidestep it simply by turning over authority to the Orthodox rabbis. The memorandum created an uproar in the community not only because of the questions it raised but also because of the obvious discourtesy in publicizing the letter before it was even received by the Israel government. The Newsletter also added: "We sincerely hope the letter was not published with an eye to the arrival here next month of the Israeli Minister of Religion, Rabbi Judah L. Maimon."

The question of the relation of Jews in the Diaspora to Jews in Israel has continued to defy resolution. As recently as January 1981, it was brought up again at the assembly of the World Jewish Congress in Jerusalem, where a report initiated by its president, Philip M. Klutznick, sought to negate the concept of the Diaspora and of Jews living in exile, much as Jacob Blaustein had sought to do thirty years earlier. The World Jewish Congress report contended that "the classic Zionist ideology which denigrates the prospects for a secure or meaningful Jewish existence in the Diaspora, and which conceives Diaspora existence as living in exile, is remote from the thinking of most Jews who live in free democratic societies." To which Klutznick's successor, the newly elected president of the World Jewish Congress, Edgar Bronfman, added in speaking to an Israeli journalist: "It is a mistake to make the Diaspora guilty for not settling here. I'm trying to be practical. I don't think my children and grandchildren will ever move to Israel."

The World Jewish Congress report, which dealt also with the rights of Jews in the Diaspora to criticize Israeli policies publicly, was not adopted by the delegates. Although widely discussed and publicized, the issue remains unresolved.

Of more immediate concern to the American Jewish Committee than the ideological question was the fund-

raising problem that it faced. Its funds were raised by
the JDA and the receipts of the annual drive were shared
with the ADL. About 98 percent of the JDA receipts came
from the New York UJA, in lieu of a separate campaign,
and from local welfare funds throughout the country. The
American Jewish Committee also collected nominal dues
from approximately 14,500 members. In 1950, the JDA goal
was $5,537,015 but it expected to raise considerably
less. JDA estimated that it would raise no more than
about $3,500,000, and by April the fundraisers began to
feel strong pressures from both of their constituent
organizations for a complete break with the New York UJA
and for a resumption of independent campaigning. At the
same time, secondary pressures were developing in-
ternally for a break-up of the JDA itself. The Newsletter carried the following report on the situation:

> At a recent B'nai B'rith convention, John
> Horowitz, of Oklahoma City, argued strongly for
> a withdrawal of ADL from the JDA. He presented
> a detailed plan for "family" fundraising within
> B'nai B'rith ranks which would free ADL from
> dependence on UJA and welfare funds. Renewal of
> the ADL-AJC contract comes up in May; it is
> automatically renewed unless protested. Efforts
> of Max Schneider, New York banker, and other
> B'nai B'rith leaders to maintain a united fund-
> raising front were successful for this year at
> least.

Efforts to keep JDA from withdrawing from the New
York UJA continued throughout the year and hope for a
satisfactory last-minute agreement was expressed by UJA
leaders, but by December the break was complete and JDA
went ahead with its plans for an independent campaign in
1951.

Meanwhile, the American Jewish Committee sought to
strengthen the range of JDA fundraising by supplying it
with accurate population statistics. Over the years, the
American Jewish Committee had funded scholarly studies
of the demography and other vital statistics of American
Jews as part of its efforts to combat anti-Semitism. Now
it apparently believed that Jewish communities would be
aided in their fundraising appeals if they had more reliable population statistics than the random estimates
they were using. These estimates were frequently based
on nothing more substantial than synagogue membership,
the number of children absent from school on Jewish
holidays, or the Jewish death rate--all multiplied by a

factor. The effort of the American Jewish Committee to set up an Office of Jewish Population Research (OJPR) ended in failure, however, and in the following report, the Newsletter summarized the reasons for that failure:

> Since 1943, a group of Jewish organizations has been discussing ways and means of establishing an agency which would spur and coordinate the efforts of local communities to compile much-needed vital statistics about Jews in America. (The United States Census does not include information on religious preference.) At the instigation of the American Jewish Committee, the Conference on Jewish Relations under Dr. Salo Baron called a Conference on Jewish Demography in December 1945, attended by representatives of the CJFWF, the Jewish Labor Committee, the Jewish Welfare Board (JWB), the American Association for Jewish Education, the Yiddish Scientific Institute and other interested bodies.
>
> Three years later, at the Second Conference on Jewish Demography, a subcommittee recommended the establishment of an Office of Jewish Population Research as an independent national agency financed by the community at large. A modest initial budget of $10,000 for a six-months trial period was decided upon, and finally in August 1949 the new organization made its bow. Appointed to the post of acting director was Ben B. Seligman, a statistician of acknowleged repute, who was granted a leave of absence by the CJFWF for the period.
>
> To meet the initial $10,000 budget of OJPR, the American Jewish Committee made a contingent grant of $5,000 to be paid in three installments provided each installment was matched by an equal sum from the other agencies. At a final meeting, held last month, JWB (which thus far had made no financial contribution to the OJPR) raised two objections to continuance of the agency: (1) JWB was dissatisfied with the setup of OJPR, which placed emphasis on actual work with the communities rather than on fundraising and publicity; and (2) JWB was in no position to participate financially in the 1949 budget or in the $20,000 requested for 1950. JWB's refusal to help foot the bill for OJPR, followed by some of the other organizations, spelled the end of the OJPR.

Asked by **Cross-Section, U.S.A.** to explain further JWB's decision, especially in view of the modest sum involved and the enormously valuable service that the OJPR could render, S.D. Gershovitz, executive director of the JWB, revealed that his organization had a deficit of $150,000 in 1949. He refused to comment on the reasons for JWB's dissatisfaction with the OJPR setup, which consisted only of Mr. Seligman and a secretary.

In an exclusive statement to **Cross-Section, U.S.A.**, the chairman of the Conference on Jewish Demography described the present position of the OJPR as "pending" rather than dead, although it now has no funds and no staff. Dr. Baron denied the possibility of rivalry between the JWB and the CJFWF as a cause for the demise of the OJPR, and stressed that no personal objections had been raised to the acting director. He reiterated that budget difficulties were the official reason for the deadlock. Another conference to reconsider the question may be called in March, Dr. Baron added.

Cross-Section, U.S.A. sincerely hopes that it will not be necessary to wait another six years before the largest and richest Jewish community in the world will be able to learn the facts about itself instead of relying on the worthless guesses hitherto passed off as "informed estimates."

The Newsletter's hope was never realized, of course, and to this day no one really knows how many Jews there are in the United States. The American Jewish Committee found itself involved not only in this controversy and the one over Jewish nationalism but also in a public rebuke from pro-Israel advocates over the standards of propriety that its publications should observe. The monthly magazine **Commentary**, which the American Jewish Committee sponsored, was the successor to the **Contemporary Jewish Record**, also published by the American Jewish Committee since 1939. It took its new name and format in 1945 with the appointment of Elliot Cohen as its editor. Cohen, who had been the public relations director for the CJFWF, was the managing editor of **The Menorah Journal** in the 1930s and had left that cultural magazine because his left-wing associations were becoming embarrassing. As editor of **Commentary**, he was given a fairly free hand by the American Jewish Committee

along with a budget in 1949 of $295,000, an extraordi-
nary allocation for the usually conservative Committee.
During the year, rumblings of discontent with the
magazine, despite its reputation as a publication of
intellectual expression, reached a climax in November
1949 when it was openly attacked by the highly respected
Rabbi Milton Steinberg of the Park Avenue Synagogue, in
New York. The following report on the rabbi's comments
appeared in the Newsletter:

> The magazine and its editor Elliot Cohen
> have been under heavy fire since the publica-
> tion several months ago of the pornographic
> "Adam and Eve on Delancy Street." Strongest
> criticism came from Rabbi Milton Steinberg of
> the Park Avenue Synagogue in New York City,
> whose precedent-shattering sermon on November
> 18, 1949, contained a scathing analysis of **Com-
> mentary** contents for one year. Said Rabbi
> Steinberg: "The list of those who have not ap-
> peared in **Commentary's** columns would coincide
> pretty closely with the names which would oc-
> cur in a Who's Who in American Jewish religious
> and cultural life."

Rabbi Steinberg's sermon, later included in his
book, **A Believing Jew,** published posthumously, sharply
attacked the magazine for its biased record against
Zionism. Rabbi Steinberg noted in the course of his remarks that out of sixteen articles in 1948 on the Middle
East, only eight dealt with policy; the others were reportorial. Of the eight that dealt with policy, said the
rabbi, "no less than six, or three quarters, are non-
Zionist, ranging from outright anti-Zionism to such bor-
derline Zionist positions as Ihud. Only two reflect
mainline Zionist thought. If ever there was an instance
of an unrepresentative coverage of a controversial
issue, this is it."
The impact of Rabbi Steinberg's sharp criticism compelled the American Jewish Committee to take some
action, but the strength of Cohen's supporters within
the organization caused it to move obliquely rather than
to tackle the problem head on. The chairman of the
American Jewish Committee's executive committee, for example, was Herbert S. Ehrmann, of Boston, a man who had
befriended Cohen in his Trotzkyite days, when he was
managing editor of **The Menorah Journal,** and had remained
his strong supporter. Ehrmann defended **Commentary** and
its editor in a letter to the **Jewish Advocate** (Boston),

citing the fact that the magazine had been endorsed by several prominent Jewish religious leaders. One of the latter, Rabbi Israel Tabak, president of the Orthodox Rabbinical Council, promptly pointed out that his endorsement of **Commentary** had been given in the early period of its publication and that he had vigorously protested publication of the controversial article.

At the American Jewish Committee's request, Dr. Louis Finkelstein, president of the Jewish Theological Seminary, and members of the faculty of the Seminary agreed to meet with Elliot Cohen and his publication committee. The meeting was scheduled for March 22, but because of the death of Rabbi Steinberg that month, and for other undisclosed reasons, the meeting was postponed until May. Asked by the Newsletter for comment, Dr. Finkelstein, who affected an air and appearance of great dignity befitting his position, made the following statement:

> I have had several discussions with Mr. Elliot Cohen with regard to the nature of **Commentary** and its future. I am trying, in cooperation with others who feel that **Commentary** is potentially a very important instrument of Jewish education but who also think that in order to fulfil itself it must reflect more effectively affirmative Jewish thinking, to solve the real problem with which it is confronted, namely, that scholars, whether in Judaism or other fields, are, generally speaking, not literary craftsmen, while literary craftsmen, generally speaking, have not had the time to obtain the scholarship necessary for effective interpretation of Judaism. I think we have worked out a plan which will be helpful. Under the circumstances, I have tried very hard to avoid participating in the present controversy, for I am sure that any participation by me would prevent us from working out a constructive solution to a real need of American Judaism.
>
> My endorsement of **Commentary**, to which Mr. Ehrmann referred, was therefore, definitely a qualified one based on hopes.

And there the matter stood. Cohen obviously had no intention of meeting with a group of rabbis, least of all permitting them to supervise his editorial judgement. When a reporter for the Newsletter called on him for his reaction to Dr. Finkelstein's proposal, he said he had no comment to make. Apparently no changes occurred after Cohen's meeting with Dr. Finkelstein, for in June, Rabbi Abba Hillel Silver denounced **Commentary** for its failure to make any policy changes that might satisfy its critics. An open letter to American Jewish Committee president Jacob Blaustein protesting the frequent use by **Commentary** of writers of the "non-Stalinist left" was also circulated by a Brooklyn, N.Y., lawyer named Nathan D. Shapiro. The only concession to its critics by the American Jewish Committee was to enlarge the publication committee of **Commentary** by six new members, three of whom were women.

Encouraged by the stonewalling of the American Jewish Committee and the support of the magazine's publication committee in the face of widespread rabbinical displease, Cohen defied his critics by publishing another article by the same Isaac Rosenfeld who had created the stir the previous year. The subject this time was Mohandas Gandhi, the Indian leader, and the Newsletter, highly indignant at what it regarded as Cohen's deliberate act of thumbing his nose at the Jewish community, exploded in the following comment:

> **Commentary** has done it again! In stupid defiance of the sharp criticism aroused last year by the pornographic "Adam and Eve on Delancey Street," the current (August) issue of the American Jewish Committee monthly carries a sex-centered review and analysis of Mohandas Gandhi by Isaac Rosenfeld. This is the same man who wrote in the **Partisan Review** (March): "The reason I cannot accept any of the current religious philosophies is that they are all crazy in one very basic respect--their denial of nature and attempt to push man out of nature."
>
> In the Gandhi article (what place has it anyway in a Jewish magazine?), Rosenfeld delivers himself of the same depraved lewd thinking that characterized his earlier writings. There are dozens of sentences in which Jewish religious concepts are held in contempt, in which hallowed beliefs are insulted in the filthiest manner.
>
> According to the sick mind of Rosenfeld, it is only the "neurotic who regard sexual intercourse without intent of producing children as a grave crime...."
>
> No one but a **meshummad**, in spirit if not in fact, would have the gall to write in a Jewish

magazine anything as foul as this: "Both 'hell'
and 'heaven' have this in common--that there,
and only there, is the dissolution of self accomplished in the sexual orgasm and in the
standing face to face with God."!

Not only Isaac Rosenfeld but also Editor
Elliot Cohen are responsible for this vicious
flaunting of degenerate paganism. The featuring
of this sophomoric pseudo-intellectual can no
longer be "explained" by Editor Cohen as an
oversight or an error. Editor Cohen has had
fair warning that the Jewish community will not
stand for this filth. Editor Cohen has deliberately thumbed his nose at the late Rabbi Milton
Steinberg, at Rabbi Abba Hillel Silver, at
Rabbi Louis Finkelstein, at Dr. Abraham Neumann and at many other leaders of American
Judaism. Editor Cohen, who was in Europe as the
representative of American Jewish culture--no
less!--must stand   ready to take the consequences of his consistently un-Jewish editorial
policy. He should be removed forthwith!

It is a Jewish duty for our readers and all
their friends to protest to the officers of the
American Jewish Committee as strongly and by
whatever means they possess Cohen's and Rosenfeld's repeated insults to Judaism. We strongly
urge you to do so.

A number of letters of criticism and protest were
sent in response to this appeal by the Newsletter, among
them, one by Rabbi Sidney B. Hoenig, professor of Bible
and Jewish History at Yeshiva University, in New York.
Rabbi Hoenig wrote to Elliot Cohen recalling the criticism by American Jewish Committee president Jacob Blaustein the previous year and the promise that Cohen and
his publication committee had made "that steps will be
taken to ensure against a similar occurrence in the
future."

A true indication of the American Jewish Committee's
real attitude in the matter was the reply of Alan M.
Stroock, a prominent attorney and chairman of the publication committee of **Commentary,** when the Newsletter
called him and protested the article. Apparently the
publication committee's promise was never intended to be
taken seriously, for Stroock's smart-alecky reply was:
"Honi soit qui mal y pense."

Stroock was also chairman of the Board of Directors
of the Jewish Theological Seminary, and this may help to

explain why Dr. Louis Finkelstein, president of the Seminary, this time refused to answer the Newsletter's telephone calls and a letter asking him to comment on the second Rosenfeld article and his understanding with Cohen. Elliot Cohen was never reprimanded and continued to serve as editor of the magazine until his tragic suicide some time later. Under his successor, **Commentary** has achieved a fine reputation as a vehicle for intellectual expression, but not as a voice for Jewish opinion. Occasionally there is an article about Israel, but only rarely will it stray from the official American Jewish Committee anti-nationalist but pro-Israel approach that Jacob Blaustein originally enunciated. The American Jewish Committee itself never deviates from that line.

5

THE "JOINT"

Few non-Zionist Jewish organizations have been affected by the establishment of the state of Israel as fundamentally as the American Jewish Joint Distribution Committee (JDC). For decades, the "Joint," as it was more familiarly known to thousands of European Jewish families, had worked tirelessly and unselfishly to rescue the persecuted and harassed Jews of Eastern Europe. Organized in 1914, some of its most important services were rendered in the troubled years between World I and World War II, and in the years immediately after that war. Its work in saving the remnants of European Jewry after the Holocaust earned it a major share of UJA fundraising campaigns, in which it was the senior partner.

The JDC was anathema to the Soviet Russian communists both because of its association with wealthy Jews and because it was American, and shortly after World War II, the Soviet Union ordered the JDC out of Poland and other Soviet satellite states. With the closing of the Displaced Persons camps, the immediate European program of the JDC virtually came to an end. Thus, cut off from its traditional and major areas of operation, the JDC was compelled to take on a new function, namely, the transportation of homeless Jews from Europe and various other parts of the world to the new state of Israel. It was an important task, and its association with the new Israel government in this effort led also to an expansion of its activities into fields it had not previously entered.

The Newsletter of January 11 disclosed the following information about one of the JDC's functions:

> Hadassah, which heretofore has enjoyed a virtual monopoly in the field of medical care in Israel, will soon face stiff competition from the JDC. At the annual meeting of the JDC in New York, January 7-8, executive vice chair-

87

man Moses Leavitt revealed plans for construction of four hospitals as part of a 15-month
program for social service for immigrants to
cost $15,000,000. Under an agreement signed
with the government of Israel last October, JDC
will share costs equally with the Jewish
Agency.

Is it naive to ask why $7,500,000 could not
have been shifted from JDC's share of UJA funds
($44,512,000) to UPA, thus sparing the Israel
government the indignity of bargaining for aid?

Probably with the encouragement of the Israel
government, the JDC also turned its attention next to
North Africa as one of the most fertile sources of immigration to Israel. A compaign to convince American
Jews that their contributions to the UJA were serving a
noble purpose in being used to help move indigent Jews
from North Africa to Israel--in reality to empty the
North African poorhouses--was promptly inaugurated.
Americans were told that these Jews were living in "sub-
human" conditions in such "Moslem countries" as Algeria,
Morocco, Tunisia and Libya. JDC news releases described
"appallingly high" infant mortality rates in these
lands, reaching as much as 50 percent in some instances;
of disease, poverty and illiteracy that was making life
miserable for the "harassed and harried Jews of Morocco
and Algiers." Their homes were described as little more
than hovels in the "evil-smelling alleys of North
Africa's ghettos" where there had accumulated "the
dreary deposits of 2,000 years of inhumanity, intolerance and filth."

With such horrendous details, the campaign was
pushed in the general as well as the Jewish press and,
for added credibility, it included a four-column spread
in the **New York Times** of February 9. The Newsletter,
after a brief investigation, promptly scored the campaign as a "prize example of gross exaggeration, deliberate distortion and rank misrepresentation of
facts." The purple-prose descriptions as well as the
population statistics supplied by the JDC were characterized as "touching but not true" by the Newsletter,
which went on to report:

"Conditions have not changed very much
since before the war," a French embassy official told this reporter. Favorable living conditions in French North Africa at the outbreak
of the war are described by Dr. Moses Jung of

the American Jewish Committee in an article
published in the **Contemporary Jewish Record,**
December 1942, page 618.

French government documents available on
request at the French Embassy Press and Information Bureau in New York City show the improvement of conditions among Jews in Morocco
despite effects of the war:

Population: 1936--161,000; 1947--200,000
Birthrate: 350 per 10,000
Infant Mortality: Low
Schools: 26,000 pupils, an increase of 36
percent since 1939 in Franco-Israeli schools
and state-subsidized Alliance Israelite Univer-
selle schools.

Agriculture: 1936--400; 1947--2,400
Trade and Commerce: 1936--3,700; 1947--
20,000
Housing: Government program has put up
5,500 buildings in Moslem areas in 1947.

We believe an explanation and apology from
JDC for its exaggeration and misrepresenation
of facts to the general as well as the Jewish
public is long overdue.

There was no response from the JDC to this challenge, however, and in fact the campaign continued unabated and unchanged. Not even a tragedy which shocked
the world brought it to a halt. In November 1949, a
plane carrying 29 Jewish children from Tunisia to a rest
home in Norway crashed in the hills near Oslo, killing
all but one of the children. They had been scheduled to
spend six months in a "rehabilitation" program before
being flown to Israel. After the tragedy, memorial services were held for the children by Hadassah and several
other Jewish organizations, but, according to the Newsletter, not one word of explanation came from the JDC,
which was responsible for the program and the airplane
trip. "Nor did anyone embarrass the JDC by asking publicly why Tunisian children couldn't have been taken
directly to Israel and rehabilitated there instead of
the expensive, roundabout and dangerous Norwegian de-
tour," the Newsletter observed.

The only reference by the JDC to the tragedy that
the Newsletter could find was a comment, made in
passing, by the distinguished Rabbi Jonah B. Wise, son
of the founder of American Reform Judaism, Rabbi Isaac
M. Wise, and a vice-chairman of the JDC. At an executive
committee meeting called for fundraising planning pur-

poses, Rabbi Wise did not hesitate to use the tragedy of the children as a reason to appeal for increased funds. The spiritual leader of the famed Central Synagogue in New York offered no explanation for the tragedy when he said: "The only manner in which we can, in some measure, express our deep sympathy to those who so tragically perished is to remember that we must provide the fullest help possible to the thousands of companions they leave behind in North Africa ghettos--hundreds of whom will go down to equally certain, if less dramatic deaths, in the face of disease and hunger."

Under continued prodding by the Newsletter, JDC officials denied that they had remained silent after the tragic airplane crash and called attention to an address by Moses Beckelman, the assistant overseas director of the JDC, delivered at a UJA conference shortly after the tragedy. Beckelman sought to answer some of the questions about JDC's responsibility for the deaths of its wards, and his address was subsequently printed in full some time later by the New York UJA in its "Year Round" report.

Despite JDC's claims that the address was available to the press, the Newsletter noted that no paper had picked it up, then added:

> Mr. Beckelman's address, like that of Rabbi Jonah Wise at a JDC executive committee meeting, used the tragedy as a take-off point for a fundraising appeal. Our check shows that no mention of Mr. Beckelman's address and explanation appeared in any of the larger English Jewish weeklies (we don't see all 50-odd of them), or in the general New York press which at the time was front-paging every scrap of information it could get on the tragedy. The general public, which read about JDC's part in the tragedy, never saw or heard of Mr. Beckelman's explanation.

> There is a vast difference between making a speech at a busy UJA conference "available" to the press, and the special effort always made by publicity men to direct the attention of newspaper correspondents to those matters they want covered. In view of JDC's enviable success in obtaining press coverage for its releases, we think it obvious that no such effort was made for Mr. Beckelman's explanation.

A more sympathetic reaction to the death of the 28

North African Jewish children came from Norway itself. There the Norwegian trade unions launched a campaign to build a memorial in Israel for the victims. Promoted by the newspaper **Arbeiderbladet,** the organ of the Norwegian Labor Party, funds were raised to erect a 35-house settlement in Israel, each house to be named after one of the victims as well as the nurses who died with them. Beyond a report that $10,000 had been raised for the project, there was no further word that it had been completed.

Confirmation of the Newsletter's charges that the JDC had willfully exaggerated the facts about living conditions for Jews in North Africa was provided by Dr. J. Gershuni, a member of the World Poale-Zion executive in France. Dr. Gershuni had spent six months in Morocco on a special mission for the Jewish Agency, and his report appeared in the January issue of **Israel,** organ of the World Poale-Zion, published in Tel Aviv. Without mentioning the JDC, Dr. Gershuni claimed that what he called the "wild **aliya**" of 1949 was responsible for the dumping of "parasitical and socially undesirable elements" of Moroccan Jewry into Israel. He recommended that a vigorous Zionist educational and training program be introduced to prepare North Africans for a normal immigration. He saw no need for hasty or emergency measures. He described Moroccan Jewry as "characterized by an overweight middle class--middlemen, merchants, clerks, artisans, etc, with a very well-to-do upper stratum and without a working class."

With regard to housing, Dr. Gershuni wrote: "Those who remember the poverty and housing conditions in Jewish towns and villages of Eastern Europe would not classify the situation in Morocco as really exceptional." In concluding, he also noted that the "more well-to-do" among the Jews of Morocco "did not move" to Israel. In short, he confirmed what many Israelis had themselves discovered to their distress, that the JDC had emptied the North African poorhouses and some jails, and moved the desperate, impoverished and often criminal elements into the Promised Land without rehabilitation and education in Zionism to help their resettlement and without adequate preparation in Israel for their arrival.

Not only did this JDC-inspired "free" immigration introduce criminal elements into Israel where none had existed previously, it also helped to bring on the growing crisis that eventually brought down the Ben-Gurion government. The Newsletter called attention to the fact that JDC's immigration program was far exceeding

Israel's capacity to absorb the new arrivals, and then added:

> JDC's concern for the centuries'-old pov-
> erty of North African Jewry has resulted in the
> following situation that highlights at least
> one of the reasons for Israel's immigration
> plight:
> In the past two years, 20,000 Libyan Jews
> have been shipped to Israel, the **Jewish Chron-
> icle** (London) reports. Another 6,000 will go in
> the next few months, leaving less than 6,000
> still in the community. Thus, says the **Chron-
> icle,** "the emigration of the poorer elements
> has improved the financial position of the com-
> munity which, for the first time in its his-
> tory, will shortly be self-supporting."
> This "wild **aliya,**" about which Israel has
> complained, is included under the JDC's "now or
> never" immigration category.

The **Jewish Chronicle's** observation about the improved financial position of the Libyan Jewish community
as a consequence of the transfer of its poor to Israel
was matched in October by the boasts of the Algerian
bureau of the JDC. Its director, 74-year-old Elie Goz-
lan, an eminent Algerian Jewish leader, told a press
conference in Paris how much better the position of the
Algerian Jewish community had become since its impoverished brethren had been shipped off to Israel. He said:
"In the past year or so, things have improved to
such an extent that Algerian Jews now indulge openly in
Zionist activities, hold public meetings to raise funds
for the Jewish State, and positively welcome Israel and
Jewish Agency emissaries, of whom we have a constant
procession....There is probably less organized anti-
Semitism in Algeria today than in metropolitan France."
His statement was made at a time when the JDC's
fundraising campaign releases were tearfully impressing
the American public with the condition of the "harassed
and harried Jews of Morocco and Algiers...the dreary deposits of 2,000 of inhumanity, intolerance and filth."
The Newsletter had been contending that "American
UJA contributions would pay all or most of Israel's immigration bill if the money was allocated for that purpose. But as nearly as we can discover, not much more
than 40 percent reaches Israel." Since the Jewish organizations refused to make public audited statements of
their receipts and expenditures, it was difficult,

though not altogether impossible, to obtain accurate
statistics. The Newsletter, nevertheless, undertook a
careful study of the statistics about JDC receipts and
expenditures that it was able to obtain. These statistics, however, raised more questions than there were
answers.

For example, the Newsletter found that the JDC had
received a major share of UJA funds for 1949 and was
slated to receive more than 50 percent also in 1950. In
1949, the JDC had received a total of $66,387,000 from
all sources. This included over $40 million from UJA and
about $9.5 million from the International Refugee Or-
ganization. The JDC also borrowed an additional $6 mil-
lion from the banks. For the first half of 1950, the JDC
had received $7.5 million from the UJA, to which it
added another $1 million borrowed from the banks. Com-
paring these statistics on income with the available
information on JDC expenditures, the Newsletter was able
to come up with the following disclosures:

> The common belief is that most of JDC's
> funds go to pay for the costs of immigrant
> transportation to Israel. The high-powered pub-
> licity department of the JDC regularly issues
> yards of statistics, but for some curious rea-
> son, it is never possible to add them up or
> relate them to other expenditures. The result
> of this obfuscation is that we usually have to
> take the word of the JDC professionals on how
> the JDC spends the $66,387,000 it received last
> year from communal funds and bank loans.
>
> Thus, we must accept Executive Vice-Chair-
> man Moses A. Leavitt's statement that JDC spent
> $24 million in 1949 to transport 240,000 per-
> sons, almost 80 percent of them to Israel.
> (Another JDC officer says that only 226,000
> persons were moved, which indicates JDC's sta-
> tistical reliability.)
>
> But what happened to the remaining $42 mil-
> lion last year?
>
> Mr. Leavitt is also authority for the sta-
> tement that JDC plans to transport 150,000
> human beings in 1950 at a cost of $14,500,000.
>
> We're grateful for every dollar saved, of
> course; but what happens to the remaining $28.5
> million the JDC expects to receive this year?
>
> Considering all the fuss JDC made this year
> over the alleged plight of Jews in Moslem
> lands, it is a little surprising to find only
> $3 million budgeted for them in 1950.

The JDC has a great history and a notable
record of achievement, but it is neither holy
nor sacrosanct. How about some honest answers,
JDC?

The Newsletter's rhetorical question failed, of
course, to stimulate a response. The JDC went on at its
Paris conference later that year to set as its goal the
emigration of 600,000 Jews in three years from Iraq,
Iran, North Africa, and the remnants still remaining in
Poland and Rumania. For this, and for "essential relief,
reconstruction and rehabilitation programs," the JDC
said it would need a three-year total of $85 million, or
an average of $28 million annually. This meant that the
costs of transporting each person had risen to $140 com-
pared with the cost of only $100 per person in 1949. In
that year, the JDC said it spent $24 million to trans-
port 240,000 persons; its total receipts in 1949 were
$66,387,000.

The tightening economic situation of the mid-1950's
finally compelled the JDC to halt its Israel immigration
program. The JDC European director, Dr. Joseph J.
Schwartz, told a New York press conference in July that
emigration from North Africa and "non-urgent" European
lands was being postponed because of lack of funds. He
disclosed that the JDC's share of the 1950 UJA campaign
funds, originally set at $44 million, had been reduced
to $35 million. To this information, the Newsletter ap-
pended a reminder to its readers that in March, it had
included among its recommendations to meet the financial
crisis the following action: "Temporary cessation of
JDC-promoted North African emigration and other non-
emergency areas; and reduction of JDC's allocation of
$44 million from this year's UJA to about $25 million."

To Joseph Leftwich in London, I had written on February 15: "This week's top story is my expose of the
JDC's campaign for North African Jewry, based on French
government documents. What a bunch of shameless liars
the JDC crowd turns out to be! I wish you were here. We
could really do a job of house-cleaning..."

As part of the Newsletter's effort to persuade Jewish organizations to observe standards of truthfulness
and responsibility in reporting their activities to the
Jewish community, attention was now directed to the
United Service for New Americans (USNA), an agency
created by the JDC and the CJFWF to help settle European
refugees, mostly victims of the Nazis, in various parts
of the United States. Settlement was to be done in an
orderly fashion so that no one community would be over-

burdened or taxed beyond its absorptive capacity. USNA's funds came from the UJA, and together with the JDC allocation, the combined amount far exceeded the amount allocated for UPA, even though the almost exclusive basis for the UJA appeal to the community was aid for Israel. The Newsletter, on January 18, therefore, took special pains to report the following facts about the USNA:

> To the accompaniment of metropolitan New York press photographer flashlights, Edwin Rosenberg, president of USNA, told assembled delegates at a recent national conference that "100,000 homeless European Jews have been brought to the United States and settled here since 1945 by the United Service for New Americans" (**New York Herald Tribune**). Rosenberg's statement, obviously made to justify USNA's slice of $18,000,000 from the 1950 UJA campaign, should be compared with the following published facts:
> (1) USNA was established in 1946, not 1945.
> (2) From May 1946 through December 1949, a grand total of 62,630 Jewish refugees arrived in this country--not 100,000 as claimed by Rosenberg. Up to this time, USNA itself claimed to have assisted only 27,502 of these refugees.
> (These statistics are from the **American Jewish Year Book**, v. 50, pp.750-752, and USNA's bulletin entitled "New Neighbors," which are based on records of steamship companies, JDC, HIAS and other Jewish agencies. These statistics show that the arrival of 13,620 DPs from May 1946 to July 31, 1948, were under the Truman Directive. To these, add 6,310 arrivals from the Far East for a total of 19,930. For 1949, USNA declared 37,700 persons arrived from all areas. The grand total, therefore, including a generous estimate of 5,000 for the second half of 1948, is 62,630).
> (3) Rosenberg boasted of USNA's expenditure of $37,000,000 for its program. This brings the cost per DP to the fantastic figure of $1,345 [i.e., $37,000,000 $\div$ 27,502]. By way of comparison, New York City maintains a man on relief for an entire year at an average cost of only $470.52.
> Contributors urging all-out aid for Israel, and local communities asked to sacrifice their

own capital fund needs may well demand a sizable "sacrifice" of USNA's allocation to the United Palestine Appeal.

Even higher than the above figures was the cost of handling the 10,000 cases between August 1946 and April 1948, for whom USNA expended $20,000,000. This sum did not, of course, include any additional expenditures by local communities for the refugees who were to be settled in their midst. It also did not include the aid provided by relatives here of the refugees. In any case, the total number of Jewish refugees who could be admitted in any one year was limited by American immigration laws to between 20,000 and 25,000.

USNA was never intended to be more than a temporary agency, but it did not wind up its affairs in June, as it had been scheduled to do. At the same time, its place was taken in April by a new organization called the New York Association for New Americans (NYANA). Initial funds for the new agency were provided by USNA, but NYANA was also listed as a beneficiary of the New York UJA. The incestuous character of the New York agencies was further exposed by an agreement under which NYANA paid ORT a fee for each one of the refugees that it sent to the ORT Trade School in New York. Understandably, ORT welcomed the agreement as "an example of excellent cooperation in the field of relief and rehabilitation." The JDC, which allocated some of its funds to ORT, also served on a special UJA board, along with representatives from UPA, which made monthly allocations to USNA and NYANA. The board was chaired by Judge Simon Rifkind, a U.S. district court justice of the Southern District, N.Y., and vice-chairman of the board of directors of the Jewish Theological Seminary.

In addition to its agreement with ORT, NYANA also arranged with the Hebrew Immigrant Aid Society (HIAS) to send newly arrived immigrants requiring temporary housing to the HIAS shelter on Lafayette Street in downtown New York rather than to the more expensive midtown Hotel Marseilles, which USNA had been using. Thus, by making use of existing facilities and organizations which had the trained personnel for accommodating immigrants, NYANA brought a degree of competence and efficiency into the process of integrating new arrivals that had not previously existed. Taking note of this development, the Newsletter complimented the agency, saying: "NYANA, which has inherited a host of operational problems from USNA, is to be congratulated for taking the initiative in this business-like arrangement that will save UJA

money." Why HIAS was not given the responsibility at the
very beginning for the reception and resettlement of the
immigrants--an operation in which it had many decades of
successful experience--why community leaders deemed it
necessary to create the cumbersome and expensive USNA
and NYANA organizations, has never been satisfactorily
explained.

Exaggerated estimates by USNA of the number of DPs
(Displaced Persons), as the refugees were regarded, that
could be admitted into the United States under an amend-
ment to the DP bill before Congress, and the secrecy
maintained over the reasons why the USNA had not been
phased out as scheduled, prompted the Newsletter to
raise several questions when the USNA and the JDC held a
joint regional conference in Miami on November 4 and 5,
and in Chicago a week later. Delegates were urged to
insist on the release "to the public of the following:
(a) verified figures of the number of DPs who entered
the United States this year under USNA auspices; (a) how
much USNA received this year from UJA; (c) why USNA did
not begin to wind up its affairs in June as planned
earlier this year; and (d) how much money the JDC actually did spend in North Africa this year and how much
financial help, if any, did it receive from France,
which governs North Africa?"

The questions may not have fallen entirely on deaf
ears because the following week the Newsletter was able
to reveal that USNA had been kept alive on the insistence of the JDC and that it had continued to receive
funds from the UJA with the consent of the special board
chaired by Judge Simon Rifkind. Noting the slow pace of
USNA's liquidation, the Newsletter commented:

"Speed" of the retrenchment was indicated
by the reduction in USNA's swollen staff from
400 in November 1949 to 250 by June 1950, and
to 162 by October 21. The executive staff has
remained almost the same. At the same time, the
staff of NYANA, which JDC and USNA set up, rose
from 483 in July 1949 to 520 by June 1950. Retrenchment moves then cut the staff to 375 by
October 15. Dismissal pay for the staff, as
stipulated in the union contract, makes retrenchment a highly expensive proposition.
USNA/NYANA rent offices at 15 Park Row, for
which they pay $200,000 annually.

These high costs and huge staff, and the fact that
the rate of immigration, as CJFWF president Stanley

Myers disclosed, had slowed considerably because of "administrative difficulties" under the liberalized DP regulations, impelled the CJFWF to insist on moves that would increase the efficiency in the way immigrants were being processed. It was at this point that HIAS was brought into the picture and negotiations were begun by USNA to merge some of their activities, and incidentally, to eliminate areas of duplication. Under a proposed plan, HIAS was to take over the port and dock work that USNA was handling and also to house the new arrivals at its shelter until arrangements could be made to place them in homes in other cities. Under USNA, the DPs had been sheltered in the Hotel Marseilles and left to their own devices without further supervision, a costly procedure. HIAS, which traditionally raised its funds through an independent campaign, was willing and able to take over the task of housing the refugees, but it flatly rejected any plan for a merger with USNA.

The full implications of the entrance of HIAS into the Israel and DP immigration situation had not yet made themselves felt as the year drew to a close. The failure of the 1950 UJA campaign and the assumption of responsibility for the 1951 UJA drive by the leaders of the JDC had consequences for that agency which could not be fully foreseen. The entrance of ORT into the Israeli scene also had the consequence of limiting the JDC's sphere of operations and of further influencing the changes in that agency's functions in the future.

6

THE CHALLENGE TO THE RABBIS

Perhaps no part of Jewish life in America has been affected as much by the establishment of the state of Israel as the synagogue, its rabbis, and the degree of religious observance. The Reform rabbinate, in particular, probably experienced the maximum impact of the new state because the basic philosophy of Reform Judaism was in sharp conflict with Zionism and had to be drastically modified. At the same time, it should not be overlooked that the Conservative rabbinate and to an even greater extent the Orthodox also were strongly affected. A relatively complacent American Jewry had previously been shaken out of its lethargy by the rapid spread of Nazism and the shocking horror of the Holocaust; by 1950, the rise of Zionism and the establishment of the new state of Israel had raised numerous questions about Judaism itself. Together with questions about the status of Jews and their observance or neglect of religious practices and beliefs, the impact was comparable in the American experience only to the soul-shaking effects of the mass immigration at the turn of the century. All Jews, from the most pious to the most assimilated, found themselves touched and involved willy-nilly.

The Pittsburg Platform of 1885, which embodied the philosophy, beliefs and practices of Reform Judaism, described itself as universal in scope and hence anti-Zionist and anti-nationalist. It stated: "We recognize in the modern era of universal culture of heart and intellect, the approaching of the realization of Israel's great Messianic hope for the establishment of the kingdom of truth, justice and peace among all men. We consider ourselves no longer a nation, but a religious community, and therefore expect neither a return to Palestine nor a sacrificial worship under the sons of Aaron, nor the restoration of any of the laws concerning the Jewish State."

Despite the finality of this credo, the Balfour Declaration and the irresistible force of Herzlian Zionism had by 1937 moved Reformed Judaism full circle. In that

99

year, the Columbus Platform, formulated at the annual meeting of the Central Conference of American Rabbis (CCAR) dropped Reform's previous rejection of Jews as a nation in exile and adopted the following resolution: "In the rehabilitation of Palestine, the land 'hallowed by ancient memories' and hopes, we behold the promise of renewed life for our brethren. We affirm the obligation of all Jewry to aid in its upbuilding as a Jewish home-land by endeavoring to make it not only a haven of refuge for the oppressed, but also a center of Jewish culture and spiritual life."

So radical a departure from the Pittsburg Platform was too difficult for many unreconstructed Reform Jews to accept, and many of them did cry that "Zionism was bootlegged into Reform." The fact was, however, that the most dedicated leaders of American Zionism were such Re-form rabbis as Abba Hillel Silver and Stephen S. Wise. Many Reform Jews, while supportive of Israel, neverthe-less took the same anti-nationalist position as the American Jewish Committee. For different reasons, anti-nationalism was also very strong among the Orthodox rab-binate. The range of Orthodoxy was marked by those rabbis who were staunch Zionists and those equally pious rabbis who believed the state was an unholy aberration and that no state in Palestine could be truly Jewish unless it were established by the Messiah himself.

Efforts to reconcile all these differences further confused an already badly shaken American Jewry and added little to soften the impact of the new state upon Jewish religious beliefs and practices. While Dr. Nahum Goldmann was telling Detroit Jews that the UJA was the barometer with which to measure Jewish attitudes, Rabbi Abba Hillel Silver, speaking in Cincinnati, was decrying the indifference of American Jews to Judaism. He warned Jews that philanthropy was superseding religion as the bond of Jewish loyalty, thus in effect underscoring the point made by Dr. Goldmann despite the difference in their approach.

The Newsletter reported some of the efforts to meet these challenges to Judaism on March 30 in the following account:

> In Cincinnati, 74 Reform rabbis and educa-tors held a 3-day Institute on Reform Jewish Theology. According to the chairman of the Institute, Rabbi Ferdinand Isserman of St. Louis, its purpose was to draw up a statement, "however imperfect it may be," on ceremonial practices and basic values of Reform Judaism,

to serve as a guide for laymen and rabbis. The
Institute, however, passed the buck to the Central Conference of American Rabbis by recommending that the CCAR formulate the code of
ritual practice. The CCAR will meet on June
7-11.

Meanwhile, in Philadelphia, Conservative
leader, Rabbi Robert Gordis, of Rockaway Park,
N.Y., countered arguments of Orthodox Rabbi
Morris Max that the Chief Rabbinate of Israel
should be the supreme religious authority for
Jews everywhere. Dr. Gordis denied the existence of a historical warrant for a chief rabbi,
calling it un-Jewish. He questioned its prac-
ticability and the possibility that the Israel
rabbinate would understand the problems and
needs of American Jewry.

And in Denver, according to the **Intermountain Jewish News,** an overflow audience listened
for over two hours to a debate between Reform
Rabbi Herbert Friedman, who advocated a **Minhag**
America which would supersede present divisions
of American Jewry, and Orthodox Rabbis Manuel
Laderman and C.H. Kauver, who insisted that
there could be no deviation from the Orthodox
code.

Reform rabbis, conscious of the influence of the new
state of Israel upon their congregations and its significance for them, continued their efforts to resolve the
issues. At the opening of the 61st convention of the
CCAR in Cincinnati, the keynote address was made by Dr.
Jacob R. Marcus, its president and a noted historian of
American Jewry. Dr. Marcus offered a number of proposals dealing not only with Reform synagogue procedure
and education but also with the broader problems of
American Jews. He was called for the formation of an
overall body to be set up by the community councils
under the aegis of the CJFWF which would "speak and act
with authority for American Jewry." Among other proposals made by Dr. Marcus, the most significant were his
"demand for the recognition of Liberal rabbis in
Israel," where only the Orthodox had authority, and his
recommendation for continued "spiritual, religious and
cultural aid to Israel." The Newsletter noted, however,
that the CCAR, like the Institute meeting before it,
tabled the "practices and values statement for further
study by the Theology Institute." The Newsletter added:

Also disappointing is the plea to the CJFWF
to form an overall body. Not only is this plan
old hat, obviously faulty and dangerous, but it
indicates CCAR abdication of its traditional
belief in the primacy of the synagogue. We hope
the Reform rabbis vote this one down.

Dr. Marcus' proposal for a central overall organization did indeed meet with a notable lack of interest and
was referred to the Executive Committee of the CCAR
where it was pigeonholed. The idea for such a central
authority that would somehow have the power to regulate
the activities of the community has long had a certain
fascination for Jewish leaders, its most complete arti-
culation up to that time having been made by Henry Hurwitz in **The Menorah Journal** several years earlier, where
he spelled out a plan for a synagogue centered community
authority. The proposal introduced by Dr. Marcus bore a
resemblance to the British Board of Jewish Deputies; it
was kept alive by the CJFWF and vigorously promoted
under another approach by the NCRAC in the following
year.

Dr. Marcus' call for the recognition of Liberal and
Reform rabbis in Israel is still being debated to this
day. Long before the independence of Israel, the Orthodox rabbinate was recognized exclusively by the Turkish
Empire authorities as the only legitimate authority to
conduct marriages, births, deaths and all other matters
involving the practice of religion. This authority was
based not on religious grounds but on the practical
reason that the only rabbis then resident in the Holy
Land were the Orthodox, and the British simply carried
on the practice as did also the Israel government.

J.S. Ackerman of Chicago, a member of the executive
board of the Union of American Hebrew Congregations
(UAHC), touched on this question in an article he wrote
for the September 1950 number of the organization's
magazine, **Liberal Judaism**, in which he described his
impressions of Israel after a 15-day visit. He contended
that the protest of the CCAR alleging discrimination
against Liberal rabbis--as distinct from Reform rab-
bis--was based on incorrect information. Ackerman said
that there were four Liberal congregations in Israel,
their membership almost entirely German in origin, who
were--in his words--"more traditional in character than
the Conservative synagogues in the United States." The
chief rabbi of Israel, he added, had found them sufficiently observant of **Halacha** (rabbinic law) to warrant
authorizing their rabbis to perform marriages. The

younger generation in Israel, Ackerman concluded, was
losing interest in religion because it was governed by
"medieval religious laws."

Perhaps the most significant consequence of the impact of Israel upon Reform Judaism was the impetus it
gave to the trend away from the limited ceremonial and
ritual practices of classic Reform, including such distinctive customs as the Sunday service in place of the
Sabbath worship. At the Biennial Assembly of the UAHC in
November, Rabbi Morton M. Berman, of Chicago, reported
on the results of a survey that had been made of the
practices of 425 Reform congregations. The survey showed
a marked trend toward increased observance of traditional rituals and ceremonies. To the question, "Is Reform Judaism Becoming Orthodox?," which was raised by
the **Jewish Layman,** the publication of the Temple
Brotherhoods, Rabbi James G. Heller responded in the
negative. Since he was the spiritual leader of the Isaac
M. Wise Temple in Cincinnati, where American Reform was
developed, his words carried considerable authority,
although the mere fact that such a question could be
raised was very significant. Heller made it clear that
in his opinion, the trend toward more ritual and observance was a "reversal...in emphasis"--a positive move--
"rather than a return to essential Jewish moorings,
common to all branches, than to Orthodoxy."

However the trend may have been interpreted, the
fact remained that before long the classic Reform of the
19th century rabbis was as dead as the Sunday morning
service which they had initiated. For Orthodox Judaism
the effects of the establishment of the state of Israel
led to a sharp split between those who were Zionists and
recognized the state of Israel as a step toward the ful-
fillment of Jewish hopes, and those who refused to have
anything to do with a state they regarded as secular and
a violation of the religious requirements of the Messianic era. At the Orthodox Rabbinical Council of
America convention in June, a report on religion in
Israel was submitted which, according to the Newsletter,
made the following points:

> (1) Our bond with Israel should be on the
> same basis as existed between Israel and **Chutz**
> **L'aretz** during the First Commonwealth and the
> beginning of the Second Commonwealth in the
> area of **Halacha;** (2) re-establishment of a Cen-
> tral Religious Authority of Torah scholars (not
> necessarily a Sanhedrin) in and outside of
> Israel which will develop into a Central Reli-

gious Authority. Their main objective, says the
rabbis, "is to do away with the chaos, the
anarchy, and the religious lawlessness...."
Unfortunately, most of the report is given
over to defensive arguments and sneers at other
analyses of religion in Israel, notably by
William Zukerman and the Conservative Rabbi
Bokser report; it is not calculated to inspire
the confidence and trust of the Jewish people.

The analysis by William Zukerman, a Yiddish journalist who also published an English language newsletter,
was hostile, colored largely by his anti-Israel, anti-
religious Bundist orientation, and therefore had little
impact. Orthodox rabbis offered a view that differed
from both the Zionists and the non-Zionists on the
controversial issue of whether Jews outside of Israel
were living in exile. Attacking a recommendation that
American Jews adopt the use of a religious flag that
would be different from the traditional flag of Israel,
the Union of Orthodox Hebrew Congregations (UOHC), in
its publication **Jewish Action,** said: "Traditional
Judaism does not recognize the existence of an 'American
Judaism' separate from K'lal Yisrael, the world community of Israel." The UOHC also opposed the adoption of
"concepts and symbols which will divide American Jewry
from K'lal Yisrael."

Conservative Judaism was shaken by the report, entitled "Religion in Israel," which was submitted by Rabbis Ben Zion Bokser, Maxwell M. Farber, Ralph Simon, and
Sanders Tofield. Essentially the report was based on a
firsthand survey of the condition of Judaism in the
state of Israel by Rabbi Bokser, and it covered non-
religious as well as religious groups of varying de-
grees of piety. In its opening paragraph, Rabbi Bokser
summarized his findings as follows:

"Religious life in Israel is a complex phenomenon
and it is difficult to describe in unitary terms. It
fluctuates from militant orthodoxy that rejects the
state as incompatible with the Torah to militant atheism
that rejects religion as incompatible with modern life.
The dominant groups in the country which have created
its unique social and cultural institutions are generally unfriendly to religion. They represent the pioneering elements who are identified with the labor movement,
and who drew their hostility to religion, at least in
part, from conventional Marxism. It must be remembered,
too, that the Zionism of the pioneers was a revolutinary
movement, that it made its way among the youth of our

people against the official Jewish communities and their religious spokesmen. The culture which these people sought to create was a secular culture. Its goals on the cultural level were the revival of the Hebrew language as a medium of common discourse and the transvaluation of Jewish tradition into national terms."

The observations of Rabbi Bokser, a distinguished scholar and author, whose congregation is located in Forest Hills, Queens, New York, offer a remarkably clear and well-defined picture of Jewish religious and non-religious beliefs and practices in Israel. Regrettably, the extent of religious complexities in Israel has not diminished in the thirty years that have elapsed since the publication of Rabbi Bokser's report. Despite the growing political power of the religious parties, very little has been accomplished in resolving religious problems, a failure which stands out when compared to the enormous advances Israel has made in agriculture, science and military power during the same period.

Efforts to link American Jews with Israel in ways other than fundraising, by the observance of commemorative occasions, for example, generally met with indifference and failure. One such attempt, for example, was the observance in Israel of the tenth anniversary of the sinking of the "SS Patria" on November 25, 1940, in Haifa harbor, a needless disaster caused by British opposition to Jewish immigration, in which over 250 European Jewish refugees lost their lives. In the United States, not a single mention of the ceremony in commemoration of the tragic event appeared in the English Jewish press.

A larger and far better organized effort, sponsored by the Synagogue Council of America, to expand the observance of the tenth day of **Tebet** (December 19, 1950) from a traditional Jewish fast day to an international day of mourning and prayer for the six million Jews who perished in the Holocaust likewise ended in failure. A ritual of prayers and special liturgical music was prepared for use in the synagogue and vigorous efforts were made to encourage widespread synagogue attendance. A survey by the Newsletter, however, showed that this memorial day was largely ignored in the metropolitan New York area as well as elsewhere. Except for an occasional reference to the Holocaust by the rabbi during the regular Sabbath service, no notice was taken of the occasion and no use was made of the special ritual.

Another event which demonstrated that American Jews were slow to react even where their religion was concerned took place in May when the famous novelist Arthur

Koestler converted to Christianity in a well publicized
ceremony. The act shocked the literary world as well as
many Israel-minded Jews throughout the world. The Newsletter observed, however, that while the writer's apostasy had become a **cause celebre** in Great Britain, there
had been no editorial reaction in the English Jewish
press in the United States. Koestler had justified his
conversion by arguing that with the establishment of the
state of Israel, only two courses of action were open to
him as a Jew: either resettle in Israel and live there
as an observant Jew, or convert and remain in Europe
without the burden of being a Jew.

Koestler's statement of his dilemma and its solution
raised a question that Zionists in America, at least,
had never been willing to confront in all their discussions about "exile" and the duty of Jews to make **aliya.**
In concluding this report, the Newsletter editorialized:

> The case was important because his reasons
> are shared by increasing numbers of American
> Jews, whose only bond is allegiance. The os-
> trich policy of ignoring or denouncing Koestler
> will not do. He must be answered, as our Eng-
> lish brethren are doing.

In a letter to my friend Leftwich, I noted the absence of any editorial reaction in the English Jewish
press to the significance of Koestler's apostasy, and
then went on to say: "Yet his defection is, I think, a
most dangerous symptom of the way a great many Jews here
believe and think. One sociologist at a meeting I attended a week ago said that one could not be correct in
speaking of Judaism in America when referring to the
majority of our people but must rather define their
position as one of 'allelgiance' to Judaism. Sad, I'm
afraid, but very true. Afraid because among our syna-
gogue-goers, even our rabbis, faith in God, a personal
God, is almost non-existent. The rabbis preach politics, Zionism, ethics, but no God. They worry about
kashruth (and the excessive cost of kosher meats),
riding on the Sabbath, and a minimum code of obser-
vance--all of which are probably necessary and certainly
practical, but I have yet to hear one preach on the belief in God. Is it as bad in England?"

One month later the Newsletter reported that two
world-renowned German Jewish writers, who had once been
ardent Zionists and who had fled when Hitler came to
power, had renounced their Judaism and returned to Germany. One was Arnold Zweig, who had been living in

Israel for about fifteen years. Zweig became a communist and accepted an appointment as head of the German Academy of Arts in the Soviet zone of Berlin. The other was the prominent novelist Alfred Doeblin, who had been living in Hollywood, California. Doeblin converted to Christianity and returned to Munich, where he became head of the German Academy of Arts in that city. "The defection of these men, in addition to the earlier apostasy of Arthur Koestler, should spur a spate of sermons, discussions, and examinations of contemporary Judaism and its relation to Israel," concluded the Newsletter.

The relationship of Diaspora Jewry to Israel also raised questions of standards and values. The death of the brilliant Rabbi Milton Steinberg at age 46 following a series of heart attacks left many American Jews with a feeling of great loss. His writings were widely read and had considerable influence not only upon his congregation but also upon his fellow rabbis. Reporting that a memorial volume of his selected sermons and other writings was being planned, the Newsletter observed sadly:

> Notice of his passing as carried by the Philadelphia **Jewish Exponent,** which is a community sponsored newspaper, appeared on page 26 in a five-inch JTA dispatch incorrectly describing the Rabbi's death as sudden. The same paper devoted an editorial and all of page 8 to eulogies of the late Ellis Gimble, a prominent local department store head. With all due respect and honor to Mr. Gimble, can there by any argument over which man's contribution to American Judaism was more valuable?

A similar question was raised in a broader context by news accounts grouping Rabbi Steinberg's death with those of Leon Blum, Harold Laski and Dr. Harry Friedenwald, all of whom passed away within weeks of each other. The Jewish press, in their obituary notices, had treated these men as if they were all prominent Jews. The Newsletter, conscious of the perennial discussions in Israel over the question of who is a Jew, brought up the same question in this instance with the following comment:

> What determines a Jew, birth or religion? Harold Laski was an avowed agnostic, disowned by his religious father Nathan Laski. Before the rise of Hitler, he declared that he would

have nothing to do with Jewish matters; after Hitler, he insisted that "as a Marxian Socialist, he held that religion was opium for the people." His funeral service was non-religious and his body was cremated.

Leon Blum likewise had nothing to do with the Jewish religion, although he was active as a Zionist and expressed strong Jewish sympathies. But in disregard of Jewish practice, he was buried on the first day of Passover after a non-Jewish funeral service.

Apart from the qualities and achievements of these men, were they worthy of the lavish praise accorded them as "great Jews?" Would our American rabbinical fathers--not to speak of Europeans--Rabbis Alexander Kohut, Isaac M. Wise, Sabato Morais, Kaufman Kohler, Adolf Huebsch--would they have eulogized these admittedly brilliant men as "great Jews?"

There are, of course, no definitive answers to these questions, yet the overall problem about the relationship of Jews to Israel and in particular the influence of Israel on Jewish religious practices and beliefs in the Diaspora continues to trouble rabbis as well as other observant Jews generally. Unquestionably Diaspora Jewry looked to Israel for its spiritual regeneration, but it had failed to reckon with the ironic twist of circumstances which allowed Ben-Gurion, Golda Meir, Moshe Sharett and other builders of Israel to be largely atheistic Marxian Socialists who believed that Israel's salvation lay with the Second International rather than the Messiah. Most of them were anti-religious and except for their ardent belief in Zionism as a revolutionary philosophy, ignorant of traditional Judaism. Yet these were the people who had assumed the responsibility of organizing the Jewish state in the Holy Land after two thousand years of exile and of developing its language, culture and Jewish character. That they were able to do so within a relatively short period of time and with a minimum of internal friction despite a hostile environment and a multitude of conflicting customs and everyday problems--that they were able to manage this was in itself as much a miracle as the establishment of the state.

In all fairness, however, it must be conceded that the scholars and rabbis apparently have been no more successful than their non-religious compatriots in reaching a consensus on the questions that plagued

Israel. Thirty-three years after the establishment of the state of Israel, a leading Israeli rabbi and scholar, Dr. David Hartman, the director of the Shalom Hartman Institute for Advanced Jewish Studies and professor of Jewish philosophy at the Hebrew University, was quoted in the **Jerusalem Post** of August 16, 1981, as expressing the following views:

"We live in a time of Jewish history when Israel could serve as the source of spiritual renewal, when Israel could mirror Judaism as a way of life that embodies the sanctifying power of Torah and the **mitzvot**. Yet, instead of its providing a framework for **kiddush ha'shem**, sanctification of God, it continues to promote the secularization of Jewish consciousness and the alienation of the Jewish people from its spiritual roots.

"Judaism will become a living reality in Israel only when we regain faith in the educational process. The Knesset and the wielding of political power cannot be substitutes for the patient processes of learning."

7

THE COMMUNIST THREAT

Efforts to combat anti-Semitism in the United States during the 1930s and 1940s were led by the American Jewish Committee and the Anti-Defamation League of the B'nai B'rith. Their philosophic and tactical approach to fighting this epidemic of bigotry that preceded World War II was followed to a large extent by the Jewish Labor Committee. Only the American Jewish Congress, led largely by Zionists, had different ideas on how to combat anti-Jewish prejudice, among them mass protest demonstrations and other measures to attract public attention. The other agencies did not regard these demonstrations and publicity as very effective in securing affirmative action, and in an effort to coordinate the activities of the American Jewish Congress as well as to some extent to control them in order to avoid conflicting actions, the ADL, the American Jewish Committee and the Jewish Labor Committee together with the American Jewish Congress set up the General Jewish Council in the 1940s with Isaiah Minkoff of the Jewish Labor Committee as its executive head.

Within a relatively short period of time, a number of community councils and other Jewish agencies which had an interest in the way anti-Semitism was to be fought joined the General Jewish Council. Eventually the name of the expanded agency was changed to the National Community Relations Advisory Council (NCRAC), and in time, NCRAC developed its own character and sphere of activities. By 1950, at its 8th plenary session, NCRAC included among its representative agencies not only the original four organizations but also 28 local community councils and six national organizations, among them the Jewish War Veterans, the National Council of Jewish Women, and the UAHC.

NCRAC described itself as a "coordinating and policy formulating body," but the Newsletter was highly critical of its activities and results. It described them in the following report:

111

On the record, NCRAC's coordinating efforts have been miserable failures; it does not make policy for its constituent bodies. But its policy-formulating efforts are developing along lines which many Jews will find dangerous. By resolutions and statements on public questions, reported in the general press, NCRAC is taking American Jews as Jews into the arena of American party politics. **It threatens Congress with a Jewish pressure bloc!** That is the clear implication of the statement by NCRAC's executive director, Isaiah Minkoff, in connection with FEPC [Fair Employment Practices Council]: "We now confront two battles: one to break the filibuster, and the other to enact the legislation itself."

Southern Democrats who happen to be Jews and who don't think FEPC is the way, as well as many other Jews who think politics is their own business as Americans, will want to know NCRAC's authority to speak for them as Jews.

As it has happened so often in the past where the vanquished eventually triumph over the victors, the effort to control the American Jewish Congress and its militant approach to fighting anti-Semitism resulted before long in the adoption of the policies and philosophy of the American Jewish Congress, through its membership in the General Jewish Council, by the ADL and the American Jewish Committee, and finally by the NCRAC. The American Jewish Congress had evolved from an agency designed largely by Louis Lipsky to offer a Zionist approach and philosophy in the fight against anti-Semitism under the leadership of the revered Rabbi Stephen S. Wise. Shad Polier, the son-in-law of Rabbi Wise, gradually assumed control of the organization and introduced a group of lawyers with strong civil libertarian views. For a time, they flirted with communist approaches to fighting bigotry and prejudice, especially in the aftermath of World War II and the destruction of Nazism. With the shift in Soviet Russian policy against the Jews and the rise of anti-communist feeling, however, the American Jewish Congress began to purge its ranks of communists and communist sympathizers. The Herzlian approach to anti-Semitism had by this time, of course, been completely abandoned.

Adoption of the civil libertarian approach by the NCRAC and its member agencies, including those who had strongly resisted it at first, was disclosed in the "Re-

THE COMMUNIST THREAT   113

port of the 8th Plenary Session" of the NCRAC. Release
of this document, according to the Newsletter, "reveals
the basis on which NCRAC believes itself justified in
plunging Jews as Jews into public politics." All the
member agencies approved the Report, which the Newsletter declared

> shows the American Jewish Congress taking the
> lead in persuading other agencies to accept its
> view in this respect. The American Jewish Con-
> gress believes "Jewish agencies are involved
> because civil rights are not secure when there
> are no civil liberties," according to its spo-
> kesman, Will Maslow. The American Jewish Con-
> gress attitude, as outlined by Mr. Maslow,
> would call for Jewish action whenever a ques-
> tion of civil liberties arose.
> American Jewish Committee spokesman Ben
> Herzberg said that the American Jewish Commit-
> tee had moved away from the "isolationist ap-
> proach" to defense problems, but insisted that
> every case had to be decided on its merits.
> Jewish Labor Committee representative James
> Lipsig, disturbed by the prevalent anti-com-
> munist hysteria, urged Jewish agencies to
> "broaden their activities to deal with civil
> liberties."
> The sole dissenter was the ADL spokesman,
> Professor N.L. Nathanson, who pointed out the
> "danger of lessening the effectiveness of our
> organization by scattering our shots over too
> wide an area"; and warned against "presuming to
> speak" for the large diversified B'nai B'rith
> membership in cases where there may be "con-
> siderable sharply divided opinion."
> In the general discussion which followed,
> Shad Polier, of the American Jewish Congress,
> chided the American Jewish Committee and the
> Jewish Labor Committee for issuing reports on
> the suppression of Jewish life in the Soviet
> Union and its satellites. He admitted that the
> American Jewish Congress had similar informa-
> tion but had decided against issuing any expose
> or denunciation.

Professor Nathanson's words of caution, inspired in
part by B'nai B'rith's large Southern membership, obviously fell on deaf ears, for the NCRAC, acting for its
constitutent agencies as well as for itself, vigorously

opposed legislation before the U.S. Congress which it regarded as restrictive. One such measure was a bill to curb communist agitation, and in September, the NCRAC wired President Truman urging him to veto the omnibus anti-communist bill passed by the Congress on the ground that it was a "violation of traditional American guarantees of freedom." The Newsletter did not disagree with NCRAC's opinion of the legislation, but it warned that "by its action in this and other public issues, NCRAC is needlessly dragging Jews as Jews into the dangerous arena of national politics."

In my weekly letter to Leftwich, I conceded that "there is a good deal of hysteria here over communism, but it isn't all that." I then explained: "Underneath there is a hard core of bitterness over Russia's refusal to work with the world for peace, a bitterness aggravated not only by the USSR's ingratitude for American war help but for plunging us into war just as we were beginning to recover from the last one. The temper of the American people is such that our leaders must hold them back--and that's a dangerous situation. At the same time, such extreme action as the ultra-anti-communist condemnation of stage folk on the flimsiest evidence was roundly condemned."

My comments on the anti-communist climate of the period were made against the background of a strong communist inspired effort by left-wingers to infiltrate and possibly take over some of the local Jewish community councils. In Chicago, for example, the Welfare Federation and Combined Appeal came under sharp attack from left-wing groups led by the local weekly **Jewish Sentinel**. These groups were agitating for the organization of a Chicago community council which would replace or supersede the Welfare Federation and which they could control. Their campaign was given an unexpected opportunity when the **Chicago Daily Tribune,** in an unprecedented display of anti-Semitism, openly attacked three prominent politically active Jews.

A front-page article by Walter Trohan, the **Tribune's** Washington correspondent, accused Supreme Court Justice Felix Frankfurter, Senator Herbert H. Lehman, of New York, and Henry Morgenthau Jr.--no less--of conspiring together to act as a "secret government of the United States." The **Tribune** headlined Trohan's article, "Three Men Called a Government in Themselves," and it shocked and frightened Jews everywhere by its blatant anti-Semitic innuendoes and echoes of such notorious anti-Jewish slanders as the infamous "Protocols of the Elders of Zion." The NCRAC, acting on behalf of its member

agencies as well as Chicago communal leaders, in one of
the few instances of such cooperation, sent a letter of
protest to Colonel Robert R. McCormick, publisher of the
Tribune. In the negotiation that followed, however,
NCRAC failed to obtain either a retraction or an
apology. Instead, NCRAC released a letter from the newspaper in which--as the Newsletter reported--it "sancti-
moniously denies that it is anti-Semitic or that any
anti-Jewish implications were intended...."
    The Newsletter pointed out that this was the way the
notorious Father Charles E. Coughlin in the 1940s used
to whitewash his anti-Semitic diatribes, then added:

> On the record, NCRAC is thus satisfied to
> let stand the **Tribune's** slander....Maybe NCRAC
> will explain to the Jewish community just how
> the **Tribune's** denial of anti-Semitic intent
> changes by one whit the Elders-of-Zion implica-
> tions of Trohan's rot.

After this unsatisfactory conclusion of the attack
from the right, Chicago successfully fought off a communist attempt to form a rival community council, in
which left-wingers would have had a strong voice. Other
community councils in various cities met the communist
inspired efforts at infiltration only with varying de-
grees of success. In Detroit, the Jewish Community
Council found it necessary to issue a statement warning
the affiliated agencies against attempts by the communist-front Civil Rights Congress to enlist their aid and
support for its appeals for peace with North Korea. The
Greater Miami Jewish Federation allocated funds for at
least two years to Ambijan, the American Birobidjan Committee, until that pro-Soviet organization closed its
doors at the end of the year. Birobidjan was established
as a Siberian Jewish province of the USSR in 1928 and
was intended to compete with Palestine as a homeland for
Russian Jews. In 1948, it claimed to have settled
100,000 Jews, but Cyrus L. Sulzberger, the chief European correspondent of the **New York Times,** reported that
the total population of Birobidjan was 100,000, of whom
less than 25,000 were Jews. The American Birobidjan Committee had also managed to get on the mailing list of
the Jewish Agency to receive the **Zionist Newsletter,**
news digests and other Israel publications which the
Agency distributed to Jewish organizations without
charge.
    In Los Angeles, the communist-front Jewish Peoples
Fraternal Order (JPFO) became a constituent member of

the Jewish Community Council and bitterly resisted
efforts by the Council to cancel its membership. An editorial in the local **Jewish Voice** by Samuel B. Gach, its
editor, denounced the JPFO as a fraud. "The Jewish
Peoples Fraternal Order is not Jewish, is not the
Peoples, and if it is fraternal, its frat is red Moscow," said Gach. The struggle over the JPFO was harsh
and intensive; not until the end of the year was the Los
Angeles Jewish Community Council finally able to oust
the JPFO from its membership.

The special target of the communists for infiltration was the American Jewish Congress. How far they succeeded in their ambitious take-over attempt before they
were stopped was first disclosed in my report, entitled
"The Red Kiss," which appeared in **The Menorah Journal**
for August 1948. The disclosures helped to focus attention on the extent of communist penetration, and after
two years of battling with the communists and fellow
travelers within its ranks, the administrative and executive committees of the American Jewish Congress voted
at the end of June 1950 to adopt a revised statement of
principles which, in effect, barred from membership any
individual or group which would not reject all forms of
dictatorship. "We...must reject every form of totalitarianism as imperiling the survival of the Jewish people
and the freedom of mankind," the statement read.

Chief among the communist-front groups that the
American Jewish Congress sought to get rid of was the
JPFO, and the effort led to a bitter fight within its
West Coast division. The newsletter reported the strug-
gle in the following account:

> Continuing to clean out the communists and
> fellow-travelers from within its ranks, the
> American Jewish Congress brought charges
> against its Southern California Division last
> week, the **B'nai B'rith Messenger** of Los Angeles
> (no connection with the national B'nai B'rith)
> reports. The Los Angeles region was accused of
> failure to carry out the American Jewish Con-
> gress program, of associating with unauthorized
> causes, of cooperating with the communist-front
> JPFO, of circumvention and outright opposition
> to national administrative directives, etc. A
> public meeting was called by the region chiefs
> after the American Jewish Congress tried to im-
> pound local funds, ordered the dismissal of
> local employees and finally closed the Divi-
> sion's offices. Alfred Buckman, president of

the Division, described the action of the
American Jewish Congress as a "purge" and submitted his resignation.

An editorial in the **Messenger** said that the
Pacific region is next on the American Jewish
Congress list. It objected to the action by the
American Jewish Congress because "we do not
want Congress to become subject to the universal hysteria and become so busy 'purging' itself that it will forget the common enemy of
the Jewish people."

Concerned over the demonstrated communist infiltration tactics and the threat to civil liberties arising
from hastily drafted anti-communist legislation, Jewish
agencies moved hesitantly and cautiously. The Newsletter
said that the "ostrich-like tactics" of the defense
agencies were "no answer to the problem of communism
among Jews." At the same time, such over-emphatic protests as the statement of the Board of Rabbis of Cincinnati denouncing communism, or the editorial in the
Intermountain Jewish News of Denver, headlined "Jewry
Opposes Communism," probably did more harm than good.

A communist monthly magazine called **Jewish Life**
scrupulously reflected Moscow's propaganda line, including such familiar efforts as an attack on Israel for
acting allegedly as an American "puppet"--a line continued to this day--and exaggerated support for Jewish
groups that circulated anti-war "peace" petitions. Said
the Newsletter:

> **Jewish Life** in itself is no danger, but the
> infiltration into the Jewish press of commu-
> nists and fellow-travelers is. Two contributors
> to the communist monthly are Morris U. Schap-
> pes, a member of its editorial board, and Jo-
> seph Brainin, alias Phineas Biron, his pen
> name. Schappes' communist-slanted stuff has
> been given respectability by being published by
> the American Jewish Historical Society.
> Brainin, alias Biron, writes a weekly column of
> comment on Jewish affairs which appears in a
> number of English Jewish papers. **Opinion**, a
> Jewish monthly edited by James Waterman Wise,
> also gives Brainin space for his communist-
> slanted views. Either deliberately or inno-
> cently, many English Jewish weeklies are pro-
> viding disguised communists with a forum for
> their propaganda. The time has come to expose

these **yevsektsias** and label them for what they
are.
Will our multi-million dollar "defense"
agencies wake up too late once more?

Communist attacks were sharpest, as might be expected, against the anti-communist bill passed by Congress over President Truman's veto. An NCRAC telegram
urging President Truman to veto the bill together with
such hysterical editorial attacks as those which appeared in the **B'nai B'rith Messenger,** the **American Jewish World** of Minneapolis and other weeklies made it
appear as if this legislation were an exclusively Jewish issue. The **Messenger** in particular warned of all
kinds of horrible consequences, predicting inter alia:
"With the so-called anti-subversive bills in Congress
about to be signed, the anti-Semites in America will
have a Roman holiday over the economic corpses of American Jewry."
NCRAC did not limit its political action to anti-
communist legislation, of course, and under the general
category of defending civil liberties issued statements
on matters as far-fetched from Jewish community interest
as a proposed American loan to the Spanish government of
General Francisco Franco. The NCRAC member agencies were
not far behind. On September 24, the **New York Times** published a letter over the signatures of Will Maslow and
Joseph B. Robinson on behalf of the American Jewish Congress criticizing Republicans and Democrats alike for
the failure of the 81st Congress to enact any civil
rights legislation. Two weeks later, the same newspaper
published a letter from Irving M. Engel, the Democratic
and Liberal candidate for Congress from Manhattan--and
also incidentally, the chairman of the executive committee of the American Jewish Committee--taking sharp issue
with the American Jewish Congress spokesman and defending the record of the "Northern Democrats."
The spectacle of the spokesmen for two prominent
Jewish organizations attacking each other in the public
press over political issues that had nothing directly to
do with Jews provided a most unhappy circumstance which
fortunately was not repeated. The entrance of these
agencies into the general field of political action,
however, combined with the fact that they employed representatives in Washington to lobby the Congress on
such issues as education, alien property, immigration
and civil rights had the unpleasant consequence of
stirring up an investigation into their tax-exempt status by the Internal Revenue Service. All the Jewish

organizations carried on their activities with tax-exempt funds, and therefore were limited in their political activity. In 1950, the immediate target of the IRS was the ADL, but the investigations were broadened and continued for the next nine years, culminating in 1960 in the hearings on the tax exemption of the UJA before the Senate Foreign Relations Committee, of which Senator William J. Fulbright was then chairman. Fortunately, all the organizations involved were able to defend their activities as in compliance with their tax-exempt status, but the experience left scars that were not forgotten.

The fight against communist infiltration was strengthened considerably by the fact that the communists were attacking Israel, then as now, as an instrument of western imperialism. Typical was Brainin's commentary on the discussions about the Israel bond campaign that took place at the Jerusalem conference. The Newsletter summarized Brainin's comments in the following report:

> While the NCRAC is playing with politics, communists and fellow-travelers are having a field day in the Jewish press. Joseph Brainin, a contributor to the communist monthly **Jewish Life** as well as a columnist for several English Jewish weeklies under the pseudonym of Phineas J. Biron, this week expounds the communist line on the Jerusalem conference and the Israel bond issue.
>
> According to Brainin-Biron, who did not go to Jerusalem, American leaders were sloganeering the Israeli government spokesmen to "join the U.S. in its cold war against the Soviet Union." Brainin-Biron explained that Israel will have to meet the U.S. State Department "demands" in order to get approval for international loans and for its bond issue.

The Newsletter also noted that while several English Jewish weeklies had dropped Biron's column, the magazine **Opinion**, which had four prominent Reform rabbis on its editorial board, continued to provide Brainin "full space for his communist propaganda." It reported with approval, however, that the ADL, the American Jewish Committee, and the American Jewish Congress had all gone on record at various times condemning communism and asserting, as the ADL did, that the "fate of the Jewish community is inextricably bound up with the fate of democracy." And a resolution adopted by the NCRAC on May 28 piously expressed "abhorrence of communism, fascism and all forms of totalitarianism." To all of which the Newsletter felt compelled to note that however praiseworthy were the sentiments expressed by these organizations, the fact remained that Jews had managed to live and even prosper under almost every form of government recorded in the annals of man.

The fine line that had to be drawn between the defenders of civil liberties and fellow-travelers was searchingly examined in the case of Rabbi Benjamin Lowell, the administrative secretary of the B'nai B'rith Hillel Foundation. Lowell had been the target of the American Jewish League Against Communism (AJLAC) and was under fire for his leftist views. When Rabbi Samuel Glasner, director of the Hillel Foundation of Georgia University, openly charged him with being a communist party member, Frank Goldman, president of the B'nai B'rith, appointed Judge Stanley Fuld, of the New York State Court of Appeals, to investigate the charges. Rabbi Glasner subsequently denied that he had accused Rabbi Lowell and instead praised his integrity and loyalty. But before any investigation got under way, Rabbi Lowell resigned. The Hillel Foundation then issued the following statement to clarify its position in the matter:

"In view of the fact that Rabbi Lowell's name has been in the press recently as the result of charges stemming from irresponsible sources, there will inevitably be a measure of speculation as to the reasons for Rabbi Lowell's resignation. Such speculation is bound to be unfair either to Rabbi Lowell or to Hillel. Rabbi Lowell resigned because of his recognition of a basic difference in approach to Hillel's aims and policies, and not because of the pressure of any outside group or individual."

With that statement which left many questions unanswered, the matter was dropped. For some time afterward, however, Hillel rabbis, most of them young men, had the reputation of being way-out liberals if not altogether sympathetic to left-wing policies. Not without its influence on the Hillel rabbis was a controversial book which was published at this time, entitled **Documentary History of the Jews of the United States**. The author of the book was Morris U. Schappes, a communist historian and editor of the communist monthly **Jewish Life**. A review of this history book in the communist monthly offered the following candid admission: "Mr. Schappes' book has the potentiality of steering the writing of American Jewish history into a more scientific, realistic path than heretofore."

Another divergent view of the American Jewish community which more justifiably deserved the description "realistic" was the book by Dr. Eli Ginzberg, published later in the year under the title, **Agenda for American Jews.** An assistant professor of economics at Columbia University and a widely recognized authority on manpower issue, Dr. Ginzberg, who was also the son of Professor Louis Ginzberg of the Jewish Theological Seminary, presented in semi-outline form his analysis of the more important issues confronting American Jews and their leadership following the establishment of the state of Israel. The book met with a cool reception, in part probably because Dr. Ginzberg minced no words in expressing his critical views of Jewish development in America. Characteristic of his sharp pen, which some critics held was inherited from his famous father, was the following conclusion:

"Judaism holds each Jew personally responsible for the welfare of the group. Until a much larger number is willing to participate actively in Jewish life, which implies that they acquire a reasonable background of facts and issues, and until they are willing to make a sizeable personal investment of time and effort, it is inevitable that the largely second-rate leadership will remain safely ensconced. The leadership, aware of its limitations, will instinctively manipulate the situation to remain in control rather than to work towards a larger and better informed participating group."

It was a harsh indictment, not altogether fair to the Jewish leadership which, with all its failings, nevertheless was making a valiant effort to resist communist infiltration while at the same time facing the enormous transitional problems resulting from the establishment of the new state of Israel. Nevertheless, it expressed a view which the Newsletter believed to be largely valid.

8

NEWS AND INFORMATION

The major source of news about Jews and events in the Jewish communities in the United States, and in Israel and other parts of the world since World War I is the Jewish Telegraphic Agency (JTA). It was founded in 1917 by Jacob Landau, a 25-year-old Austrian immigrant, as an independent business venture to service the Yiddish dailies and the growing number of English Jewish weeklies. I first met Landau in the early 1940s in the office of the American Jewish Committee, where I was then employed. He was a short, very fat man with shiny blackeyes, and I was impressed by his quick mind and sharp tongue. Apparently he had early recognized that without the financial help of major Jewish organizations he could never realize his ambition of establishing a world-wide Jewish news service, and he managed therefore to interest Morris Waldman, the secretary of the American Jewish Committee, in his ideas for a Latin American service. In 1940, Waldman, who described him in the annual report of the Committee as "a keen and reliable student of international affairs," made it possible for Landau to spend five months in South America surveying conditions in the Jewish communities that had grown up there since the turn of the century. At the annual meeting of the American Jewish Committee in January 1941, Landau delivered a very informative report on his findings which fully justified Waldman's confidence in him.

Helped substantially by an annual subsidy from the American Jewish Committee, Landau was able to undertake a very considerable expansion of the JTA during the second World War, when information about what was happening to the very large European Jewish communities was scant and rumors were frightening. One result of the South American survey was to provide Landau with a base on which to build the Overseas News Agency (ONA), one of his most ambitious ventures, which was designed to serve the general press with news about South America as well as Europe. It proved to be a very costly enterprise, and

123

along with the Seven Arts Feature Syndicate, another JTA affiliate which Landau developed at this time, led to increasing financial difficulties. The various maneuverings and schemes devised by Landau to keep ONA and JTA in operation, and his increasing efforts to obtain the support he needed from Jewish community funds without at the same time considering any change from his personal ownership and control of JTA were analyzed in considerable detail by this writer in **The Menorah Journal** for Spring, 1949.

Much of the problem arose from the fact that ONA, established in 1941, failed to get the general press to subscribe to its service. Although ONA was not Jewish oriented--its most valuable asset was a comic strip called "Louie"--Landau, in a desperate effort to save it from bankruptcy, appealed for help to the Jewish community funds. In a "Report on the ONA," he tried to justify his appeal by claiming that it was largely because of ONA's "indispensable job" that "Israel has not disappeared from the general non-Jewish press in recent months." He could not conceal the embarrassing fact, however, that the only New York daily taking ONA service at the time the report was issued was the leftwing **New York Daily Compass**. The appeal failed and Landau was compelled to separate ONA completely from JTA. In the first of a succession of JTA corporate reorganizations, ONA was left to shift for itself. At the same time, JTA president George Backer submitted his resignation; no reasons were given and no official announcement was made to mark his departure despite his long support for and personal friendship with Landau.

Landau's best opportunity to obtain the funding he needed to continue his news service was to have JTA included as a beneficiary of the New York UJA. His claim that the JTA served the cause of Israel undoubtedly was persuasive because it gained him the support of Louis Lipsky, chairman of the American Zionist Council, when he submitted a bid for a minimum allocation of $150,000. Lipsky may very likely have been won over by his son Eleazar, a former New York district attorney and writer of popular detective novels, who was a strong supporter of the JTA. The younger Lipsky had accepted Landau's invitation to act as JTA's representative on a trip he was making to South Africa. In Johannesburg, Lipsky met with the South African Board of Jewish Deputies and appealed to them for funds for the JTA, emphasizing its service to South African Jewry by keeping them informed of events affecting Jews throughout the world. At its meeting in January, however, the executive council for the

Board recommended that "the question of further financial aid to the [Jewish Telegraphic] Agency" be tabled
until March when, according to the **Jewish Times** of
Johannesburg, "it was hoped by then that the Agency
would have been satisfactorily reorganized."

The problem obviously was Landau's corporate ownership and control of the JTA which he refused to give up.
His failure to reincorporate the JTA on a non-profit
basis blocked all efforts to transform it into a genuine
communal agency and also resulted in a break in his
long-time relationship with the American Jewish Committee. Since the JTA was not a non-profit communal agency,
it was not eligible to receive tax-exempt funds on a
membership basis, and subsequently it was also dropped
as a beneficiary of the New York UJA. This was noted by
the Newsletter when it reported the fact that among the
agencies listed by the New York UJA in full page advertisements on February 1, the name of the JTA was conspicuous by its absence. The JTA was not without its defenders, however, which the Newsletter observed in the
following report:

> Mordecai Danzis, editor of **The Day**, New
> York Yiddish daily, who recently devoted his
> column to pot-shots at famous violinist Yehudi
> Menuhin, last week fired a broadside at the New
> York UJA and local welfare funds throughout the
> country for dropping the JTA from their list of
> beneficiaries. Accusing all welfare funds in-
> discriminately of being undemocratic, destruc-
> tive of the Jewish **zedakah**, and a veritable
> **Golem** that straddles American Jewish life and
> arbitarily "tramples over organizations and
> institutions," Danzis claims that they have cut
> off JTA without a hearing and simply because
> its director, Jacob Landau, had a fight with
> Jacob Blaustein, former chairman of the JTA
> Board and president of the American Jewish
> Committee.
>
> Lauding the work of the JTA to the skies,
> Danzis prefers to remain silent on the basic
> issue which led to JTA's downfall: should a
> privately owned organization masquerading as a
> communal institution continue to receive public
> charitable tax-exempt funds without adequately
> accounting for them? Nor does Danzis refer to
> the fact that the attempted reorganization of
> the JTA following the resignation of Blaustein

and others is still pending more than six months after it was first announced.

None of this inner communal struggle was reported in the English Jewish press. According to a survey made by the Newsletter, "editorials in a sampling of English Jewish weeklies of March 9 and 10 demonstrate a remarkable determination to avoid current issues and controversies in communal life, both local and national." Difficulties continued to mount for JTA during this period as Landau's financial situation became more and more critical. In my letter to Leftwich, I pointed to a new development that could affect the future of the JTA and observed:

"The American revolution is gaining momentum but in an atmosphere of extraordinary calm--or is it just apathy, a hangover from the halcyon days during the last years of the war when everyone was a Zionist and Israel a seemingly impossible dream. Now we have Israel, and American Jewry willy-nilly is being swept to God knows where by the powerful forces that the achievement of statehood has let loose. Anti-Semitism no longer absorbs the efforts of our 'leaders'; now it's 'nationalism' that is the issue of the moment. And with the JTA being taken over by the 'nationalist' Jewish Agency (I can't prove it yet, but the evidence so far points pretty definitely to it), the fight must come out into the open. Add the rabbinical ferment that's stirring the country, place it all under the pressure of declining charity funds, including UJA, and you have all the elements of a first-class blow-up."

Landau's extraordinary flexibility in keeping afloat financially without sacrificing his ownership of the JTA was demonstrated afresh by his turn, this time, to the Jewish Agency for help. Progressing from the American Jewish Committee to the local welfare funds and the New York UJA, Landau now recognized that his salvation most likely lay with Israel, and in my letter of March 31, I told Leftwich about some of the preliminary details of the newest "reorganization" of the JTA. In the following report, I also pointed out how hard it was to pin down Landau:

"The reorganization of the JTA will be announced in a few weeks following the return of Rudolf G. Sonneborn from Israel, where he is now. Mr. Sonneborn, a wealthy American oil magnate, prominent anti-Silver Zionist and chairman of the Board of the UPA, has now accepted the chairmanship of the new Board of Directors of the JTA.

"Mr. and Mrs. Jacob Landau have transferred their controlling shares of JTA stock to the new Board and have completely severed all connection with the JTA. Landau, however, still owns ONA, whose major financial asset at present is a cartoon strip without words called 'Louie,' and a paper organization formed during the war called the American Institute for International Affairs, or something like that. He is now campaigning to set up the latter as a research institute and is seeking $450,000 for it. He has Albert Einstein set up as the head of the Institute, and former State Department official Spruille Braden and Ben Javits, brother of Representative Jacob K. Javits, working with him on it. Nothing small about the Landaus!

"JTA, of course, now goes into the hands of the Jewish Agency, and may actually set up its head office in Tel Aviv. Victor Bienstock will be retained as the chief editor. What the Landaus were paid, I don't know, but I suspect that they were the same terms reported at the time of the Blaustein blow-up: cancellation of Landau's debt to JTA (about $40,000, I think) and a life pension. What the anti-Zionist American Jewish Committee will do about the situation even they don't know yet, but I have little doubt that they will try in some way to counter Israeli control of the American Jewish press. The new JTA plan is along the lines outlined by Eleazar Lipsky, I am told. Unfortunately, Lipsky is out of town and I can't get hold of him for a story. I suspect, however, that there is a good spot for him in the new set-up."

Another report making the rounds was that Dr. Nahum Goldmann had accepted an invitation from Landau to become chairman of the JTA board of directors in the new reorganization. When he was reached by the Newsletter, however, Dr. Goldmann angrily denied the rumor as well as the reports that he had had a hand in the reorganization. "It's a lie," he said. "I have nothing to do with it." He pointed out that the new chairman was Rudolf G. Sonneborn, thus confirming the information I wrote Leftwich.

In the next weeks, the sensational information contained in my letter was fleshed out in the Newsletter. Reporting on April 13 that control of the JTA had passed into the hands of the Jewish Agency, the Newsletter pointed out that top priority was now being given to news coverage about Israel in the JTA over domestic American news. It also noted that the reaction of the American Jewish Committee had been swift: "...this week [it] discontinued distribution of the daily **JTA Bulletin** which it had been sending to a selected list of officers," and for which it had been paying $100 a subscription.

Details about the JTA reorganization were not officially released until the middle of April. Reported to

the press by Adolf C. Robison, the information promptly
stirred up doubts about the extent of the changeover and
about the degree to which Landau had given up control.
Robison, a well-meaning New Jersey textile manufacturer
who was active in Materials for Israel and other Zionist
organizations, confirmed the Newsletter's suspicions when
he disclosed the fact that Jacob Landau was still very
much in charge of JTA and had also assured himself of a
lifetime income. My information in the letter to Leftwich
obviously had not been correct; Landau had not only not
given up control of the JTA but had also arranged to have
himself appointed as executive secretary of the new board
of directors and his brother-in-law Victor Bienstock
named the managing director, thus insuring his control as
firmly as ever. Apparently, the only concession Landau
had made to his new financial sponsors was to turn over
his shares in the JTA to the board of directors--in short
to sell his shares for a lifetime pension!

Moreover, the list of new directors included enough
Landau friends and supporters to guarantee his control
over the news service. For example, among the new directors were Benjamin A. Javits, a lawyer, who had been
associated with Landau in the effort to promote the
American Institute for International Information; S.H.
Scheuer, a Landau supporter and holdover from the previous JTA board; and Philip Slomovitz, editor of the
Jewish News of Detroit and president of the Anglo-Jewish
Press Association. Slomovitz was a privileged client of
JTA and for some time had enjoyed last-minute JTA news
coverage by virtue of a special wire service not avail-
able to other English Jewish weeklies. The other members
of the new JTA board were George Alpert, a Boston com-
mual leader associated with Brandeis University; A. Good-
man, a wealthy Miami communal leader; Professor Horace
Kallen, of the New School for Social Research; Robert
Szold, of Baltimore, a former ZOA president; and Rabbi
Samuel Wohl, a Labor Zionist leader and an associate of
Rabbi James Heller of the Isaac M. Wise Temple in
Cincinnati.

The wily Landau, moreover, had made sure that the
basic corporate structure of the JTA would remain unchanged, thereby leaving also unchanged the fact that the
JTA was no more eligible for tax exempt funds now than it
had been previously. Whether there was more reason for
Landau's obvious unwillingness to change the JTA structure than his fear of losing control I was never able to
discover, but in my letter to Leftwich, I observed that
"Landau has pulled a fast one, which leaves him in full
control and guarantees himself a life pension besides.

The Zionist window dressing is not fooling anyone, if I can help it. I'm sending the Newsletter to all local welfare funds as well as to organization leaders in New York."

The Newsletter report that I distributed to the welfare funds made it crystal clear that Landau had saved his organization from bankruptcy at the expense of the tax-exempt community funds. The Newsletter reported:

> Mr. Robison's statement adds that the JTA will sever all connections with other news agencies, presumbly the ONA, but goes on to disclose that the Palestine Telegraphic Agency will take over JTA's European and Israel offices and service JTA with news from these sources. No mention is made of the fee that JTA will have to pay for this service, but in view of the manner in which ONA "legitimately" milked JTA for services rendered, the possibilities inherent in the PTA setup should not be overlooked. PTA, which was also organized by Mr. Landau, has yet to be "reorganized."
>
> Boris Smolar, editor-in-chief of JTA, is not mentioned in Mr. Robison's statement. From other sources, it was reliably learned that negotiations over severance pay are now going on between JTA and Smolar.
>
> Queried about the reaction of local welfare funds to the new JTA setup, a spokesman for the CJFWF told **Cross-Section, U.S.A.** that no statement would be issued by the CJFWF until it had full opportunity to examine all documents and agreements relating to the new JTA setup.
>
> The Zionist coloration of Mr. Landau's new Board of Directors indicates an alliance with forces headed by Henry Montor and Dr. Nahum Goldmann, but does not represent the approval of the ZOA. Some veteran Zionist leaders have indicated privately to this reporter their disapproval of the new JTA move.
>
> Some months ago, Mr. Landau was reported to have told a subscriber: "You ought to know that I give away nothing that I have." The current JTA maneuver indicates that Mr. Landau has made good his boast. His "reorganization" reorganizes nothing save the Board of Directors. These new faces will not obtain New York State or New York City tax exemption for JTA. They will not be able to transform JTA into the independent

objective news service for which American Jewry
has been paying hundreds of thousands of dollars. Honorable men though they may be, there
is no reason to believe that they will be able
to control Mr. Landau's actions any more than
his previous board of honorable men. Surely
there must be good reason why George Backer and
Ralph Lazarus, who defended Mr. Landau so ardently at the time of his fight with Jacob
Blaustein (then chairman of the JTA board and
president of the American Jewish Committee)
would not stomach Mr. Landau's present setup.
     By this alleged reorganization, Mr. Landau
in effect is thumbing his nose at the American
Jewish community, which has already demonstrated its disapproval of his methods. JTA
will soon appeal to the Jewish communal funds
for a substantial subsidy. Will our communal
leaders let Mr. Landau get away with it once
more?

The following week, the Newsletter noted that not a
single English Jewish weekly--with one exception--car-
ried the complete story of the reorganization of the
JTA. It reported that the JTA had deliberately delayed
releasing the information on Monday, which meant that
most newspapers did not receive the story in the mail
until the following day at the earliest, a day beyond
their deadlines and too late for them to include it in
their weekly editions. The sole exception was the Jewish News of Detroit, whose editor, Philip Slomovitz, was
one of the new directors of the JTA and therefore privy
to the entire action. What the weeklies did carry was a
report on the general outlines of the reorganization,
but with no details. The Seven Arts Feature Service, a
JTA affiliate, did send some details out in time to meet
the weeklies' deadline. Seven Arts said that the reorganization had established a "public trust" status for
the JTA; it did not, however, disclose the appointment
of Landau as executive secretary nor Bienstock as managing director of the JTA.
     The Newsletter minced no words in charging that the
labelling of the JTA as a "public trust" was an "attempt
to perpetuate a fraud upon the public" because nothing
had changed in the corporate structure of the organization. Apparently the Large City Budgeting Conference
(LCBC), an independent body made up of some of the
largest welfare funds, also could not stomach the alleged reorganization of the JTA. Their reaction was

noted in what must be regarded as a masterpiece of understatement, by **The American Jewish Year Book** (vol.53, 1952, page 223), which said that "the LCBC, finding itself unable to clarify and evaluate these structural and financial arrangements, recommended that its affiliated welfare funds treat the JTA on the basis of purchasing its service rather than granting it philanthropic allocations as a communal agency. The JTA continued to appeal to welfare funds for communal support, maintaining that its reorganized setup qualified it for such consideration. Community practice varied...."

The Newsletter's reference to the Zionist coloration of the JTA reorganization, which indicated "an alliance with the forces headed by Henry Montor and Dr. Nahum Goldmann," must have struck sensitive nerves because Henry Montor promptly and unpleasantly denied it. Writing to the Newsletter, Montor said: "In a letter dated April 23, 1950, which you circulated, you mention my name in connection with the Jewish Telegraphic Agency. Only because you assume an air of authenticity which may lead people to believe you, I find it necessary to say that there is not one iota of truth in your reference. I have not had and do not have--directly or indirectly, publicly or privately--any connection with JTA, old or new."

The Newsletter, of course, published this denial, but added that the "source of our information is a highly respected Zionist official in whose reliability and authority we have the utmost confidence." To this comment there was no rejoinder; the identity of my source, which I could not reveal at the time, was Louis Lipsky. As subsequent events proved, it was probably Nahum Goldmann who, in all likelihood, had advised Montor to deny the connection with JTA.

The new reorganization of the JTA was shortlived. In a letter to Leftwich dated May 23, I described a startling phone call that I had received from a fellow journalist and editor of a rival newsletter named William Zukerman. To Leftwich, I wrote the following: "It was Zukerman on the phone to tell me that Sonneborn and Robison have just resigned from the board of JTA after a spat with Landau, which apparently followed a blow-up by Nahum Goldmann (just returned to these shores) who was furious that the name of the Jewish Agency should be linked to the JTA. At least, that is the confused story I got from Zukerman. I'll have to start checking tomorrow to get the real dope on it. If, as Zukerman says, his information is absolutely reliable, it means a victory for us. I'd like nothing better than to knock JTA

out of the picture completely. Then, maybe, we would
have a chance to get a decent honest news service. But,
as you have pointed out, it may be too early to call
Landau out entirely."

My wishful thinking was inspired in part by the efforts of the London **Jewish Chronicle** to establish its
own news service in this country. Zukerman had been approached by David Kessler, the publisher of the **Jewish
Chronicle**, at one point but the negotiations had been
inconclusive. I had also had a similar experience. The
Jewish Chronicle had indeed developed its own highly
selective news service, especially expert in covering
Jewish events in Europe and particularly what was happening behind the Iron Curtain, where JTA had very in-
adequate coverage. Kessler was visiting New York and
other American cities in a first-hand effort but was
unable to find sufficient financial support on his terms
to replace the JTA with a proposed extension of the
Jewish Chronicle news service.

In this respect, unfortunately, neither Zukerman nor
I was able to help. I complained to Leftwich about
Kessler's unrealistic attiude in assuming that he could
get started here without making a financial investment
along with the new service. I wrote: "Kessler doesn't
seem to realize that while there is dissatisfaction with
JTA here, the powers that be are quite content to wait
until Landau is starved out and then pick up the remains
and reorganize it to their liking. That is the plan of
the CJFWF now, and local funds have been allocating but
not disbursing special amounts for a news service, if,
as, and when. But someone would have to come in and
knock out JTA first if they expect to get any of that
money. That is what I would be willing to gamble my time
and work for--as little as I can afford it. But if even
a small sum is going to stand in Kessler's way, then obviously he is not the man for the job or the opportunity
here."

As subsequent developments proved, Kessler never did
obtain the opportunity he was looking for. I had duly
reported the failure of the new JTA reorganization and
had even managed to reach Rudolf Sonneborn and asked him
for a statement on his resignation. He denied that there
had been any disagreement between himself and Jacob Landau, but when I pressed him, he refused to comment further on the reason for his resignation. Robison also
refused to comment. He had been asked by the CJFWF for
details of the JTA reorganization but had never supplied
the requested information. Obviously Landau was trying
to stonewall the situation as were his friends.

Meanwhile, an editorial in the **National Jewish Post,**
a weekly published in Indianapolis by Gabriel Cohen, expressed considerable dissatisfaction with the JTA reorganization and recommended the establishment of an
independent Jewish news service free from organizational
sponsorship and ties. It was the only English Jewish
weekly to express an independent opinion on the JTA
situation. The Newsletter picked up on the **Post's** editorial and went on to say:

> The **Post** might have gone a step further and
> asked by what right did JTA turn over to Mr.
> Jacob Landau as his private property the Over-
> seas News Agency and Press Features, both or-
> ganized and developed with Jewish community
> funds! How come this free gift to Mr. Landau of
> a business worth almost $100,000?
>   By what right, also, is Mr. Landau entitled
> to a pension not only for his lifetime but for
> his wife's as well, which will eventually cost
> the American Jewish community several hundreds
> of thousands of dollars?
>   Where are the voices of American Jewry who
> will cry out against this criminal exploitation
> of public charity funds!

The Newsletter's challenge was never picked up;
there were no threats of court action, no angry letters; but the expose did compel the CJFWF to take some
action. The Newsletter made a number of attempts to get
a reaction from the Jewish Agency, but its spokesman
refused our request for a statement on the failure of
the JTA reorganization. He was silent also when the
Newsletter asked how the Agency expected to collect the
$50,000 it had advanced to Landau. Sonneborn did ask
the CJFWF to call a special meeting and promised that he
would give a full report on the JTA situation, but when
he met with the delegates of the community funds at the
CJFWF meeting on June 18, which had been arranged at his
request, he pleaded with them to support the reorganized
JTA instead of making the explanation he had promised.
He was also less than frank with the delegates in
responding to the question that was on everyone's lips
when he said that he had resigned from the JTA board
only because he felt he could be more helpful outside
the agency. His answer to questions about Landau's lifetime pension was equally unsatisfactory. All he would
say was that no further changes in JTA's reorganization
were expected--which was no answer at all. Moreover,

Sonneborn was obviously being a good soldier in an embarrassing cause when he assured the delegates that Judge Simon "Rifkind had agreed to become his successor as president of JTA if he could be assured of community support." The reply of the delegates to his appeal for support, according to the Newsletter, "can be summed up in one word, 'No.'"

The same issue of the Newsletter explained to its readers that it had made an error in reporting the size of the "loan" that the Jewish Agency had made to JTA: instead of the $50,000 as reported, the amount actually loaned to JTA was $110,000. Jewish Agency officials, added the Newsletter, when confronted with this information, "refused to comment on how or when they expected repayment of these communal funds."

The Yiddish daily newspapers were major beneficiaries of the JTA service, and therefore their defense of the news service against the decision of the CJFWF not to support JTA was not unexpected. David Meckler, the editor of the **Jewish Morning Journal**, advanced an unusual argument to his editorial and it drew the following response from the Newsletter:

> If ZOA president Browdy's suggestion for greater democracy in Jewish fundraising were effected, says David L. Meckler in last Sunday's **Morning Journal**, then the JTA would be able to appeal from the decision of the "Welfare Funds" not to give funds to JTA. This verdict, says Meckler, was handed down at the request of the former chairman of the JTA board who "suddenly declared war on JTA."
>
> (The former chairman, whom Meckler does not name, is Jacob Blaustein, also president of the American Jewish Committee.)
>
> Meckler underestimates the intelligence of his readers if he thinks they will believe the cock-and-bull tale he has concocted. JTA's flagrant misuse and waste of communal funds over a period of many years is sufficient reason for the long overdue action of the welfare funds. Nor will phony "reorganizations" save it. There will be no confidence in JTA as long as Jacob Landau controls it. The JTA case above all represents the true workings of democracy, where "you can fool some of the people some of the time, but you can't fool all of the people all of the time."

Editorial comments defending the JTA similar in tone to the one written by Meckler were published by the German language weekly, **Aufbau**, and by Mordecai Danzis, editor of the **Tog**. To which the newsletter added the comment: "Though the bylines are Meckler and Danzis, the voice is the voice of Landau." Of the English Jewish weeklies, most gave full play to the JTA attack on the welfare funds and in their editorials lauded Landau for his services to the community.

Meanwhile, the JTA went ahead with still another "reorganization," this time installing Dr. Isador Breslau as the president of the board of directors to succeed Sonneborn. Breslau, a rabbi and a wealthy businessman, was president of the Jewish Community Council of Washington, D.C., as well as a member of the national executive committee of the UJA and a former chairman of the allocating committee of the American Fund for Israeli Institutions. It was believed at the time that Breslau, a dedicated Zionist, had accepted the appointment at the behest of Dr. Nahum Goldmann. To a Newsletter inquiry about these developments, the CJFWF expressed complete disinterest in either the JTA attacks on the welfare funds or in the new JTA president.

None of the editorials mentioned the Jewish Agency's loan of $110,000 to JTA, and the Detroit **Jewish News,** which attributed JTA's financial difficulties to "personality problems," also failed to tell its readers about the possibility of a conflict of interest arising from the fact that its editor, Philip Slomovitz, was a member of the JTA board of directors. By August, all of the $110,000 had been expended, and JTA was once more sending frantic appeals for funds to wealthy individuals around the country. Confirmation of the Newsletter's exclusive report of the Jewish Agency loan came from Julian Freeman, of Indianapolis, who was chairman of the CJFWF Committee on Stable and Unified Fund Raising. Speaking at the Israel Bond conference in Jerusalem, Freeman sharply criticized the Israelis for failing to eliminate waste in raising and distributing funds, and as an example, he cited the fact that the Jewish Agency had made a "loan" to the JTA at a time when the welfare funds were refusing to include JTA as a recipient of communal funds.

As JTA's financial situation became increasingly desperate, responsible communal leaders were compelled to consider the consequences of its impending collapse. It is very likely that Israel was particularly concerned because it regarded the JTA as more comprehensive in reporting news about Jews than any other news service. A

hint of possible negotiations under way to rescue the
JTA was contained in a provision of the allocations by
the United Jewish Welfare Fund of Los Angeles. It announced the distribution of $6 million among 47 local,
national and overseas Jewish agencies. Included in the
list was the following curious item: "A Jewish News
Agency, $5,000. (Set aside for a reorganized JTA or
other news gathering group that may be considered.)"

A check of the Newsletter's sources was unable to
turn up any information that might explain what other
"Jewish news gathering group" was being considered.
Instead, as I wrote Leftwich on October 12: "One of the
men at the CJFWF here tells me that they still have
hopes of reorganizing JTA satisfactorily, ousting Landau
and making a communal agency out of JTA. In that case,
an independent agency would have a very rough time if it
depended to any extent on customers among the Jewish
press, as little as that means financially at
present...."

Meanwhile, in the absence of any other news service,
JTA was kept alive by handouts from the Jewish Agency.
Landau was also successful in obtaining funds for the
floundering ONA by persuading the United States Economic
Cooperation Administration to approve a grant of $31,000
to ONA on his proposal to provide a German language news
service for the press in Western Germany. The government
agency had made an advance payment to Landau of $23,000
late in 1949 and another payment of $7,840 in June 1950
as part of its overall program to subsidize exports to
Europe by American periodical, book and motion picture
companies.

By the end of the year, however, Landau was in such
desperate straits that for several weeks he was unable
to pay salaries to his staff. I wrote Leftwich that Landau had been turned down again by New York UJA after
another intense effort to get help, and that at this
point no one seemed to care whether or not there was a
JTA news service. The English Jewish weeklies had already taken independent steps to protect themselves by
recruiting a young journalist named Joseph Harrison
Fried; his job was to provide them with coverage of the
American community as well as a weekly comment column,
areas in which JTA had been weak especially since the
demise of the Seven Arts Feature Service. Fried's news
service was slugged AJP, the initials standing for
American Jewish Press, and it was formally sponsored by
the American Association of English Jewish Newspapers,
the president of which was the same Philip Slomovitz who
was also a member of the JTA board.

At the turn of the year, I wrote to Leftwich describing the impending collapse of the JTA. There seemed to be no way this time for Landau to survive, I wrote, adding: "A golden opportunity [for the **Jewish Chronicle**] is going to waste here because it's only a matter of months--maybe less--before JTA goes under. They almost did a couple of weeks ago; their employes were suing for non-payment of salaries and had they been allowed to obtain a judgment, Landau would have had to go into bankruptcy. At the last minute, the Jewish Agency bailed him out, but it won't last. Smolar wants out--his salary has been cut along with all the others at a time when the cost of living is going sky high. And since the defense agencies definitely do not want a Jewish news agency--so one of their executives told me--no one with enough money is willing to step into the field in place of JTA. There are several scribblers like myself trying to peddle news, but we're all starving and hanging on for the 'break' that never seems to come."

Landau had demonstrated beyond any doubt that a privately owned Jewish news service could not exist on the fees it charged its subscribers, and that without communal funds to subsidize it, a news service could not be maintained. At the same time, JTA would have been allowed to die if it had not been for Israel's insistence that it was essential for the Jewish state to know what was happening to Jewish communities throughout the world. On this disconsolate note, the year ended for the Newsletter.

9

EDUCATION AND OLD CLOTHES

Efforts of the UJA with the cooperation of the Jewish Agency to limit fundraising appeals by Jewish organizations to one national campaign in which all American communities would take part met with a large degree of success up to this time. Persuading an organization to accept a certain percentage of UJA funds instead of running a separate and expensive campaign of its own was successful largely because local communities simply balked at the prospect of a number of individual organizational appeals. Nevertheless, apart from the JDA, some local charities, many small Orthodox religious groups, and a very small number of national organizations continued to insist on conducting their own campaigns outside of the UJA fold.

The Union of American Hebrew Congregations (UAHC) was one of the larger organizations which annually launched a separate drive for the combined institutions of Reform Judaism. In 1950, its stated goal was $1,875,000, to be raised for the most part from members of the Reform congregations themselves. At this period, many of these members were not Zionists and might have balked at the thought of raising funds through the Israel-oriented UJA. The UAHC campaign, however, did not raise more than $1,013,503, of which about $300,000 was in membership fees which would have been collected in any case. Expenses for the campaign, which included a national Town Hall Meeting radio broadcast, were expected to run as high as $200,000. In 1949, the UAHC had raised about $750,000 at a cost of approximately $100,000. In its report about the campaign, the Newsletter said:

> In view of the regrettable public apathy toward the needs of this important religious institution as well as others, the streamlining of the administration, faculty and publicity departments seems to be the only solution to

139

the financial difficulties of the Reform institutions, which, in addition, are compounded by
the obligations of the recently acquired Jewish
Institute of Religion.

A greater degree of success seemed to be in store
this year for the separate campaign of the American
Friends of the Hebrew University, which had been limping
along for several years. The new president of the Hebrew
University in Jerusalem, Dr. Selig Brodetsky, a British
scientist of note and a dedicated Zionist, had gained a
reputation for rough-and-tumble fighting when he cap-
tured the leadership of the Board of Deputies of British
Jews some years earlier. He launched the campaign personally at the beginning of the year with a Friday
evening address at the fashionable Park Avenue Synagogue
in New York, and followed it with a speaking tour of
some of the principal American communities.
      Prior to his arrival, there had been some prelimi-
nary talks about a joint campaign with the Weizmann
Institute of Science, which Dr. Brodetsky had initially
opposed, but he was soon persuaded by the community
leaders he visited to accept the fundraising advantages
of a united effort. Accordingly, on January 31, announcement was made of the joint drive by the two Israeli institutions toward a goal of $5,000,000. In this
effort, they were joined very shortly after by a third
prestigious Israeli school, the Hebrew Institute of
Technology, better known popularly as the Haifa Technion, and the campaign goal was raised to $7,000,000.
Among the reasons underlining the appeal was the fact
that the Hebrew University received only 15 percent of
its budget from the Israel government, and in 1949, had
incurred a deficit of $200,000. The average salary of a
full professor at the Hebrew University was only about
$3000-$4000 a year.
      During his stay, Dr. Brodetsky also made an effort
to recruit prominent American scholars for the University faculty but without much success. In particular, he
sought out and offered Dr. Max Weinreich an appointment
as head of the newly endowed Chair of Yiddish. Dr. Weinreich was director of the Yiddish Scientific Institute
(YIVO) in New York and was widely recognized as probably
the foremost scholar in the field. Before Dr. Brodetsky
returned to Israel, their talks left him with the impression that Dr. Weinreich had accepted the appointment, but, as the Newsletter subsequently reported, he
was not correct. I related the details to Leftwich in
the following letter:

"I checked Brodetsky's story with Max Weinreich, who would not speak directly with me. Weinreich says definitely that while he had received an invitation to take the Chair in Yiddish, he has not accepted it. He gave no reason, but I suspect YIVO's bad financial position. I don't understand Brodetsky's comment on 'big' Jews in medicine. What about Waxman at Rutgers? He's only one. There is always a scramble for top position, of course, and very likely a Jew has to work harder and be better to get there, but get there he does. It's too pat to blame difficulties on anti-Semitism. America has no genteel tradition when there's a top position at stake; anything goes in a fight, a relic of our pioneer tradition, I think. Money is probably the root cause of Brodetsky's inability to get the men he wants for the University. What else could he offer a **goy** in a top post here? His school has no prestige yet."

When the University celebrated its 25th anniversary in May, it boasted an enrolment of 1400 students, the largest in its history up to that time. In London, Dr. Brodetsky voiced confidence in the success of the tri-school joint campaign, noting that it would help substantially to solve the University's financial problems. "All the forces and institutions in Israel which are concerned with intellectual life and with moral things," he said, "are starved financially and unable to exist. We have neglected it. We are bringing Jews to Israel. What are those Jews to become? The creation of a state is not itself a great service to the world and to humanity. The world has too many states already. Will Israel be a second Egypt or Syria? If Israel is not going to be a state in which all Jews all over the world can be proud, it will be a very serious matter. And I fear that is what is happening."

Dr. Weinreich, of course, never did accept the invitation to join the University. And Dr. Brodetsky, in spite of his prophetic appeal, suffered a similar disappointment when he approached one of his fellow countrymen, Dr. Sydney Goldstein, the former chairman of Great Britain's Aeronautical Research Council and one of Britain's most brilliant mathematicians. Despite a generous offer from Dr. Brodetsky, which was reinforced at the time by Sir Leon Simon, Dr. Goldstein rejected the invitation. Instead, he decided to accept an appointment as the head of the Haifa Technion's new department of Aeronautical Engineering. A year later he became the vice president of the Technion, a post in which he would be directing the Technion's ambitious $1.5 million project to make Israel the aviation center of the Middle

East. To this project, the Israel government had also contributed a grant of 200 acres of land to be used for a testing field and for extension buildings. Dr. Brodetsky's reaction was not reported.

The joint fundraising drive of the three Israeli educational institutions, dubbed the U.I.T., made slow progress despite the direction of Meyer Weisgal, one of the most flamboyant personalities in Israel and the director of the Weizmann Institute. In New York, where the appeal hoped to raise $2.5 million, it ran into competition from the Federation of Jewish Philanthropies of New York, which during the same month of October had launched a campaign for $50.5 million. The high point of the U.I.T. drive was reached on November 29, when it held a special fundraising dinner at the Waldorf-Astoria Hotel. Subscription for the dinner was set at an unprecedented $500 per plate, and as late as November 16, the Newsletter reported that the "U.I.T. campaign so far is not doing as well as expected."

To Leftwich, I wrote about the campaign on January 5, 1951: "The joint appeal of the University, Technion and Institute has been going badly, and I understand that different arrangements will be sought this year, although the joint appeal idea will remain, at least on the surface. Complaints, apparently, are against Weisgal and too much fundraising overhead without adequate results. The Technion people, of course, have most to complain about since they are the best organized and the wealthiest group here. They are fearful that the Jewish Agency will appoint a political deadhead as their next president about one year hence."

To the list of separate campaigns, the Newsletter added its own drive--not for itself--and like the U.I.T., it too was not successful. At the urging of Leftwich and in recognition of the great need of the immigrants in Israel, many of whom arrived--as an old Yiddish saying goes--"naked and barefoot," the Newsletter in October called on Zionist organizations to undertake a collection of old clothes from their members for shipment to Israel. I pointed out that such clothing drives were under way in Great Britain and in South Africa. In New York, however, just one organization, the Pioneer Women, was willing to ship such used clothing to Israel, and then only if it was delivered to the Pioneer Women's warehouse on West 68th Street. No organization was willing to launch a drive to collect, sort and ship the clothes. Individuals who had tried to send clothing to an Israeli relative or friend through the postal service soon learned that the Israeli recipient had to pay an import tax before he could pick up the package. Israel had not arranged any provision for prepaying the tax by the sender, thus effectively cancelling any benefits for the recipient, who obviously was an impoverished person.

The following week, the Newsletter called attention to the efforts of Mrs. Shoshanah Persitz, a member of the Knesset, who singlehandedly was trying to publicize the desperate need in the immigration camps in Israel for clothes for men, women and children; she listed over 200 items that were needed immediately before the beginning of the rainy season. In London, the Federation of Jewish Relief Organizations responded by launching a used clothing appeal. In New York and other parts of the country where the Newsletter was circulated, there was no response whatever to Mrs. Persitz' appeal or to its own call for a collection.

I told Leftwich about the failure of my efforts and some of the reasons for it, saying: "Although more than a week has gone by since I ran the story about Mrs. Persitz, such is the pulling power of this Newsletter that I have not had a single inquiry about the clothing drive. Actually though, there are several reasons why my item was ignored. For one thing, UJA--meaning Montor--frowns upon the practice, and there are few who will oppose him. Secondly, I understand that WIZO [Women's International Zionist Organization] asked Hadassah to undertake such a drive here and the latter refused. I am trying to get more details on that story and may have them next week. In any case, I'm not going to drop the issue because, among other reasons, I am hopeful that I can force some action."

Accordingly, the Newsletter again called attention to the desperate need of immigrants in Israel for clothing "in amounts which cannot be supplied by Israel even if the actual dollars were available." The report went on to point out that in New York City alone, the used clothing that was given away or sold in one day could provide every needy Israeli with more clothes than he would need to see him through the winter. The Newsletter then added the following comment:

In Newark, N.J., last Sunday, the National Council of Jewish Women enlisted the aid of three 15-ton trailer trucks, 62 smaller trucks and hundreds of passenger cars in a one-day clothing drive that brought in "mountains of clothing." Numerous volunteers helped to sort and pick the used clothing. The eventual wear-

ers, however, will not be the needy Israelis
but "new Americans" who are settling in Essex
County, N.J.
Council and the local organizations which
assisted in the drive are to be commended for
their public spirit. But is it true that in New
York, Hadassah, the Women's Zionist Organization, rejected a request from WIZO to conduct a
clothing drive for Israel here?

Clothing drives for Israel were being held in Canada
and other parts of the English speaking world. The
Canadian Zionist Organization responded by launching a
two-year clothing collection campaign for needy immigrants to Israel, and as a first installment, shipped
43,000 pounds of clothing and footwear. They also contributed to the "Materials for Israel" drive, which
included clothing. The chairman of the Canadian campaign, J.A. Klein, in his appeal pointed out: "There is
a dire need for wearing apparel for adults and children
in Israel. One shudders to think of immigrants reaching
Israel at the rate of 20,000 a month, living in tents
without adequate protection against the rain and cold of
the coming winter months."
All this was duly reported by the Newsletter, but in
the United States no appeal could prevail against Henry
Montor's opposition. In Washington, D.C., the B'nai
B'rith Women, after a month-long campaign made a first
donation of clothing and shoes--but it was for the needy
children of South Korea! To this information, the Newsletter added: "We are sure that the kindly B'nai B'rith
Women would do as much for the needy children of Israel
if they were permitted to do so." These incidents
prompted me to send Leftwich the following complaint:
"I've had no response to my **Cross-Section** appeal for
a clothing drive, but I expected none. I haven't the details of the Hadassah-WIZO story, but it is true. And
none of the others will dirty their hands or dare to
defy the powers. Probably the latter, for I notice that
the National Council of Jewish Women is running a clothing drive in some cities--but for 'new Americans'!!! And
as for volunteers--they would rather write out a check
than handle or sort used clothes! But let me not explode
on the shortcomings or our apathetic community here.
Besides, right now, those who can do anything are worried about the finances of their pet organizations and
really devote little more than lip service to Israel's
problems."
The Newsletter's efforts to publicize the need for
clothing for Israel's immigrants eventually began to

make some impact despite the opposition that I was convinced came from Henry Montor and the UJA. In Sioux
City, Iowa, the local chapter of the National Council of
Jewish Women conducted a drive for clothing and blankets
for Israeli chidren. And the **Hadassah Newsletter** at last
carried an item, however unobtrusive, informing people
how to send clothing, tax prepaid, to relatives and
friends in Israel. But no American Zionist organization
made a genuine effort to collect clothing. By the end of
the year, the Newsletter was finally able to unearth the
details of this disgraceful American episode, and under
the heading, "Top Secret," it reported the following:

Repeatedly, since October 5, **Cross-Section,**
U.S.A. has been pointing to the urgent need for
a clothing drive for needy men, women and
children in Israel, particularly those in the
mabarot, the work villages which have largely
replaced the immigrant camps. We have said many
harsh things about American Zionist organizations in our failure to understand why they refused to undertake such a drive in the face of
mounting evidence of the need and the existence
of such campaigns in South Africa, England and
Canada.
This week we learned on very reliable information that a solicitation has been under
way in New York City for about one month following an urgent request from the Israeli
government itself. Carefully avoiding all publicity, an independent committee drawn from the
Zionist organizations, has been soliciting
clothing, footwear and other needed materials
from manufacturers, wholesalers and other business sources in the city. Donations are not
necessarily of new clothes but all are in good
condition. Deadline for the--er--solicitation
is March 1.
Basic reason for the secrecy: UJA's demand
that no major drive other than its own be given
publicity! Now we understand.

Thus, by costly and sometimes painful experience,
did the Newsletter, the Hebrew University, the Haifa
Technion, and the Weizman Institute learn that Henry
Montor's control of fundraising in the United States was
complete!

10

THE MACIVER BLUNDER

It is not easy to understand why a distinguished Christian scholar with a well-deserved reputation as a philosopher, sociologist and teacher, enjoying the initial years of his retirement, should be willing to step into the arena of competing Jewish community organizations and risk his reputation by undertaking to bring about order, efficiency and the logical allocation of functions in their local and national activities. It becomes even more difficult to understand when you add that this scholar was not only a fundamentalist Protestant but also had little or no intimate knowledge of the history and development of the modern American Jewish community. Notwithstanding these considerations and perhaps because his only previous experience with Jewish groups had been his participation in the proceedings of the Conference on Science, Philosphy and Religion, which was sponsored by the Jewish Theological Seminary, Robert M. McIver, Lieber Professor Emeritus of Political Philosophy and Sociology, of Columbia University, permitted himself to be persuaded by his friend, Dr. Louis Finkelstein, Chancellor of the Seminary, in June 1950, to accept such an assignment.

Professor MacIver was the author of several books in the field of sociology, one of which--**The More Perfect Union,** a study of the effects of prejudice--undoubtedly was a factor in the decision of the Special Committee on Evaluative Studies of the National Community Relations Advisory Council to invite him to undertake the proposed study. This committee had been set up in January at the request of the Large City Budgeting Conference (LCBC) and directed "to inquire into the areas of activity of the national and local agencies, relationships, objectives, assumptions on which they rest, methods and results." No doubt, too, the committee was influenced by the fact that Dr. MacIver was not Jewish, and therefore in their opinion was likely to be more objective in his findings and recommendations than a Jewish scholar.

147

On May 11, 1950, the Newsletter noted that the Evaluative Committee, after deliberations and consultations over a period of three months, had begun negotiations to appoint a "chairman of study." According to a spokesman for the NCRAC, the chairman, or director, was to be a "person from the academic world, who will consult with the scientific research departments of the American Jewish Committee, the Anti-Defamation League and the American Jewish Congress."

The choice of Professor MacIver, therefore, was a carefully considered selection, made presumably after a number of other scholars had been considered or interviewed--no other names, however, were ever mentioned or reported. In fact, however, the choice of Professor MacIver proved to be a colossal blunder, and the Evaluations Committee members--who included the community welfare fund leaders as well as the executive directors of the national defense agencies, namely John Slawson, of the American Jewish Committee; Benjamin R. Epstein, of the ADL; David Petegorsky, of the American Jewish Congress; and Isaiah M. Minkoff, of the NCRAC--all had to bear responsibility for the decision.

Obviously, in setting up the Evaluative Committee, there had to be agreement that some duplication in defense agency activities did exist and that ways in which costs could be contained should be explored. In 1946 and 1947, several of my articles, published in **The Menorah Journal**, had been based on analyses calling for the reform of the defense agencies and their budgets. The pressure for change and reform was further emphasized by Israel's need for funds and the problems this created for the welfare funds. Moreover, within some of the larger cities, separate community relations councils had been organized to deal with local problems of prejudice and discrimination, and the need for coordinating their actions soon became embarrassingly evident.

In all these considerations, there must be included the traditional Jewish yearning for a centralized coordinating and governing body which had the power and authority to guide the community. In times past, religious observance was the unifying force. The Kehillah governed the Jewish community; and as late as the turn of the century, a form of Kehillah functioned in New York City as the representative of the Jewish community. With the increasing secularization of Jewish life in America, however, and the development of fundraising as a function of Jewish identification equal to, and in some instances, surpassing religious identification, control and direction were to be exerted by separate bodies, such as the welfare funds, and UJA, and the rabbinical boards. Nevertheless, the aspiration for a centralized governing body persisted, and, as we have noted, as late as 1950, Dr. Jacob Marcus presented a proposal for such an organization at the annual conference of the UAHC.

Some residue of this tradition may have been in the back of the minds of the leaders of the NCRAC and the LCBC when they set up the Evaluative Committee and appointed Dr. MacIver. It took the Columbia sociologist about six months to complete his analysis and write his report, and on January 4, despite the efforts of NCRAC to keep the report secret, the Newsletter was able to disclose that it was being edited and prepared for submission to the Evaluative Studies Committee by April. It was not until the end of May, however, that I was able to see a copy of the MacIver Report. It was given to me by an officer of the ADL who asked me to analyze and review it. No conditions were placed on me and no favors were requested in the way I should publish my review of this extraordinary document.

I was naturally very excited about the sensational news scoop that I had been privileged to get, and I hastened to write about the Report to my London friend Leftwich as soon as I had read it. On June 7, I wrote him in great excitement: "The big news this week is the MacIver Report, and I think I'm the only Jewish newsman who's had a chance to read and study the entire document so far. I hated to do a job on it--I'd cut the defense agencies to the bone if I had the chance--but the well-meaning professor really stepped in with both feet. The net result of his recommendations would have been bigger and better budgets for all concerned, more appeals and more money than ever on useless 'defense' work. The Anti-Defamation League, which opposes the Report, is ready to roll out the plush carpet for me, but the company makes me uncomfortable. They have bought several hundred copies of the Newsletter for national distribution."

The Newsletter had prepared its readers by disclosing the previous week that the Report had been completed and that copies were being read by the members of the Evaluative Studies Committee. I also advised them that it was regarded as a secret and would not be released without further extensive editing. Its recommendations, moreover, were to be withheld until some time in November, when the plenary session of the NCRAC had scheduled a meeting.

This was by far the most sensational story that the Newsletter had ever reported, and I had very high hopes

that it would attract enough subscribers to be the salvation of the Newsletter itself. The recommendations of
the Report would have resulted in revolutionary changes
in the future shape of the Jewish community if they were
carried out, and I was fully aware of the unpleasant
consequences that could follow my unofficial disclosure
of them. Many long hours of study and analysis went into
my summary review of the MacIver Report, and the entire
issue of the Newsletter of June 7, 1951, was devoted to
it. I had come to the following conclusions:

> Although the 135-page "Report on the Jew-
> ish Community Relations Agencies," prepared
> after a 10-month survey by Professor Robert M.
> MacIver for the Special Committee on Evaluative
> Studies of the NCRAC, will not be released for
> publication, **Cross-Section, U.S.A.** is able to
> bring you the following exclusive summary and
> review, based on a reading of the entire docu-
> ment by our editor, Allen Lesser, author of "On
> Anti-Defamation Hysteria" (**The Menorah Journal,**
> Spring 1946), and other critical analyses of
> communal agencies.
> To a student of defense agency development,
> the Report by Dr. MacIver, retired sociology
> professor of Columbia University, comes as a
> disappointment though not as a surprise. Its
> approach is superficial, its recommendations
> naive for the most part, and its attitude of-
> fensively assimilationist. It criticizes Jew-
> ish life needlessly and ignorantly. The Report
> attacks Orthodoxy as separatist, as alien to
> American life; it scores Jewish education for
> failing to portray Christianity favorably; it
> terms "isolationist" many forms of Jewish so-
> cial groups. To solve the defense agency prob-
> lem, it urges a pattern of allocation of func-
> tion but repeatedly violates its own criteria
> for reorganization.
> Notwithstanding Dr. MacIver's authority in
> the social sciences, he has had neither the
> background nor the experience to cope with the
> maze of national and local interrelations and
> intra-relations of the defense agencies. And
> in many subtle ways, his Protestant Christian
> background has presented an additional handi-
> cap.
> To Dr. MacIver, anti-Semitism is largely a
> matter of misunderstanding and misconceptions

for which Jews themselves are in considerable
measure to blame. But it would take a very
brash, very ignorant Jew to state with the Professor's positiveness: "The religious faith of
Jewry is one that, in its more strict, or more
traditional interpretation has a particularly
elaborate expression in dietary prescriptions
and social observances. This tends to limit
at some points the community life of those who
cling to orthodox ways. Moreover, the festivals
of the Jewish people are very distinct from
those observed by nearly all Western peoples"
(pgae 47, our emphasis).

As part of his analysis of the "Anti-
Jewish Prejudice Complex"--in which, among
other things, he offers an apologia for Goyim
--Dr. MacIver plunges fearlessly into the deli-
cately balanced field of Jewish education.
Without intending insult, he urges development
and teaching of a "philosophy for minority
living" (a phrase he credits to Commentary
magazine). Without appreciating the missionary
implications, he wants Jewish schools to teach
Christian observances, "for it can hardly be
denied that in some Jewish households they im-
bibe the notion that there is something intrin-
sically hostile to them in the celebration of
the Christian faith."

Dr. MacIver is on firmer ground when he
demolishes the "ideological differences" argument of advocates for separate defense agencies. But between page 5 and page 80 of his
Report, he weakens his own cogent argument by
admitting that the "distinctive ideology of
the Congress does have some influence on its
approach to problems of civil rights." Apart
from specific examples, Dr. MacIver presents
little that is new in the duplication, friction and lack of cooperation among defense
agencies, calling attention especially to the
"scrambling for membership, an insistence on
the merits of independence and, on the part of
certain agencies, an exaggerated bid for exclusive credit in advancing the cause in which
they are all enlisted."

The broader approach to the direction and
scope of defense activity--succinctly and
clearly expressed by Dr. Eli Ginzberg in his
recent Agenda for American Jews--is never

touched upon. The Anti-Defamation League and the American Jewish Committee bear the brunt of Dr. MacIver's strictures, but he apparently does not realize that **his recommendations would impose a far greater burden of cost upon the community** for defense work than exists now. With a rather naive acceptance of each organization at its own face value, Dr. MacIver would take certain activities from the large defense agencies and turn them over exclusively to the smaller organizations, irrespective of the latter's obvious weaknesses or inability to cope with the size of the task given them. Thus, he recommends that all veterans activities be turned over to the Jewish War Veterans; all labor work to the Jewish Labor Committee; all legislative reporting to the American Jewish Congress (which, he says, in another connection, "is not interested in good 'public relations' as such"). Despite admitted lack of funds, he would turn over all interfaith work to the Union of American Hebrew Congregations (a member of NCRAC) and invite the Synagogue Council (!) to join with it. (Apparently he does not realize that the Jewish Theological Seminary carries on its interfaith work in large measure through the American Jewish Committee.) Again, irrespective of competence, Dr. MacIver would give the nod to local defense agencies whenever a conflict arose with the national agencies.

Over all this network, Dr. MacIver would set an enlarged and greatly empowered National Community Relations Advisory Council--in effect a new agency--with national "strategy" to be set by a board of social scientists, which would be **"entirely free, without any ties, with no obligation except its own sense of responsibility."**

(Shades of the late Technocracy fad of 20 years ago!)

Dr. MacIver's report is a regrettable failure. May we suggest to the Special Committee when it begins its deliberations that it first take to heart the following acute observation by Dr. Eli Ginzberg: "The individual Jew's approach to the Gentile world is determined by his approach to Judaism."

The impact of this disclosure upon community leaders and the English Jewish press, all of whom, we made sure, received copies of the Newsletter, was enormous. As might be expected, however, their reactions varied widely, depending to a considerable extent on their attitude toward the defense agencies and the NCRAC. On one specific criticism of the MacIver Report, however, feelings ran especially high. This was Dr. MacIver's attitude toward Jewish Orthodoxy, which I had quoted from the Report, and it eventually aroused enough anger to discredit the entire work despite the efforts of the NCRAC to salvage it.

On the Tuesday following the appearance of my review, the Evaluative Committee was called together for a special meeting with Dr. MacIver at the Harmonie Club in New York. There Dr. MacIver defended his Report, and in answer to a question from a representative of the UAHC, he denied that he had intended to cast a slur against Orthodox Jews. He insisted, however, that it was a "scientific fact" that "separatist" actions did help to stimulate prejudice. One member of the committee, in his defense of the Columbia professor's report, described the analysis by **Cross-Section, U.S.A.** as "mendacious."

During the discussions at the meeting, it became quickly obvious that those Jewish organizations which would gain in power and influence if the MacIver recommendations were implemented strongly favored the MacIver Report, while the defense agencies who had the most to lose in the reallocation process, and a few religious bodies who were offended, strongly opposed the recommendations. The CJFWF, which had paid Dr. MacIver $25,000 for the study, naturally defended it as did the American Jewish Congress, the Jewish War Veterans, the Jewish Labor Committee and the UAHC as well as the local welfare fund representatives attending the meeting. In reporting the meeting, the Newsletter predicted that compromises all along the line were likely to result from the talks among the organizations if the plan were to go into effect. In addition to these developments, the LCBC met the following week and decided to make the hitherto secret MacIver Report available in its submitted form to local community council leaders for study and discussion. The Newsletter, noting that the LCBC was made up of representatives from Baltimore, Boston, Chicago, Cleveland, Detroit, Newark, Philadelphia, Pittsburgh, St. Louis and San Francisco, offered the following conclusions:

Effect of the decision is to exclude New York City because it has no community council. The Brooklyn Jewish Community Council, however, is a member of the NCRAC and has asked for and received additional copies of the Report. In other communities, notably Los Angeles, the Report has been duplicated and distributed by local authorities without NCRAC permission. The LCBC decision reverses its former position and is a direct consequence of the expose by **Cross-Section U.S.A.** The reversal graphically demonstrates the need for an aggressive, independent Jewish press.

The edited MacIver Report, published by NCRAC in February 1952, contained a foreward by Irving Kane, the NCRAC chairman, and the following table of contents:

SECTION I

"Part One: **The Background of the Investigation**

1. Range and character of the investigation
2. General characterization of the national agencies
3. Overtures for unity

Part Two: **The Question of Strategy**

1. Conspectus of agency programs
2. The anti-Jewish prejudice complex
3. The need for reassessment

Part Three: **The Need for Integration of Programs**

1. General considerations
2. Mass appeal activities
3. Group appeal activities
4. The role of the specialized agencies
5. Civil rights activities
6. Fact-finding and reportorial activities
7. Research and evaluation activities
8. Review of the question of integration

Part Four: **The CRCs**

1. Character and role of the local agencies
2. The national agencies and the CRCs
3. Some conclusions

Part Five: The Role of the NCRAC

Part Six: Conspectus of Major Recommendations

Appendix to Section I - Clarification by Professor
            MacIver

SECTION II

Statements of View by Participating Agencies
            Prefatory note: Statements by
            communities
            American Jewish Committee
            American Jewish Congress
            Anti-Defamation League of B'nai B'rith
            Jewish Labor Committee
            Jewish War Veterans of the U.S.
            Union of American Hebrew Congregations
            Large City Budgeting Conference

SECTION III

Statement Adopted by NCRAC Plenary Session on November
26, 1951

Despite the Newsletter's sensational scoop, and the
revolutionary character of the MacIver Report, most English Jewish weeklies withheld any account of the study
until they were handed an official release from the
NCRAC or the LCBC. A survey of the Jewish press that
June by **Cross-Section, U.S.A.** disclosed that barely a
handful of the papers had made any mention whatever of
the existence of the MacIver Report. The two Yiddish
dailies, based in New York, remained completely silent
on the subject despite the fact that each had received
a copy of the **Cross-Section, U.S.A.** review and in addition they had also received a brief summary of the Mac-
Iver Report in the weekly column of Boris Smolar,
editor of the JTA; an account of the Report from the
American Jewish Press; and a two-page release sent out
by the NCRAC on the June 12 meeting of the Evaluative
Studies Committee in New York.
The Newsletter reported on June 28 that out of about
65 English Jewish weeklies, only the **Jewish Press
(Omaha)**, the **Jewish News** (Detroit), the **Jewish Advo-
cate** (Boston), the **Jewish Examiner** (Brooklyn) and the
Sentinel (Chicago) provided coverage that could be con-

sidered minimally adequate. Boris Smolar's column appeared in the **Jewish Chronicle** (Kansas City), but the
Jewish News (Newark N.J.), which usually carried it as
a regular feature, this week omitted it. The **Jewish
Press** (Omaha) also carried an editorial which urged
that the Report should be made public as soon as possible, adding: "We know of no one in American or Jewish
life, on a national or local level, into whose hands we
would place the power to decide what the public is wise
enough or mature enough or informed enough to read or
hear."

The self-imposed censorship of the Jewish press was
not lifted until the second week in July, almost two
months after the Newsletter's analysis of the MacIver
Report was published. The Newsletter of July 5 reported
that the English Jewish weeklies would finally break
their silence the next week, then added:

> The July 6 column of Seven Arts editor
> Nathan Ziprin will sharply attack the MacIver
> Report for its slurs upon Jewish education and
> Orthodoxy, while JTA editor Boris Smolar in his
> column will report factually on Dr. MacIver's
> recommendations. (JTA and Seven Arts are both
> owned and controlled by Jacob Landau.) At the
> same time, the **National Jewish Post** will break
> its long silence by publishing an analysis fa-
> voring the MacIver Report. Although the identi-
> ty of the analyst was not available at the time
> of going to press, informed quarters noted that
> Editor Gabriel Cohen had recently admitted
> yielding in news judgment to local community
> professionals.

> Earlier, a strong defense of the MacIver
> Report was voiced by the LCBC which thanked
> the Professor "for his objective, penetrating,
> and comprehensive analysis of Jewish community
> relations work," and pointed out that the indi-
> vidual responses of the members of the Evalua-
> tive Committee to the Report must be submitted
> not later than August 1.

> In Newark, at the General Assembly of the
> Jewish Community Council last week, executive
> Director Herman Pekarsky defended the Report as
> an "earnest, impartial attempt to evaluate the
> entire field of community relations"; made no
> reference to the Report's attack on Jewish edu-
> cation despite the fact that Michael A. Stavit-
> sky, prominent Newark leader, is president of

the American Association for Jewish Education
(AAJE).

At the same time, in Boston, Lewis H.
Weinstein, a communal leader and member of
the Evaluative Committee, in a statement to
the local Jewish press, took exception to the
analysis by **Cross-Section, U.S.A.** and said:
"To call the MacIver Report an attack on
Orthodoxy or Jewish education is untrue. One
of its premature critics, a journalist, purports
to find contrast in **Agenda for American Jews,**
recently published by Professor Eli Ginzberg,
also of Columbia. I have just re-read Professor Ginzberg's book and I find a general pattern
of agreement in the basic issues between Profe-
sors MacIver and Ginzberg."

Asked for comment on this statement, Profe-
sor Ginzberg told **Cross-Section, U.S.A.** that
he had only the highest regard for Professor
MacIver; added that he could not comment because he had not seen a copy of the MacIver
Report despite efforts to obtain one.

(In an article on Professor Ginzberg's
book in the current issue of **The Menorah
Journal,** Allen Lesser, writing long before
the appearance of the MacIver Report, says:
"Without a sound analysis of basic problems
that will provide perspective and clarity, no
constructive evolution, no long-range planning
is possible. **This is a task for the social
scientist who must also be a Jewishly learned
Jew, a combination not too easily discovered
these days.**")

It soon became clear that the Newsletter's attack on
the MacIver Report had put the NCRAC and the welfare
fund leaders on the defensive and that they were hard
pressed to provide a satisfactory explanation of Dr.
MacIver's criticisms of Jewish education and Orthodox
religious practices. A great deal of information about
the reactions of these community officials was given to
me by Nathan Belth, the public relations director of the
Anti-Defamation League, which strongly opposed the
MacIver recommendations. Contrary to some of the rumors
which were circulating in an effort to discredit the
Newsletter's analysis, I had had no contact whatsoever
with the American Jewish Committee during this period.
I had stated clearly in the Newsletter that my review
of the MacIver Report was based on my own first-hand

reading of the entire official NCRAC offset copy of the
Report, and that the judgments were entirely my own. The
rumors continued, however, and were kept alive by Joseph
Brainin, alias Phineas Biron, among others, who hinted
broadly in one of his columns in August that the ADL was
paying me off. At the same time, the public relations
director of the Jewish Welfare Board told me that he had
been busy denying that I was in the pay of the American
Jewish Committee. In point of fact, the only benefit
that I received from anyone was the ADL's purchase of
2,000 copies of the single issue of the Newsletter containing the analysis and review of the MacIver Report.

Statements by the organizations sponsoring the Report to explain away some of the Professor's damaging
opinions kept the controversy alive during the hot summer months. Spokesmen for the NCRAC and the CJFWF,
responding to an inquiry by the Newsletter, said that
they had no idea who the anonymous author might be of
the analysis and defense of the MacIver Report that appeared in the **National Jewish Post** on July 6. Gabriel
Cohen, the editor of the weekly, denied authorship and
described the author of the review simply as a man
"closely connected with the Report from the very beginning." Persistent inquiry, however, led the Newsletter two months later to disclose that the anonymous
author was Sidney Hollander of Baltimore, a former CJFWF
president and the NCRAC representative on the Evaluative
Studies Committee. Why he insisted on anonymity remained
his secret.

Isaiah Minkoff, executive director of the NCRAC, had
notified its affiliated agencies to submit their opinions of the MacIver Report by August 1, but some of the
agencies responded in advance of that date. On July 26,
the Newsletter carried the following details about their
briefs:

An exclusive report from usually reliable
sources said that the American Jewish Committee's response will applaud Dr. MacIver's "integrationist" approach, criticize the LCBC for
circulating the Report among its community
board members, and approve Dr. MacIver's stress
on CRCs. But the American Jewish Committee will
defend at length its "ideology" as sufficiently
different to warrant its separate existence and
reject completely Dr. MacIver's recommendations
for allocation of functions, financing and
voting.

Similar in many respects but considerably
sharper in tone is the ADL's analysis. It at-

tacks Dr. MacIver's "assimilationist criteria";
charges him with writing a partisan brief for a
rejected view in communal life; and notes that
the Report generally shows a lack of understanding of Jewish life. The ADL will defend
its "ideological" approach and flatly reject
the recommendations of the Report; and charge
that the recommendations would vastly increase
defense expenditures. The ADL admits errors of
omission and comission, says they can be cor-
rected and improvements made, but insists that
the MacIver Report is not the way.

At the American Jewish Congress, a spokesman said that only Dr. David Petegorsky (its
executive director) was in a position to comment on the Report and he was out of town.
At the Synagogue Council of America, which
nominally represents the three major branches
of American Judaism, executive director Rabbi
E.L. Freund told **Cross-Section, U.S.A.** that
its board members had had an opportunity to
read and study the Report but that the
Synagogue Council would not make an official
statement at this time. He added that the NCRAC
had not asked the Synagogue Council for its
opinion. Rabbi Freund said that the Report
would be discussed at the Council's executive
committee meeting in September and that it
would also be on the agenda of the plenary
meeting in October.

From reliable sources, **Cross-Section,
U.S.A.** learned that some local community opinion is sharply opposed to Dr. MacIver's integrationist approach and to his recommendations
for allocation of function, particularly in the
case of the Union of American Hebrew Congregations. Some CRC members also feel that they are
being squeezed out in the fight looming up
between the LCBC-CJFWF forces and the ADL-
American Jewish Committee representatives.

Meanwhile, because of the insistence on
the secrecy of the Report, it has become the
subject of widespread misunderstanding, misin-
terpretation and misrepresentation throughout
the country. Typical were reports that the
defense agencies had sought to suppress the
Report, that Dr. MacIver recommended the
complete elimination of the defense agencies,
that the June 7 analysis published by

Cross-Section, U.S.A. had accused Dr. MacIver
of being an anti-Semite, and similar comments.
Efforts by this reporter to obtain statements
from Jewish education leaders in New York
failed. This reporter has positive knowledge
of at least two lengthy statements attacking
the MacIver Report which Jewish education
leaders had prepared and had held up. At a special meeting last month, the LCBC urged welfare
funds to give full consideration to the
$181,500 drive by the American Association for
Jewish Education.

The Newsletter had reported in an earlier issue that
an LCBC recommendation to its members to increase their
allocations to the Association was made in order to head
off the attacks by prominent Jewish educators on Dr.
MacIver's opinion of Jewish education. The bribe,
however, was not enough to silence all the educators and
their unhappiness with Dr. MacIver's criticism managed
to find expression in the Jewish press. Even the Yiddish
press, which had delayed until July 15 before allowing
their readers to learn that there was such a thing as a
MacIver Report--the first notices appeared in the
Forward--subsequently picked up the fight of the Jewish
educators. While the Newsletter regarded the Report as
the outward evidence of a struggle for power in the
leadership of the community, and especially as an effort
to reduce the influence of the defense agencies, the fate
of the MacIver Report was eventually decided not because
of its recommendations but as a result of its criticism of
Orthodoxy and education as barriers to assimilation.

The full meaning of the MacIver Report, however, had
not yet touched the Jewish public because the NCRAC was
successful in keeping much of the controversy out of the
press. Probably all of the agencies concerned would have
preferred to keep it that way, thus giving themselves
time to work out a compromise solution before the NCRAC
plenary in November. They might have succeeded had it
not been for Dr. Joshua Bloch, the chief of the Jewish
division of the New York Public Library since 1923. A
short slight man with bright black eyes, Bloch was a
Jewish scholar of considerable distinction as well as a
teacher and an editor. A man of strong liberal views, he
was fully supportive of the aims and objectives of
Cross-Section, U.S.A. Although he had as little regard
for the defense agencies as I did, he nevertheless
agreed with me that the MacIver route was not the way
for the community to go.

One day in July, he called my attention quite casually to one of Dr. MacIver's books. It was a college sociology textbook which I would never otherwise have bothered to examine. But in this book I discovered the literary bomb that effectively blasted the MacIver Report out of the communal picture altogether. It completely demolished the joint LCBC-CJFWF effort to reduce the power of the defense agencies and to build up the NCRAC and the CRCs. I hinted at the new explosion that I was preparing in my letter to Leftwich on July 28, in which I said:

"In another envelope I'm sending you the Newsletter and several clips. One of them is from the front page of the **National Jewish Post** and will give you some idea of the furore my June 7 analysis of MacIver is creating. It has helped a little financially but not nearly as much as the noise would indicate. The **Jewish Chronicle** story on MacIver (7/13) was entirely inadequate--didn't even spell MacIver's name correctly. This is the biggest thing to hit the American Jewish community in years and it will continue to be the subject of considerable discussion until the plenary meeting of NCRAC in November. Basically, it's a struggle for control of the community purse strings and eventually will force the rabbinate as well as the Zionists--who are now deaf to the issue--to step in willy-nilly.

"Next week I'm going to blast MacIver's head off with a quote from one of his own books attributing to Jews racial characteristics--physical as well as emotional--comparable to the colored peoples! And that's the man who was chosen to advise the Jewish community! In any case, I'll have to keep the Newsletter going now!"

The latter comment was a reference to my increasingly difficult financial situation and the prospect that I would have to suspend publication of the Newsletter. Had it not been for Dr. Bloch's findings, I probably would have dropped the MacIver controversy at this point and sought other employment. My hopes that the MacIver expose would stimulate subscriber interest in the Newsletter had so far not been borne out, and the response to the 2,000 copies which the ADL had bought and which I had sent out was especially disappointing. Promotion costs were high and my personal resources were almost at an end. At the same time I refused to compromise my independence by seeking a sponsor. In any case, none came forward to test my resolution.

As far as the ADL was concerned, my analysis of the MacIver Report had reinforced their position in opposing

its recommendations and had placed them in a strategic
position to effect a compromise to their liking.
Probably they would have preferred to have me drop the
controversy at this point, but Professor MacIver's textbook to which Dr. Bloch had referred me contained
expressions and opinions that were highly offensive to
Jews, and I felt it was my duty at this juncture to tell
the community just what the man chosen by responsible
Jewish community agencies really believed about Jews. On
August 2, therefore, the Newsletter carried the
following startling information:

Disclosure that Professor Robert M. MacIver
stated as a scientific fact that Jews, like
Negroes and other colored peoples, stand out as
a race because of physical differences reinforced by social discrimination was made this
week in an exclusive report to **Cross-Section,
U.S.A.**
Informed circles question whether the
Evaluative Committee of the National Community
Relations Advisory Council would have selected
Professor MacIver to conduct his now controversial study of duplication among defense agencies
had it known of this publicly expressed attitude
toward Jews. Professor MacIver received $25,000
for his "Report on the Jewish Community Relations Agencies."
Professor MacIver's statement is especially
important because of the pro-assimilationist,
anti-Orthodox approach expressed in his Report.
It appears on page 67 of Professor MacIver's
book, entitled **Society: Its Structure and
Changes,** published in New York in 1931, and it
reads:
"It is only when we find marked social
barriers between human types exhibiting physical
differences, in other words where on a basis of
physical differences reinforced by social-
historical discrimination race-consciousness
develops, that the tendency to intermixture is
checked, and the discriminated groups stand out
as races. This has determined the distinc-
tiveness of the Jewish race, and is obviously
at work in maintaining the broad color-
divisions of humanity."
On page 66 of the same book, Professor
MacIver says: "The Jews, for instance, are a
race-conscious people, but we would not apply
to them the term **nation**" (his emphasis).

In order to maintain as objective a posture as possible, the Newsletter appended no comment of its own to
to this astounding disclosure. It did conclude the dispatch, however, with the following appropriate observation from Rabbi Milton Steinberg:

> Some years ago, the late Rabbi Milton
> Steinberg, of sainted memory, uttered the fol-
> lowing wise council:
> "Most of the Gentiles who rally to our aid
> are pure idealists. But some are our friends
> only because it pays. And we are never quite
> sure which is which. The sad truth is that we
> are in danger of creating a new and profitable
> business, the business of being a professional
> friend of Jews, a merchant trading in Jewish
> fears."

The obvious corollary to Professor MacIver's candidly expressed view--and one which none of my readers,
I am sure, failed to appreciate--was that if anti-Semitism were aggravated by "physical differences reinforced
by social-historical discrimination," then it could be
substantially reduced by making Jews look and act like
their Gentile neighbors; in other words, assimilation
and eventual conversion to Christianity. Furthermore, if
this opinion failed to anger some Jewish readers, Dr.
MacIver's view that Jews were not a nation, disclosed at
a time when even non-observant Jews were proud of the
establishment of Israel as a Jewish nation, would have
been sufficient to offend them.

What most failed to appreciate, however, was that
Dr. MacIver's views were strikingly parallel to those
held by the American Jewish Committee--up to the point
of conversion, of course--in its "scientific" approach
to the problem of combating anti-Semitism in the United
States and in its attitude toward the new state of
Israel. Like Dr. MacIver, the Committee believed that by
minimizing Jewish differences and mannerisms, by developing a Jew whose manners, dress and speech were as far
away as possible from the Jewish stereotype and as close
as possible to the Anglo-Saxon American prototype, the
incidence of anti-Semitism would be substantially
reduced. The Committee also believed, and still does to
this day, that it is possible to do this while at the
sme time faithfully observing the tenets of the Jewish
religion.

I pointed out some of these considerations the
following week when the Newsletter presented a lengthy

report on Dr. MacIver's belief in proselytizing Jews. It
was expressed quite candidly in another one of his textbooks, one which was in current use in a number of
colleges. By this time, however, a shocked Jewish
ledership was much too embarrassed by the Newsletter's
disclosures to respond--it was just beginning to try to
defend Dr. MacIver against my review of his Report--when
the publication of the most damning of all quotations
from one of Dr. MacIver's books completely destroyed his
credibility and authority. The Newsletter reviewed some
of the attempts to support Dr. MacIver, noted the
American Jewish Committee's reaction to the Report, and
then went on to say:

> When the NCRAC's Evaluative Studies Com-
> mittee appointed Columbia University Profes-
> sor Robert M. MacIver to analyse Jewish defense
> operations, it assumed without investigation
> that his attitude toward Jews was beyond
> reproach.
> In answer to criticisms of his Report,
> notably our June 7 analysis, such prominent
> members of the Committee as Lewis H. Weinstein,
> of Boston, defended Professor MacIver as one of
> America's leading social scientists and said:
> "To call the MacIver Report an attack on Ortho-
> doxy or Jewish education is untrue."
> In Newark, N.J., Herman Pekarsky, Jewish
> Community Council director, told his community
> that the Report was an "earnest, impartial
> attempt to evaluate the entire field of com-
> munity relations."
> In its "secret" analysis, the American
> Jewish Committee--which has a competent staff
> as well as all the facilities for a thorough
> investigation--not only describes the MacIver
> Report as an "impressive document" but goes on
> to endorse the Professor's views on "how Jews
> should relate themselves to the American
> scene." The American Jewish Committee also
> agrees largely with his "philosophy with re-
> spect to Jewish integration." (The American
> Jewish Committee, apparently, takes for granted
> that American Jews, even at this late date, are
> still immigrants who need to be "integrated"
> into the American scene; ignores the anti-
> Semitic implications of such a view.)
> And the Anti-Defamation League, too,
> acknowledges Professor MacIver to be "one of

the most eminent social scientists in America today." The ADL, however, is the only NCRAC agency openly to attack Dr. MacIver's anti-Orthodox, assimilationist approach.

But **not one** of the agencies on the Evaluative Committee--so quick to allocate $25,000 of the community's funds--took the trouble to make the simplest, most elementary check of Professor MacIver. NOT ONE BOTHERED TO LOOK INTO PROFESSOR MACIVER'S WIDELY USED TEXT-BOOKS ON SOCIOLOGY FOR HIS PUBLISHED STATEMENTS ON JEWS. This is what **Cross-Section, U.S.A.** found:

Unimpeachable evidence of Professor Mac-Iver's prejudiced view appears in his **magnum opus**, the book upon which his reputation as a sociologist is based. In this book, using language more in keeping with the mouthings of Father Coughlin, Professor MacIver condemns Jews for their "exclusiveness" and their refusal to accept the "message of Jesus."

With the fanaticism of a Gerald B. Winrod (Kansas Fundamentalist preacher), this same Professor MacIver proclaims: "WHILE PAUL PREACHED THE MORE UNIVERSAL LAW ... THE JEWS PURSUED THAT STUBBORN PRINCIPLE OF EXCLUSIVE-NESS WHICH BROUGHT UPON THEM THE DESTRUCTION OF THEIR TEMPLE AND CITY, AND ENDED IN THEIR DISPERSAL THROUGHOUT THE WORLD, TO BE THE HOMELESS DEPENDENTS OF ALL OTHER NATIONS. **NEVER WAS THE NEMESIS OF UNYIELDING EXCLUSIVENESS MORE COMPLETE.**"

That's not all.

With no more regard for quoting in context than a college freshman, Dr. MacIver asserts that Jews were forbidden by "Yahweh" to have any dealings with "the Gentiles," then quotes as proof the biblical **cherem** against mingling with the Canaanites (Deut. vii,3)--whose immorality and human sacrifices outraged the Israelites--and concludes by saying, as if it were an historical fact: "With scarce a protest, this spirit rules throughout Jewish history."

You may find these and other shocking expressions in full on pages 292-293 of Dr. MacIver's **Community: A Sociological Study, Being an Attempt to Set Out the Nature and Fundamental Laws of Social Life.** The volume used was the 3rd edition, published in London by MacMillan in 1924. The American edition appeared in 1928. This is a standard textbook on sociology, currently in use in many colleges throughout the country.

Professor MacIver's "facts" about Jews appear in a section headed "General survey of the problem of coordination," and are intended as an example of the sociological consequences of the "spirit of exclusiveness." (Last week, **Cross-Section, U.S.A.** quoted from Dr. MacIver's book, **Society: Its Structure and Changes,** in which he states as a scientific fact that Jews, like Negroes and other colored peoples, stand out as a race because of physical differences reinforced by social discrimination.)

For their inexcusable blunder and shocking carelessness in selecting a man with these hostile sentiments about Jews, NCRAC and its affiliated agencies owe the community a most humble public apology.

And if the communal leaders involved in this dereliction of responsibility genuinely desire to do "what is best for the community," they can begin now by throwing out the MacIver Report!

Although I anticipated that this latest revelation of Dr. MacIver's opinion about Jews would discredit his Report completely, and--as I wrote Leftwich--"give the NCRAC the black eye it deserves," I did not expect much immediate reaction on the part of the agencies or the community leaders. The August weather in New York was hot and sticky, with the temperature up in the 90s, and most of my readers were away on vacation. What I did not expect, however, was the effort by some communal leaders to defend their choice of Dr. MacIver even in the face of the devastating disclosures that the Newsletter had published. In my letter to Leftwich of August 11, I made only a passing reference to the MacIver controversy; I was much more concerned over my increasing financial difficulties. I wrote:

"The Almighty has helped me get through the summer, so I guess I shouldn't complain. At the end of June I didn't see myself this far, and now, thanks to MacIver, I'll probably get through all right. This week's blast ought to knock the bottom out of his adherents, but how much good it will do me financially is another story.

"ADL is sending out about 2,000 copies, but they're not paying anything above the regular cost of copies. I'm hoping the distribution will bring in a few more subscriptions. But withal, the circulation remains pitifully small; what public there is simply won't pay $10 a year. And if I cut the price, I'll find myself squeezed by constantly rising costs--every time I reorder envelopes or stationery the price is 5-10 percent higher than it was a few weeks ago."

The letter went on in much the same vein to describe my only prospect at the time: my hope that Louis Lipsky and his Progressive Zionist friends would provide me with enough part-time work in the following months to enable me to keep going. Dr. Bloch also promised to bring a group together to help the Newsletter. And my good friend Bernard G. Richards, a veteran Zionist and the director of the Jewish Information Bureau, used his connections with the **New York Times** to secure me an interview with its editor, David Joseph. That effort to get a job came to naught, but I never told Richards that Joseph, who was Jewish, had given me a long discourse on why the **New York Times** did not think it wise to have too many Jews on its staff!

The controversy over the MacIver Report finally reached the general public on August 22 when the **New York Herald Tribune** carried a report by Paul Tobenkin, one of its best informed men on Jewish affairs. A less detailed account of the MacIver Report also appeared in the **New York Post**. Neither of them, however, brought up the subject of Dr. MacIver's views about Jewish "exclusiveness." I advised Leftwich about these developments in the following letter:

"The MacIver story hit the daily press this week-- **Tribune** and **Post**--and my report on MacIver's anti-Semitism was frontpaged by the Brooklyn **Jewish Examiner;** and completely distorted by Slomovitz in the Detroit **Jewish News.** The [**National Jewish**] **Post** didn't carry a word, although I released the story to all the papers including the **Jewish Chronicle.** There's really going to be hell to pay now, and my information is that the bigwigs simply don't know what to do or say about this fantastic--to them--turn of events. I've sent out about 2,000 promotion letters on the basis of the scoop, and if they don't pull, then absolutely nothing will."

Only slight attention was paid to an NCRAC release the same week in which its chairman, Irving Kane, was quoted as saying that he deplored "the tendency to quote excerpts of the MacIver Report out of context, to attribute judgments to Dr. MacIver which are not borne out by

the full text of his report and, on the basis of partial
and incomplete evidence, to prejudge the conclusions he
sets forth." His statement contained no reference to the
disclosures about Dr. MacIver's attitude toward Jews.

Earlier that month, Joseph Brainin, writing in the
B'nai B'rith Messenger (Los Angeles) under his pseudonym
of Phineas Biron, described an interview he had with Dr.
MacIver during a visit to the professor's summer home in
New England. Brainin said that the professor was
"completely oblivious" of the storm he had aroused in
the Jewish community and quoted him as saying: "I have
finished my work; now it is up to those who wish to
implement it." Nevertheless, Dr. MacIver was apparently
willing to defend his Report, for the **Jewish Exponent**
(Philadelphia) announced in August that Dr. MacIver was
expected to appear as the principal speaker at the
annual dinner meeting of the Philadelphia Jewish
Community Relations Council on September 25.

A press roundup by the Newsletter at the end of the
month confirmed my belief that community leaders would
try to stonewall the controversy and play down any reaction to the Newsletter's quotes from Dr. MacIver's
books. The English Jewish press, however, finally began
to take sides in the controversy as the following
Newsletter report demonstrates:

> Neither of the Boston weeklies nor any of
> the community-owned weeklies surveyed this week
> carried any reference whatever to Dr. MacIver's
> anti-Jewish statements as quoted by **Cross-Sec-
> tion, U.S.A.** Out of a score of English Jewish
> weeklies surveyed this week, only three pub-
> lished an accurate version of the **Cross-
> Section, U.S.A.** disclosures, and only six
> carried the distorted version put out by the
> AJP news service. Neither the JTA nor the Seven
> Arts carried the story.
>
> The **American Hebrew,** published in New York
> City, incorporated the **Cross-Section, U.S.A.**
> report in an editorial headed, "About Prof.
> MacIver," noted that most readers of the Eng-
> lish Jewish press know what the MacIver Report
> is about, cited the **Cross-Section, U.S.A.** quote
> from Dr. MacIver beginning "While Paul preached
> the more universal law," attempted a brief
> answer to Dr. MacIver's accusations, and
> concluded:
>
> "If full justice has not been done to Prof.
> MacIver in repeating the above statements, which

it is possible he may have outgrown, then the
way to settle the matter is to see that the
report gets immediate publication and
distribution."

The **Jewish News** of Detroit accorded our
report a straight news treatment under the
headline, "NEW CHARGE HURLED AT MACIVER:
'MOUTHINGS THOSE OF A FR. COUGHLIN'"; stressed
our demand that NCRAC apologize to the community for its "inexcusable blunder and shocking carelessness." The **News,** which is the chief
sponsor of the AJP, placed the story on page 7
and rounded it out with the AJP's report on the
Brainin interview with Dr. MacIver (in **Opinion**
magazine) and the Irving Kane release, cited
here last week. The **News** did not use the AJP's
inaccurate version of our report.

The **Jewish Examiner** of Brooklyn was the
only weekly to give the sensational story the
frontpage treatment it warranted. Under the
3-column headline--"APPOINTMENT OF MACIVER
WITHOUT A CHECK-UP SEEN AS SHOCKING BLUNDER"--
the **Examiner** said:

"Are the faces of the lay leaders of American Jewry red?

"If not, they should be.

"Because the joke is on them.

"They pulled an awful boner when they, that
is, the National Community Relations Advisory
Council, consisting of the heads of community
organizations in all the large cities of the
country, appointed Prof. Robert M. MacIver ...
without first checking on the professor's fit-
ness for the job with respect to his attitude
toward Jews and Judaism."

The **Examiner** then went on to quote and
report on our disclosures. An editorial in the
same issue, entitled "Facts of Life," comments
on the statement of NCRAC chairman Irving Kane,
notes that it was released eight days after
Cross-Section, U.S.A.'s revelations, and asks
NCRAC: "Now, with the truth about the professor
known and documented, will they have the de-
cency and the courage to recognize their error,
make a public apology for it and toss the Mac-
Iver Report into the ashcan?"

No such apology was ever forthcoming, of course, the
community leaders involved seeking instead to find ways

to justify their selection. The weeklies noted in the above report were the exception as far as I could learn, most of the others preferring to wait for the response of the official establishment. The establishment, however, was hard pressed to justify its position even within such powerful units as the Boston Jewish Community Council. There after a bitter debate, a resolution to postpone for 60 days any vote .on the MacIver Report so that members would have time to study it was barely defeated. Proponents of the resolution sharply criticized the assimilationist approach of the Report to Jewish problems and argued vainly against what they regarded as the Council's unseemly haste in voting on the MacIver recommendations. They pointed out that in Los Angeles the community council had discussed the Report for three days before voting on it. The resolution nevertheless was defeated but only by the narrow margin of 18 to 14 with three members of the Council abstaining. The Newsletter account of the meeting contained the following observation:

> Assent of the Council members for submission of its own report was obtained only after the inclusion of a clause reserving the right of the Council to amend its opinion at a later date and indicating the tentative nature of the vote it was taking.
> A strong advocate of the Report in the Boston Council was Rabbi Joseph Shubow, who was also an editor of **Opinion** magazine. The current issue of **Opinion** contains an interview with Professor MacIver by fellow traveler Joseph Brainin (alias Phineas Biron); the former admits that he had the ADL and the American Jewish Committee in mind when he charged agencies with exaggerated claims; also charges that attacks on his Report in the press before it was made public were "unethical--especially the statement by Judge Meier Steinbrink that the Report is "unobjective."

In spite of Professor MacIver's admission in this interview that he was highly critical of the major defense agencies, Robert E. Segal, the executive director of the Boston Jewish Community Council, appealed to the public to withhold judgment on the MacIver Report and refrain from entering the controversy before the NCRAC held its plenary meeting in November. In letters

to the **Advocate** and the **Jewish Times,** the two Boston
weeklies, Segal pleaded for patience; and neither of the
papers, accordingly, carried any report of Dr. McIver's
anti-Jewish comments.

Such self-imposed censorship was not limited to
Boston. The **National Jewish Post,** which frequently
boasted of its independence and objectivity, also made
no mention of the disclosures of **Cross-Section, U.S.A.**
despite the fact that its editor, Gabriel Cohen, as well
as every weekly editor in the country had received a
copy of the August 9 issue. The Newsletter reported that
the **National Jewish Post** was explaining its silence by
saying that it needed more time to prepare an adequate
answer to tne Newsletter's disclosures but would respond
in its issue of September 7, a rather lame excuse for
withholding news of vital importance to the community.
According to information leaked to the Newsletter, the
National Jewish Post in its reponse would seek to persuade its readers that Dr. MacIver's anti-Jewish statements in his sociology textbooks were torn from their
context by the Newsletter. In defense of Dr. MacIver the
Indianapolis weekly also would publish a statement by
Irving Kane, NCRAC chairman, as well as testimonials
from other community leaders to prove that Dr. MacIver
was "a good friend of Jews." The Newsletter also charged
that the **Post** would not quote the offending sentences in
Dr. MacIver's books and offered to send any reader of
the **Post** a copy of those sentences as quoted by
Cross-Section, U.S.A.

In my letter to Leftwich of August 31, I described
my unhappiness over what I felt was public apathy to the
controversy. I said: "Out today is the first--but I'm
sure not the last--attack in the press on me and the
Newsletter for the expose of MacIver. It comes from the
communist fellow traveler Joe Brainin and appears in the
B'nai B'rith Messenger of Los Angeles, the only weekly
that still carries his Biron column. I hit below the
belt, he claims, when I quoted the professor on that
'Paul preached' business; the sentence was taken out of
context; in any case it is a 'theological interpretation
which one can find in many Jewish books'!! He ends by
hinting broadly that the ADL is paying me off. Incidentally, this morning, the JWB publicity man told me
he's been busy denying that I'm in the pay of the American Jewish Committee! Apparently, it's inconceivable for
anyone in the field to have an independent opinion and
sheer madness to proclaim it.

"The sad part about the whole affair, however, is
the complete apathy of the Jewish public. Would you be-

lieve that apart from the ADL and the **National Jewish Post** no one has asked for a copy of the August 9 issue with the MacIver expose! True, I mailed out 2,000 copies to the rabbis and to a B'nai B'rith list with a promotion letter asking for subscribers, which got into the mails about two weeks ago. But there, too, to date results equal exactly one new subscription, received this very afternoon! And this, after reports of the controversy also appeared in the **Tribune** and the **New York Post**.

"Each time I run into this blank wall of public apathy, I react with the same astonishment. It seems I never learn--or can't accept--a fact that has been hammered home to me since 1946, when I wrote my anti-anti-defamation article for **The Menorah Journal**. The power of the printed word is a mighty thing and it has given me a coast-to-coast reputation as well as a great deal of power in the shaping of the community; but apparently only television can stir up enough public feeling these days to mean anything."

A week later I was still complaining to my English friend about the apathy of the Jewish public and the rabbis to the controversy. "There isn't enough interest even for people to start abusing me," I wrote. "Apparently even the Jew who is fairly active in communal affairs doesn't care a hoot one way or the other, and what's worse, simply refuses to see or try to understand that he will inevitably be affected adversely if the recommendations of the Report are adopted. There's nothing that can crush a writer or a crusader, if you will, more quickly than indifference and apathy; and I'm beginning to get more than I can take...."

I quickly stopped complaining, however, when the **National Jewish Post** finally unleashed its big guns to counter my attack. William Cohen, a friend and the public relations director for the Haifa Technion organization, telephoned me late one afternoon to alert me to the fact that I was being lambasted in the **National Jewish Post** by Dr. MacIver and his friend Rabbi Louis Finkelstein. This is the way I described the character of the attack and my reaction to it in my letter to Leftwich on September 7:

"I ran uptown to get a copy of the paper, then home. MacIver on page 2 under the headline: 'MACIVER HURLS SLANDER CHARGE; LESSER SAYS SCIENTIST HOSTILE,' does not deny that I quoted him correctly, but explains that the passages I quoted were 'merely an application of the well-recognized sociological fact that small peoples, exposed to environing greater powers, could not survive as territorial unities unless they were willing and able to establish contacts and make agreements and alliances with such powers.' He also denies that he is an anti-Semite: 'The charge is as ridiculous as it is vicious.'

"Finkelstein, on page 3, likewise does not deny the accuracy of my quotes, but unlike his friend, he tries to explain it away. Thus, he points to the 1928 date on MacIver's book and says: 'No scholar would like to have to answer for every statement expressed in books published two and three decades ago.' He then tries to show what a good democrat MacIver is, denies he is hostile, and attempts to explain what he has in mind. Also that there is a difference between 'assimilation' and 'integration,' the latter 'is not an evil concept.'

"At the same time, he admits that the concept of Jewish exclusiveness as expressed by MacIver 'is, unfortunately, a concept commonly held among persons reared in the belief that Judaism was an exclusive religion, and that it was against its exclusiveness that Paul revolted.' Finkelstein then tries to show how MacIver has changed since then and concludes by 'citing Lesser's attack as a hillul ha-shem [desecration of the Name of God] and a violent transgression of Jewish morality.'

"So the abuse has begun--at least in the Post, as I predicted two weeks ago. I shan't answer, naturally, because both men really confirm what I said (I never did say, deliberately, that MacIver was an anti-Semite). I don't intend to let Finkelstein get away with his contradictory remarks, though, and I am trying to arrange to get Horace Kallen to answer them both through the American Jewish Press agency. Kallen, whom you probably know about, is the sociologist at the New School--you must have read his review of Finkelstein's book in The Menorah Journal. If all this newspaper publicity meant anything by way of more subscriptions--as it would probably in any other field--then I'd be all in favor of bigger and better controversies, but I'm very much afraid that it won't mean any more now than it did in the past."

Dr. Finkelstein's denunciation and charge that I had desecrated God's name in attacking MacIver was a religious judgment and in a more cohesive Orthodox community such as those that existed in Eastern Europe before the war would have condemned me to ostracism. My decision to ignore the attack was made in the realization that despite the risk to my reputation, it would be a tactical blunder and divert attention away from the issue of MacIver himself. Rabbi Finkelstein's imprecations would have little effect in New York or in other cities because the Jewish community was widely dispersed and Jews were less observant than their European fathers. Furthermore, as the sharply critical article on the MacIver Report by M. Shoshani, which appeared in the Hebrew weekly, **Hadoar**, demonstrated, I was not without support in defense of my criticism even within religious circles.

I continued the attack on Dr. MacIver by directing my fire on his textbooks. On the occasion of the Jewish Youth Conference, sponsored by the JWB during the first week of September, I called attention to the failure of the textbook commissions of the ADL and the American Jewish Committee as well as the National Conference of Christians and Jews to do anything about the anti-Jewish statements in Dr. MacIver's textbooks. The youth conference had passed resolutions urging the elimination of prejudicial statements about minority groups in textbooks in use in schools, and it was in this connection that I pointed to the failure of the textbook commissions to act on the MacIver textbooks. None of the agencies affiliated with NCRAC, however, was willing to take any action that might be construed as criticizing Dr. MacIver. Instead, the Newsletter noted, the shocked embarrassment that greeted its disclosures of Dr. MacIver's attitude toward Jews was giving way only to an effort by communal leaders to cover up their error. The issue of September 20 contained the following report:

> The weekend meeting of the NCRAC's Exaluative Committee, which was to have discussed briefs on the MacIver Report, spent most of its time instead on an effort to concoct a cover-up for its colossal blunder in selecting a sociologist whose textbooks not only contain statements hostile to Jews but also currently defends those statements as "scientific fact."
>
> (Defense agencies as well as other NCRAC bodies admittedly failed to check Professor MacIver's views on Jews, knew nothing at all about his anti-Jewish textbook statements, which were first quoted by **Cross Section, U.S.A. To date, no action on Dr. MacIver's textbooks has been taken by the textbook commissions of the American Jewish Committee and the ADL.**)
>
> After a sharp debate over phraseology, NCRAC adopted a resolution expressing its "gratitude" to Professor MacIver, applauding his

integrity but "deploring" and "denouncing" anyone who dared to attack him. With true Gilbert
and Sullivan pomposity, NCRAC complained that
such attacks "attempt to subvert the impar-
tiality of the NCRAC evaluative study process."
(And doing a good job of it, too, if that
statement means what we think it does--Ed.)
     On the subject of "impartiality," the ADL,
which voted for the resolution, stated earlier
in its brief: "The MacIver Report is not a true
survey but a partisan and impressionistic brief
for a point of view that has been rejected time
and again in Jewish life." (Maybe ADL's representatives didn't understand NCRAC's English
when they voted for the resolution--Ed.)

In my letter to Leftwich I noted that the vehemence
of the attacks against the Newsletter's disclosures and
the efforts to defend MacIver were finally beginning to
create some reaction in my favor. There was a feeling
that the MacIver recommendations would have dangerous
assimilationist consequences; at least one rabbi, a subscriber whose name, unfortunately, I did not record,
took the Newsletter's disclosures as a basis for his
weekly sermon. The Zionists, who had stayed as far away
from the controversy as they could, began to realize
that they too might be affected. It was at the suggestion of Louis Lipsky, who I continued to see regularly, that the Newsletter quoted the entire passage
about the Apostle Paul as it appeared in Dr. MacIver's
books. In effect, this became my answer to Rabbi Finkelstein's charge that in exposing Dr. MacIver I had committed a grievous sin. The full flavor of the quote left
no doubt about the Professor's views. In his textbook,
entitled **Community: A Sociological Study**, pages 292-3,
the passage reads as follows:

     "'And who is my neighbor?' asked the Jewish
lawyer who would justify himself. The answer
has been clear enough to the Jew of the Penta-
teuch. Did not Yahweh command him to have no
dealings with the 'Gentiles'? 'Thou shalt smite
them and utterly destroy them; thou shalt make
no covenant with them, nor show mercy unto
them.' (Deut., vii, 3) With scarce a protest,
this spirit rules throughout Jewish history.
Bound to this exclusive creed, and yet blindly
seeking the Messiah who would save him from the
impotence and failure it ensured, the Jew heard

in vain the message of Jesus, bidding him see
in every man his neighbor. That any salvation
should come with the breaking down of exclusiveness seemed foolishness to him. So the
message passed to his more universal-minded
neighbors. 'Seeing ye put it from you,' cried
Paul--who himself had lived 'after the most
straitest sect of our religion'--'lo, we turn
to the Gentiles.' (Acts xiii, 46)
  "So while Paul preached the more universal
law 'where there is neither Greek nor Jew, circumcision or no circumcision, Barbarian, Scy-
thian, bond nor free' (Col. iii, 11), the Jews
pursued that stubborn principle of exclusiveness which brought upon them the destruction of
their temple and city, and ended in their dispersal throughout the world, to be the homeless
dependents of all other nations. Never was the
nemesis of unyielding exclusiveness more
complete."

This was, of course, a complete refutation of the
charge that I had quoted Dr. MacIver out of context. But
the obvious theological overtones of the MacIver statement were greeted with silence once more by the Jewish
establishment. My letters to Leftwich disclose the great
bitterness and discouragement that I felt over the
failure of the Jewish community to react positively.
Nevertheless, I was able to inform Leftwich that "the
MacIver business has finally paid off with about 35 new
subscribers since July," adding that most of them were
rabbis, "maybe because of Finkelstein's denunciation."
The **National Jewish Post** played up every attack on the
Newsletter and upon me but published no letters defending my disclosures. "Another indication of American
apathy," I complained to my friend, was the fact that
"not one periodical has asked me for a piece on the Mac-
Iver report! Could you imagine anything like that happening in the general magazine world?"
  In advance of the NCRAC plenary session in November,
where the decisive action on the MacIver Report was to
take place, the American Jewish Committee had submitted
its final brief after a heated debate on what its contents should be. It had taken place at its policy meeting in Chicago in October and was resolved by rejecting
without qualification all of the MacIver recommendations.
  The ADL did not disclose the contents of its brief
until its policy meeting on October 19 and 20. Its 23-

page "Statement of Views" carried an implied threat to walk out of the NCRAC if the welfare funds attempted to control its policy. While ADL admitted some duplication of effort, it defended the various agencies on the basis of ideological differences in their approaches to anti-Semitism. The brief noted that the ADL had 25 regional offices while the welfare funds had established only 22 community relations councils. Unlike the American Jewish Committee, the ADL then went on to reject the MacIver assimilationist approach as well as his recommendations, contending that the one followed directly upon the other. The brief contained the following warning:

"It is noteworthy that both the Anti-Defamation League and the American Jewish Committee raise approximately 60 percent of the funds outside of federations and welfare fund communities. ADL sees no advantage to Jewish life in the destruction of the idea of federated fundraising any more than in the destruction of national defense agencies. It is the opinion of ADL that should the welfare funds seek to curtail unduly funds allocated to these agencies, independent fundraising will result and the effectiveness of federations will diminish."

The brief of the American Jewish Congress displayed what the Newsletter called "a remarkable feat of intellectual gymnastics" because it indignantly rejected Dr. MacIver's integrationist suggestions but, at the same time, accepted his recommendations. None of the agencies, however, anticipated that the November meeting would be acrimonious or uncompromising. The American Council for Judaism criticized the ADL's position because it rejected Dr. MacIver's assimilationist approach. A prominent member of the anti-Israel organization named Moses Lasky, a San Francisco attorney, noted: "The Council is not the only organization that perceives and professes the philosophy expressed by Dr. MacIver—the American Jewish Committee is another—but the Council does seem to be the only one that is based upon that philosophy, has been created to forward it, and hews closely to it in its day to day work." Still another point of view came from the communist monthly, **Jewish Life,** which analysed Dr. MacIver's recommndations and arrived at the following conclusion: "MacIver's proposal, then, would only take power from Tweedeldum and give it to Tweedeldee."

In advance of the plenum the NCRAC Evaluative Studies Committee held a meeting in New York on November 2 to 4, during which it reviewed the entire series of developments surrounding the MacIver Report. Although the meeting was held privately and without publicity,

the Newsletter learned enough about the discussions to be able to announce proudly on November 8: "The MacIver Report is dead!"
What had happened was that after a bitter debate between representatives of the defense agencies and the LCBC, the Evaluative Committee decided to drop the Mac-Iver Report altogether and thus avoid the controversy by replacing the Report with a proposal incorporating a new 5-point program of principles, which the NCRAC plenum would be asked to approve. Boasting that this "marks the complete triumph of the fight against the MacIver Report which was begun by **Cross-Section, U.S.A.** in June and carried on throughout the summer months," the Newsletter then went on to issue the following statement:

The Evaluative Committee's report, which was adopted by majority vote, is remarkable for its omission of Professor MacIver's name throughout--with the sole exception of thanks at the beginning of the report. This puts the capstone on the crushing defeat suffered by the LCBC and the CJFWF, and bears out reports that the MacIver study is now considered a public relations liability.
The five-point program of principles--details were avoided--put forward by the LCBC and the CJFWF members and adopted by the Evaluative Committee for the NCRAC plenum on November 23 are: (1) Recognition of the need for a continuing study of community relations work; (2) establishment of a central planning and coordinating committee which would work toward development of an integrated program for the entire defense field; (3) primacy for community relations councils, which should be established in communities which do not yet have them; (4) strengthening of NCRAC's authority, to include the setting up of new criteria for membership and voting; and (5) central NCRAC committee to be set up to funnel all defense agency information to welfare funds and aid the latter in allocating total funds in the field on the basis of an integrated program of activity, the plan for this new body to be drawn up by a joint LCBC-NCRAC committee for the 1952 plenum of the NCRAC.

The CJFWF did program further discussion on the Mac-Iver Report for its annual assembly in December, but the success of the Newsletter in exposing the author of the Report and in demolishing it was complete. In spite of my own feelings about the waste and ineffectiveness of the defense agencies, the Newsletter had made it possible for them to escape MacIver's scalpel, and at the same time, had blunted the clumsy NCRAC-CJFWF attempt to take over control and direction of the community, a strategy which had the silent assent of the Zionists.

The veteran Zionist and satirist, Bernard G. Richards, a one-time reporter for the **Boston Globe**, offered the MacIver **coup de grace** in a humorous comment in the **Congress Weekly**. In a discourse entitled "Keidansky Reports on MacIver," Richards offered the following dialogue:

"Karabas: 'What will happen to the Report, I mean finally?'

"Keidansky: 'It will be properly filed.'

"'Only filed?'

"'To have a thing properly filed--that's no small achievement.'"

11

A RABBINICAL DISPUTATION

In the aftermath of the rejection of the MacIver Report, threats of drastic reprisals, sharp words and bruised feelings scored the relations of national and local Jewish community agencies. Some of the wounds inflicted by MacIver took years to heal, especially since some diehard opponents of the defense agencies persisted in trying to put the MacIver recommendations into effect under the guise of implementing the five principles adopted at the NCRAC plenum. Especially bitter, however, was the quarrel between the Reform rabbis of the UAHC and the Conservative rabbis along with some Reform rabbis of the Synagogue Council.

The dispute was instigated by the recommendation of the MacIver Report that all interfaith work should be done by the UAHC. Almost as an afterthought, Dr. Maciver also recommended that the UAHC, which was a member of NCRAC, should invite the Synagogue Council, which was not a member of NCRAC, to cooperate with it in the interfaith effort. It was a most unfortunate display of Dr. MacIver's obvious ignorance of the tensions among Jewish organizations, and it has never been explained why the professional staff people working with Dr. MacIver allowed it to happen. The Synagogue Council of America is the overall representative body of Conservative, Reform and some Orthodox rabbis. The UAHC represents only the Reform movement. Although both groups had engaged in interfaith work to a limited extent, neither body had the resources, the staff or the experience to initiate and execute interfaith activities on a national scale. This was done primarily by the defense agencies. Thus, the MacIver recommendation helped to intensify the latent rivalry that existed between the two rabbinical organizations and bring them to a confrontation that did neither one credit.

In its brief on the MacIver Report, the UAHC recorded the fact that it had received Dr. MacIver's recommendations with enthusiasm and "heartily concurs"

181

particularly in the allocation of the Union as the
"sponsor and director in the inter-faith area." The UAHC
further offered its "ardent" hope that the recommendations would be adopted. It had only one reservation:
that section of the recommendation which suggested that
the Synagogue Council be invited to participate in sponsoring efforts in the interfaith area. The UAHC justified its objection to the Synagogue Council in the
following blunt statement:

"In seeking to further cooperation with other Jewish
religious groups, it would seem unwise to include in
that endeavor the Synagogue Council.... It is...unable
by its very structure to assume a function such as a
community relations program. The measure of cooperation
achieved within the Synagogue Council has been largely
due to the presence of a unanimity clause in its constitution. Each constituent agency has the power of the
veto....There are deep and, at present, unbridgeable
gaps in the ideology of the member groups in the Synagogue Council."

It was a most unwise, most inappropriate declaration. In their enthusiasm over receiving the MacIver
nomination, the men responsible for this statement obviously went overboard in their anticipation of the assumption of responsibility and power in the interfaith
field. Not content with minimizing the effectiveness of
the Synagogue Council, the UAHC proceeded to call upon
all congregations, Conservative and Orthodox as well as
Reform to break away from their national associations
and join the UAHC in its interfaith work. Without referring to Dr. MacIver's evangelistic attitude toward
Jews, the UAHC went on to say in its brief: "Though the
Synagogue Council is not the proper vehicle for such
desired cooperation, there will be no difficulty in
gaining the active and full-hearted partnership of individual congregational bodies and of congregations dif-
fering in this matter with their own national congregational organization. These will be invited to join the
Union in a joint interfaith community relations program."

The anger and bitterness with which this insensitive
statement was received, especially by the Conservative
rabbinate, found full expression a few weeks later at a
meeting of the Synagogue Council. It was made, surpris-
ingly enough, by a Reform rabbi, Rabbi Bernard J. Bamberger, in his capacity as chairman of the committee to
evaluate the MacIver Report. In the statement which he
submitted to the full membership, the Synagogue Council
declared itself ready and able to take on the full re-

sponsibility for communal interfaith activities. According to the Newsletter account of the meeting, Rabbi
Bamberger limited his comments only to the MacIver recommendation on interfaith work and in his brief, left
no doubt about where he stood. The Newsletter summarized
his brief as follows:

> It did not express an opinion on the Mac-
> Iver Report as a whole. With obvious references
> to the brief submitted to the NCRAC by the
> UAHC, Dr. Bamberger--himself a member of the
> UAHC--pointed out that the Synagogue Council
> had been engaged in interfaith work to the ex-
> tent of its financial ability; that such work
> should be carried on by a religious agency,
> specifically an overall body such as the Syna-
> gogue Council; that such work is being carried
> on at present not only by the UAHC but by the
> Jewish Theological Seminary and by Yeshiva Uni-
> versity as well as by a number of individual
> congregations.
>   In the discussion which followed the Bam-
> berger report, the UAHC brief was bitterly
> criticized. The UAHC had charged that the
> Synagogue Council was "unable by its very
> structure to assume a function such as a com-
> munity relations program"; added that there
> were deep and "unbridgeable gaps in the ide-
> ology of the member groups of the Synagogue
> Council." The UAHC will discuss the Bamberger
> report at its own executive board meeting next
> week and submit its answer at the October 30
> meeting of the Council.
>   Asked by **Cross-Section, U.S.A.** to comment
> on the UAHC statement, Rabbi Hirsch Freund, the
> executive director of the Council, said: "It is
> a complete and gross misrepresentation, and an
> ungentlemanly kind of publicity."

The Bamberger report was never submitted to the
NCRAC; it was vetoed by the UAHC, which took advantage
of the unanimity clause in the Synagogue Council's constitution, the same provision which it had charged in
its brief made it impossible for the Council to undertake communal interfaith work. The consequence of the
UAHC veto was that five other constituent members of the
Synagogue Council, the New York Board of Rabbis, the
Orthodox Rabbinical Council, the Union of Orthodox Jewish Congregations, the Conservative Rabbinical Assembly

and the United Synagogue, all handed in reports recommending that the Synagogue Council be designated as the religious body to be charged with responsibility for interfaith work. At the same time, the Synagogue determined that it would now undertake a fight to replace the UAHC on the NCRAC membership role.

At no time, however, did the Synagogue Council express an opinion about the MacIver Report itself, both Conservative and Orthodox rabbis carefully sidestepping the other controversial issues. There was, however, one important exception, especially significant because the MacIver Report had been given the stamp of approval by Rabbi Louis Finkelstein. The exception, alone among the Synagogue Council members, was contained in the statement of the United Synagogue, which seemed to go out of its way to say that it was "inclined to question the basic thesis of the MacIver Report because its implications regarding the nature of the Jewish community...go far beyond what appears on the surface." The statement was signed by Rabbi Simon Greenberg, the vice chancellor of the Jewish Theological Seminary. Despite this indication of differences within the Seminary itself, Dr. MacIver nevertheless was given the opportunity to address the Seminary's Institute for Religious and Social Studies on his impressions of the Jewish community on November 7, presumably on the invitation of the Chancellor of the Seminary, Rabbi Louis Finkelstein.

The division of opinion within the Seminary, however, was never allowed to surface. Neither were the resentment and divisions caused by the rabbinical squabble over their ability to carry on interfaith work, and the Jewish public generally had no knowledge of it. At the NCRAC plenum, every effort was made to avoid fireworks, and the discussion from the floor proceeded with deliberation and in an atmosphere of unnatural restraint. The critical sessions on November 25 and 26 were closed to the press and to the public, and that was where a bitter debate took place over the only document under discussion, namely, the five-point program of principles. The MacIver Report itself never came up for discussion. It was referred to only in the NCRAC news release, which said that the agencies would discuss the "evaluative study of the Jewish community relations agencies, based on the MacIver Report." Rammed home to all the participants in the discussion, however, was the realization—in the words of the Newsletter report of the meeting—"that the voluntary character of the American Jewish community effectively bars the use of sanctions against any organization, but at the same time compels them to live together and cooperate."

Contributing to this realization was the fact that several large community councils, among them Los Angeles and Columbus, had also in effect rejected the MacIver Report. Columbus went as far as to appeal to NCRAC to continue acting as an advisory body rather than as a functioning agency. In contrast to this recommendation, the Jewish Community Council of Essex County (Newark, N.J.), swayed by its executive director, Herman Pekarsky, decided to withhold its allocation of funds for the defense agencies pending action by the NCRAC plenum, a decision which violated an agreement by the LCBC, of which Essex County was a member, not to take such action. The possibility that the Jewish community as a whole would be torn apart over the MacIver Report, as these examples made clear, contributed to the pressure on NCRAC to drop the controversial study and confine its discussions to the five-point program compromise. The Newsletter made a note of this in its report on the plenum, as follows:

> Debate was over the Evaluative Committee's five-point "Report on the Jewish Community Relations Agencies"--not on the controversial **MacIver Report**--and it was unanimously adopted as amended only after opposing sides had retreated considerably from their original positions. By decision of the NCRAC Executive Committee, taken Friday night, the plenary sessions were open to the press. At no time during the plenum was the MacIver Report under discussion. Professor MacIver was not present at the meeting. The final compromise proposals--after a debate lasting into the wee hours of Monday morning--were submitted by Leon Mesirov and Daniel L. Ullman of Philadelphia. Also noteworthy as a peacemaker was Mendel Silberberg, of Los Angeles.
>
> Details of the five-point program were reported exclusively by **Cross-Section, U.S.A.** on November 8. Amendments stipulated that "the autonomy of the member agencies will be fully respected and maintained"; that the Evaluative Committee is to attempt to work out a plan "on the logical and practical division of labor" by May 1, 1952, to which all can agree; and that in the event of no unanimous agreement, the entire matter shall be thrown back into the lap of the NCRAC 1952 plenum, to be held no later than June 15. The adopted report is known as the Ullman Report.

The defense agencies were jubilant about what they regarded as a victory over the efforts of the CJFWF to limit the range of their activities and their power in the community. The Newsletter concluded its report with the following note of caution:

> With the costly and ill-advised MacIver Report out of the way, we sincerely hope that the NCRAC agencies can now come to some practical arrangement which will eliminate the duplication, waste and other evils about which the community has been concerned. Only the cynical will say that the NCRAC debate has not had a sobering effect upon those responsible for our community welfare; and that it was not of great educational value in demonstrating that walk-out threats and power-drive tactics alike have no place in a community where all must work together for the common good.

The CJFWF refused to take its defeat lightly, and at its Chicago Assembly the following week, it demonstrated its attitude by loudly applauding the remarks of its featured speaker, none other than Professor Robert M. MacIver. The Assembly also adopted a resolution on community relations which was practically a restatement of the MacIver recommendations. To this action the Newsletter raised the following question: "Does this mean that the CJFWF is refusing to go along with the compromise Ullman Report which it voted for, along with the other NCRAC agencies, just a week before, and plans to battle defense agencies to the finish?"

Most English Jewish weeklies followed the line taken by the CJFWF, and their headlines fully reflected the Assembly's action. A Newsletter survey revealed the following:

> The bitterness engendered by the MacIver Report controversy was exemplified at the CJFWF Assembly by unofficial talk of "victory" over the defense agencies and dismissal of the Ullman Report as "postponement" of inevitable "defeat."
> This type of slanting and distortion of the action taken at the NCRAC plenum was reflected in the flagrantly inaccurate reports published in a number of English Jewish weeklies. Guiltiest was the **National Jewish Post** (Indianapolis) which frontpaged a three-column head reading,

"LAST MINUTE RETREAT BY COMMITTEE, ADL, BRINGS UNANIMOUS O.K. OF MACIVER REPORT." The **Jewish Advocate** (Boston) headline gave the story a slightly different twist with "NCRAC VOTES ACCEPTANCE OF MACIVER'S GENERAL DIRECTIONS." The **American Hebrew** (New York) said flatly: "MACIVER REPORT APPROVED."

An old, rather dishonest trick was pulled by the **Jewish News** (Newark), a community-owned paper, which carried an early JTA report under a two-column headline reading: "MACIVER REPORT IS DEBATED AT NCRAC," then printed a correct box report in the second column headlined: "ADOPT REPORT." Two papers ignored the story altogether: the community-owned **Jewish Press** (Omaha) and the **Review and Observer** (Cleveland).

Among the papers sampled, only the **Jewish Exponent** (Philadelphia) carried the official NCRAC account under an accurate headline. This release said that the plenum had "unanimously approved a report providing for re-assessment and reorganization of the Jewish community relations field"; added that it was "based on a study" by Professor MacIver. Text of the approved report, which was appended to the release, does not contain a single line of the MacIver Report itself.

None of the weeklies pointed out to their readers that the MacIver Report was at no time under debate at the NCRAC plenum, that it was never voted upon, that the delegates debated a report brought in by the Evaluative Studies Committee and adopted it after amendments were made which in effect put the situation back to where it was when the Evaluative Committee first began its work in 1950.

Also hidden from the Jewish public and from the press as well was the determined effort made by the LCBC and the CJFWF in the Evaluative Committee meetings that preceded the plenum to "force a strait-jacket program on the Anti-Defamation League and the American Jewish Committee," an effort which was, of course, soundly defeated. As disclosed in the minutes of the March 1952 meeting of the Evaluative Studies Committee, the large cities community leaders had offered a plan at the November 1951 meeting which would have assigned to the ADL the task of combatting anti-Semitism; to the Ameri-

can Jewish Committee, the task of conducting intergroup
relations; legal services to the American Jewish Congress; veterans contacts to the Jewish War Veterans; the
Jewish Labor Committee for labor groups; and interfaith
work to be assumed "by an instrumentality involving the
various Jewish religious bodies." In short, this was a
modified MacIver program in which neither the Synagogue
Council nor the UAHC was mentioned by name in an obvious
effort to avoid further controversy. According to this
plan, which was promptly rejected, the NCRAC was to have
had the exclusive authority to allocate funds to each
constituent agency out of a central pool, in effect
giving NCRAC supreme control over the entire field of
community relations.

The effort to conceal the resentment and anger
brought on by the MacIver Report was best exemplified by
the way the **American Jewish Year Book** for the years
1951, 1952 and 1953 tried to whitewash the entire controversy. Volume 52 referred only briefly on page 82 to
the reasons for the probe into the community relations
field. "A significant development was the initiation of
an evaluative study by Professor Robert M. MacIver under
the joint auspices of NCRAC and the Large City Budgeting
Conference, a group of eleven Jewish federations and
welfare funds affiliated with the CJFWF," was the way
the **Year Book** first described the study.

A much more detailed elaboration of the reasons for
the study was contained in volume 53, on pages 222-223,
but nothing was reported in this or any other volume of
the expose by **Cross-Section, U.S.A.**. Its name was never
mentioned. The **Year Book** for 1952 confined its observation to the following sentence: "Professor MacIver's
report quickly became a focus of sharp controversy and
widespread community discussion was developing around
the report and the issue it raised." To this was added a
note to the effect that an account of the discussions
was not included because the period covered by the
writer extended only until June 30, 1951.

It was not until the **American Jewish Year Book** of
1953, volume 54, almost two years after the event, that
the MacIver Report and the subsequent controversy were
made the subject of a special article. It was written by
Selma G. Hirsh, a former member of the staff of the
American Jewish Committee, and her lengthy account
proved to be a bland, highly biased review favorably
describing the MacIver Report and its recommendations.
"MacIver's report had several sections," Hirsh observed.
"One consisted of his own philosophy and a theoretical
analysis of Jewish community relations needs, with some

general observations on the kind of program which, in
his view, would meet those needs. A major portion of the
report, however, consisted of a series of concrete recommendations.... These recommendations, MacIver pointed
out, did not 'stand or fall with acceptance or rejection' of his views concerning the nature of anti-Jewish
prejudice and the need for re-examination of the fundamental objectives of the agencies presently in the
field."

Hirsh noted that the reactions of the local community relations councils to the MacIver Report were
"scattered and varied." She recognized that the American Jewish Committee approved of Professor MacIver's
description of Jewish life in the United States despite
the fact that together with the ADL it opposed his recommendations. Apart from the complete omission of any
reference to the role of **Cross-Section, U.S.A.** in bringing the Report to public attention and in stirring up
opposition to it, Hirsh also is silent on the prolonged
controversy aroused by MacIver's attack on Orthodox
Judaism and the one created between the Synagogue Council and the UAHC. Public and press reaction to the Report is limited to a footnote on page 168--the 15-page
article extends from page 162 to 177--and Hirsh describes it in the following terms:

"While the MacIver report was being studied by the
national agencies, the Anglo-Jewish and Yiddish press
devoted considerable attention to it--both in criticism
and support. The criticism was levelled mainly at Mac-
Iver's analysis of the nature and causes of anti-Jewish
prejudice and his concept of Jewish life in America.
MacIver, however, was widely supported for his attack
upon 'waste' and duplication'; and his recommendations
for a division of labor among the agencies were regarded
by some commentators as a needed step in the direction
of the eventual establishment of a central organization
for American Jewry. A particularly extensive analysis of
the report, especially the theoretical concepts expressed in it, and their relation to the Reconstructionist program was prepared by Abraham G. Duker for the
Jewish Reconstructionist Foundation."

Hirsh's effort to rewrite history was part of the
continued struggle by the CFJWF and the NCRAC to limit
the power of the defense agencies and to allocate some
of the responsibilities they had assumed to other
organizations. The Ullman recommendations, which were
formally proposed at the March 1952 meeting of the
Evaluative Studies Committee, were vigorously debated at
the NCRAC plenum the following September over the bitter

opposition of the ADL and the American Jewish Committee. Eventually, in spite of efforts at compromise, the controversy led to the withdrawal of the ADL and the American Jewish Committee from the NCRAC in a spirit of considerable anger and resentment, the fruit of the MacIver Report.

The rabbis were not content to drop the issue. Oblique references to the controversy over the way the community should be organized continued to appear in sermons and articles, although the name of MacIver no longer was mentioned. One of Reform Judaism's leading spokesmen, Rabbi Jonah B. Wise, the spiritual leader of Central Synagogue in New York, used the occasion of the Founders' Day exercise of the Hebrew Union College-Jewish Institute of Religion, to declare in his address:

"I am convinced that there can be no dignity and no peace for American Jews unless their religious life is adjusted on a national scale and with consecrated authority. This certainly brings the Union of American Hebrew Congregations forcibly into the picture. The Union was originated as a means of presenting Jewish life in the United States on a national level. The need for this was obvious....It is more apparent now when so many crudities and so many misinterpretations of Jewish life harass us on every side. Unless our religious life can be organized on a national level, we shall present too weak and too feeble a front in the battle for a dignified interpretation of all of us as Jews."

Dr. Wise's statement was made early in the year at a time when it was useful in bolstering the Union's effort to secure authority in the field of interfaith relations in keeping with the MacIver recommendation. A statement of the Conservative rejection of this claim was made shortly before the NCRAC plenum by Dr. Simon Greenberg, vice chancellor of the Jewish Theological Seminary. Writing in the **United Synagogue Review,** organ of the Conservative synagogues, Rabbi Greenberg offered the following observations:

"Now we make bold to suggest that in the group of institutions and organizations centered around the Jewish Theological Seminary, the United Synagogue and the Rabbinical Assembly of America, we have the closest approach on the American scene to a program and an organization whose scope embraces almost all possible Jewish interests and whose ranks attract in good numbers, Jews of all ages. We have here the possible core around which an integrated Jewish community may develop."

In this controversy, Dr. MacIver's friend, Rabbi Louis Finkelstein, the chancellor of the Seminary, pre-

served a dignified silence. By coincidence, Dr. Greenberg's challenging declaration was reinforced by the
simultaneous appearance of Rabbi Finkelstein on the
front cover of **Time** magazine against a rainbow-like
background. **Time** also featured a six-page article about
the Seminary and its current leader which recalled,
among other facts Rabbi Finkelstein's anti-Zionist but
pro-State of Israel statements, a position which
paralleled that of the American Jewish Committee. The
Newsletter, in revealing that the **Time** magazine publicity had in fact been arranged by the American Jewish
Committee, included the following comment: "The faces of
former Seminary presidents Dr. Cyrus Adler and Dr. Solomon Schechter look down unhappily on page 53 on all this
'publicity.'" The Jewish press greeted the **Time** magazine
display with mixed reactions, at least one weekly hinting that the publicity might have been arranged by the
American Jewish Committee in return for Rabbi Finkelstein's defense of Dr. MacIver. A sharply critical observation appeared in **Hadoar**, the Hebrew language
weekly; the consensus of the press, however, was that
the publicity would undoubtedly enhance the Seminary's
annual appeal for funds.

The basic weakness of the rabbinate in the American
Jewish community was fully demonstrated at the NCRAC
plenum. In the debate that took place between the defense agencies and the forces aligned with the community
welfare fund leaders, the rather undignified quarrel between the UAHC and the Synagogue Council was completely
ignored. And if the rabbis raised their voices at any
point in the discussion, it was not reported.

12

NEW GOALS FOR BONDS

The attention of community welfare fund directors and defense agency executives may have been absorbed in the fight over the MacIver recommendations, but at the headquarters of the Israel bond campaign, no one ever heard of MacIver. The greatest concern of Henry Montor and his staff at the beginning of the year was the resignation of Prime Minister Ben-Gurion and the effect that his government's fall might have on the 1951 Israel bond campaign which they were planning. Although Ben-Gurion was asked to head the interim provisional cabinet before the elections were held for a new Knesset, there was deep concern when the cabinet crisis caused the value of the Israel pound to nosedive on the New York money mart to a new low of sixty cents from its nominal value of $2.80.

Other problems soon arose. While preparations for the campaign went ahead at full speed, local community leaders expressed their fears over the probability of a conflict with the UJA drive. In Newark, N.J., the community council appointed a three-man committee to coordinate the two-drive efforts, and all local and national agencies were urged to clear their own appeals in the area with this committee in order to provide "maximum cooperation and integration." The formation of this committee set the pattern for other communities to follow, where it was adapted to fit local needs. Despite questions and doubts, all community leaders set out in good faith to fulfil what they regarded as a solemn responsibility toward Israel.

Prime Minister Ben-Gurion himself provided them with a new definition of that responsibility, one which contradicted the agreement he had made with Jacob Blaustein the previous year. In a speech reported by Sidney Gruson, the **New York Times** correspondent in Tel Aviv, on January 28, 1951, Ben-Gurion was quoted as saying that Jews everywhere belonged to the Jewish nation and were as directly obligated as the citizens of Israel themselves to pay the costs of the "ingathering

193

of the exiles." Gruson was obviously reflecting informed Israeli opinion when he concluded his dispatch with the observation: "It can be expected that the new tone will penetrate the efforts of the Israeli Government to raise funds in the United States even though this may bring conflict with the efforts of the United Jewish Appeal."

Commenting on Israel's attitude, I wrote to Leftwich: "Your diagnosis of Israel is correct; they make no secret of it themselves. They're out to get what they can and wherever they can, and they'll get a great deal because—well, for all the reasons. If we feel outraged because of the Sharetts and the Lockers and the Eliezer Kaplans—perhaps that's the price we have to pay for losing sight of our Jewishness, the values which kept us together and distinctive.

"Most Americans are still inclined to be tolerant of Israeli blunders, waste, impudence, etc., simply because they feel Israel is doing a swell job of 'rescuing' the Jews of Europe and Asia. And if they weren't worried stiff about the war and its effect on business, they would put over the bond issue. But present indications are not good. The big givers are flatly saying 'no'—they'll give to UJA because that's tax exempt, but the bonds are a very poor risk."

The issue of Israel bonds was authorized by the Knesset at the end of February when it approved the sale of 15-year coupon bonds paying 3½ percent, and 12-year savings bonds with a maturity value of 150 percent. Henry Montor and the Israel bond directors officially scheduled the start of their campaign for May 1, despite the danger signals of a possible conflict with the UJA. Unofficially, the campaign was launched as early as March 11 at a conference sponsored by the ZOA which was attended by Zionist leaders from all parts of the country. At the same time, bond sales committees were already in the process of organization in many communities, and some were busy at work collecting pledges. This was an action that was clearly in violation of arrangements Montor had made with the UJA and with local welfare funds.

To insure the success of the campaign, Montor and the Israel government mobilized Israel's best talents. Meyer W. Weisgal, the colorful executive vice chairman of the American Committee for the Weizmann Institute, and the guiding force behind the U.I.T. (University-Institute-Technion), the joint fundraising arm of the three major Israeli institutions of learning, was drafted to direct the Israel bond drive in the New York

metropolitan area. Another bond drive recruit was I.L.
Kenen, the press officer at the Israel consulate in New
York. To give the Israel bond campaign its greatest
incentive, Prime Minister Ben-Gurion himself decided to
fly to the United States in May to deliver the opening
speech. Accompanying him was to be Gershon Agron, the
brilliant editor of the English language **Jerusalem Post,**
who had resigned his office as Israel's Minister of
Information in order to lend a hand to the bond effort.
The Newsletter explained the reasons for these preparations in the following report:

> The desperate economic situation in Israel
> is the basic reason for the speed-up pressure
> put on UJA by the Bond campaign leaders all
> over the country. ZOA officials, protesting
> "no conflict" with UJA, explain that pre-
> campaign organizing for the bond drive is
> essential if the sale is to open successfully
> on May 1. (Jump-off date originally mentioned
> was May 11, Israel's Independence Day.)
> Secondary political reason, according to well-
> informed sources, for speed-up is Ben-Gurion's
> desire to present Israeli voters with success-
> ful campaign results **before** the Israel
> elections.

Henry Montor brushed aside any questions about the
encroachment of the bond campaign on the UJA drive.
Following his customary strategy, he boasted before a
special bond conference of one hundred representatives,
called by ZOA in New York on March 11, that he would
personally hand over $50 million in cash to Prime
Minister Ben-Gurion at the Madison Square Garden rally
scheduled for May 10. At the time he made this promise,
I advised my friend Leftwich, all that Montor had on
hand were pledges for $5 million. The Prime Minister
was scheduled to be the guest of honor at the ZOA
celebration in Madison Square Garden, headlined as ZOA's
"Salute to Israel Pageant." At least five Israeli cabinet ministers were also expected to take part in the
launching of the bond drive, all of which was widely
publicized as unprecedented in the annals of American
fundraising. Among the cabinet ministers scheduled to
accompany the Prime Minister was the popular Mrs. Golda
Myerson. Also expected to arrive in New York to add to
the fanfare were two Israeli warships and their handsome, smartly outfitted crews. S. Dingol, writing in
the **Tog,** New York Yiddish daily, took note of all the

high Israeli officials arriving in this country and asked wryly whether Ben-Gurion intended to form an Israeli government-in-exile as long as they were here!

The Israelis obviously were pinning all their hopes for financial solvency on the success of the bond drive, but, as I wrote my friend Leftwich, the first signs of resistance to the campaign were becoming evident. "Initial reports from the outlying eastern areas received by yours truly indicate that big givers won't buy government bonds because they're not tax exempt and do not represent a sound investment," I wrote. "But I would like to see the bond drive successful and the UJA a failure. We need a cleanup of the charity situation here and that's the only way it will be done thoroughly. Also, a successful bond sale would probably mean the demise of the half a dozen Zionist agencies and drives with which we are saddled here, not excluding Hadassah, ZOA and JNF."

Future events were to prove that I was wrong in my prediction, of course, the eventual success of the bond campaign resulting in the opposite development. At the time, however, UJA leaders were watching the bond campaign extravaganza with increasing bitterness. They charged Montor with double-crossing them and with breaking his promise not to interfere with the UJA campaign which he had made the previous October. Israel was bringing considerable pressure for quick sales on Montor, however, and, as I wrote Leftwich: "Things look very rough in this field now. I don't think UJA is doing very well and the bond campaign boys aren't helping matters by going ahead with their plans immediately. Montor never kept his word to anyone, so why should he worry now about possible conflicts with UJA. The bond campaign may do well despite worsening economic conditions. Inflation is eating everyone out of house and home, and the government isn't really doing anything to stop it."

The feelings of the UJA leaders were allayed only temporarily by the three-quarter page advertisements in the New York newspapers announcing a "Zionist Mobilization Rally for the UJA," which was set for April 1. New York UJA leaders, according to a Newsletter report, "have been pointing proudly to record-breaking collections thus far this year." They were properly fearful, however, that the bond competition would have an adverse effect on their future collections. Echoes of their concern were heard in Israel during the Knesset debate on the authorization of the bond sale, and in a comment on the situation, the Newsletter said:

Wall Streeters are watching with con- siderable interest the wholly unorthodox--and highly extravagant--steps being prepared by the American Financial and Development Corporation for Israel (AFDCI) to sell Israeli bonds next month; noted the rapidly expanding, high- salaried staff which necessitated removal from the quarters at 2 Park Avenue to larger (21,000 square feet), considerably more expensive offi- ces in the swank Equitable Building on lower Broadway, where AFDCI will pay an annual rental of $84,000!!

Expenses of the bond sale are currently being covered by loans to be paid out of pro- ceeds of the bond sales.   Meanwhile, in the Knesset debate over the authorization of the bond sale, General Zionist speakers complained that American Zionist leaders had been bypassed when Finance Minister Eliezer Kaplan chose Henry Montor to head the bond drive, and accused Mr. Montor of being an "assimilation- ist."   Their complaint was seconded by Mapam leader Dr. Moshe Sneh, who charged that Mr. Montor had "sabotaged" the UJA by transferring its administrative staff to the bond headquar- ters.   In reply, Mr. Kaplan said that Mr. Montor had taken only six UJA officials with him when he left the UJA!

Community welfare fund leaders complained bitterly about the developing conflict and competition between UJA and Israel bonds at the New England regional con- ference of the CJFWF as early as March, and their fears were not allayed by the assurances they were given that the UJA campaign would be given priority.   They also got small solace from the advice they received to follow the example of Newark, Boston and Bridgeport, and set up coordinating committees to eliminate as much fundraising competition as possible.   The Newsletter pointed out that there was little doubt that the early launching of the bond drive had already hurt the UJA.

With the single-minded determination for which he was famous, Montor ignored the complaints that came across his desk and pushed forward with the build-up for the bond sale.   In March he announced that sixteen state governors, headed by New York Governor Thomas E. Dewey, would attend the launching of the bond drive.   Its goal was set at the enormous sum of $500 million, and in a comment about this to Leftwich, I said:

"The bond drive is in full swing here, and by next month it will be a regular circus, complete with well-trained Israeli ministers. The UJA people are furious but they can do nothing with Montor, who is determined to make his name as the greatest fund raiser in Jewish history no matter who gets hurt in the effort. Incidentally, there will be terrific speculation in these bonds after 1954, when they can be changed into negotiable 'Bearer Bonds.' I suspect an investor could pick them up at about 50 percent or less of face value. Buying them now is, of course, an **auto da fe** in more than one sense."

No one in the United States had ever seen a bond drive launching like this one. The campaign in New York was actually opened on Tuesday, April 17, when in the first mail delivery on that morning, thousands of New Yorkers received a "Special Memorandum" signed by Henry Morgenthau Jr., appealing to them to buy Israel bonds. The prospectus of the Israel Independence Issue, as it was called, was described by the Newsletter as a remarkable document, distinguished by its clear terse summary of Israel's history, resources and development plans. It listed the receipts and expenditures of the Israel government, and also disclosed that the AFDCI was to be limited to a commission of 3½ percent on the bonds it sold. This percentage was to be reduced if the corporation's net profits after taxes exceeded $10,000 in a year. Nothing was said about expenses.

On Tuesday night, April 17, at a dinner in the Waldorf-Astoria Hotel, the Israel bonds campaign in Greater New York was officially launched. The featured speaker of the evening was Israel's Labor Minister, Mrs. Golda Myerson, who told her distinguished audience in no uncertain terms why it was imperative that they should buy substantial quantities of Israel bonds. In keeping with Montor's practice, most of the diners had already pledged in advance to do just that. The Newsletter cited the following reservations, however, by UJA leaders:

> The opening of the bond campaign comes at a time when the New York UJA drive is just getting under full swing, with numerous trade meetings being held. Negotiations between UJA and AFDCI for postponement of the bond drive long enough for the UJA to complete its campaign have been going on for some time without result, informed circles said. They pointed out that the choice of the April 17 opening date, in spite of repeated assertions of the

primacy of the UJA and of mobilization rallies,
put the bond drive in direct competition with
the   UJA   and   would   damage   the   latter
considerably.

The ZOA reported at this time that for its part in
the Israel bond campaign it had established Bond
Campaign Committees in 550 districts throughout the
country, and that these committees were prepared to send
out an army of thousands of volunteer salesmen. Not to
be outdone, the Religious Zionists, the Mizrachi, announced that their annual dinner on June 5 would be
devoted to promoting the sale of bonds.   The only sour
note in the chorus came from Lessing Rosenwald, the president of the anti-Zionist American Council for Judaism,
who protested against "Zionist political pressuring,"
and attacked the "spectacle of American Jews being mobilized for Israel bonds."   He was promptly
answered by ZOA president Benjamin G. Browdy, who
retorted:
"It is nothing but comical to see this negligible
minority assume the role of super-patriots at the
expense of five million loyal members of the American
Jewish community."
The elaborate preparations and the gala dinner for
the launching of the bond sale had one consequence which
the fundraisers had not counted on.   By drawing public
attention to their activities with their flamboyant
publicity, they provided the impetus for several newspaper articles criticizing the expenses involved in
raising funds.   The **Forward,** a New York Yiddish daily,
opened the inquiry by focussing especially on the high
cost of raising funds for the UJA.   The newspaper estimated that in 1948, a peak fundraising year, fundraising
costs for all Jewish agencies totalled over $8 million,
of which the largest share was incurred by the UJA.   At
the same time, an investigation of all fundraising in
New York was frontpaged by the **New York World Telegram,**
a Scripps-Howard newspaper, under the byline of Allan
Keller.   He stressed the growing irritation of New
Yorkers at the number of overlapping appeals of which
they were the targets, adding that they were "beginning
to feel that they are being bled white for sweet
charity."   Keller pointed out the excessively high costs
of some campaigns, where expenses ran as high as 40 percent, and compared them with the very low costs of community chest drives, which rarely went above 4 or 5
percent.   He emphasized that public scrutiny of the campaign expenses, administrative costs and "other tech-

niques now cloaked with virtual secrecy" of the various
appeals was a vital necessity.
After calling attention to these articles, the
Newsletter went on to point to the huge amounts of money
that Jews in New York were called on to contribute, and
continued:

> Within the same week, the Federation of
> Jewish Philanthropies of New York announced
> that its 1950-51 campaign, which closed on
> February 1, will probably total $14,500,000.
> Statisticians noted that Federation actually
> ran two campaigns in the 14 months from
> December 1949 to February 1, 1951; and
> according to Federation figures, raised a total
> of $39,500,000 in both campaigns ($25 million
> for the first; $14.5 million for the second).
> Federation maintains 116 hospitals and agencies.
> (Despite the letter-writing campaign of the
> Committee for Kashruth in the planned Long
> Island Jewish Hospital, Federation officials
> and hospital officers have not budged so far
> from their position on serving **trefa** food; they
> will probably ignore Long Island congregations
> as long as the Yiddish press and the Jewish
> public itself do not protest.)
> At the same time, New York Catholic Chari-
> ties announced that it had raised $2,124,405 in
> 1950 and had spent slightly less than $3 mil-
> lion for 186 Catholic institutions and agen-
> cies. The Catholic population in New York City
> is approximately one and one half times larger
> than the Jewish population.
> No doubt there are sound reasons for the
> difference between the Jewish expenditure of
> $39,500,000 and the Catholic expenditure of $3
> million in New York City, but we do not know
> what they are.

The Newsletter does not record any public or private
reaction to this sharp contrast in charity expenditures.
It did go on to note, however, that May was the peak
month for at least four other major fundraising drives
in New York City. These were the Joint Defense Appeal of
the ADL and the American Jewish Committee, which raised
over $1 million; the New York UJA, which said it had
raised a total of $14 million; the appeals of the Jewish
Theological Seminary, and the UAHC Combined Campaign. At
the same time, Jews and other New Yorkers were faced

with the 1951 campaign of the Greater New York Fund with
a goal of $9 million, and by a drive by the U.S. Trea-
sury for the sale of United States bonds, with May
designated as Defense Bond Month.

In the midst of all this fundraising activity, Prime
Minister David Ben-Gurion arrived in New York on Thursday, May 3, and was greeted with great excitement. In
addition to his appearance at the opening of the Israel
bond drive, he was scheduled to make a cross-country
tour in which he would also include an appeal for the
UJA. The Newsletter noted that his schedule on behalf of
the Israel bond drive included the following events and
cities:

> The opening of the $500 million Israel bond
> drive and the arrival in Washington today of
> Prime Minister David Ben-Gurion made the news
> headlines this week. Mr. Ben-Gurion will see
> Secretary of Defense George C. Marshall and
> lunch with President Truman on Friday, arrive
> in New York the following Wednesday, and parti-
> cipate in the Madison Square Garden Independ-
> ence Day and Bond rally on Thursday, May 10,
> according to the schedule released by the
> Israel Office of Information.
> In a cross-country tour, the Israel Prime
> Minister will meet bond drive leaders in Phila-
> delphia, May 13; Boston, May 15; Pittsburgh,
> May 17; Chicago, May 19; Detroit, May 21;
> Cleveland, May 22; Los Angeles, May 23; and
> back to New York on May 27.
> The May 1 opening of the bond drive in-
> cluded a report by ZOA president Benjamin G.
> Browdy that his organization had sold $15 mil-
> lion worth of bonds toward its quota of $100
> million.

The Prime Minister was also scheduled to stop off in
Chicago on May 26, en route from Los Angeles to New
York, in order to attend a big national UJA rally, where
he was to be the guest of honor. On that occasion, the
UJA director Dr. Joseph J. Schwartz said he would hand
the Prime Minister over $20 million "in cash" as part of
the UJA collections to that date. Beyond doubt, Israel
was benefitting from the spirit of competition between
funds and among organization which, to his credit, must
be attributed to the efforts of Henry Montor. The desperate urgency of the success of the bond campaign for
Israel was underlined by **Ha'aretz**, an Israeli inde-

pendent liberal daily, when it emphasized that "the Independence Loan is the last effort we can expect from
American Jewry for a long time."
The Newsletter raised the question about whether
Henry Montor could make good his boast of March 11 when
he said he would present Prime Minister Ben-Gurion with
$50 million in cash at the Madison Square Garden rally.
Noting that expenses for the rally were running as high
as $500,000, the Newsletter went on to describe the
highlights of the meeting in the following report:

> At the Madison Square Garden bond rally
> last Thursday, not cash, not $50 million--as
> some overeager weeklies headlined last Friday
> and as bond drive director Henry Montor re-
> peatedly boasted he would hand over to Prime
> Minister Ben-Gurion (as recently as 10 days
> before the bond rally during a Chicago meet-
> ing)--but $32,125,000 "committed" was the total
> of the roll-call of states (of which ZOA this
> week claimed credit for selling $25 million).
> Recipient of the loudest, warmest and most
> spontaneous ovation of the evening was Franklin
> D. Roosevelt, Jr., according to one observer.
> The tangible thrill that passed through the
> audience when the flag of Israel was unfurled!
> ...Meyer Weisgal beating Henry Montor to the
> microphone when Jascha Heifetz finished playing
> the Bruch Concerto....**The only reference all
> night to the President of Israel, Chaim
> Weizmann, was made by Mr. Weisgal....**
> Best speech of the evening was delivered by
> Ambassador Abba Eban (who was so exhausted by
> his efforts for the bond drive as well as at
> the U.N. that he yawned three times during the
> Prime Minister's address)....The shower of Miz-
> rachi protest leaflets from the balcony just as
> the festivities ended....

Montor's failure to collect the amount of cash he
had boasted about, and the suspicion that a good part of
the money he gave to the Prime Minister had been raised
by borrowing from the banks in anticipation of bond
sales--**Ha'aretz** had earlier revealed that European banks
had extended loans and credit to Israel on the assurance
that the bond drive would be successful--tempered the
enthusiasm that the bond rally had sought to arouse.
Additionally, criticism was voiced by Hayim Greenberg,
highly respected editor of the influential New York

weekly, **Yiddisher Kempfer,** who charged the bond drive
management with bad taste because it had hired Israeli
night club singer Miriam Jaron, who had won a bathing
beauty contest in Tel Aviv, in order to display her
charms as "Miss Israel of 1950." Ben-Gurion, Golda Meir
and other Laborite leaders had never made a secret of
their agnostic views, with the result that when the
Prime Minister made a much-publicized appearance at the
Sabbath service of the Orthodox East Fifty-First Street
Synagogue, in New York, some observers charged him with
using the occasion to appease the religious Zionists.
But when the women's division of the bond drive tendered
a non-kosher breakfast in Boston in honor of Mrs. David
Ben-Gurion, it was sharply protested by the Women's
Branch of the Union of Orthodox Jewish Congregations,
which also demanded that Sabbath meetings for bond sales
be discontinued.

My own private feelings about the opening of the
bond drive were reserved for a letter to Leftwich in
which I wrote: "How do you like our bond drive circus
here? Strangely, most Jews here aren't the least offended by the spectacle of the Israel government acting
like a bunch of mountebanks under the direction of chief
clown Henry Montor. The UJA people are furious, but no
one will say a word for publication. Montor is virtual
dictator of the American Jewish community today, and his
pitchman standards apparently have become our values.
And despite his ruthless crippling of UJA, his careless
breach of his pledged word not to compete, there is no
one to protest, least of all the people who choose not
to see the implications of his conduct. They'll give him
more than most people think they will, but not as much,
of course, as he boastfully anticipates. And as long as
his drives are successful, the Israel government will
back him up to the hilt. He is running up a terrific
advance bill for staff, etc., at least $2-3 million, I
would guess."

After the bond rally, according to the Newsletter's
"informed sources," there were "long faces" at the headquarters of the AFDCI despite all the optimistic reports
of the sale of bonds. The Newsletter revealed that contrary to all the boasting, the actual cash returns from
bond sales throughout the country were not likely to
reach as much as $12 million by the end of May, when
Ben-Gurion was scheduled to return to Israel. Nevertheless, bond directors outwardly maintained a display of
enthusiasm and confidence in the success of the campaign. Ben-Gurion, returning from his nationwide tour,
described his reception by the Jewish community as "mag-

nificent" and unhesitatingly predicted that the bond
issue would be oversubscribed. And on his last day in
the United States, he received a delegation of ADL leaders headed by Judge Meier Steinbrink, who said: "We hope
that your visit to our shores has given you renewed understanding of the aspirations of American Jewry."

The Prime Minister's response to Judge Steinbrink
was not recorded, but in the speech made before leaving
New York, Ben-Gurion once more called on American Zionists to mobilize American Jewry for the upbuilding of
Israel, to promote **chalutziut**, and to foster Hebrew
education. He had no problem in assuring Jews that
Israel would not become a theocratic state--an obvious
acknowledgement of the feelings of the American Jewish
Committee--and described the results of the bond sales
so far as an "encouraging" beginning. Adding that he was
confident that "it will bring full results," he appealed
to leaders of the bond drive and the UJA to cooperate
with each other, insisting that they needed each other
and that Israel needed both of them.

In Israel, the reaction to the opening of the bond
campaign was described by the Newsletter as being initially "over-optimistic," in a report in which it said:

> Over-optimism about the results of Premier
> David Ben-Gurion's visit here and the launching
> of the Independence Bond drive mark the initial
> reaction of the Israel press, but the man-in-
> the-street suffered a decided let-down when
> actual returns became known, according to a re-
> port from our correspondent in Tel Aviv.
>
> Returning to the United States early last
> month, Dr. Dov Joseph, Minister of Communica-
> tions, set the pace by telling Israeli newsmen:
> "Jews in the United States have been waiting
> for the Independence Bond issue; they don't
> need to be persuaded to buy--they have only to
> be told of the need."
>
> **Davar**, the Mapai daily, said that the Pre-
> mier's tour was likely to have "a considerable
> effect" on Jewish life here, while the **Jerusa-
> lem Post**, Israel's only English language daily,
> cited new hopes for an increase in private in-
> vestments and a rise in the value of the Israel
> pound as some of the "first reactions" to the
> bond drive here. The liberal daily **Ha'aretz**,
> the largest morning paper, said the Premier's
> visit was a "special event" in American Jewish
> life, then went on to tell Israelis that be-

cause American Jews now "have their own state
to symbolize their best original traits, they
were thus at least equal to all other Americans
not only in citizenship but as immigrants."
        On the reaction of the man-in-the-street,
our correspondent writes: "Everyone is proud of
Ben-Gurion's popularity in the United States.
The businessmen are enjoying a lift, but professionals and working men feel that so important a personality as Ben-Gurion should not be
giving his time and using up his energy to
collect money. They ask over and over again:
'Don't the American Jews know and understand
what it is to absorb so many thousands of Jews
who must be helped and that we cannot do it
alone?' But now that the parades and receptions
for Ben-Gurion are over, they are suffering a
deep feeling of disappointment over the low
level of bond drive investments. The tremendous
fanfare has been completely out of proportion
to the results. The contrast between the huge
receptions and the actual money invested
reminds us of Nero fiddling while Rome burns."

This early pessimism, however, was soon dissipated
by the news that through June 30, sales of Independence
Bonds had reached a total of $60 million, while actual
cash receipts up to that date totalled $22 million. Mon-
tor's strategy was vindicated, and when the bond office
managers met that summer they were told that bond sales
would reach a total of $100 to $200 million by the end
of the year. Prime Minister Ben-Gurion also exuded confidence when he arrived in Israel, and he predicted that
the original goal of $500 million in bond sales would be
achieved because the bond drive, he said, was "a popular
one as compared with the United Jewish Appeal, which
concentrated only on the wealthy."
        To the dismay of community leaders, the Prime Minis-
ter's gauche statement was reported by the Jewish
Agency's **Digest**. Fortunately, in the same statement, he
went on to express the hope that UJA and bond drive
officials would work in harmony and reach agreement on a
solution to all their differences. But the damage caused
by his off-hand remark was already done: from other
sources, the Newsletter learned that differences had
reached the breaking point and that by the end of June,
the UJA leaders Edward M.M. Warburg and Dr. Joseph J.
Schwartz were threatening to resign. The Newsletter
summed up the situation that was causing the break in
the following report:

Bond drive competition and increased allocations for local needs are cutting into
chances of the UJA matching its 1950 total, and
indicate that any hopes of exceeding the 1950
total are highly over-optimistic, according to
a reliable national survey released exclusively
to **Cross-Section, U.S.A.**

For example, Baltimore raised more this
year than last, but the UJA will get about
$200,000 **less** because of higher allocations for
local needs. Philadelphia also raised more than
last year's $5 million, but about $500,000 will
be allocated for its new Medical Center. Cleveland has over $200,000 more than last year's $4
million, but how much more UJA will get is
doubtful. Pittsburgh, Miami and Cincinnati will
reach the 1950 totals, but Detroit, with more
pledges than last year, is still short of
1950's total of $4,615,000 by about $300,000;
and Newark, N.J., is running under last year's
$2,250,000.

Israel bond competition, however, has seriously damaged the drive in Los Angeles, which
has so far raised little more than 60 percent
of 1950's $6,844,000. Also badly hit are New
Haven, with less than half a million ($700,000
in 1950), and Paterson, N.J., with half a million dollars against last year's $618,000--and
both drives are practically over. Running behind but not so badly are the drives in San
Francisco, St. Louis and Buffalo. The survey
notes that the most successful Spring drives
were those which--like Baltimore and Cleve-
land--got under way earliest and thus beat the
bond drive competition.

The big question marks are New York, which
recently announced a total so far of $24 mil-
lion, and Boston, which has a Fall campaign.
Informed opinion there believes privately that
the Fall campaign will be hurt by the successful bond drive just completed there.

As early as April, Israel's Ambassador Abba Eban had
found it necessary to issue a statement affirming the
priority of the UJA contributions. Referring to "some
confusion" existing in connection with the two drives,
Eban said: "The government of Israel does not want
anyone to take money which should go to UJA and buy
bonds with it." Shortly afterward, Israel's Finance

Minister Eliezer Kaplan recommended the establishment of
a committee to coordinate the two drives, consisting of
Henry Morgenthau, Jr., Henry Montor, Julian Venezky, Edward M.M. Warburg, Dr. Joseph J. Schwartz, Morris Bernstein, Rudolf G. Sonneborn, and Dr. Nahum Goldmann.
Almost immediately, however, the committee found itself sharply divided over a recommendations, attributed
to Henry Montor, to allow purchasers of bonds to turn
them in as payment for pledges to UJA. Since the UJA
contributions were tax exempt, this meant that the donor
would be able to write off his bond purchases in spite
of the fact that they were not tax exempt. The welfare
fund, which accepted the bonds, however, would have to
take a discount on their face value when it sought to
cash them. It was the kind of a scheme which Montor--
who had instructed large contributors to UJA on the way
they could reduce their income tax payments by making
sizable contributions to UJA--was justly credited for.
Trouble arose, however, when Chicago welfare fund leaders flatly refused to accept Israel bonds in payment of
UJA pledges. Other welfare funds indicated that they
might accept only a small percentage of bonds as payment, but none was ready to make a flat decision on what
the percentage might be. In May, the Newsletter learned,
however, that an official statement would be issued with
the knowledge and approval of Israel's Finance Minister
Eliezer Kaplan accepting up to 25 percent of Israel
bonds in payment of UJA pledges. It was argued that the
UJA would be helped rather than hurt by this concession.
The UJA campaign, however, was in trouble. While Dr.
Goldmann was optimistically predicting that the UJA in
1951 would raise about $95 million, 70 percent of which
would go to Israel, the Newsletter carried the following
report:

> Up to the beginning of June 1951, the UJA
> sent only $27 million cash to Israel. This re-
> port was made to the Jewish Agency Executive in
> Jerusalem last month by Gabriel Hammer, execu-
> tive director of the American section.
> It will be recalled that at the UJA rally
> in Chicago, May 27, chairman Edward M.M. War-
> burg announced that the UJA had raised over $44
> million; had handed over to visiting Prime Min-
> ister Ben-Gurion checks totalling $15,731,135.
> The report by Mr. Hammer is especially note-
> worthy in view of the earlier prediction by Dr.
> Nahum Goldmann that Israel would receive only
> $30 to $35 million from the 1951 campaign. Dr.

Goldmann had made his prediction at the National Planning Conference in Washington, D.C. in October 1950.

Dr. Goldmann's forecast of the success of the 1951 UJA campaign appeared to be part of an orchestrated effort to reassure the Jewish community. In Boston, for example, Harry L. Lurie, the executive director of the CJFWF, told his audience that while the total fund raising for the year would probably decline by about five percent below the 1950 total, the Israel bond drive had not cut into the efforts of the local UJA drives throughout the country. He said the total of all Jewish philanthropy would level off at about $150 million for the year, and added: "The bond campaign has had practically a negligible effect on Spring campaigns this season."

Similar optimism was expressed by Julian Freeman, president of the CJFWF, in an article on the UJA campaign in the CJFWF publication, **Jewish Community**. Statistics offered at the annual ZOA conference, however, told a different story. According to the Newsletter, Rudolf G. Sonneborn, in his capacity as chairman of the UPA, reported that from January 1 through June 13, UPA received from UJA and "distributed" $25,238,746, almost $5 million more than the previous year. However, JNF director Mendel N. Fisher reported that he had received only $15,713,312 from UPA, and that JNF had raised $1,643,277.59 through its own collections from October 1, 1950 to June 1, 1951, a drop of over $3 million from its receipts the previous period. Expenses of the organization were reported at $353,987. JNF president Harris J. Levine told delegates: "The financial returns this year for the Jewish National Fund from the ZOA have not been what we had a right to expect since we met at our last convention in Chicago."

It should be noted that at this convention the ZOA director, Dr. Sidney Marks, made available to each delegate an audited financial report of the organization, probably the only major Jewish organization to provide this public accounting and one which the UJA refused to make available to this day.

From various communities around the country, reports indicated that the Fall campaigns of the UJA were falling short of their goals. Boston was shocked by the drop in receipts by the end of October to $3,506,588, and in order to approach the $6 million it had raised the previous year, extended its campaign to November 9. By that time, it was able to close its drive with total

pledges of $5,096,550. Minneapolis cut its allocation to
UJA to $537,500, but the biggest disappointment was the
drive in Los Angeles. Its special Cash Month Drive in
October, which had the objective of obtaining payment of
$1 million in pledges, actually raised less than half
that amount despite a warning to contributors that
"without cash, some agencies will be unable to function
beyond the next few weeks." To meet the urgent needs of
local agencies, the Los Angeles Jewish Community Council
borrowed $1.5 million from local banks. And at a UJA
conference in New York, at the end of October, Dr. Nahum
Goldmann warned the delegates that Israel faced a choice
between two crises, "a moral crisis if it stops immigration, or a financial crisis if it goes on with immigration." Carefully choosing his words, Dr. Goldmann
predicted: "If Israel chooses between the two, it will
choose the financial crisis and will not choose the
moral crisis."

His prophetic words gave unexpected emphasis to the
later announcement that the Fall campaign of the UJA had
raised less than $20 million toward its goal of $35 million. Altogether in 1951, UJA had raised $55 million of
which $38 million was allocated to Israel, Edward M.M.
Warburg announced while on a visit to Israel with other
UJA officials. Indicative of Israel's financial problems
was the report in mid-September that the economic advisor, David Horowitz, had left for the United States with
$7 million in American and Canadian securities which he
planned to sell there. The securities had been turned in
by their Israeli owners in exchange for Israel government dollar bonds. By the end of November, however,
Israel disclosed that it had exhausted its frozen
sterling balance and was seeking a loan of L20 million
from the British government.

Some hard-nose observations about Israel and its
neighbors appeared in the **New York Herald Tribune** on
November 23 and 25 under the byline of noted correspondent Stewart Alsop. The Newsletter described his report as "incisive" and unsentimental, and went on to
say:

> Alsop takes no sides, points out that talk
> of peace and cooperation between Arab states
> and Israel at present is "wishful nonsense" and
> "politically dangerous." He notes that Israel
> is "flat broke and getting broker all the
> time," but adds that there will be no economic
> collapse thanks to aid from the American Jewish
> community and U.S. government. Alsop predicts

that to avoid Middle East chaos, the U.S. government will subsidize Israel to the tune of about $100 million a year "for a good many years," and concludes: "It is...in the essential American interest to make it certain and obvious to all concerned that the state of Israel is here to stay."

Equally pessimistic about Israel's financial position was the analysis delivered by Harold Glasser at the General Assembly of the CJFWF in Chicago in December. Glasser, who was the director of the CJFWF Overseas Studies, pointed to the rising imbalance of Israel's exports and imports, and warned the delegates that foreign aid would not be sufficient in 1952 to cover Israel's needs, noting that Israel imported almost six times as much as she exported in 1951. He emphasized that Israel would have to increase the level of her agricultural development tremendously in order to improve her situation.

Dr. Joseph J. Schwartz, the UJA director, who also addressed the Assembly, tried to present a more optimistic picture of Israel's situation, pointing out that the crisis was caused largely by the fact that a number of bank loans had fallen due "almost every day this month, with the largest due on December 10." He announced, however, that UJA had received a total of $75 million in 1951, of which $60 million had been raised that year. Of the remainder, $15 million was collected on 1951 pledges while $6 million of the 1950 pledges and $20 million of 1951 pledges were still outstanding. There was no attempt to reconcile these statistics with the numbers reported earlier in Israel by UJA chairman Edward M.M. Warburg, or to explain why they were different.

The Newsletter compared these and other community statistics, which had been submitted by the CJFWF for inclusion in the **American Jewish Year Book**, volume 53, and offered the following conclusions:

1. Welfare fund drives in 1950 raised $140,500,000, to which New York (i.e., Federation and New York UJA) gave $48.5 million. This total is about 32 percent below the 1948 peak. Estimated total for all community drives in 1950 is $168 million.

2. National agencies--defense, health, welfare, culture, religion and education--had a total income of $20,600,000. Specific agencies were not named in this tabulation.

3. Largest beneficiary of the welfare funds was the "community relations" group, who received $5,897,907 from all funds including the New York UJA. The American Jewish Congress and the World Jewish Congress got $998,018; the Jewish Labor Committee, $800,350; and the Joint Defense Appeal of the ADL and the American Jewish Committee, $3,886,340. The last named agencies also received over $212,000 from non-JDA sources.

4. Largest income went to the religious institutions group, but most of the total of $6,600,000 was raised from congregations and individuals rather than from welfare funds. The total includes the Jewish Theological Seminary for $1,364,800; and the Reform UAHC-HUC for $1,552,019.

5. For the fifth consecutive year, CJFWF failed to give exact figures for UJA. The "Estimates" in the summary and tables are given variously from $77,900,000 to $88 million, with no indication of cash or pledges.

6. The CJFWF also does not provide audited figures for the JDC; gives only meaningless "allocation" statistics.

It should be noted that none of the above statistics as reported in the **American Jewish Year Book** and provided by the CJFWF are audited figures. It is an extraordinary fact that except for the ZOA, to this very day none of the major Jewish organizations, including the UJA, provides audited figures for its collections and expenditures. Since these funds are tax exempt, they are not required by law to report these statistics. This is also true of most synagogues--with only a few exceptions--and is invariably the sad truth about the statistics recorded each year by the **American Jewish Year Book**. Thus, the American Jewish community is never accurately informed about the amount of money it raises, the amount received by the tax-exempt charitable funds or about the way the money is spent. Moreover, the community does not know how much it had been placed in debt to the banks by agencies which borrow funds on the credit of collections they anticipate. For example, the Newsletter disclosed in December 1951 that American Jews owed various American banks between $35 and $45 million, payable in 1952 out of their welfare fund contributions. These funds had been borrowed within the last six months of the year by the UJA and the Independence Bond agency.

Earlier in the year, the Newsletter had offered the following comment on CJFWF responsibility in providing accurate fundraising statistics:

> In tables prepared by the CJFWF on the 1949 receipts of national Jewish agencies (**American Jewish Year Book**, volume 52, p.162), only "estimated pledges" are given for UJA. **Cross-Section, U.S.A.** gave exact cash totals last May for UJA receipts from January 1, 1949 to March 1950, a total of $115,160,571. We also cited total receipts for JDC.
> Our figures, we may reveal, came from the JDC itself! If they existed last May, why couldn't the CJFWF publish something more convincing than "estimated pledges"? Why are audited figures withheld?

There was, of course, no response to our questions. Optimism was the keyword for all Jewish fund raisers that year despite differences between UJA and Israel bonds, and the depressed American economy, which affected all contributions. The Newsletter reported:

> At the weekend conference of the UJA in Atlantic City, a goal of $151,500,000 was adopted. JDC asked for $23.5 million; USNA/NYANA, for $4,048,200--of which USNA would get $779,200 and NYANA, $3,269,000--the remainder is to go to the UPA. The total 1951 funds announced by the UJA, and the 1952 budget figure of UPA should be viewed in the light of the statement by Keren Hayesod chairman Eliahu Dobkin, who said last month that the 1951 income for Israel from UPA "should reach $50 million." Dobkin also pointed out that Israel was planning for only 120,000 immigrants in 1952 (about 200,000 entered this year).
> UJA will open its 1952 drive on February 23 at a Miami Beach "conference." A resolution calling for greater coordination in planning UJA and bond drives remained silent on the acceptance of bonds for UJA pledges. UJA leaders feel they have established the primacy of UJA as the fund raiser for Israel.

Israel bond directors also continued to issue optimistic reports. Israel Finance Minister Eliezer Kaplan was quoted by the **National Jewish Post** at the end of

July as saying that bond sales totaled $75 million, and
that over $30 million had been paid in by 70,000 buyers
of bonds. But in August, ZOA president Benjamin G.
Browdy announced that 40,000 American Jews had bought a
total of $67 million worth of bonds up to that month and
had paid in a total of $27 million. Puzzled by these
statistics, the Newsletter called the AFDCI office and
asked for confirmation of these reported sales. An
authorized spokesman, however, refused to verify Mr.
Browdy's totals and added that his organization would
not release any statistics on sales until the national
conference which it had scheduled for September 20. On
that date, the Newsletter carried the following report:

> In a report to the Israel cabinet, Finance
> Minister Eliezer Kaplan outlined the "expendi-
> tures and appropriations of the first fifty
> million dollars received" from the Independence
> Bond drive in the United States. His statement
> was made in the presence of the bond drive di-
> rector Henry Montor last week.
> Mr. Kaplan's latest statement should be set
> alongside his report in July, when he was
> quoted by the Jewish Agency as saying that the
> bond drive had collected $30 million in cash
> and had total pledges of $75 million. It should
> also be placed alongside the early August re-
> port of ZOA president Benjamin G. Browdy, who
> said $67 million in bonds had been sold, and
> $27 million collected in cash.
> Perhaps, as Mr. Kaplan's report would seem
> to indicate, $20 million or more in cash was
> collected during the vacation month of August
> by Mr. Montor's minions. Perhaps Mr. Browdy's
> figures are inaccurate. But in any case, the
> contributing American public is entitled to
> know the facts. The Independence Bond drive is
> a deadly serious matter, and its results should
> not be juggled around like a theatrical public
> relations stunt.

At the bond conference, held that night in Washington, D.C., what appeared to be the accurate statistics
were finally disclosed. Henry Morgenthau, Jr., president of the bond corporation, announced that Israel had
indeed received $50 million in cash from the bond drive.
However, while the total sale of bonds reached $75 mil-
lion, only $35.5 million had actually been paid for, the
Newsletter reported. Of the $50 million transferred to

Israel, $14,500,000 was a loan granted by the Chase National Bank in New York on the credit of the United Palestine Appeal!

No one bothered to explain that transaction to the assembled delegates, and none of the English Jewish weeklies reported it. But the Newsletter had at least smoked out the basic facts of the bond sales. The Newsletter also observed that several million dollars in expenses--the actual amount remained a deep secret as far as the public was concerned--had been paid out of the total announced sum. In a report at the end of the year, the Newsletter noted that expenses of the bond campaign were rumored to have reached "the fantastically extravagant rate of $600,000 a month," but there was no confirmation of the rumor. An unofficial report, circulated by a CJFWF Assembly at the end of the year, put the total amount raised by the bond campaign in 1951 at about $80 million, with half in cash and $18 million in loans from the banks, borrowed on the collateral of the pledges to buy bonds. But verified statistics were never revealed.

In any case, Israel apparently did receive from the UJA campaign and the sale of bonds, in addition to bank loans, almost $100 million for the year 1951 from the American Jewish community. It unquestionably helped save the young state from bankruptcy though the Israel economic situation continued to be marked by the frantic financing of its ever-growing mountain of debt. Orthodox American Jews had been outraged by the public flouting of **kashruth** regulations by Israel government officials and the bond campaign organizers, but they nevertheless continued to purchase bonds and contribute to UJA. As the following report by the Newsletter in November indicates, bond officials ignored Orthodox protests:

> Protest against the **trefe** [non-kosher] dinner to be given this week by bond drive sponsors in Cleveland, Ohio, was made in the form of an open letter in the current **Jewish Review and Observer**, inserted by Young Israel and Rabbi Shubert Spero. The chief speaker at the dinner is Ambassador Abba Eban. (The protest recalls a similar occurrence last May when Orthodox women in Boston protested a bond drive breakfast [trefe] given in honor of Mrs. David Ben-Gurion.)
>
> At the same time, the Cleveland Jewish weekly editorially criticizes Ambassador Eban for his failure to observe **kashruth**; cites the

Saturday Evening Post article as saying that
"ham sandwiches are served at the [Israel] embassy," and that "this tolerance is generally
true of life in Israel"; notes that when Mrs.
Golda Myerson was the Israeli envoy in Moscow,
she made a point of maintaining a kosher
kitchen there as a matter of principle. The
weekly suggests that Ambassador Eban might do
the same and thus save "a great deal of embarrassment for many of Mr. Eban's co-reli-
gionists in this country."

In sum, however, neither this nor any of the other
problems encountered by the bond campaign in its first
year can be regarded as critical, and in succeeding
years it was possible for both Israel bonds and the UJA
campaigns to be conducted successfully and without conflict. Together they contributed huge sums toward the
financial well-being of Israel.

13

SEARCH FOR A PROGRAM

It is a phenomenon of Jewish community life that its national organizations rarely disappear; somehow they manage to survive decade after decade despite changing leadership and changing circumstances. Such is the case of the American Jewish Joint Distribution Committee as well as its affiliates, USNA and NYANA. By 1951, the function of the JDC in Europe and North Africa was virtually completed, and its efforts to establish new programs in Israel were meeting with increasing competition from other Jewish organizations. Moreover, its European director-general, Dr. Joseph J. Schwartz, was now the director of the UJA and its chairman, Edward M.M. Warburg, was devoting at least half of his time and attention to his new responsibilities as UJA chairman.

Nevertheless, at its annual meeting in New York during the first week in January, Moses A. Leavitt, the executive vice-chairman of the JDC, told delegates that as much as $22,350,000 was still needed in 1951 to assist "at least 400,000 Jews in Europe, Israel and the Moslem countries." Delegates were also told about JDC's projects in the displaced persons camps in Germany and among refugee rabbis in Israel, which included several costly Hebrew publishing ventures. The DP rabbis produced an edition of the Babylonian Talmud, sumptuously printed in two colors, in 19 folio volumes. The edition of 700 sets of the Babylonian Talmud, of which one set each was presented to the Yeshiva University in New York, and to the Jewish division of the New York Public Library, was produced at a cost of $85,000, to which the JDC contributed $35,000 and the U.S. Army, $50,000.

In Israel, the JDC was supporting a group of refugee rabbis who were at work in Jerusalem on the **Otzar Haposkim**, a digest of all rabbinic **Responsa** bearing on Jewish law and ritual. The compendium was supervised by Chief Rabbi I.H. Herzog and was expected to total forty volumes, two of which had already been published. The third volume in preparation was concerned with the problem of the **Agunoth**, which was explained as the problem

217

faced by "wives whose husbands are missing" as the result of war or other disaster. Under Jewish law, certain
procedures must be followed before a woman in that situation can be declared a widow and therefore free to
remarry. JDC's responsibility for the care of the DPs
was summarized by the Newsletter on February 1 in the
following report:

> Fifteen months ago, JDC and the Jewish
> Agency agreed to share a $15 million program to
> rescue 4,000 "hard core" DPs in Germany, among
> them 1,500 tubercular cases. At a press confer-
> ence on November 21, 1949, JDC said that Israel
> needed "at least 1,000 **more** hospital and con-
> valescent home beds to care for them properly."
>   In December 1950, JDC reported that MALBEN
> (the organization created to care for these ill
> and aged DPs) had set up facilities to care for
> 2,500 cases, including a new 500-bed TB hospi-
> tal and a village at Gedara for one hundred
> blind men and their families.
>   At the same time, however, JDC announced
> that it needed $8 million for MALBEN in 1951;
> that it was assuming sole financial respon-
> sibility for the program, which now called for
> 2,000 beds for TB treatment, and new facilities
> to take care of 5,000 persons in addition to
> 1,000 "over age" persons now being cared for
> and 2,500 more it expects in 1951.
>   Any organization that plans to spend 23
> million American dollars in two and half years
> for what was originally said to be 4,000 per-
> sons but which now seems to include all the old
> folks in Israel owes the Jewish community here
> a much fuller explanation than the statistics
> and plans released thus far show.
>   And, incidentally, why does this Israel job
> have to be assigned to the JDC?

Two weeks later, the Newsletter observed that no
explanation of JDC's role in MALBEN had been forthcoming. It also noted that despite the intent to limit
MALBEN's treatment of tuberculosis to "hard-core" DP
cases, Israeli organizations were referring all their
tubercular patients to MALBEN. The result was that
MALBEN soon found itself without sufficient funds to
provide all the arrested cases of tubercular DPs with
the follow-up care necessary to prevent a recurrence of
the disease. Consequently many such cases were forced to

return to the hospital within six months of their release. What had not been made public, however, was the
fact that MALBEN's authority had been expanded to include in addition the care of all the aged and invalid
immigration cases, particularly those from North African
and Middle Eastern countries. To meet this new burden,
MALBEN's 1952 budget was raised accordingly to "well
over $10 million," according to its director, Charles
Passman. All of its funds were obtained from the JDC.

Meanwhile, despite statements to the contrary from
the JDC as well as the Jewish Agency, immigrants continued to be brought in from North Africa, though more
selectively and in smaller numbers. Nevertheless, the
Libyan Jewish community leaders complained that Israel
was refusing to admit as "hard-core" cases about one
thousand aged and sick Libyan Jews. A report in the
Jewish Chronicle (London) noted that only a few Tripoli-
tanian Jews in this category had been admitted to Israel
because they were required to provide maintenance
guarantees. Moreover, under the MALBEN program, European
"hard-core" refugees were given priority. In this connection, Israeli sources disclosed that the Jews of
Libya had invested over $1.5 million in Israeli industry
and transport, a report obviously intended to show that
the Libyan community was well able to care for its own
indigent members.

Questions about expenditures for immigration to the
United States were raised also in connection with the
USNA and NYANA, as the following report in the Newslet-
ter early in January indicates:

> Although six times as many Catholic DPs
> reached the United States in 1950 as Jewish
> DPs, the USNA spent over ten times as much as
> the Catholic War Relief Services, an investiga-
> tion by **Cross-Section,U.S.A.** disclosed this
> week.
>
> Official statistics provided by the War
> Relief Services show that for 72,635 Catholic
> DPs, only $208,675 was spent in 1950.
>
> Statistics provided by the Church World
> Service, which performs a comparable function
> for Protestants, show $405,000 spent for 19,390
> DPs in 1950. (Both services arrange for spon-
> sors in advance; inland transportation is paid
> for by these sponsors who are later reimbursed
> out of wages earned by the DPs.)
>
> **United Service for New Americans** spent
> **over $3 million for less than 12,000 DPs who**

arrived in 1950. (Of the 12,000 arrivals, some were serviced by HIAS while others went directly to relatives.)

THESE COMPARATIVE COSTS INDICATE THAT A FULL-SCALE INVESTIGATION OF USNA IS LONG OVERDUE.

To the delegates attending USNA's annual meeting in New York, January 20-21, we respectfully submit these verified statistics of Catholic and Protestant costs. **Our request to USNA for its figures has not been answered to date.** (To test the willingness of the respective agencies to disclose their figures, a telephone request was made in each case.)

For 1951, USNA is presenting Jewish communities with a bill for $7,288,577 in expectation of 20,000 immigrants.

For 1951, Church World Service (Protestant) has budgeted $485,000 for 30,000-35,000 anticipated arrivals.

Communities which allocate additional funds (over $300,000 in Newark, N.J., for example) for resettlement of DPs owe their contributors an answer for USNA's waste of UJA communal funds. Next week's annual meeting is as good a place as any for UJA leaders to start explaining.

Earlier issues of the Newsletter had frequently questioned USNA's expenditures for housing and resettling Jewish refugees, but this survey marked the first attempt to assemble all the facts and compare them with a parallel operation by the Catholic and Protestant agencies. The report was published to coincide with the annual conference of the UJA and it created almost as dramatic a sensation as the Newsletter's expose of the MacIver Report. In my letter to Leftwich, I described what I had done in the following manner:

"The fat is in the fire; I'm stirring up the witch's brew--mix in a few more metaphors and you'll begin to have some idea of the explosion I created with my USNA story in the January 11 number. From coast to coast, the repercussions have been felt, and the end is not yet in sight. I've already scored one notable victory, and there are more to come.

"The victory is USNA's apology for not giving me the facts when I asked for them, and the submission of its financial report. NYANA is also eager to give me all the facts it can (as long as I try to shift the blame elsewhere), and the facts are shocking beyond belief. I'm going to blast the whole DP scandal out into the open and force an investigation; there's been a fantastic waste of money--how many millions we'll never really know--in 'resettling' immigrants here. At a rough guess, I would say that close to $15 million was spent in 1950 for about 10,000 immigrants; it's impossible to get exact figures anywhere. That's one of the things wrong with the way our professionals handle the public's money.

"Now I'm going to hang on to this DP story as long as I can shock our good citizens into action. When that shows signs of beginning to pall, I'll throw in a shocker about the Joint and the money it is spending for MALBEN. Eventually the boys in Israel may get wise to the fact that the philanthropy spree at American expense is over; but if they don't, don't be too surprised if an accounting of funds is requested from the Jewish Agency and the CJFWF."

The Treasurer's Report of USNA was not only delivered to the Newsletter, it was printed in the report of the annual meeting of the USNA, which was held at the Hotel Roosevelt in New York on January 20-21. It showed among other facts that 15,000 Jewish immigrants arrived in the United States in 1950, but that USNA handled only about 9,500, of whom 7,479 came in under the DP act. In 1950, USNA spent a total of $2,341,126, of which $675,714 was expended for "Port Reception Services and Temporary Assistance." For 1951, USNA budgeted for the same service only $371,550, although it anticipated the arrival of about 20,000 immigrants. USNA's total budget request for 1951 was $1,580,800, and it explained the sharp drop in these budget estimates as stemming largely from "the discontinuance of settlement payments to communities, the transfer to the local NYANA of the New York shelter operation and...the discontinuance of the national shelter."

A better perspective on expenditures for settlement was provided by William Rosenwald, honorary president of USNA, when he told a UJA conference in December 1950 that for the next year USNA "would have to spend $7,288,577 to carry out its program." According to a UJA spokesman, Rosenwald meant by this figure--and UJA had been using it ever since--to include only $1,580,000 for USNA and $5,707,777 for NYANA. UJA had lumped these two amounts together because, they said, it was "simpler" to explain them to the public this way. What the spokesman did not comment on was the fact that heretofore the UJA had told contributors that there were only three benefi-

ciaries of the campaign, namely, UPA, JDC, and USNA; now
apparently there were four. To which the Newsletter observed: "We are simple enough to believe that the public
would rather have all the facts, including the arrangements whereby national UJA now admits to at least four
major beneficiaries instead of the advertised three."

One of the Newsletter's readers, Maxwell Abbell, a
prominent Chicago attorney and accountant, and the newly
elected president of the United Synagogue of America
(Conservative), expressed great indignation over the
expose of USNA's financial arrangements in a letter to
the Newsletter. He wrote that "the figures you include
in your article tell only part of the story. Many
cities, like New York and Chicago, have their own separate appropriations for the refugees out of the local
combined appeals. I know that we do in Chicago. I don't
believe these figures get into the grand totals at all."
Abbell's indignation was completely justified, as
the Newsletter was quick to admit. Additional inquiries
by the Newsletter on the basis of Abbell's complaint
resulted in the disclosure that "no Jewish organization
has either a grand total or even an estimate of the
amount of money spent for immigrant resettlement here by
our local and national agencies in 1950 or 1949!" The
best figure that the Newsletter could come up with was
that USNA and NYANA together had spent a total of almost
$12 million in 1950, a truly shocking expenditure for
the relatively small number of immigrants serviced by
these organizations. Charging that communal funds had
been squandered irresponsibly, the Newsletter reported:

> Here are some facts which show that the
> problem is larger than the efficiency of a par-
> ticular organization:
> 1. USNA claims that it spent $675,714 in
> 1950 for "Port Reception Services" (for 1951's
> anticipated 20,000 immigrants, USNA has bud-
> geted for the same service only $371,550). Per
> capita cost for the 10,000 arrivals in 1950 is
> thus $67.57 approximately (not counting the
> services volunteered by 150 members of the
> National Council of Jewish Women), spent for
> meeting the immigrant, collecting his baggage,
> seeing him through customs and shipping him off
> to his destination.
> In Israel, the cost per capita is only
> $18.20 for disembarkation, transportation to
> and maintenance for ten days in Shaar Aliya--
> the clearance center. Services include regis-

tration, screening, medical examination and vocational counseling (this information is from a
UJA bulletin entitled, "1951 budgetary needs").
A USNA spokesman had no ready answer to our
query for the difference in cost--$67.57
against $18.50--as well as service, even if all
other differences between the two countries
were to be taken into account.

2. Before the establishment of NYANA, it
was USNA practice to maintain supervision over
immigrants for a period of five years, including cash relief in some instances over the
entire period!

3. NYANA has provided the statistics presented below. From July 5, 1949 (when it was
organized), to June 30, 1950, NYANA discloses
expenditures of $11,707,055 for 30,800
immigrants.

For the 1950 calendar year, NYANA claims it
spent $9,655,926 for 29,932 immigrants, of whom
25,750 got weekly relief checks--about $25 per
family (2.6 persons) per week.

NYANA begins 1951 with "6,888 newcomers of
whom 5,166" get cash relief up to one year;
expects 9,300 new clients in 1951; and wants
$5,700,777 to cover its costs. It claims that
almost any European immigrant (except France,
Great Britain, etc.) whether DP or not, has a
right to get NYANA help, including direct relief; points out that only about half of the
immigrants are "persuaded" to settle outside
New York City.

4. NYANA's entire operation, including
staff, social workers, etc., is entirely separate and distinct from the New York Federation
of Jewish Philanthropies, which was recently
described by the **New York Times** as "the largest
network of allied social work institutions in
the world working on behalf of the people in a
single city." Federation's agencies (which collected over $24 million last year, and seek $20
million this year) won't touch an immigrant
until he has lived here at least one year (it
formerly was five).

**Thus, Jews of New York City enjoy the
luxury of two distinct charity setups--at a
total cost in 1950 of more than $36 million!**

5. Although the International Refugee
Organization (IRO) is scheduled to wind up its

affairs by June 30, neither USNA nor NYANA
expects to be "going out of business" for some
years to come.
Explanations, no doubt, will be forthcoming
and voluminous. **But they cannot explain away
the flagrant duplication, lack of central
planning and extravagant waste of communal
funds** shown by the facts uncovered thus far by
Cross-Section, U.S.A.
WHAT IS YOUR COMMUNITY GOING TO DO ABOUT
IT?

The Newsletter's expose may have caused concern in
some quarters of Jewish community leadership, but there
was no immediate public response to the Newsletter's
challenge. After the disappointing MacIver experience,
however, I was skeptical about whether there would be
any substantial reform in this instance. What change
there was in succeeding years may or may not be entirely
attributed to the Newsletter's efforts, but there was
some change. USNA was eventually merged with HIAS to
form the United HIAS Service, which is still a beneficiary of the UJA. But NYANA has managed to justify its
separate existence, supported by New York UJA, because
allegedly more than half of the Jewish immigrants decide
to stay in New York City.
My discouragement and doubts about the effectiveness
of the Newsletter's disclosures were expressed in my
letter to Leftwich on January 26, in which I said: "Now,
my final (I hope) blast at the refugee situation here
has been written and next week I shall try to relax a
bit. Whether some good will come of the row I've raised
or whether the whole business will be double-talked to
death is still a moot question. It all depends on how
many questions are raised throughout the country and who
raises them. A certain number are expected and the public relations staffs of USNA and NYANA are both ready
and waiting with a full barrage of the neatest and
slickest double-talk you ever heard. I suspect, though,
that the Zionists may hop on the issue in order to get
more money for their funds."
This time, however, there was much more of a reaction to the immigration scandal than I had anticipated.
The veteran Zionist, Dr. Samuel Margoshes, in his
English column in the **Tog** of January 27, took the USNA
to task, though without referring to the Newsletter as
his source, because it "expects to spend this year more
than a million and a half; that is still a huge sum for
work that HIAS has conducted for years very efficiently

at a much smaller expense. To me, the whole idea of two organizations handling the same task, where no ideological differences are involved, seems a waste of good money and energy. Why wasn't HIAS permitted to handle the problem in the first place?"

It was a question that many were beginning to ask with increasing frequency. In fact, however, negotiations between USNA and HIAS had been initiated the previous year but had got nowhere primarily because HIAS had insisted, quite understandably, on maintaining its identity, among other reasons. USNA's reaction to the Newsletter's expose was, as I had anticipated, largely an evasion of the problems that were revealed. An advance report in the Newsletter on February 15 included the following comment:

> United Service for New Americans and UJA are issuing a "Memorandum on Cross-Section Articles on Jewish Immigration" to persons requesting it, which purports to present "verifiable facts" as answers, **Cross-Section, U.S.A.** learned this week. The memorandum takes special issue with Catholic and Protestant statistics, accuses **Cross-Section, U.S.A.** of inaccuracy and failure to obtain all the facts, then proceeds to present a series of half truths in rebuttal. Examples of USNA's current distortions:
> 1. USNA employs statistics from the DP Commission to refute our statement based on Catholic War Relief Services (WRS) telegram that--and we quote from the telegram--"WRS-NCWC HAS BROUGHT HERE 72,635 DPs AT A COST OF $408,675 REPRESENTING 35% OF THE GRAND TOTAL BROUGHT HERE UNDER IRO AUSPICES." USNA does not tell readers that the DP Commission's figures do **not** include all war-victim immigrants--for example, the DP Commission's figure of Jewish immigrants for 1950 is only 10,352 (of which USNA handled only 7,479 and HIAS the remainder). Total Jewish immigrants numbered 15,000.
> 2. In citing Catholic and Protestant expenditures, USNA fails to point out that aid for needy persons in Korea is included in the totals. To document the statistics used in our reports, we are prepared to furnish copies of WRS telegram and Church World Service letters as well as USNA's 1950 financial report (unaudited) and 1951 budget to anyone on request.

3. USNA's honorary president William Rosenwald first used the figure of $7,288,577 as USNA's share of the 1951 UJA and the UJA conference last December, and the UJA has been using it ever since. We humbly suggest to UJA to use an adding machine on the sums it now allocates to USNA and NYANA. UJA will find that its figure of $7,288,577 as the total is $7,000 more than the organizations asked for.

Undeterred by USNA's "Memorandum," the Newsletter continued to attack the reliability of the statistics issued by the agency and by NYANA as part of its overall effort to compel Jewish agencies to issue audited reports annually. When the CJFWF **Social Service Yearbook** was published later that year, for example, the Newsletter was quick to point out that while NYANA was credited with spending "nearly" $6,900,000 for immigrant aid in 1950, NYANA itself the previous January had claimed that it had spent $9,655,926 for 29,932 immigrants in 1950. The Newsletter had no explanation for the discrepancy in the figures, but went on to add that fifty communities outside New York had spent an additional $2.5 million on direct aid for these immigrants and that USNA had spent almost $3 million, while HIAS had spent a smaller sum--all apparently for the same number of new arrivals.

A much more drastic impact on USNA/NYANA than the Newsletter's reports was made by news of the suspension of the International Refugee Organization, and the realization that it was scheduled to close out all its activities by the end of the year. Arthur Greenleigh, director of USNA, made a special trip to Europe to investigate the problems affecting the remaining displaced persons that would be created by the closing of the IRO. And at the regional conference of the CJFWF in Memphis in October, associate director of that organization, Philip Bernstein, predicted that local community planning would be sharply affected by "the decline in immigration to the United States with the entry of displaced persons to end in June 1952." He also called attention to the impending changes that would take place in Jewish family welfare agencies "whose services in the past several years have concentrated largely on aid to immigrants." When the Newsletter called the offices of USNA and NYANA, however, their spokesmen said that they had no knowledge of any "impending changes" in their agencies.

A week later, the Newsletter was able to attribute to a reliable source the information that four top exe-

cutives of the NYANA had received notices that their
jobs would be terminated by February 1, 1952, and that
NYANA itself might be shut down by midsummer of that
year. One unnamed executive had already resigned, the
Newsletter said, and pointed out that the contract which
Louis Bennett, the head of NYANA, had signed when he
undertook the responsibility of directing the agency in
July 1949, was for only three years and therefore was
due to expire in July 1952. Bennett was quite frank in
explaining the situation when we interviewed him, and
the Newsletter summarized our talk in the following
report:

> NYANA will **not** suspend operations on July
> 1, 1952, but talks are going on with other
> agencies over which one will take on the re-
> sponsibility for immigrant resettlement in the
> New York area after NYANA does close, Louis
> Bennett, executive head of NYANA, told **Cross-
> Section, U.S.A.** after correcting our report
> last week. Among the organizations being con-
> sidered are HIAS, National Council of Jewish
> Women, Jewish Family Service, and the New York
> Federation of Jewish Philanthropies, Mr. Ben-
> nett added. The major obstacle in the takeover
> is the question of cash relief which NYANA pro-
> vides for a maximum period of one year.
> The proposed terminal date for NYANA is
> December 1952, but it may be extended if the
> immigration rate continues heavy, Mr. Bennett
> explained. He said that 15,000-16,000 would
> enter under the DP act this year, a greater
> total than last year. Although IRO expires on
> December 31, 1951, DPs will be entering the
> United States under the present act until the
> end of June 1952.

As we have noted in the above report, the inability
of the agencies handling immigration to reach an agreement on the question of cash relief led to the decision
to continue NYANA indefinitely, with funding provided by
UJA. Since this would lead to an increase in the American share of UJA proceeds, complaints soon began to be
heard from Israel. In Jerusalem, the head of the Jewish
Agency, Berl Locker, accused American Jewry of not doing
enough to help Israel and added that their donations
were not a form of charity but a responsibility which
they shared with all the Jewish people for the "ingathering of the exiles." There was never a possibility

of imposing any compulsory fundraising, Locker said, but American Jews should regard themselves in the same light as citizens of Israel in the discharge of their responsibility in this matter.

Similar comments came from Eliahu Dobkin, also a member of the Jewish Agency, who blamed the drop in funds from the United States on the "race" among Jewish communities to build luxurious Jewish civic centers. He alleged that the local communities retained 56 percent of the funds raised in this country in 1950, whereas in 1947, they had reserved only 20 percent. In another Israel reaction, however, a call for a strict censorship on pessimistic reports about American fundraising was made by Israel Schen in the Zionist **Newsletter** of December 26, 1950. Schen recommended that a ban be placed on "gloomy appraisals of future prospects" for UJA and other Zionist fundraising appeals, and also on discouraging reports of prospects for **chalutziut**. He argued: "The prospects ... should be regarded as inside information: no word should leak out to the general public....As far as the mass of contributors is concerned, the prospects are invariably excellent; the target will be attained."

While this strategy was generally followed by fundraisers, not even Henry Montor would have been so brash as to call openly for censorship of adverse reports. One prominent editor of an English Jewish weekly, however, frankly admitted that he did suppress news that might have a negative effect on fundraising drives. The Newsletter indignantly reported his admission in the following comment:

> When the publisher and editor of an influential English Jewish weekly, which is proud of its independence as well as of its national circulation (14,599 in its official report), frankly admits suppressing news allegedly for the good of the community, and literally turning over to local campaign directors its local editions "to handle the news the way they think it will most stimulate sacrificial giving"-- that's news!!
>
> The publisher is Gabriel Cohen; the weekly is the **National Jewish Post**. In the "Editor's Chair" of June 22, Mr. Cohen openly confesses yielding to UJA pressure not to publish news "showing where drives were flopping." Fearing to trust the American Jewish public with the facts, Editor Cohen explains that in his opin-

ion publication of unfavorable trends in giving would harm local drives all over the country. **"We know about it, but we do not publish it,"** he admits.

Such censorship makes Editor Cohen unhappy, and he therefore notes: "The question warrants discussion, perhaps by the American Association of English Jewish publishers so that something more definitive can be arrived at."

Like not publishing any account of the MacIver Report, Mr. Cohen?

Fortunately, the national UJA decided that more rather than less information was a far more rewarding tactic. It invited nine journalists to tour Israel as the guests of the UJA with the hope that on their return they would publish their impressions of Israel, with special emphasis, naturally, on the good works to which the UJA funds were put. The Newsletter listed the journalists on this initial venture as George Carroll of the **New York Journal American;** Harry B. Wilson, **St. Louis Globe Democrat;** G.S. Davidson, **Boston Post;** Dixon Preston, **Cleveland Press;** Max Wiener, **Newark News;** David Carno, **Chicago Sun-Times;** Richard Pierce, **San Francisco Examiner;** and George Cassidy, **Brooklyn Eagle.** They were the first of a continuing list of American newsmen who were invited by the UJA to see Israel first-hand.

The practice did not go unopposed. The first to raise a question was the venerable Dr. Samuel Margoshes of the **Tog,** who expressed approval of the UJA junket for journalists, but then unabashedly went on to complain: "What's the matter with Yiddish newspapermen? Why weren't they included?" He was not alone in recognizing a good thing; within the week there was an editorial in the **National Jewish Post** headlined, "Why Not Anglo-Jewish Newspapermen, Too?" Apparently, the UJA placed the English Jewish weeklies in a separate category, because free trips to Israel were subsequently given to at least four men from each of the Yiddish dailies, including Dr. Margoshes and Mordecai Danzis, editor of the **Tog,** but none from the other group.

Obviously, the UJA has found the free-trips-to-Israel program worth the expenditure because it has been continued to this day. So, too, have the UJA beneficiaries, which have remained substantially unchanged. The JDC continues to operate an expanded MALBEN program in Israel while going on with its search for new areas to service. NYANA is still helping refugees and Russian immigrants who choose to settle in New York's metropoli-

tan area. Only USNA is gone, for it has been merged with
HIAS to form a vastly enlarged United HIAS Service, with
the task of helping Jewish immigrants on a world-wide
basis. No one is trying to find out--as far as we know--
what the overall cost of resettling the estimated 55,000
Russian immigrants in all the American communities has
totalled thus far.

14

THE JEWISH AGENCY TAKES CHARGE

"Within a period of two months, there were and are being held in this country thirteen (count 'em, 13) national conventions and conferences relating in whole or in part to Israel and Zionist affairs. Most, if not all, of the delegates to all these conferences and conventions are the same individuals. The cost of these perpetual, endless, duplicating, overlapping and repetitious conferences, figures for which are never made public ... must be enormous. The cost in manpower, lost motion and wasted energy is beyond calculation....How vain can people be to have their pictures (the very same pictures) printed over and over again?...Poor Mr. Everyman, who stays home and for whom these planners and conferees are perpetually planning and conferring, is bewildered and stunned by the plethora of words, pleas, 'blueprints,' plans, slogans, appeals, exhortations, denunciations and commands...."

The anonymous complainant, quoted by the Newsletter, was the author of "Ben David's Views," a column which appeared in the **B'nai Zion Voice** of January 1951. As its name implies, B'nai Zion is a fraternal Zionist organization which, among its activities, provides its membership with life and health insurance as well as an opportunity to sponsor various projects in Israel. Ben David's exasperation with Jewish communal activities reflected a rising tide of public impatience with the multiplicity of Jewish organizations and the consequent duplication and waste. His complaint, moreover, may have also served to prepare Zionists for some of the drastic proposals for change and amalgamation which were on the agenda of the Jewish Agency. At an executive session in Jerusalem at the beginning of the year, Jewish Agency heads discussed plans for the future of the Keren Hayesod (Palestine Foundation Fund) and the Keren Kayemeth (Jewish National Fund), whose amalgamation had frequently been discussed. Both organizations were holdovers from pre-state days and had served to provide

231

the Yishuv with essential funds. The JNF, in particular, had built a huge constituency by placing distinctive blue and white tin boxes for small coin collections in thousands of Jewish homes. The money thus donated was used to purchase land from the Arabs and to plant trees in the denuded hills of Israel. Since this function could now be taken over by the state, the merging of the JNF into the Keren Hayesod was recommended by Dr. Nahum Goldmann, chairman of the Jewish Agency. The entire matter was referred to a special committee for further study and reported to the World Zionist Congress, which had the power of final decision.

In the hierarchy of Zionist organizations, the Keren Hayesod served as the beneficiary of the UPA (later renamed the United Israel Appeal) and in turn distributed the funds it received according to the directions of the Jewish Agency. The machinery for Zionist fund collection and distribution had developed on an ad hoc basis as special needs arose over the years of Palestine colonization and settlement, but as organizations outgrew their functions, there was an increasing reluctance to dissolve them in part because of the sympathetic allegiance of their followers and in part also out of a sense of loyalty to the dedicated men and women who had created these organizations and directed them over the years. The Zionist funds had made no provision for retirement of staff or for pensions.

The Jewish Agency was itself an anachronism in the year 1951, and as the following Newsletter report discloses, also came under fire:

> Almost unnoticed in the American Jewish press has been a revolution in Israel's immigrant absorption and settlement policy, which went into effect on December 1, 1950. On that date, the Israel Army took over from the Jewish Agency the responsibility of caring for immigrants in the new **ma'abaroth**, work villages, of which 56 are permanent settlements and 52 are assembly points near towns. Another 28 **ma'abaroth** are being organized at present.
>
> Current plans are to leave the Army in control until April 1, 1951. This leaves the Jewish Agency without another of the great tasks assigned to it last year, the first to be taken away being immigrant housing. The action recalls the statement of Prime Minister David Ben-Gurion last April that immigration and absorption were the work of the state, not the

World Zionist Organization or the Jewish
Agency. It also recalls the forecast by Israel
Schen, editor of the **Zionist Newsletter**, that
month, casting doubt on the future of the Jewish Agency and describing it as an anomaly.

As we have noted in an earlier chapter, the Jewish
Agency was originally created to accommodate American
non-Zionist leaders like Louis Marshall who wanted to
work with the Zionists toward the establishment of a
Jewish state but did not want to be associated with the
World Zionist Organization or any of the Zionist groups.
After the establishment of the state, its leadership and
essential functions became identical with those of the
WZO. Unlike the JNF, however, which managed to survive
because of the appeals and demands of its large number
of loyal contributors who remembered with nostalgia the
household collection boxes of their childhood days, the
Jewish Agency had no constituency to plead for its
survival. It did, however, have in the person of the
head of the American section, Dr. Nahum Goldmann, one of
the most extraordinary personalities in the history of
contemporary Zionism. And it undoubtedly owed its survival through this period to his efforts.

Nahum Goldmann may best be described as an international Zionist statesman. He was born in Lithuania in
1895 and was given a traditional Jewish education before
he went off to Heidelberg University, in Germany. There
he studied philosophy and law, and eventually received
his Doctor of Laws degree. He became an ardent Zionist
as a result of his associations at the university, and
in 1913, he was invited to go to Palestine with a group
of his fellow Jewish students. He went intending to stay
four weeks and remained for five months. In his autobiography, subtitled **Sixty Years of Jewish Life,** which
was published in 1969, he described the impact that this
first visit to the Holy Land made upon him. His life
thereafter, except for a brief period after World War I,
was devoted to Zionist activities. He was the representative of the WZO to the League of Nations; he played an
active role in the negotiations leading up to the independence of Israel; and he was also closely associated
with Rabbi Stephen S. Wise in the leadership of the
World Jewish Congress.

Dr. Goldmann became actively involved in Zionist
negotiations with the U.S. State Department, according
to Dr. Emanuel Neumann, only after Rabbi Abba Hillel
Silver took over the direction of the American Zionist
Emergency Council. "Goldmann took to that like a fish to

water," said Neumann in his own autobiography. "What interested and attracted him most were the occasions for negotiations--a field in which he considered himself a past master."

And it was as the chief negotiator not only with the United States but also with the Federal Republic of Germany over the restitution that was to be made to Israel and to the individual Jews who had survived the Nazi holocaust that Goldmann made his greatest contribution. He had succeeded Rabbi Silver as head of the American section of the Jewish Agency but at the same time had retained his position as president of the World Jewish Congress. Based on the authority of both offices, he was able to claim, and succeeded in getting German agreement to pay, substantial compensation for the Jewish property the Nazi's had confiscated. At this critical time in Israel's economic situation, he was successful in obtaining millions of German marks and considerable machinery and other equipment for Israel.

To represent all Jewish organizations which also had claims against Germany, Goldmann helped to organize the Jewish Restitution Successor Organization (JRSO). Agreement was reached that the Jewish Agency would receive 67 percent and the JDC 33 percent of the compensation the German government would pay for heirless Jewish property. In 1950, JRSO collected over eight million Deutsche marks, of which one and one-half million marks had been paid by the Bremen State government and the equivalent of $5,800,000 by the State of Hesse, an amount believed to be about one-third of the estimated full value of the confiscated property. The Orthodox Agudath Israel, which was one of the constituent organizations of the JRSO, demanded that 20 percent of the JRSO proceeds should be turned over to a "Torah Fund in Memory of the Victims of Nazi Persecution." This fund, according to Dr. Isaac Levin, chairman of the Agudath Israel and a vice president of the JRSO, was to be used for the support of religious institutions and immigrant children's homes in Israel. Dr. Levin's proposal was supported by all of the American Orthodox groups. Another demand for a similar percentage of the JRSO proceeds was made by the Council for Protection of the Rights and Interests of Jews from Germany.

Faced with these and other claims, Dr. Goldmann decided to call a conference in New York under the auspices of the Jewish Agency that would fix a common policy on the numerous claims of Jews and of Israel against Germany. It was also hoped that the conference would unite on a program that would influence the Bonn government to take stronger steps to combat an increase in anti-Semitism in Germany. Dr. Goldmann made it clear that the conference would not go beyond the scope of its immediate program when he said: "It would be insulting to the memory of the six million Jews slain by the Nazis, and an insult to the dignity and self-respect of the Jewish people to imagine that less than a decade after the greatest crime in history, the Jewish people would even consider normalizing relations with Germany."

Among the twenty major organizations from seven countries, including Israel, that took part in the conference were the American Jewish Committee, the American Jewish Congress, the Jewish Labor Committee, the World Jewish Congress, the Agudath Israel, the American Zionist Council, the B'nai B'rith, the Jewish War Veterans and the Synagogue Council. The JDC sent observers. Dr. Goldmann made it clear that the "conference cannot in any way commit the Jewish people with regard to other aspects of the German problem."

On the question of what course to follow in the event that German Chancellor Konrad Adenauer were to make an overall indemnification offer, the conference decided to insist on satisfaction for all Jewish and Israeli claims for losses inflicted by the Nazis. Two committees were set up to plan and take action if the situation were to develop along anticipated lines. However, the conference failed to make what became the critical decision: whether the American Jewish Committee or the Jewish Agency was to be the spokesman for all Jewish claims other than those made by the Israel government. Instead, it set up an executive committee to arrive at a decision that was made up of 12 members, among them Dr. Nahum Goldman, Dr. Israel Goldstein, Dr. N. Barou--all leaders of the World Jewish Congress--and Rabbi Irving Miller, of the American Jewish Congress, thus giving the World Jewish Congress representatives virtual dominance over the committee.

Shortly after the conclusion of this conference, Dr. Goldmann left for a meeting in London to arrange for a conference of the WJC. While there, he met Chancellor Adenauer for the first time. Unfortunately, no details about the conversation between the two men were included in the Israel radio newscast which reported the meeting. Just prior to this meeting, Dr. Goldmann had met with U.S. High Commissioner John J. McCloy in Bonn and had told him about the conference of the Jewish organizations in New York and about Israel's demand for $1.5 billion in German compensation. In that connection, the Newsletter reported:

Despite the Israel government ban on anything German, Dr. Nahum Goldmann, head of the
American section of the Jewish Agency, recently purchased German machinery for Israel
with Restitution Marks, an exclusive report to
Cross-Section, U.S.A. said this week. Described
in England as a "leader of American Jewry," Dr.
Goldmann, who is also president of the World
Jewish Congress, has been urging the Israel
government to authorize the WJC to negotiate
with the Bonn government for a cash settlement
of Jewish claims, estimated in the United
States zone alone to total over 150 million
marks. (Dr. Goldmann may have used some of the
3 million Restitution Marks blocked by the
Allies, over whose release he had negotiated
last month with the U.S. High Commissioner John
J. McCloy, for the purchase.)

It was in March, shortly after this agreement, that
the Israel government filed a claim with the United
States, Great Britain, France and the USSR for overall
reparations from Germany in the amount of $1.5 billion,
based on the cost to Israel of resettling 500,000 European Jewish survivors of the Holocaust. Israel claimed
that the total value of the property seized by the Nazis
from the German Jews was estimated at $6 billion and
suggested that the payments be made over a period of
years and partially in manufactured products. Also in
securing reparations from Germany, the JRSO sought to
act as quickly as possible because Dr. Goldmann had
reason to believe that the Allies were about to restore
German independence as part of its arrangement with the
Soviet Union.
With the prestige gained from his successful negotiations for restitution, and in his capacity as head of
the American section of the Jewish Agency, Dr. Goldmann
was able to give that organization a new lease on life,
and it is very likely that his activities warded off the
threat of its dissolution at this time. A strong personality, Dr. Goldmann also did not hesitate at times to
take matters in his own hands and act on his own responsibility, a practice which frequently exposed him to
criticism. Thus, when he signed an agreement with the
WJC in his capacity as head of the Jewish Agency to give
the WJC a share in Jewish Agency funds on condition that
it cease fundraising activities in all countries except
Canada, South Africa and the United States, the American
Jewish community and the press remained silent, but he

was met with a barrage of criticism from the Jewish com-
munity of Great Britain. The London **Jewish Chronicle**
made no bones about its displeasure over the conflict of
interest that it saw in the deal, and in an editorial on
February 16, it said:
"The similitude of reciprocity need deceive no one.
As far as this country is concerned, if the Joint
Palestine Appeal is to be transformed into a United
Jewish Appeal, then the decision is one for the Anglo-
Jewish community to take; there is no case for giving
one Diaspora organization a 'cut' off the proceeds of
Israeli appeals. If the World Jewish Congress were to be
so privileged, then the Board of Deputies (and its coun-
terparts in other countries) which work in a similar
sphere, would also be entitled to a share. Self-inter-
est and its constitutional link with the Agency should
impel the Board of Deputies at least to elicit the facts
about the proposed arrangements; and it has the higher
and more compelling duty of acting as Anglo-Jewry's
watchdog in this matter."
After reporting the editorial, the Newsletter commented that at a previous press conference, Dr. Goldmann
had unequivocally insisted that "it was the prerogative
of the Jewish Agency to decide how the proceeds of the
various Joint Palestine Appeals should be allocated."
The Newsletter also added that the Jewish Agency was not
required to clear any of its grants with any higher
authority and could act entirely on its own responsibility, which in effect meant giving Dr. Goldmann almost
dictatorial powers over vast sums of money. It was in
the exercise of this power, for instance, that Dr. Goldmann "loaned" the JTA $110,000, a loan which the private
news agency up to that time had not repaid.
At a press conference in the last week of March, Dr.
Goldmann disclosed that the Knesset, Israel's parlia-
ment, would be asked to approve a bill giving the Jewish
Agency legal status in connection with immigration,
absorption and resettlement in Israel--in effect, a
power similar to the one that the ZOA had previously
requested in vain. The bill, which Dr. Goldmann said had
the advance approval of all Israeli political parties,
would mean that all programs of American and other overseas Jewish organizations operating in Israel would have
to be coordinated with and secure the advance approval
of the Jewish Agency. No organization would be permitted
to work in Israel without the consent of the Agency, Dr.
Goldmann explained. In addition, the name of the Agency
would be changed to Jewish Agency for Israel, and an
enlarged Joint Development Authority would be set up to

include government and Jewish Agency representatives. In
response to a question, Dr. Goldmann said that although
the World Zionist Organization and the Jewish Agency
were identical, legal status was being given only to the
Jewish Agency because its structure permitted participation by non-Zionist organizations.

At the same press conference, Dr. Goldmann responded
to a question about the controversial deal he had made
with the WJC by saying that he could not see what all the
fuss was about since the arrangement was no different
from the one he had made with Agudath Israel in 1950
under which that organization received $1 million in
lieu of its own campaign. The WJC agreement, like the
one with the Agudath Israel which was not renewed, was
for one year. At the same time, the Newsletter disclosed
that the Palestine Foundation Fund, acting on the request of the Israel government which was forwarded
through Dr. Goldmann, borrowed $10 million from the
Manufacturers Trust Company in New York, of which half
was retained by the Jewish Agency and the other $5
million was given to the Israeli Agriculture Minister
Pinhas Lavon for the purchase of certain basic com-
modities from American companies.

Despite this and other frantic finance arrangements,
the economic situation in Israel continued to grow more
desperate from day to day. Zionist leaders finally
decided to appeal to the U.S. Congress for additional
help. In March, Senator Irving M. Ives, Republican, of
New York, told the annual meeting of HIAS that a group
of senators was drafting a bill under which Israel would
receive a substantial grant-in-aid from the United
States. And a few weeks later, it was learned that Representative John W. McCormack, Democrat, of Massachu-
setts, a powerful friend of Israel for more than twenty
years, had introduced a bill authorizing a grant-in-aid
for Israel of $150 million. In the Senate, an identical
bill was introduced by Senator Paul Douglas, Democrat,
of Illinois, with Senator Robert A. Taft, Republican, of
Ohio, as its chief cosponsor. These bills marked the
beginning of Israel's participation in the foreign aid
program in the United States.

How desperate Israel's situation was at this time
was graphically described for the Newsletter by a correspondent writing from Tel Aviv. It is probable that
few Americans in or out of government fully appreciated
the following circumstances:

I'm convinced that the "delegates and representatives" who come here for a few months

and return to the U.S.A. to report on the state
of conditions do not and cannot give the full
picture....Israel's economy is battered; it
just is not. Human tempers are sharp and
strained to the breaking point in the struggle
for survival. The gathering-in of the exiles
has been going on almost in a vacuum. **The suffering of the newcomers in the transit camps
and in ma'abarot is fierce.**
     I am aghast at the policy of housing for
newcomers. **In place of shelter, there are only
promises;** human beings are left bewildered and
overwhelmed. Three factors are obvious: (1)
There is not enough money for housing; (2)
There is difficulty in getting building materials; (3) It is not at all clear what the Jewish Agency does with the money, or would do
even if they had more of it.
     It is obvious that sums of UJA money are
being spent to support paid propagandists to
encourage the "ingathering of the exiles." This
may be a very important activity, but it is
clear that **money raised for the settlement of
human beings should not be drained off for
other purposes; that other sources should be
used to raise funds for Zionist and internal
political activities.**
     I believe strongly that the five million
Jews in the United States **should know more
about the doings and involvements of the Jewish
Agency** without necessarily controlling the
policies long-distance.

The letter came at a time when my own spirits were
at a low ebb because of the failure of the Newsletter to
be supported by the Jewish public--renewal subscriptions
were lagging and new subscribers were few. My correspondent, who insisted on anonymity, confirmed my own insistence on the need to concentrate aid for Israel, and
I needed the encouragement he provided by implication
that my crusade for honest reporting about Jewish community developments was worth the trouble and personal
sacrifice. At the same time, I confided to my friend
Leftwich that I had "a very juicy scandal involving the
Jewish Agency and the Palestine Foundation Fund in the
works," an expose which demonstrated once more the careless manner in which money and position were being mani-
pulated. When I told Louis Lipsky what I was planning to
do, he raised no objection--in effect, encouraging me to

go ahead. The details of the scandalous scheme and the people involved were described in the following Newsletter report:

The amazing success story of "Service for Palestine," which has grown from a modest food and consumer goods agency organized with communal funds three years ago by the Keren Hayesod (Palestine Foundation Fund) to a private firm currently doing a business of over $2.5 million annually, was disclosed this week by Charles Ress, president of Service for Israel (as it is now called), in an exclusive interview with **Cross-Section, U.S.A.**

(Keren Hayesod is a beneficiary agency of the United Palestine Appeal and serves to collect and transfer funds exclusively to the Jewish Agency.)

Mr. Ress, a New York attorney and an active Zionist for many years, told how he had suggested and organized Service for Palestine in 1948, while holding office as president of Keren Hayesod, the object being to stimulate trade between the United States and Israel. Business flourished, but in October 1949, the Jewish Agency ordered Keren Hayesod to get rid of Service for Palestine because of complaints that it had become too commercial and was competing with private firms in Israel, Mr. Ress declared, adding that he had protested the order in vain.

Subsequently, because the Keren Hayesod board considered it "improper" to auction off the successful subsidiary, Mr. Ress said that he and Mr. Abraham Krumbein, another Keren Hayesod officer, offered to take over the Service for Palestine as their private business. **No cash compensation was paid Keren Hayesod,** Mr. Ress pointed out, adding that he and Mr. Krumbein personally assumed full responsibility for the "liabilities" of Service. The question of the propriety (or conflict of interest) of the president of Keren Hayesod taking over the flourishing communal enterprise he had organized and continuing it as his private business was fully gone into by the Jewish Agency and the Keren Hayesod, Mr. Ress said.

No controls over salary or distribution of the proceeds of Service were retained by Keren

Hayesod in the contract effecting the transfer, Mr. Ress explained. Asked whether he would care to comment on present salaries or distribution of proceeds of Service for Israel, which is organized as a New York non-profit membership corporation, Mr. Ress replied sharply: **"Service for Israel is our private business; it is not a public Zionist organization."**

Mr. Ress' account was corroborated for the greatest part by the Jewish Agency executive diretor, Gottlieb Hammer, who added that the Jewish Agency had not specified how Keren Hayesod should dispose of the Service. Mr. Hammer insisted, however, that there had been no joint meeting of the boards of the two organizations on the question of the propriety of the sale to Mr. Ress.

Efforts to obtain a statement on the liabilities and assets of Service at the time of sale, and to learn the terms of the contract from Keren Hayesod proved unsuccessful. Miss Sarah Behrman, executive director of the organization, said that the contract was not in her files, and that she would have to consult other officers before issuing any financial data on Service for Palestine. Previously, Miss Behrman told **Cross-Section, U.S.A.** that she did not like the way or approve of the "deal" by which the sale of Service was effected.

The actual transfer of Service for Palestine to the control of Mr. Ress was dated December 31, 1949, the date of the expiration of his term as president of Keren Hayesod. Both Mr. Ress and Mr. Krumbein are currently members of the executive board of Keren Hayesod; Mr. Krumbein is also associate treasurer of the UPA.

In concluding the interview, Mr. Ress threatened **Cross-Section, U.S.A.** with a lawsuit for damages if any allegations were made which in his opinion would be harmful to Service for Israel.

The transfer of this enterprise, which had been started and financed with public tax-exempt funds, to a private corporation without compensation or controls--in effect, as a free gift--to the man who had used his public office to start the business which he then carried on for his personal profit is a striking example, though

not the only one, of the blatant disregard of the public
interest by the UJA and the Jewish Agency, and the careless way in which their funds were being handled. Despite Mr. Ress' threat, the Newsletter continued its
investigation of Service for Israel in an effort to
determine just what kind of service it was really of-
fering. The fact that the Keren Hayesod refused to open
its files and disclose the terms of the sale of the Service or any other financial information did not increase
my confidence in the innocence of the deal or the vera-
city of the Keren Hayesod officials. Unfortunately, its
refusal to account for the way it expended public funds
was a part of the same pattern that was being followed
by most national Jewish organizations then, as it is
now. To my friend Leftwich in London, I offered the
following account on September 14:

"I've been working on the Service for Israel business deal again, checking their price list for scrip
merchandise against the costs here, and it is really an
outrage to see how far out of line they are. They are
charging Israelis two and three times the price of the
very same item in American stores, and getting away with
it so far. And they don't pay retail prices for their
merchandise to begin with. I'm strongly tempted to go
into the Israel scrip business myself, with a relative
or two providing the grocery know-how. But I feel so
discouraged these days that I've been asking myself
seriously why I should go to the trouble of exposing
Ress' racket. What am I going to get out of it? And when
one begins to think that way, it's not good. Bartley
Crum has organized a similar company, but it's been very
slow to get under way and still hasn't been properly set
up although they've begun advertising for business. I
couldn't get a price list there last week."

It was most discouraging to find very little
response or other reaction from my readers and no
cooperation from the Israelis themselves in my efforts
to expose Mr. Ress' scheme for the way in which it pro-
fited from the hunger of the Israelis and the generosity
of their American friends and relatives. Had it not been
for the enthusiastic encouragement of Louis Lipsky, who,
I suspected, may have had his own score to settle with
Mr. Ress, I might not have continued the investigation.
It was a good news story, however, too good to drop, as
the Newsletter's report early in October demonstrated. A
great deal of investigation and hard work had gone into
the following account:

Unless the new Israeli Ministry of Agriculture takes prompt steps to control basic food prices in so-called "dollar shops" in Jerusalem, Tel Aviv, Haifa and other cities, ruthless profiteering by the New York private business firms which own and operate these shops is inevitable, a month-long survey by **Cross-Section, U.S.A.** reveals. The Ministry is in full charge of all agreements under which these firms do business in Israel.

The survey indicates that under proper supervision, the plan by which gift certificates sold in the United States are redeemed for scarce food and merchandise in Israel can help Israelis enormously in overcoming the hardships of austerity while providing the Israel treasury--at no extra expense--with an estimated maximum of $10 million annually in desperately needed hard currency. Moreover, the plan has the additional virtue of providing American Jews with a direct personal method of sharing with their fellow Jews in Israel some of the basic commodities of decent living which they enjoy in abundance.

(Gift certificates are being sold at present by three companies; by the end of the year five are expected to be in the field. Purchasers airmail these certificates to Israeli relatives or friends who may then buy what they want without giving up ration points in the special "dollar shops" for which their certificate is issued. Dollar shop merchandise can only be sold for these certificates or scrip; no other currency will be accepted. Under existing contracts, 42.5 percent of all dollar receipts are turned over to the Ministry of Agriculture which in turn credits each company with an equivalent sum in Israeli pounds. The latter are used to pay customs duties, expenses and for Israeli manufactured products. The Ministry has the right to audit company books.)

Since there is no limit to the amount of script which can be sent to an Israeli, the possibilities for abuse of the dollar script plan are many. Against the more obvious opportunities for corruption and fraud, the Ministry is constantly on the alert; it records details of all purchases and has on occasion confiscated excessive supplies of a particular commodity acquired by an individual.

Regrettably, the Ministry has not been as quick to protect the Israeli housewife against the dollar shop profiteering, although price lists are submitted to it for approval. Vaguely hoping that competition will keep prices down, the Ministry has looked the other way when the New York firms—which are technically non-profit, tax-exempt corporations—in most instances charge two and three times as much money for the same product as the New York shopper has to pay. Although these firms buy at wholesale by the shipload, the following prices are charged in Israel compared with retail prices here:

PRODUCT	AMERICAN PRICE	DOLLAR SHOP
Evaporated milk	14-15¢ per can	30¢ per can
Prepared oatmeal	17¢ per 20 oz.	35¢ per 8 oz.
Strained baby food	10¢ per 4¼ oz. jar	15¢ per 4½ oz.
Oleomargerine	23-35¢ per lb.	70¢ per lb.
Sugar	23¢ per 2 lbs.	25¢ per lb.
Pure cocoa	50¢ per 28 oz.	90¢ per lb.
Instant coffee	37¢ per 2 oz. jar	70¢ per 2 oz.
Rice	19¢ per lb.	30¢ per lb.
Dried prunes	26¢ per lb.	50¢ per lb.
Peaches #2½ can	33¢ per can	65¢ per can
Oil in 11 lb. cans	$3.52 (domestic)	$8.80
P & G Ivory soap	21¢ for 4	15¢ per bar
P & G Ivory Flakes	27¢ two 5 oz. pkg.	30¢ 5 oz. pkg
toilet tissue	25¢ for 3 rolls	25¢ per roll
Corn starch	11¢ per lb.	30¢ per lb.

Because of the absence of comparable brand names, no effort was made to compare meat and poultry prices or quality. In the opinion of one executive of a large grocery firm who was interviewed by a **Cross-Section, U.S.A.** investigator, and who was informed of all the factors in dollar shop operation, **dollar shop prices should be no more than 10-15 percent higher than American retail prices in a truly non-profit enterprise.**
One of the three New York firms selling dollar scrip was unable to offer a price list to a prospective purchaser; a second firm, well

established in the field, provided a complete printed list of prices; the third company, a newcomer, twice said a price would be forthcoming in a week to ten days, failed to produce one but did quote prices on selected items. Company A claimed stores were established in four Israeli cities; Company B said it now had eight stores; Company C, which plans to stock clothing, shoes and other rationed merchandise in addition to food, has so far opened only three stores in Israel.

Hope for corrective action rests with American purchasers and Israeli recipients of dollar scrip, the **Cross-Section, U.S.A.** survey concludes. It warns American donors against buying scrip unless they can see prices that will be charged their Israeli relatives; it urges Israelis--however grateful they may be for dollar shops--to protest excessively high prices to the Ministry of Agriculture.

While the existence of a capitalist scheme of this character in a country governed by a dedicated socialist administration may not have disturbed the Israeli officials, the abuses to which the dollar shop scrip lent itself did. Outgoing Minister of Agriculture Pinhas Lavon had reported that food parcels were coming into the country at the rate of 120,000 per month in spite of very high duties, and before long illegal practices began to make their appearance. Despite the fact that austerity was a severe burden for all the people of Israel to bear, the new Minister of Supply, Dov Joseph, in a radio speech on the food policy of Israel, revealed that the government was reconsidering its policy toward the dollar shops because of the large number of scrip purchases that were making their appearance on the Israel black market. He admitted that at least ten percent of the scrip packages had found their way to the black market.

The existence of this rapidly growing black market spelled the end of the dollar shops. The Newsletter may have helped by exposing the operations and the possibilities they offered for abuse, but if it did, no one troubled to inform it of that fact. In publishing the summary of the survey, the Newsletter was careful not to mention the companies by name because of the possible legal action that Mr. Ress, for one, had threatened to take. One group did indicate privately its approval of the Newsletter's report on the dollar script operation. As I said when I wrote to Leftwich asking him what he thought of the story: "It's got the Zionists nodding approval, but I don't know yet what they're going to do about it."

Israel's economic difficulties were reflected in the policy changes that were made, particularly with respect to immigration. As announced at a Jewish Agency meeting in Jerusalem in November, the new policy left untouched the basic commitment to admit into the country any Jew who could reach the shores of the Holy Land. However, assistance in getting to Israel would now be provided only to young able-bodied persons except for Jews in lands where persecution is threatened or actually exists. In those cases, the new selective policy would not apply. The so-called Black Jews of Malabar, India, who claim to have settled there after the destruction of the Second Temple, were prepared to take advantage of the new policy, but no attempt was made to explain how this policy would affect countries like Rumania, where the Soviets had virtually banned the emigration of young workers. In Hungary, over 50,000 Jews had registered for emigration.

The flap over Service for Israel and other dollar scrip businesses was a relatively minor upset compared to the shocking charges of mismanagement, carelessness and dishonesty brought against the Jewish Agency in Israel by its comptroller, Dr. Emil Schmorak. Full details of Dr. Schmorak's accusations were published by the Israeli newspapers, but only brief mentions appeared in the English Jewish press in the United States. Dr. Schmorak not only charged the Jewish Agency with mismanaging its funds and failing to keep proper accounts, he also went on to accuse Jewish Agency executives of incurring swollen expense accounts, exploiting Jewish Agency facilities for personal transport and insurance; and illegally extending loans in foreign currency in order to repay them at a later date in depreciated Israeli pounds. He also charged the Jewish Agency administration with laxity and favoritism in checking bids by contractors, taking inventories of stocks and storage facilities, in fraudulent assessments of such Jewish Agency property as ships before selling or transferring them, and in testing the quality of merchandise purchased abroad or in Israel.

These sweeping charges, covering so broad a range of activities, were met by the Jewish Agency Executive not by denials but by countercharges, accusing Dr. Schmorak of "many inaccuracies and distortions in the Comptroller's report." To which the highly respected and incorruptible Dr. Schmorak replied with all the dignity at

his command: "I assume all responsibility for the cor-
rectness of the facts therein stated. These facts, by
the way, were determined after the receipt of explanations from the executives of the department examined."

The Jewish Agency Executive in response said that it
welcomed "honest and relevant criticism," but it continued to charge that the revelations in the Israeli
press were inaccurate. It no longer charged Dr. Schmorak
with inaccuracy and referred his report to the praesid-
ium of the Actions Committee of the World Zionist Organization for further study. This was tantamount to
moving the report from one desk drawer to another in the
same desk, and it was no surprise to find that the report was unceremoniously buried by the Actions Committee, never to be heard from again. If there were any
inquiries from American organizations or the English
Jewish press other than the Newsletter's report, they
never reached my desk.

Long after Dr. Schmorak's accusations, successive
Jewish Agency comptrollers continued to complain about
the way the Jewish Agency funds were being mishandled
and about the failure of the Jewish Agency to take "real
steps" to correct abuses in line with their recommendations. Thirty-one years after Dr. Schmorak's charges,
the **Jerusalem Post** on June 27, 1982, reported that the
1980-81 report of the Jewish Agency comptroller, Meir
Ben-Zion Meiri, included the following charges: "In-
adequate co-ordination among Jewish Agency departments
resulted in double payments of 'considerable amounts' to
outside contractors; 'needy' Jewish Agency employees
were given loans without reasons being properly given,
and Galilee lookout points were poorly constructed by
firms that had no experience in residential building....
The comptroller notes that in earlier reports he offered
recommendations to the treasury on how to improve its
supervision, but 'no real steps were taken' to implement
them." This report was tabled by the board of governors.

At the time of the Schmorak revelations, the Newsletter wrote to the Jewish Agency Executive requesting a
copy of its annual report. Early in January 1952, I told
my friend Leftwich that I had finally received it. It
was a huge tome, which I commented on in the following
letter:

"Did I tell you that I got the complete Jewish
Agency report from Jerusalem--about five months after
asking for it? Curious item buried in the middle of its
1,000 pages discloses a plan to erect a 'Central National Synagogue' in Jerusalem 'to serve as a center for
Jewish religious and national life, a national house of

prayer, and as an institute for research into Jewish liturgy...as well as a place from which guidance would emanate to all synagogues throughout the world.' It is planned for construction after the completion of the convention center (Binyamey Ha'Ooma). Money would be raised, among other ways, by urging the transfer of title to the Central Synagogue committee of the 'hundreds (sic) of abandoned synagogues in New York and throughout the United States...now in the hands of trustees.'!!!

"I wonder what it will take to establish sanity in Israel."

15

THE ZIONIST CONGRESS

No one questioned whether Zionism would continue to be a force, but ever since the establishment of the state of Israel, the survival of the Zionist movement in the United States and the form in which it could survive became a matter of increasing concern. The issues which had been raised in 1950 at the meetings of the Zionist General Council and other Zionist bodies were left unresolved, and in preparation for the first World Zionist Congress to be held in Jerusalem, scheduled for August 1951, intense discussions and maneuverings for political advantage consumed the early months of the year. Under Prime Minister Ben-Gurion's fire, American Zionist leaders were badly divided; opinions were firm and fiercely fought over.

Former ZOA president Dr. Emanuel Neumann in his memoir provided his own keen appraisal of Ben-Gurion's attitude in the following summary: "There were at least two such controversies in the early 1950's. The first of these grew out of the **hafrada** [separation] issue of 1948 and our victory in that skirmish. Mapai, and Ben-Gurion in particular, did not take kindly to the outcome. The latter, entrenched in a position of great strength and prestige as Prime Minister, had begun shortly thereafter to fulminate against the Zionist movement. He seemed to sense in our continuing Zionist leadership a challenge—an actual or potential rivalry for the position of decisive influence in the Jewish world. The claims of the Zionist movement for worldwide recognition and acceptance derived, as he saw it, chiefly from our relationship to the nascent Jewish State; but that place of honor and power he claimed and sought exclusively for the State of Israel and himself as its active head. For several years, in many speeches and statements, he challenged the authority of the World Zionist movement, and more particularly, our habit of referring to ourselves as 'partners' in the upbuilding of the State. 'You are not partners,' he insisted, 'but only helpers.' At a later stage he went further, describing the Zionist

249

movement as a mere 'scaffolding'--useful in the process of erecting the edifice of the State, but now that the building was complete the 'scaffolding' was superfluous and could be discarded."

Determined to make a last-ditch effort against the Ben-Gurion onslaught, Dr. Neumann and Mrs. Rose Halprin, president of Hadassah, met in Israel with Dr. Nahum Goldmann in February to decide on the strategy they would follow in talks with Israeli officials on what was euphemistically termed the future of the Zionist movement. They agreed that Dr. Goldmann would act as the spokesman for the American Zionist movement and that he would present the demands of the Zionist organizations to the Knesset for a charter to legalize their status in Israel.

They were promptly rebuffed once more by the Prime Minister. Speaking at a Mapai party conference in Tel Aviv in March, Ben-Gurion disparaged the Zionist movement outside of Israel and its Zionist members, saying that they had no other reason for existence than to help the state of Israel by providing for the "ingathering of the exiles." He pointed out that "whether there will be one or two million Jews here shortly may decide the future of the country." His view was promptly echoed by Berl Locker, who was the chairman of the Jewish Agency Executive in Israel.

The Prime Minister's criticism of American Zionists, and in particular of the ZOA, was noted by Israel Schen, editor of the **Zionist Newsletter,** who said: "Even if the ZOA has a justifiable cause for grievance, it will not get very far by continually harping on it." Comment in the liberal Israel daily, **Ha'aretz,** seemed to reinforce that view, pointing out that while Mapai apparently approved of the granting of legal status to the Jewish Agency, the Prime Minister was opposed to it. Mapai had pledged itself during the Zionist Congress election campaign to "do its utmost in the second Knesset in order to influence the government to grant legal status to the Zionist movement." But, continued **Ha'aretz,** while Mapai called for "unified Zionist organizations in every country," its leader, Mr. Ben-Gurion, would like to see the Diaspora parties abolished altogether.

Most American Zionist leaders avoided personal attacks on Israeli government officials, but at least one veteran Zionist did not hesitate to tell this reporter exactly what she thought about the Prime Minister. I told my friend Leftwich about my meeting in the following letter:

"I had a long interview with Mrs. Rose Jacobs the other day. She is a past president of Hadassah--you must

know her. A very fine woman, good mind and a strong
temper. She has no use for the present Hadassah crowd--
they, in turn, won't have anything to do with her. She
knows most of the Israeli government from the old Jewish Agency days, and she agrees with your characterization of Ben-Gurion as a megalomaniac. She goes farther
and calls him a fascist; also an ill-mannered boor who
hasn't even decent eating habits. Sharett she terms a
clerk. She is planning her own history of Hadassah,
which will also be somewhat autobiographical--and she
asked me to help her with it."

A handsome statuesque lady, Mrs. Edward Jacobs was a
close friend of Henrietta Szold and also of Dr. Judah
Magnes. As president of Hadassah in 1940, she organized
the Hadassah Emergency Council in Palestine at a time
when the Nazis under General Rommel were threatening to
take over the Middle East. Dr. Magnes was appointed
chairman of the Council, while Miss Szold took a leading
role in its activities. At the time I interviewed Mrs.
Jacobs, she was retired, but as far as I know, her projected history of Hadassah regrettably was never published. On the political scene, Hadassah was an organization to be reckoned with especially in 1951, when the
American Zionist movement was undergoing its severest
crisis. Not the least of its accomplishments was the
fact that it had raised $9,250,000 for Israel that year.

This was also the year marking the one hundredth
anniversary of the death of Mordecai Manuel Noah, the
colorful American politician, journalist, playwright and
ardent Zionist of the early nineteenth century. His cen-
tenary was observed in Israel by a special broadcast
over Kol Yisrael, the Israel radio, of a play entitled
"Ararat, U.S.A.," a reference to Noah's grandiose plan
for an island refuge where Jews could prepare for resettlement in Palestine. The Newsletter noted that no
American Jewish commemoration was held. And again, in
July 1951, only the Newsletter called attention to the
fact that it was the 47th year since the death of Theo-
dor Herzl, the founder of modern Zionism.

That month was also important for the election that
was held in Israel for a new government. The Newsletter
carried the following report about it:

Early returns of the Knesset election in
Israel followed expected lines with Mapai leading. A surprise was the very large General
Zionist vote, which can be interpreted as a
protest against the government's socialist
economic policy and a warning to any new

government against more stringent controls. Now
the second largest party, displacing the pro-
communist Mapam, the General Zionists will
probably refuse to join the Mapai coalition, if
the usual party pattern is followed, and leave
Prime Minister Ben-Gurion with the problem of
forming a two or three vote majority government. The latter's gamble on forming a government before the convening of the World Zionist
Congress on August 14 now seems lost, and the
Congress may have to mark time until a government is formed. Without a government with whom
it can negotiate, the Congress becomes a mere
debating society.

   The American press and radio treated the
Israeli election as a major news event, with
hourly bulletins and full cable treatment. At
the same time, British Foreign Minister Herbert
Morrison took the first step to implement the
British plan for a Middle East command by
urging the Arab states to work for peace with
Israel. He reiterated Britain's traditional
friendship for the Arabs, but on Israel, said
simply: "We wish her well."

   The report is noteworthy because it is possible to
compare it with the way the American press, in similar
fashion thirty years later, treated the election of
Menahem Begin and the Likud party. The comment of the
British Foreign Minister and his proposal for establishing peace in the Middle East also demonstrates how
little progress Israel has made in changing the attitude
of the Western nations. Not helping the situation then
was the way some Orthodox Jewish groups staged public
protests against the Ben-Gurion government. In May 1951,
for example, the Agudath Israel (which is today a part
of the Israel government coalition) held a mass meeting
in New York to protest the arrest of about fifty Orthodox Jews in Israel on charges of plotting allegedly to
bomb the Knesset. The rally listened to several
emotional speeches and sent a cable to Israel accusing
the government with using "terror" and "vilification"
against the Orthodox. The charges were reported in the
general press here but stirred little or no reaction in
Jewish organizational circles.

   Jewish education in Israeli schools also became an
issue here with repercussions that were felt not only by
the Israel government but also by the Jewish Agency.
Religious Zionist groups, which helped to make up the

Religious bloc in the Ben-Gurion coalition government, fought bitterly with secular Jews over the direction and degree of religious education in the **ma'abaroth,** which was provided, nominally at least, by the Jewish Agency. A conference of the Mizrachi Federation of Great Britain and Ireland sharply attacked the Jewish Agency for its efforts allegedly to "secularize" the education of Jewish children in the Diaspora through the selection of textbooks it distributed as well as the children's periodicals and other study materials. The Mizrachi also charged that the study of the Hebrew language alone without its religious associations, as advocated by the Jewish Agency, would degrade the holy language.

Leon Gellman, chairman of the World Mizrachi, indignantly denied that the Mizrachi demands on the Ben-Gurion government for religious education had been made for political reasons. He pointed out that Mapai, the Labor party, had refused to apply to the **ma'abaroth** the same compromise on education that had been worked out the previous year for the immigration camps, and he charged that Mapai's education system was irreligious "and at the worst anti-religious." Despite the validity of his complaint, the controversy was not reported by the English Jewish press here, but its repercussions were felt nevertheless by the Jewish Agency heads because they moved promptly to appease the religious parties. Its Department of Education and Culture in the Diaspora was headed for several years by Dr. Hayim Greenberg, a venerable Labor Zionist and the editor of the **Jewish Frontier** and the **Yiddisher Kempfer,** both Labor Zionist organs. Despite his widely recognized reputation as a scholar and teacher, he came under the fire of the Mizrachi, who wanted control of the department. To keep the peace—and probably the Ben-Gurion coalition cabinet as well—the Jewish Agency replaced Dr. Greenberg in a matter of weeks with Rabbi Zeev Gold, a Mizrachi member of the Jewish Agency Executive, and a co-founder and president of the Mizrachi.

The religious education controversy was one of the factors that inspired a prominent American Conservative rabbi to call for the formation of a new Zionist party along the lines of Conservative Judaism. At the Rabbinical Assembly in June, Rabbi Max Davidson, president of the organization, said in his opening address: "The whole Zionist movement is changing its form and purpose. We should like to join with like-minded persons of every religious complexion in America and form in this country a new Zionist party. There are parties dedicated to protect the rights of labor, and parties to protect the privileges of private enterprise, and parties to support a state religion. I propose a party dedicated to restore and revive religion for the modern Jew in the Holy Land. We have had the experience of working through the existing Zionist parties....The Reform movement has had a Silver opportunity, and the Conservative movement has had two Golden opportunities.... Where is the impress, their impress of religion on the work that they have done for Israel?"

Rabbi Davidson's words were prophetic; there is today a Conservative Zionist organization in the United States. But it took about twenty-five years after Rabbi Davidson's proposal to bring it into existence.

The World Zionist Congress, where the issues of Zionist survival, religion and other problems would presumably be dealt with, was scheduled to convene on August 14. Election of delegates to that critical meeting began in Israel where shekel holders went to the polls two months earlier. Israel was to be represented at the Congress by 210 delegates; the delegates from the Diaspora were distributed among 110 for the Progressives, General Zionists and Hadassah; 60 for Mapai, or Labor Zionists; 39 for the Mizrachi and Hapoel Hamizrachi, the religious Zionists; 16 for the Hatzoher-Heruth; 12 for the Mapam; and 6 from other groups. According to Eliahu Dobkin, a member of the Jewish Agency Executive, the Agency proposed that the Congress take up the following four issues: (1) the area in which the Zionist Organization should work; (2) its relations with the Israel government; (3) the Zionist funds; and (4) the replacement of the Basle program with the Jerusalem program.

The Israel election, however, was marked by the abstention of the General Zionists and the Mizrachi, who boycotted the voting allegedly because of fraud. Less than 284,000 votes were counted, a much smaller number than had been expected, for which the boycott of the General Zionists and the Mizrachi was blamed. From New York, ZOA president Benjamin G. Browdy issued an appeal to the World Zionist Congress to allocate a number of seats for the Israeli General Zionists despite their boycott of the election.

First reports when the World Zionist Congress was finally convened as scheduled were pessimistic. The Newsletter pointed out that the Congress would not take any definitive action, among other issues, on the question of merging the JNF, the Palestine Foundation Fund and other fundraising agencies for Israel or on the question of the establishment of a central Israeli budget and fund as recommended by the CJFWF. A proposal to recommend that the Jewish Agency be empowered by the Knesset to control the use of all Diaspora philanthropic funds in Israel, in effect, the charter or "status" requested by Dr. Goldmann and approved earlier by the Israeli political parties, was also likely to be sidetracked because of the opposition of the Prime Minister. Similarly considered doomed was a proposal to enlarge the Jewish Agency by permitting it to include representatives of such non-Zionist communal agencies as the CJFWF.

The accomplishments of the World Zionist Congress after about two weeks of discussion and debate were summarized by the Newsletter on August 30 as follows:

> The World Zionist Congress closed this week without achieving any of the six major planks on its agenda. Compromise resolutions left in status quo essentially the question of "status" for the Movement and the Agency, and watered down almost beyond recognition what had started out as the Jerusalem program. Opposition of some American Zionists and a warning cable from American Jewish Committee president Jacob Blaustein against tampering with the "exile" concept led to the adoption of a resolution in which for the original "Zionist aims" there was substituted "tasks of the State of Israel," and the traditional, much-discussed "ingathering of exiles" was weakened by the substitution of the phrase "fostering of the unity of the Jewish people" for the historic "redemption of the Jewish people."
>
> The split in the Confederation of General Zionists, created before the opening of the Congress when Dr. Abba Hillel Silver walked out, was healed last Saturday with the reelection of Dr. Israel Goldstein as president, and a new agreement was signed between Progressives and General Zionists. At stake was a $1 million UPA plum which now will be equally divided. The money is used for colonization in Israel.
>
> It is anticipated that an effort will be made here to blame the deadlock at the Congress on the attitude of Hadassah.

The Jewish Agency meeting in Jerusalem after the adjournment of the Congress ignored the intra-party fight.

It adopted a revised budget for 1951-52 of IL50 million
(about $137 million at the official exchange rate) and
at the same time decided to put off discussion on the
division of functions among the Zionist funds. In the
opinion of ZOA president Benjamin G. Browdy, reporting
on his return from Israel, the World Zionist organization had emerged "stronger than ever" from the 23rd Congress. He emphasized that the ZOA would continue its
efforts to send technical and professional workers to
Israel, but added that he had told Prime Minister Ben-
Gurion that "we do not plan or aim or contemplate any
mass exodus of Jews from the United States."

The whole question of what is a Zionist and what was
his obligation to Israel obviously troubled all the
delegates to the Congress. The conflicting views of the
Israelis and the Americans as represented by Prime Minister Ben-Gurion and by Jacob Blaustein, with American
Zionists deeply concerned about their own relation to
Israel over the questions of **chalutziut** and political
affiliation, surfaced on almost all occasions. Such efforts at a compromise solution as the speech at the Congress by Dr. Hayim Greenberg only added to the ideological confusion. Dr. Greenberg was reported to have told
the delegates that emphasis in Israel and in the **Galut**
should be on the spiritual values of Judaism rather than
on Zionist propaganda. His conclusion was: "Where there
is Jewishness, Zionism flows therefrom quite naturally."

Dr. Greenberg's conclusion satisfied no one although
it was in keeping with traditional Jewish thought. Indeed, as early as 1904, long before there was hope for
anything more than a Jewish homeland, the famous scholar
and founder of the Jewish Theological Seminary, Dr.
Solomon Schechter, explained his position in a letter to
Israel Zangwill. Dr. Schechter wrote:

"You scold me for not having joined the Zionists in
America. One may be a Zionist without wearing a label.
If Zionism means admiration of Israel's past and hope
and faith in its future, devotion to the national
literature and reverence for the national institutions,
if Zionism means this--and I dearly hope that we are not
merely forming a gypsy camp--then I am trying in my humble way to be a Zionist. I have neither the money nor
the practical mind to deal with such questions.... I am
neither a rabbi nor a poet and thus lay no claim to be
on special confidential terms with the Almighty. I don't
even choose to be clever this time. But I have spent
nearly fifty years on the study of Jewish literature and
Jewish history and I am deeply convinced that you cannot
sever Jewish nationality from Jewish religion. The

destruction of the latter will end in the destruction of
the former." (**The Menorah Journal,** VIII, 183)

In all the complex maneuverings before the World
Zionist Congress of the Zionist parties in the United
States and Israel, I was fortunate to have as my guide
and adviser one of America's greatest Zionists, Louis
Lipsky. For almost half a century he had been a powerful
force in the practical development of Zionism in America, a creative leader in the expansion of the Jewish
Agency, the Zionist floor leader in the first American
Jewish Congress, and a close associate of Rabbi Stephen
S. Wise in the growth of the later American Jewish Congress, of which he had been a vice president for many of
its early years. He was a powerful speaker, and once
when I asked him how he could speak for over an hour
without a note and apparently without intensive preparation, he replied: "What do I need notes for? I have been
living Zionism all my life. I just get up and talk."

A tall, sharp-featured man, his spare figure topped
by a shock of white hair, Louis Lipsky, in contrast to
most of his fellow Zionist contemporaries who were of
East European origin, was as American as baseball. A man
of many talents, his first love was the American
theater, and he used to regale me with tales of the
actors and the plays he saw as a boy from the balcony of
the theater in Rochester, New York, his home town, where
he was born in 1876. He began his career, however, as a
writer and journalist, serving as the managing editor of
the **American Hebrew,** a widely read weekly, for about
fifteen years. During that time he also wrote a weekly
column for the **New York Sunday Telegraph,** and frequented
the Yiddish theater where he became the close friend of
many of the famous Yiddish thespians of the early decades of the century.

My friendship with Louis Lipsky had its roots in our
mutual interest in the American theater. I had written a
biography of Adah Isaacs Menken, a world-famous American
actress of the mid-nineteenth century, which was published in 1947 under the title, **Enchanting Rebel.** Although Menken had died in 1868 at the age of 35 after a
spectacular career in Europe as well as the United
States, Lipsky knew about her acting and her role in the
American theater, and was convinced that my book could
be the basis for a fine motion picture or play. He was
especially pleased when I told him about the Menken's
early championing of Zionism and the poems she wrote
heralding the return of Jews to the Holy Land.

At the time I got to know Louis Lipsky, he was about
74 years old and in semi-retirement. In addition to all

his activities, he was also the founder and president of the Eastern Life Insurance Company, and each day he would leave his office at noon for the cafeteria on Madison Avenue, where he would hold court. There, surrounded by friends and eager listeners, he would hold forth on the topic of the day affecting Israel and Zionism. In the evening, he would be surrounded by a similar ad hoc gathering at the Tip Toe Inn at 86th Street and Broadway, near his residence.

Our mutual friend was Bernard G. Richards, also a veteran journalist, Zionist, and former secretary of the American Jewish Congress, who introduced me to Lipsky. There was something very warm and inviting about Lipsky and I was very strongly attracted to him. He had also been the founder and editor of the **New Palestine** and before that an editor of **The Maccabean**, and therefore had a sympathetic appreciation of the Newsletter and its objectives. Because he took considerable interest in the work I was doing, I made it my business to see him at least several times a week, and to listen carefully when he talked about developments in the Zionist organization. He was careful never to say anything that I could quote with attribution, but quite deliberately nevertheless did put me on the trail of several worthwhile stories, including such tidbits as the way Service for Israel and other dollar shop organizations came into being.

It was from Lipsky that I first learned about the split in Zionist ranks over the question of affiliation with the General Zionist party in Israel, a division which for a time threatened the existence of the ZOA. Although the controversy had been brewing for years, it was news to me, and I hinted at it in a letter that I wrote to Leftwich early in March, in which I said: "I hope to have...a story I can't publish yet about a split in the Zionist ranks here--the Progressives will shortly launch an attack on the present Browdy-Silver administration, and I may give them some professional assistance."

The possibility of ZOA affiliation with the General Zionist party in Israel had been under discussion for some time, spurred in some measure by the fact that American Labor Zionists, though relatively small in number and limited in power, exerted a far greater influence in American Zionist circles than their membership warranted because of their affiliation with the ruling party in Israel, namely, the Mapai. Prime Minister Ben-Gurion's brusque dismissal of the ZOA confronted Dr. Abba Hillel Silver with a challenge he could not ig-

nore. To add insult to injury, **Ha'aretz** early in March
quoted the Prime Minister's rejection of a proposal to
invite Dr. Silver to Israel as a guest of the government. According to the Hebrew daily, Ben-Gurion had
said: "Dr. Silver would not come to Israel as a leader
of American General Zionists but as a spokesman for
those General Zionists who conduct anti-government activities both in Israel and abroad."

Asked by ZOA president Browdy to clarify this statement, the Prime Minister said that he had not authorized
the **Ha'aretz** quote, but did not deny it; as far as he
was concerned, he said, Dr. Silver was as welcome as
anyone else to visit Israel. His reply, however, did not
include an official invitation.

Dr. Silver did go to Israel but as the guest of the
General Zionist party, which accorded him the honors be-
fitting a man in his position in the Zionist movement.
The speech that Dr. Silver delivered on his return to
New York was reported by the Newsletter as follows:

> In the light of reports on violence in the
> pre-election campaigning in Israel, the most
> interesting observation in Dr. Abba Hillel Sil-
> ver's speech last week was: "The General Zion-
> ists in Israel have been stressing the concept
> of nationhood instead of the concept of party."
> He viewed critically the "intensified economic
> difficulties and political strife" in Israel,
> deplored the existence of four school systems
> instead of one, and the teaching of children to
> regard as strangers those holding different
> political views. He warned: "You will be build-
> ing a series of tribes instead of one happy
> united people."

To this summary, the Newsletter added reports of the
intention of the General Zionist party to open an office
in New York. Dr. Joseph Serlin and Major Shalom Zysman,
General Zionist leaders, disclosed shortly before their
return to Israel that the purpose of the office was to
"enlarge and strengthen the cooperation between our
party in Israel and the Zionist Organization of America." During his stay in Israel, Dr. Silver had committed the ZOA to support the General Zionist party and
had given "definite assurances that the Zionist Organization of America would soon, and increasingly, manifest
its attachment to the General Zionist party in Israel by
practical and closer cooperation."

Not least among the reasons for the ZOA affiliation
was the fact that the Ben-Gurion government was a

socialist government while most ZOA members were middle class people, committed to the American capitalist, or free enterprise, system. Dr. Silver, as we have noted, was himself a Taft Republican. In Tel Aviv, however, he had found it necessary to assure the General Zionists that he was not a "reactionary Republican" but a Republican who had used his party affiliation as a lever on the Democratic Truman administration in Washington. None of his predecessors could do this, he explained, because all of them were Democrats. It was at this meeting that Dr. Silver also renewed his attack on Henry Morgenthau, Jr., and on Henry Montor, including criticism of Prime Minister Ben-Gurion for supporting these "non-Zionists," as he termed them.

The Progressives in the ZOA were led by Louis Lipsky and Judge Louis Leventhal, and included most of the past presidents of the ZOA. They also had the support of Hadassah. Their opposition to the Silver-Neumann faction was based in part on their unwillingness to affiliate formally with any Israeli political party and thereby become involved in all the complexities of Israeli politics. They believed that their responsibility to support Israel should not be modified in any way because of their feelings about the Israel government. They were convinced that their Zionism had to stand above government; their exclusive loyalty was to Israel.

The first gun fired in public in what was to be a bitter unresolved fight came from Dr. Silver in an article attacking the Progressive group in the ZOA. The article was distributed by ZINS, the Zionist Information News Service, and was published in the **Jewish Mail**, a New York weekly, in May 1951. In the article, entitled "The Rift in Zionism," Dr. Silver defended the ZOA alliance with the General Zionist party in Israel and observed that in view of the split with the Progressives, "the World Confederation, a union of all General Zionist parties in Europe and South Africa as well as Israel and the United States, had among its objectives the maximum encouragement of private enterprise and capital in Israel; it also advocated a compulsory, free, united school system in Israel.

The Progressives took their name from the Progressive General Zionist party in Israel, a liberal center party, with which they maintained "close relations" but with which they were careful not to affiliate. Early in June the fight within the ZOA broke out into the open. At the conference of the Southern Pacific Region of the ZOA, held in Los Angeles, its president-elect Jacob M. Alkow said: "We, the General Zionists of America, do not have and do not share any common political program with the so-called General Zionists of Israel."

At the same time, Bernard Kaplan, president of the Pittsburgh Zionist district, protested any "drastic change in the policy of our organization" and urged that the forthcoming convention take up the question of policy change. In a letter to ZOA president Browdy, he said: "Most of us...have rather seen ZOA as the organ and instrument for furthering the aims of the **entire** Zionist movement and aiding **all** the people of Israel."

The ZOA response was reported in the following Newsletter account on June 14:

> In a clever tactical maneuver calculated to put the Progressives on the defensive, the ZOA this week released a statement calling for "unification of the Progressive Party with the General Zionists of Israel." The statement, issued jointly with the Zionist Organization of Canada, is signed by the twenty heads in Australia, South Africa, Brazil, Mexico, Chile, Belgium and France. It denied the existence of ideological differences between the two parties, concedes the willingness of the General Zionist party to "entertain proposals for unification" and for participation in the post-election anticipated coalition government of Israel.
>
> The statement follows the disclosure that such leading figures as Louis Lipsky, Rudolf G. Sonneborn, Morris Margulies, Ezra Shapiro and others had pledged support to the Progressive General Zionist party in Israel, and that the Zionists in Los Angeles, Chicago, Pittsburgh and elsewhere had protested the ZOA alliance with the General Zionist party. The issue will be fought out in the resolutions committee behind closed doors and probably will not be allowed to reach the floor of the ZOA convention Saturday night, when the political resolutions are to be submitted to the delegates. The convention, in Atlantic City, opens today and concludes on Sunday night.
>
> (Progressive General Zionists are similar to American New Deal Democrats in political philosophy; General Zionist party is led by men resembling Taft Republicans. American Progressives insist upon the neutrality of the ZOA, would exclude all political alliances with

Israeli parties and support whatever government
the Israelis elect irrespective of party.)

The ZOA convention in Atlantic City fulfilled all
expectations of a bitter fight, and it led shortly
thereafter to the establishment of a new Zionist organization called the American Jewish League for Israel.
Despite predictions of its early demise, and sharp
criticism because it omitted the word "Zionist" from its
name, the League exists to this day as a non-party Zionist organization, although the party alignment in Israel
in the recent decade has been altogether different from
what it was in 1951. In anticipation of the creation of
the League, Lipsky had asked me to put together a newsletter for the Progressives and for that purpose had invited me to attend the convention. Notwithstanding this
association, however, I did try to be as objective as
possible in my coverage of the convention, as the following Newsletter summary of the event shows:

A once-great movement in American Jewish
life, its high ideals distorted and dissipated,
its weakening structure torn by internal strife
but still held upright by an embittered old
man, its remaining energies wasted in a vain
pursuit of an authority that would be imposed
rather than acknowledged--that is the picture
of the Zionist Organization of America impressed upon this observer at its Atlantic City
convention, June 14-17.

The 54th annual convention--probably the
smallest in recent years--heard Dr. Abba Hillel
Silver set the tone of the meeting Thursday
night with a bitter attack on Prime Minister
Ben-Gurion, whom he charged with seeking to
destroy the movement. Delegates shifted uncom-
fortably as Dr. Silver, the undisputed leader
of the organization, injected his personal
feelings of anger and disappointment into the
larger issue.

A firm alliance with the General Zionist
party of Israel, insisted upon by Dr. Silver
and his chief advisor, Dr. Emanuel Neumann, was
put through Saturday night after a sharp debate. Despite the announcement that only 409
delegates were registered and eligible to vote,
the tally on the resolution to affiliate was
329 in favor, 127 against--a total of 456. A
protest by Morris Margulies was brusquely waved

aside by Dr. Silver. The resolution in effect changes the character of the ZOA from a non-political organization to the American wing of the General Zionist party.

The only fireworks of the convention were set off by the opposition group led by Jacob M. Alkow, president of the Southern Pacific region, who was joined by the Progressives including Louis Lipsky, Fred Monosson, Ezra Shapiro, Rudolf G. Sonneborn, Morris Margulies, Robert Szold and others. Alkow's resolution reaffirming ZOA's traditional political neutrality and urging a ban on collections here for political campaigning in Israel was defeated, but obtained the votes of one-third of the delegates.

The split in the ZOA ranks was not the only bad news at the convention. The Newsletter also noted that the ZOA executive director, Sidney Marks, in his report to the delegates, tried to put the best possible face on the figures that showed a continued decline in membership and revenue. His report disclosed that the ZOA membership, which had peaked in 1946 at almost 500,000, now stood at 163,971, a drop from the previous year's figure of more than 165,000. In order to meet rising costs, Dr. Marks urged the delegates to raise the membership fee from $5 to $10.

Most English Jewish weeklies avoided any discussion of the controversy between the General Zionists and the Progressives, but the **Intermountain Jewish News**, of Denver, strongly supported the Progressives and Jacob Alkow in an editorial headlined, "Keep Out of Israeli Politics." The editorial then went on to say: "If the ZOA can't find any more constructive things to do than to interfere in Israel's election, it ought to say **kaddish** for itself at Atlantic City and, in the immortal words of Albert Cohen and Douglas MacArthur, 'just fade away.'"

Back in Los Angeles that month, Alkow announced that he would call a national conference later in the year to continue the fight against political intervention in Israel by the ZOA. At the same meeting, Rabbi Max Nussbaum urged that the Zionist movement be reorganized on a territorial basis and without parties. "This means," said the rabbi, "that there would be, in the future, an American, a British, a French, and an Australian Zionist movement of which the future World Zionist Congress should be composed."

Another voice to join in the controversy was that of
Dr. Nahum Goldmann. Shortly before the convening of the
World Zionist Congress, Dr. Goldmann held a press conference in Jerusalem in which he warned that there would
be a new American Zionist organization if the ZOA continued to follow a policy of interference in Israeli
politics. Most American Zionists, he insisted, were opposed to the ZOA policy. But ZOA president Browdy, in
New York before leaving for Israel, pledged that the
efforts of his delegation would be directed toward
reaching an agreement uniting the General Zionist and
Progressive General Zionist parties in Israel. He said:
"If we are successful in promoting such joint action at
the Congress, then there is every reason to expect that
the two groups can unite on the Israel internal
political scene."

On August 11, the Newsletter reported that Dr. Silver had split the World Confederation of General Zionists, an action which brought the fight out into the
open. In a harshly critical speech, he had charged once
again that the Israel government had undermined the
American Zionist movement. Before the week was out, however, Louis Lipsky, speaking in his capacity as chairman
of the America Zionist Council, responded sharply to Dr.
Silver, saying: "Dr. Silver's address at a press conference in Jerusalem on Monday, cabled to the **New York
Times** on Tuesday by Sidney Gruson, was not good for Jewish interests in Israel or the United States.

"The record will show that all Zionist and Jewish
groups--all Zionist groups in the American Zionist Coun-
cil--have been helpful to Israel in a harmonious and cooperative spirit as never before. Favorable opinion,
notably in Washington and throughout the country, has
been won to an extent rarely witnessed in recent Zionist
history. The report of the House Committee on Foreign
Affairs, including a substantial allocation of a grant-
in-aid to Israel is certainly no indication that 'the
mobilized force of organized Jewry has been undermined'
by Israel.

"We have not found in the course of the past two
years the slightest indication of a desire on the part
of Israel's American representatives--headed by Ambassador Abba Eban--to resent or reject American Jewish or
Zionist efforts in public relations.

"Dr. Silver seems unable to adjust himself to the
historic fact that there is a Jewish state in existence
which has its legal representatives in Washington and at
the United Nations; and that the initiative for action
and responsibility rests with them and not with American
Jews or Zionists.

"In my view, he is rendering a disservice to the American Jewish community **by seeking power in Israel's political affairs**--in Israel as well as in the United States--which they do not want and should not have.

"It is discouraging to find the preliminaries of the first Zionist Congress held since Israel was born marred by contentiousness and uncontrolled partisan passions unworthy of the historic occasion."

My letter to Leftwich that week added some details to the fight that was marked by Lipsky's open attack on the leadership of Dr. Silver. In the letter, I said: "Unless JTA has sent out the text, the enclosed Newsletter is the only source of the full text of Lipsky's blast against Silver. He called me yesterday to give it to me after the **New York Times** had printed only part of it. On page 3 you will also find the paragraph in Silver's address which roused the old boy's ire.

"Lipsky told me that in September the movement to take over the ZOA or else start a new Zionist organization would definitely be started, in California by Jacob Alkow, and in New York through my office. I don't know yet who will take Chicago, but it will not be one of the old Progressives if that can be avoided. The slogan of the group will be 'Keep Out of Israeli Politics,' or some such phrase, and that will be its basic policy.

"Lipsky is convinced that Browdy is fed up with Silver and his disruptive tactics and will come along with the new group if it is possible for him to do so. I'm not so sure Browdy won't be persuaded by Silver, though he said he was a fool for continuing a hopeless battle on a senseless issue. He exploded in part at least because he had just come back from Washington the week before with a tremendous triumph in his cap: the additional $50 million for Israel which he persuaded the House to grant. Not he personally, though he did appear at an early hearing, but he did direct the lobbying and the button-holing of Congressmen at the last minute to get them to vote for more money for Israel when they were cutting everybody else's demands to the bone. This $50 million, plus $23.5 million previously agreed upon and about $42 million in military aid just about bails Israel out of the bankrupt spot she was heading for. It's much more than they'll get from the UJA and the bond drives combined--no wonder Lipsky was proud; and all along he had worked hand-in-glove with Eban.

"Incidentally, he told me off the record for the present, that he was planning to resign as chairman of the AZC as soon as the Senate completed action on the foreign aid program--this time he said he would give no reason, but actually he feels that other Zionist organizations are continuing to bypass the Council, and he wants to bring matters to a head. He's quite a guy, despite his understandable personal idiosyncracies."

The paragraph on page 3 of the Newsletter, to which I had called Leftwich's attention, first appeared in the **New York Times**. It quoted Dr. Silver as saying: "If the mobilized forces of organized American Jewry had not been undermined, it would have been helpful to the cause of Israel's foreign relations. The Israeli government, however, wanted non-interference from United States Zionists in political matters and nothing pleased Washington more."

At the Zionist Congress, where Dr. Nahum Goldmann was elected president as expected, the first real test of strength came over the question of the admission of delegates. The forces led by Dr. Silver lost the first battle when the Zionist Congress Court, which governs admissions, ruled that members of the General Zionist party of Israel and members of the Mizrachi party were not entitled to representation because they had not voted to elect any delegates. Dr. Silver then turned to the Progressive General Zionists and when they refused to agree to his demand for the admission of 60 Israeli General Zionist delegates, he angrily walked out of the meeting followed by most of the ZOA delegation and the other General Zionists. At the same time, the Zionist Congress Court reduced the number of Israeli delegates to 185 because it found certain irregularities in the election returns.

The action of the Court was followed by the opening speech of the Prime Minister in which he reiterated his consistent position that Jews who want to have a voice in Israeli policy should become Israeli citizens, an obvious slap at Dr. Silver and his fight for special recognition. The controversy left Lipsky more determined than ever to oust the Silver-Neumann administration and put his own people in control. He had also told me that the reason he was planning to resign as chairman of the AZC was that he wanted to be in a position to reorganize it and assign to the chairman the express power to command greater coordination among the constitutent organizations. One of his constant complaints about the AZC was its failure to act in a unified manner on any course the representatives had agreed to take, and he had about reached the limit of his patience. He had also asked me again to work for the Progressives if the fight he anticipated were to take place. On September 7, in a letter to Leftwich, I wrote about our conversation:

"Lipsky let slip two important developments yesterday. The first is that Browdy will announce on or about
September 20 that the ZOA resolution affiliating with
the General Zionists of Israel has been nullified by the
Administrative Committee of the ZOA--which means that
Silver is through after the defeat he received at the
Congress, and that the fight which the Independents
started at the ZOA convention last June has been won
without a real struggle.

"It also means the end of my prospects for work with
them, to which I had looked forward all summer.

"The second development I stumbled upon in conversation and Lipsky confirmed indirectly. We were talking
about the Jewish Agency effort for status in Israel,
which Goldmann wants, when I said that if he gets it
there, he will then complete his deal with the CJFWF
here, and with them jointly control the community funds
here. I also pointed out that Goldmann had better watch
his step because the CJFWF crowd is much too smart for
him, or any man that Landau could swindle out of
$100,000.

"Lipsky must have suspected that I knew more than I
was saying for he immediately cautioned me against
damning the CJFWF or trying to check them. (I had just
finished saying that the CJFWF attempt at national budgeting had been stopped three years ago, again last
year, and now once more when I had checkmated the Mac-
Iver maneuver, which was also a national budgeting
move.)"

Lipsky's first tip was confirmed on September 23,
when ZOA president Browdy introduced a motion at the
Administrative Committee meeting in Washington, D.C., to
nullify the resolution affiliating the ZOA with the
General Zionists of Israel. This was in line with an
agreement reached at the Zionist Congress to restore
unity in the Confederation of General Zionists. No formal action was taken, however, on Browdy's motion although the delegates heard Browdy and Abraham A. Redelheim appeal for an end to the factional strife that was
tearing the ZOA apart. Later, the Newsletter reported
that on November 23, when the ZOA Administrative Committee held its fourth quarterly meeting in Chicago, Louis
Lipsky would urge the appointment of a committee of 15
to work out the policy details connected with the nulli-
fication of the resolution to affiliate. Lipsky repeatedly emphasized that the function of the ZOA was to
work for the triumph of Israel by concentrating its
efforts in support of Zionist funds. In his view, the
fight over ZOA affiliation with the General Zionist

party was now a dead issue. The Newsletter carried the
following report at the end of the month about this
meeting:

> In about two weeks, ZOA president Benjamin
> G. Browdy will announce appointments to the new
> Policy and Scope Committee which was finally
> decided upon at the National Administrative
> Committee meeting in Chicago, November 23-24.
> This committee, which will formulate the future
> program and organization of the ZOA, will in-
> clude members from all parts of the country.
> Among issues it is expected to decide formally
> is the matter of ZOA affiliation with the
> Israeli political parties, which was vigorously
> fought at the last convention by a group headed
> by Jacob M. Alkow of Los Angeles.
> The meeting heard Mr. Browdy criticize the
> American Jewish Congress for its protest
> against the naming of a United States ambassa-
> dor to the Vatican as "headline hunting"; he
> disavowed any Zionist opposition, as implied in
> the American Jewish Congress resolution.
> The projects program under the direction
> of Louis A. Falk, which was budgeted at
> $1,950,000, will include the establishment in
> Israel of ten trade schools and a business ad-
> ministration college; and the shipment of
> 20,000 food packages to immigrant families
> under an arrangement with Service for Israel, a
> New York private firm. Some criticism was
> voiced here over such an arrangement without
> making provision for competitive bidding by
> other firms in the field.

The meeting was also marked by considerable speculation over a successor to Mr. Browdy, whose term expired
at the national convention. Among the names mentioned by
the delegates were those of Abraham A. Redelheim, Louis
A. Falk and Mortimer May. The only concrete action to
come out of the meeting, however, was the decision to
ship early the next year the equipment for the needle
trades school, the beauty culture school and the elec-
tronics trade school, which was part of the entire projects program. By the end of the year, although it was
not apparent that any formal action had been taken on
the resolution to affiliate with the General Zionist
party, the issue, as Lipsky said, was dead.

And there the issue might have been allowed to rest
had it not been for a renewed attack on American Zion-

ists by Prime Minister Ben-Gurion. In a speech before the Knesset toward the end of the year, the Prime Minister unexpectedly and harshly denounced American Zionist leaders for their alleged failure to come to the rescue of Israel in her economic plight. The white-haired Prime Minister charged that American leaders were bankrupt and had failed to do their full share in assuming the costs of absorbing the immigrants. There was nothing new in his accusations, and ZOA president Browdy described the Prime Minister's speech as "unfortunate and ill-timed." He defended the ZOA's projects program and said that Ben-Gurion's "attack can only bring rejoicing into the hearts of the enemies of the Zionist movement and the State of Israel." The best informed opinion among American leaders was that this attack was probably made for domestic consumption in answer to political attacks against the government.

Hadassah president Mrs. Samuel Halprin denied the Prime Minister's charge that anti-Semitic discrimination in the United States was so intense that professional American technicians were emigrating to Israel. And Dr. Nahum Goldmann, speaking at a UJA conference in Atlantic City, retorted that the outburst could be blamed on Ben-Gurion's anger at his political opposition. Dr. Abba Hillel Silver made only a passing reference to the speech in his own address, but most of the delegates at this UJA conference felt that Ben-Gurion had committed a major blunder, especially since his attack was published in the general press. The Newsletter commented that "things had come to a pretty pass when an attack on American Zionists is effective in halting internal Israeli criticism of government policy."

Lipsky replied to Ben-Gurion's attack through the **New York Times**, bluntly expressing his opinion in characteristically sharp terms. I wrote to Leftwich about it in the following letter: "Lipsky told the **New York Times** that such talk needlessly stirs up muddy waters and serves no purpose at this time. American leaders were really shocked, and I'm sure nothing else was talked about at the UJA conference this weekend. It's going to do a great deal of harm among the lukewarm, who are beginning to realize that they don't mean any more to Israel than money bags--the very things you said months ago.... Apparently Lipsky no longer can do what he wants--his Zionist Council committee holds the purse strings and that's what controls him."

Thus the year ended with the Zionist organizations in much the same relation to Israel as they had been twelve months earlier. Despite all the maneuverings and

the speeches, they had not been able to obtain the much
sought after "status" from the Israel government; Ben-
Gurion was continuing his denunciation of their efforts;
and the only positive action they seemed to be able to
take credit for was the expansion of their projects in
Israel.

16

ZIONISTS TAKE POLITICAL ACTION

In the opinion of Louis Lipsky, the **Zionist Review,** a London weekly, was "a very good paper, much better than anything the Zionists have here." Apparently he did not disagree with its observation that there was a marked shortage of information about Israel and not a little confusion over the influence upon Prime Minister Ben-Gurion of what it described as "an American Jew of avowedly non-Zionist orientation," an obvious reference to the president of the American Jewish Committee, Jacob Blaustein.

In an unsigned article on October 5, 1951, the **Zionist Review** went on to say: "We feel over here, and American Jews have done little to disillusion us, that your controversies are conducted more in the light of your attitude to America than in your strength of feeling as Jews. It may reasonably be supposed that your views on pioneer immigration into Israel are coloured by a feeling that chalutziut involves a negation, perhaps a betrayal of Americanism. No English Jew need fear that England will take personal offense in the existence of a virile Zionist youth movement organized with emigration in view. This issue of 'Americanism' in relation to Jewry confuses us not a little, for it is hard to say from this remote distance whether General MacArthur or Molly Goldberg is the best representative of that quality."

Characteristically, American Jews were not particularly concerned about what their English cousins may have thought of them, but some American Zionists realized at a very early date that there was a need to provide the American government and the general press with information that would help Israel to be better understood and to counter policies that could be harmful to Israel. With the Jewish Agency's attention focused on Europe and Israel, the task of providing good public relations for Israel on the domestic scene became the responsibility of the American Zionist Council primarily because Louis Lipsky, its chairman, made a deliberate

271

effort to assume it. This body had originally been set up during World War II as the Zionist Emergency Council in order to coordinate the activities of the Zionist organizations in the United States. Before the end of the war, it was reorganized to include representatives from every American Zionist group and renamed the American Zionist Emergency Council. After the state of Israel won its independence, the "Emergency" was dropped from its name, and Louis Lipsky was chosen to serve as its chairman.

The freshly reorganized AZC was given three major functions to perform: it was to serve as a coordinating body for Zionist activities as originally planned for it; it was also to conduct public relations for American Zionists as well as for Israel; and most important of all, it was to work actively with the Congress of the United States in order to obtain foreign aid for Israel under the Mutual Security Act. The responsibility was given to Lipsky because it was felt that only he, as an elder statesman, had enough prestige among American Zionists to get the rival Zionist groups to work together. Almost from the beginning, however, he faced a challenge to his efforts to coordinate the actions and the public statements of the Zionist members. After several warnings to the group to work together, he resigned in November 1950 in protest against their continued violation of the agreement to work together, but he was persuaded to withdraw his resignation when the members promised to abide by their agreement.

In the early months of 1951, Israel was the target of Syrian attacks along the eastern shores of the Galilee, and especially against Israeli efforts to drain the Huleh swamps. The Israelis promptly began a series of retaliatory raids, and these attacks just as promptly brought forth a rebuke from the American Department of State. In April, the AZC issued a sharp response to the State Department's protest, which the Newsletter summarized in the following report:

> The American Zionist Council this week strongly protested U.S. Assistant Secretary of State George C. McGhee's rebuke to Israel for its aerial bombing of Syria in retaliation for the fatal shooting of seven Israeli policemen by Syrian troops; charged the State Department refused to acknowledge that the basic cause of Middle East unrest is the Arab failure to negotiate peace with Israel. Council chairman Louis Lipsky issued a statement which read:

"Assistant Secretary of State McGhee would have
served the cause of peace in the Middle East
much better had he called--without partisan-
ship--upon Syria and Israel to make peace."
    On Wednesday, Israeli Ambassador Abba S.
Eban pointed out to Deputy Assistant Secretary
Burton Y. Perry that blame for the border
shootings rested on Syria, who had fired on
Israelis "carrying out an Israeli project on
Israeli soil."
    Informed circles, recalling repeated re-
ferences by **Cross-Section, U.S.A.** to the State
Department's cool attitude toward Israel, observed that the failure of the foreign policy
of the Ben-Gurion government was emphasized by
the Syrian situation and the U.S. State Department's attitude.

Shooting in the Huleh area between Syria and the
Israelis continued, however, despite a cease-fire order
from the United Nations and "warnings from U.N. Secretary General Trygve Lie and the American Jewish Committee president Jacob Blaustein that world peace depended
upon peace in the Middle East," as the Newsletter reported. At the same time, the State Department decided
to send Harold B. Hoskins on a tour of Middle East countries in order, said the **New York Times**, "to help coordinate United States planning in that area." Hoskins,
a consultant to Assistant Secretary of State for the
Near East McGhee, was also president of the board of
trustees of the American University of Beirut, and had
consistently displayed his pro-Arab, anti-Israel
sentiments.
    A growing distrust of American policy by the
Israelis was noted early in the year by the British M.P.
Richard Crossman. He had just returned from a visit to
Israel and his report appeared in the **London Sunday Pic-
torial** on January 7. Leftwich sent me a copy of the
report, and the following excerpt appeared in the
Newsletter:

    "Israel is pro-British now. There is a new-
found enthusiasm for everything British. Two
years ago, Sir Knox Helm was warned to keep off
the streets of Tel Aviv for fear of being
stoned. Today the British Minister is by far
the most popular diplomat. Even officers of the
Israeli Army, who were waging underground war
against us only a few months ago, ask you when

Britain proposes to move troops from Egypt to this country, where they would be most welcome. "This pro-British feeling is due not only to our own merits, but to the unpopularity of the Americans. A world war here would not only halt the work of building a Jewish state, but would mean almost certain occupation by the Soviet Union. MacArthur's handling of the Korean campaign and the apparent inability of Truman to prevent him from dragging America's allies into a hopeless war against China have created nothing but alarm and despondency. Nor can the American determination to re-arm Germany seem anything but insanity to the Jews, who are most of them survivors of the Nazi gas chambers and extermination camps. Distrusting American policy, men and women who for years denounced British imperialism as the root of all evil now feel that the Commonwealth is a safer and more reliable ally than the inexperienced, unpredictable United States."

Crossman had a well-earned reputation as a liberal on both sides of the Atlantic, and his views carried considerable weight, a fact which was emphasized when the chairman of Israel's Knesset Foreign Affairs Committee, Zalman Aranne, told the **New York Times**, in an effort to soothe ruffled feelings, that Crossman's report was based on "dangerous gossip" and that it was not true that Israel distrusted American policy. At the time, Israel was officially following a policy of neutrality, but its greatest fears were stirred up by the Soviet Union and its policies. Both Egypt and Syria were in the Soviet camp, and Soviet propaganda with its hostile anti-Semitic overtones revived ancient Jewish fears of the Russians. Moreover, the Ben-Gurion government was coming increasingly under criticism for its attempt to steer a middle-of-the-road policy which, the Newsletter noted, succeeded only in offending both the United States and the Soviet Union. It was also criticized for failing to develop friendly relations with any of the Arab states. Moreover, Egypt's refusal to allow Israeli ships to pass through the Suez Canal in violation of the 1948 armistice agreement provided an additional negative factor in the economic crisis that Israel was experiencing.

Then, as now, the State Department was making strenuous efforts to keep the Middle East quiet and stable by appeasing the Arabs. In the Congress, however, where the desire for peace was equally strong, sentiment for the fledgling state of Israel was almost unanimous.   One of the younger members, Representative Jacob K. Javits, Republican, of New York, was moved to offer a foreign policy plan designed to help the State Department achieve its objective of peace in the Middle East.   The Javits' proposal--the first of a long series in a most distinguished Congressional career that covered more than thirty years--was described by the Newsletter in the following report:

> Representative Jacob Javits (R., N.Y.) last week proposed a six-point foreign policy plan to be pursued by the U.S. State Department in the Near East designed to prevent a resumption of hostilities between Israel and her Arab neighbors. Policy calls for U.S. to tell Great Britain to stop shipment of arms to Arab States, review of arms situation in Arab States and Israel, U.N. consideration of the Near East arms race, insistence on "full British coopera- tion in a renewed drive for peace treaties," separation of U.S. policy from British imperial interests in the Near East, and international control of holy places and establishment of U.S. Near East Development Commission.

The State Department, however, remained as deaf to Congressional proposals in 1951 as it did in succeeding years. Israel continued to drain the Huleh swamp area and Syrian gunners repeatedly fired on the Israeli work- ers. Israel's retaliatory attacks promptly brought the State Department's condemnation of the action and a United Nations protest as well. No one blamed the Syrians, while the Russians launched a vicious propa- ganda offensive against Israel that followed essentially the same line as the one they use today. To its readers the Newsletter offered the following analysis of the situation:

> Suspicions held here and in Israel that the U.S. State Department's Bureau of Near East, South Asia and African Affairs is responsible for the unfriendly United States policy toward Israel (in defiance of Congress and President Harry S. Truman) as well as for the United Nations ban on Israel's attempt to drain the Huleh swamp grew stronger as the result of the State Department's reaffirmation of the United

Nations action this week. Chief of the Bureau is Assistant Secretary of State George C. McGhee, whose close adviser and Near East representative is Harold B. Hoskins, chairman of the board of the American University in Beirut, Lebanon.

(The university president, Stephen Penrose, blamed Israel for the Arab refugee problem and said that the friendly U.S. actions toward Israel were creating Arab hatred of the United States. The university, a privately endowed arm of the New York State educational system, has long been a hot-bed of anti-Israel, pro-Arab propaganda. President Penrose spoke in San Francisco earlier this week on a fundraising tour.)

United Nations failure to censure Syria for aggressive acts in the Huleh area may be due, inter alia, to annoyance with Israel for creating new problems at a time when the Iran powder keg threatens to blow, informed circles said, adding that there was no great urgency about the Huleh swamp question. Israel has insisted upon her rights in the area, which only the Arabs deny, and will obey the United Nations order only in the seven Arab-owned acres of the Huleh area.

Irrespective of rights, Israel's action adds up to another foreign policy blunder which has resulted in intensification of the Arab boycott (which Lebanon unofficially has been sabotaging) and a stiffening of the U.S. State Department's unfriendly attitude toward the $150 million grant-in-aid in behind-the-scenes negotiations. The United Nations action has been the subject of protests to President Truman by the American Zionist Council and the American Jewish Congress.

Meanwhile in New York last week, Senator Paul H. Douglas (D., of Illinois), mentioned frequently as a candidate for President next year, told the China Institute diners that a new alliance in the Near East should include Turkey, Greece and Israel, with as many Arab states as would come in. (The State Department's bid two weeks ago went only to Greece and Turkey.) Iraq, which has strongly supported Syria, this week received tanks and other military equipment from Great Britain.

Commenting on the Huleh question, the official Soviet paper **Pravda** charged that the incident was "staged" by American imperialism which allegedly wants to intensify the "war psychosis"; it added that U.S. diplomats are trying to strengthen the American position in the Middle East by dictating to Israel and Syria, and trying to keep the [Huleh] question out of the Security Council.

Drainage of the Huleh swamp area became an international issue because this part of the Galilee bordering Syria had been designated as a demilitarized zone under the 1948 armistice agreements. Syria feared that once the area was cleared and reclaimed, it could serve as a staging area for an Israeli thrust into Syria in the event of war. In fact, Syria was even then preparing for a second round against Israel, aided and abetted by the Soviet Union. The AZC became involved because Lipsky feared that all the unfavorable publicity occasioned by the United Nations resolution and the State Department's rebuke to Israel would seriously affect his efforts to persuade the House of Representatives to approve a $150 million grant-in-aid bill for Israel. A delegation headed by Lipsky and including Dr. Joseph J. Schwartz, the UJA director, and Robert Nathan, a prominent Washington economist, braved the July heat to testify before the House Foreign Affairs Committee on Israel's needs and why it was entitled to American aid; also why the State Department's offer of $23.5 million was not enough.

At the same time, the AZC submitted a memorandum to the Congress citing among the reasons why Israel should receive American assistance, the military importance of that nation as a bulwark against the advance of communism in the Middle East. The memorandum was especially timely and significant because the subject of how to meet the Soviet Russian threat was due to be thrashed out at the impending meeting of the Supreme Council of the North Atlantic Treaty Organization (NATO). British policy, backed by the Scandinavian states, regarded the Middle East as a defensive zone in the event of war with the Soviet Union, with Turkey and Israel as the two strongest powers in the region. The American view, formulated by our top naval strategists, differed sharply from the British. It discounted the importance of Israel because it regarded the Mediterranean as the gateway for an offensive straight into the heart of industrial Soviet Russia. In the American plan, Egypt,

Syria, Greece and Turkey--not Israel--were essential to protect the navy's flanks and therefore were the key powers in our strategy. In the event of war with the Soviet Union, the State Department and the Pentagon practically wrote off the Middle East entirely.

In line with this strategy, the Newsletter observed, an important part of the U.S. Navy was concentrated in the Mediterranean, while the State Department continued to ignore Zionist arguments about Israel's military importance. It is noteworthy that except for modifications made necessary by the development of nuclear weapons, American strategy has not changed over the years in any essential factors. Had the British strategy prevailed in NATO, however, Israel would have become a major pillar in the Middle East defense plans, and the course of history over the next thirty-odd years might have been considerably different.

Despite State Department opposition to an increase in aid to Israel, the efforts of the AZC met with striking success. A declaration supporting the $150 million grant-in-aid bearing the signatures of 163 Congressmen was submitted to the House Foreign Affairs Committee by Representative Jacob K. Javits. ZOA president Benjamin G. Browdy was received by President Truman and urged him to support the grant-in-aid for Israel. Browdy argued that the allocation of $23.5 million for Israel under the proposed $8.5 billion foreign aid bill was a "poor substitute" for a grant-in-aid bill. House Speaker John W. McCormack, long a champion of Israel, also went to the President to urge support of the higher sum for Israel. But President Truman remained silent on the request although he did say that he favored increased aid for Israel. Eventually the House committee decided to earmark $50 million for Israel in refugee aid, this sum to be in addition to the $23.5 million in economic aid originally allocated. For the first time, Israel was also to receive $20 million in military assistance, for a total of $93.5 million--a huge sum for a nation in the desperate economic plight that Israel found herself in at that time. Lipsky, of course, was enormously pleased at the result, especially in view of the fact that other parts of the Mutual Security bill had been slashed. After a conference with the Senate, however, the bill as finally passed by the Congress and signed by the President left the military aid stand but cut refugee and economic aid from $73.5 million to $64,950,000.

The importance of the AZC's achievement in obtaining substantial American assistance for Israel was fully appreciated by Louis Lipsky, but there were few others who recognized its long-term potential. Out of a score of New Year statements released by Jewish organizations and Jewish leaders, only one referred to this achievement and to the role played by the American Jewish press. That was the AZC, whose chairman, Louis Lipsky, was quoted as saying: "The Anglo-Jewish press has been an important factor in the task of developing the strong bond of friendship between the Jewish communities of Israel and the United States."

An editorial in the **New York Times** when the foreign aid bill was signed set a tone that was considerably less complimentary. On November 15, the Newsletter commented on that editorial as follows:

> When the **New York Times** pulls one, it's likely to be a lulu--if the editorial on the Middle East aid program in today's **Times** is only a boner! Discussing the Congressional grant of $160 million for Middle East aid, the editorial said: "Congress not only made deep slashes in the requested amounts **but insisted on dividing what little was left equally between Israel on the one hand and all the Arab states together on the other.**"
>
> Apart from the fact that the nasty implications in the statement are hardly worthy of a great newspaper like the **Times,** the statement simply is not true. The only section of the grant-in-aid bill which contains the equality clause is the one providing for refugee aid, which gives Israel and the Arab states $50 million each. Arab states actually got more in economic aid than Israel.

This information came from Louis Lipsky who, during one of the cafeteria luncheon sessions, pointedly criticized the **New York Times** editorial to all and sundry who were present to hear him, not excluding the editor of the Newsletter. It was his way of imparting information but never indicating how it was to be used, if indeed it was to be used at all. In the same way, he made no secret of his personal gratification at having made an important contribution to Israel's economic welfare at a time when that country was in dire financial straits.

Success in getting Israel included in the foreign aid program encouraged Lipsky to embark upon an aggressive public relations program for Israel. An installment of the "Forrestal Diaries" in the **New York Herald Tribune** on October 10 described the pro-Arab attitude of the

former Secretary of Defense particularly on the Palestine partition issue, and also disclosed the political
jockeying for the Jewish vote that took place between
President Truman and Senator Taft. The former Defense
Secretary also quoted New York Governor Thomas E.
Dewey in this installment as saying that the Palestine issue
could not be made non-partisan "because of the intem-
perate attitude of the Jewish people" and "because the
Democratic Party would not be willing to relinquish the
advantages of the Jewish vote."

These observations drew a prompt and very profound
reply from Lipsky. In a letter to the **New York Herald
Tribune**, he pointed out that Forrestal's assumption was
incorrect, and that political pressure had little or
nothing to do with the development of American policy on
Palestine. That policy, Lipsky said, was based on America's traditional interest in the Holy Land and in the
fate of European Jewry as well as on President Woodrow
Wilson's sponsorship of the Balfour Declaration. At the
same time, Lipsky issued a "white paper" through the AZC
providing factual information on the Israel-Arab relationship entitled, **Israel and the Arab States: The Issues in Dispute,** which was given a wide circulation.

To keep the record straight, the Newsletter disclosed in a later report that Defense Secretary James
Forrestal, notwithstanding his pro-Arab sympathies, had
expressed considerable admiration for Israel's military
achievements. It quoted from a letter to the **New York
Herald Tribune** by Eliahu Elath, in which the former
Israel Ambassador to the United States described his
discussions in the early months of 1949 in which Defense
Secretary Forrestal said that "he had found his earlier
misgivings regarding Israel had been largely dissipated." At the time he wrote this letter, Elath was
Israel's Minister to Great Britain.

American Zionists honored Louis Lipsky on the occasion of his 75th birthday at a dinner sponsored by the
Weizmann Institute in New York on November 29. To mark
the occasion, Harry Scherman, president of the Book of
the Month Club, had the honor to announce the establishment of a Louis Lipsky Fellowship Fund. On December 4,
the actual date of his birthday, Lipsky was the guest of
honor at another New York event sponsored by the AZC. On
that occasion, Lipsky called on the ZOA to cast off the
confusions created by the economic pressures and other
negative developments that followed in the wake of the
creation of the State of Israel and to resume its time-
honored leadership of the Zionist movement. He characterized the current ZOA projects program as a throwback

to the Hadassah program of thirty years earlier and
urged the ZOA instead to foster and encourage full
Jewish living in the Diaspora and in Israel. The ZOA, he
emphasized, had never been concerned only with itself
but rather addressed itself to the totality of the
Zionist movement. The speech was really the farewell
counsel of the veteran American Zionist, but at the
time, Lipsky's vigorous delivery disguised the illness
that was to end his life a few months later.

In my letter to Leftwich, I noted briefly that I had
attended "the Zionist Council party for Lipsky; met
everybody who was anybody. Lipsky gave the ZOA hell, and
they all took it as nicely as they could. Nobody will
carry my version, I promise you."

The Israelis moved swiftly to take advantage of
Lipsky's successful campaign to win a grant-in-aid for
them because of the terrible economic pressures that
they were under. Early in December, following an appeal
by Ambassador Abba Eban to the State Department, over
$25.5 million of grant-in-aid funds were made available
to Israel notwithstanding the fact that Congress had not
yet appropriated the authorized funds. To get around
this delay, the funds were drawn on the account of the
$50 million grant for refugee relief. The Newsletter
disclosed that out of the $25.5 million about $6 million
was set aside to buy desperately needed foodstuffs; $3
million was to be used for the purchase of power plant
parts; $2.5 million went for irrigation equipment; and
the remainder, about $14 million, was to be used to pay
for raw materials which Israel had previously purchased.

The Newsletter blamed the foreign policy of the
Ben-Gurion government for Israel's economic plight. As
early as April 1951, in a roundup of Israel's economic
situation, the Newsletter was able to make the following
points:

> Although Israel is potentially a rich na-
> tion and has excellent long range prospects,
> the complete failure of the Ben-Gurion govern-
> ment's policies in economic affairs and in for-
> eign policy has set in motion a runaway infla-
> tion which threatens the country with complete
> bankruptcy, it was learned here this week.
> The foreign policy failure is marked by the
> collapse of the so-called "neutrality" policy,
> which succeeded only in offending both the
> United States and the U.S.S.R., and by the
> complete lack of progress in developing
> friendly relations with members of the Arab

bloc nations, a basic requirement for Israel's economic development. The Syrian border incidents and the economic strangulation of the Egyptian blockade emphasize the failure of Sharett's foreign policy.

Internal economic policy, frequently criticized, led to new peaks in currency inflation and panic buying of gold last month. Commenting on the government's failure to check runaway inflation, the **Jerusalem Post** says: "Despite individual measures taken by the responsible authorities, the question remains whether the Cabinet is following a well thought out economic line. It is well known that the very fact of financing a development budget by means of the printing press must operate as an inflationary factor, but it is also known that there are certain measures capable of countering this pressure that are either not being introduced or left until too late."

(Speaking before the Dropsie College Institute on Israel in Philadelphia last week, **Jerusalem Post** publisher Gershon Agron stressed that the unprecedented immigration to Israel had doubled the population roughly in three years since the state was founded.)

Israeli economic expert Dr. A. Barth, general manager of the Anglo-Palestine Bank, who accurately foretold Israel's financial crisis of last summer, said that an improvement in Israel's position would be felt soon, but warned that Israel's present situation was comparable to that of France in the 1920s. (At that time France devalued the franc drastically in an effort to stop inflation. The Israel pound is tied to the British pound, with a nominal value of $2.80; it was selling in New York this week at 95 cents. Dr. Barth's comment may indicate that the Israeli pound is due for devaluation soon.)

Another report on Israel's desperate financial situation was made this week by Harold Glasser, director of the Overseas Institute of the CJFWF, who pointed out that Israel's foreign exchange position was still critical. (In 1950, Israel sold the United States $7,815,536 worth of goods; it imported from the United States alone $93,009,535.) Returning from a six weeks' first-hand study of economic

conditions in Israel and Europe, Mr. Glasser
said that Israel had maintained itself during
the last nine months only through $50 million
in loans, large gifts of U.S. surplus foods,
and increased austerity.

To avert financial disaster, Israel was fortunately
able to get through the emergency by putting together
the combined help of the UJA, the Israel bond sales, the
reparations payments by Germany and perhaps most important of all for the long term, the American foreign aid
program. At the same time Israel had to contend with the
foreign policy maneuverings of the British, the United
States, the Egyptians, and the Arab nations as well as
the Soviet Union. When Iraq and Saudi Arabia contrived
to bypass the oil pipeline to Haifa in order to cut off
Israel, the famous British owned Haifa oil refineries
were compelled to depend for their supplies of crude on
the oil tankers. Egypt, however, flatly refused to allow
the tankers and all other ships bound for Israel to pass
through the Suez Canal. The blockade further delayed the
oil shipments from Iran to Israel. Egypt remained ada-
mant in the face of an American protest against the
restrictions it had imposed on the oil tankers. Major
General William E. Riley, the United Nations truce chief
in Israel, denounced Egypt's blockade as an "aggressive
and hostile action" which should be condemned by the
U.N. Security Council, but Egypt refused to budge.
Most seriously affected by the Suez blockade was
Great Britain, which needed the Haifa refining capacity
because of a shortage of such refining facilities in
other parts of the world. The Abadan refineries in Iran
were shut down because of a dispute between the British
and the Iranian government, and British efforts to
reopen the pipeline from the Kirkuk oil fields were
foiled by the Baghdad government. The Haifa refineries,
therefore, had to operate on oil imported from Venezuela
in a quantity sufficient only to operate the refineries
at a quarter of their capacity. Their output could be
increased from 20,000 barrels to over 80,000 barrels,
according to a youthful Walter Levy, then the oil consultant to the United States Materials Policy Commission. Iranian or Iraqi oil, shipped through the Suez to
Haifa, could easily solve Britain's problem, hence the
increasing British government pressure for swift action
by the U.N. Security Council to force Egypt to change
its policy.
Britain's hand was forced when Iraq rejected the
British demand to reopen the Kirkuk oil pipeline to

Haifa, and in a desperate move, Britain submitted a resolution to the U.N. Security Council which would have condemned Egypt for refusing to lift its illegal blockade of the Suez Canal. Israel had also submitted a complaint, but before the U.N. could act, a new situation was created in the Middle East in July when King Abdullah of Transjordan was assassinated. Using this new crisis as a reason, the United States persuaded British Foreign Secretary Anthony Eden to postpone his presentation to the Security Council by arguing that a compromise could be worked out with Egypt. Israel's Foreign Minister Moshe Sharett was insistent that all restrictions on passage through the Suez had to be removed, but the British seemed to be willing to consider the American proposal under which Egypt would permit a limited amount of oil to go through the canal to Haifa provided that an international commission would be set up to supervise the output of the refinery and guarantee that none of the oil would be used by Israel in any action against an Arab state.

The American hold on the British determination to bring U.N. pressure to bear on Egypt was part of a larger plan by Secretary of State Dean Acheson to bring about peace in the MIddle East. Repeated efforts to persuade the Arabs to negotiate a treaty with Israel following the 1948 armistice had failed up to this time despite separate efforts by the United States, Great Britain and the United Nations. The Newsletter summarized the American effort in the following report:

> The U.S. State Department is holding up United Nations action against Egypt on its blockade of the Suez Canal in part because it fears that a strong resolution may upset efforts to establish a workable peace formula acceptable to Israel and the Arab states, it was learned this week from a reliable U.N. source. The plan calls for Israel to pay Arab refugee claims.
> Under this formula, Israel will ask the United States and the United Nations for a loan covering the total claim of the Arab refugees. Arab states will then accept as settlers the refugees now within their borders. London and Paris, as well as Israel and several of the Arab states, are reported to have accepted this plan tentatively. A similar plan, attributed to U.S. officials several weeks ago by Jon Kimche in the **Jewish Chronicle** (London), said that

Egypt, Syria, Lebanon and Jordan had given their approval in principle to the scheme.

Meanwhile, the United States has sought at all costs not to offend Egypt, and despite British pressure for U.N. action, has persuaded Britain and France to agree to ask, not direct or order, Egypt to call off its blockade.

Throughout the hot summer of 1951, the jockeying between the United States on the one hand, and the British and the French on the other, with Israel bringing up the rear, over Egypt's blockade of the Suez continued unabated. Unspoken was the realization by all the parties involved that the seeds of another Middle East war were being sown in this dispute, a war for which the United States would be responsible at least in considerable part. The Newsletter reported that there was speculation which indicated that Egypt ws using the blockade not as much because of enmity toward Israel but as a lever to pry loose Britain's hold on the rich Sudan and the Suez Canal. Apparently this situation became the subject of discussion at Lipsky's luncheon table because it led to the following observation in the Newsletter:

> United Nations action on the Suez Canal resolution was put off once more this week at Turkey's request for time. Despite U.S. pressure, Egypt was standing pat until she gets concessions in the Sudan... Have you noticed the glaring contrast between the U.S. State Department's speed in acting against Israel on the Huleh-Syrian problem and the current snail's pace against Egypt? Louis Lipsky would like to know what Egypt's got that it has to be appeased for.

Meanwhile, the British were putting forward their own plan for the defense of the Middle East, a plan which would bring the Arab states and Israel together. Anthony Eden proposed a Middle East command structure embracing Israel and the Arab states but built around Greece and Turkey. It was intended that this structure would be linked with NATO through Turkey, and would also be linked eventually with an African defense organization, including Egypt, which Great Britain planned to set up at the eight-power conference scheduled to be held in Kenya on August 20. It was a bold, far-sighted strategy based upon Great Britain's many years of experience in these exotic lands. In order to win

American support for this ambitious plan, the British
agreed to accept the U.S. Navy's proposal for the
defense of the Mediterranean against the Soviet Union, a
plan which, as we have noted earlier, rejected the
Middle East entirely as a defense position except for
Egypt and Syria.

Linked with the British effort to set up a Middle
East command was the meeting of the United Nations
Conciliation Commission for Palestine (PCC), set for
September 10 in Paris, where a determined bid for peace
between Israel and the Arab states was expected to be
made. Formal peace was regarded as a necessary prere-
quisite to the British strategy, which was to be
directed by a special defense board. Members of this
board were to be Turkey, Israel, the Arab states and
Iran; and a Turkish general was to be the head of the
combined land forces. Israel had accepted the invitation
of the PCC but had expressed considerable pessimism
about its chances for success. Egypt, Jordan, Lebanon
and Syria were also expected to attend the meeting.

When the Paris peace conference opened, the chairman, Ely Palmer, an American, made it clear that after
three years of effort, this was to be the PCC's last
attempt to bring the parties together. Nevertheless, the
Arab delegates defiantly continued their policy of
refusing to sit at the same table with the Israeli
representatives. This Arab inflexibility compelled
Palmer to offer his proposals first to the Arab delegates, then later and separately to repeat the process to
the Israelis. His plan called for the return of some
Arab refugees to Israel; compensation for abandoned Arab
property and bank accounts to be paid by Israel to the
remaining number of bona fide refugees; economic aid for
the countries in which the refugees were to be
resettled; free port facilities in Haifa for the Kingdom
of Jordan; and revision of the borders of the Arab
states and Israel. The results of Palmer's negotiations
were reported by the Newsletter in the following
account:

> Despite strong United States pressure,
> including special talks with Egypt, the Arab
> states are balking at the peace plan offered by
> the United Nations Palestine Conciliation
> Commission in Paris; and have refused to deal
> directly with the Israelis. The PCC plan calls
> for a declaration of non-aggression, mutual
> cancellation of war damage claims, admission by
> Israel of a "specified" number of refugees and

payment to others of compensation for abandoned property, release of blocked bank accounts and their payment in pounds sterling, considerable territorial revisions, a free port at Haifa for Jordan, disposition of the Gaza strip, and establishment of a Water Authority to govern the use of the Jordan and Yarmuk rivers.

Israel has rejected only the demand for the return of the Arab refugees on the ground that they would create an internal security problem. Speaking at the Hadassah convention last week before he was taken ill, Israeli Foreign Minister Moshe Sharett warned against a possible PCC attempt to "penalize" Israel for her survival by imposing one-sided concessions on her; thundered: "Israel has not achieved her independence by the sacrifice of blood and treasure only to see it crippled by a political settlement." But in Washington, ZOA president Benjamin G. Browdy called for an "alliance between Israel and the Arab states."

Despite Sharett's fears, the recommendations of the PCC were eminently reasonable, and had they been accepted by the Arab states, the course of Middle East history for the next three decades would have been considerably more peaceful and beneficial for all concerned. But after weeks of fruitless negotiations with the Arabs, who proved to be rigid and intransigent in their rejection of peace with Israel, the PCC decided on November 16 to abandon the effort. With its failure went the defeat of American policy in the Middle East. Assistant Secretary of State George C. McGhee, who was responsible for that policy, was expected to be "exiled" to the U.S. Embassy in Turkey, the Newsletter reported. But in fact, McGhee was sent to Greece instead.

The British apparently had discounted the PCC effort and had continued with their plan for a Middle East command. Under a Paris dateline, the **New York Times** reported that Israel had conditionally agreed to enter the Middle East defense alliance with the Big Three and Turkey. The report added that Israel had told the United States, France and Great Britain that it "wants no fanfare about such an arrangement.... It does not want high-level foreign military missions, a grandiose international headquarters, nor well-publicized visits by foreign defense officials to its shores." Israel was exceptionally sensitive and fearful about the alliance it had entered because this meant complete abandonment of its neutrality policy. It also meant that Israel was giving up its immediate hopes for a deal with the Soviet Union for the emigration of large numbers of Russian Jews. Israel also feared Soviet penetration of the Middle East more than any other nation.

A report in the Newsletter in September outlined additional developments that increased Israel's feeling of insecurity:

> Contributing in very large part to Israel's economic plight is the large secret military expenditures occasioned by the intensified Arab "second round" threat.... Israel watched with concern possible moves indicating that Syria, Iraq and Egypt might foment internal revolt in Jordan, leading to its division and loss of independence. It is unlikely, for example, that Israel would stand by passively until Iraqi or Syrian troops marched into old Jerusalem. Israel notified the United States, Great Britain and France last week that she would feel free to act if the Arab states moved. The three powers had guaranteed Jordan's boundaries last year in a joint pact.
>
> Israel is also affected by Egypt's blunt refusal to comply with the U.N. resolution calling on her to end the blockade of the Suez Canal, which the Security Concil adopted Saturday after delays of almost two months. In Alexandria, the Arab League called for intensification of the blockade against Israel and issued reckless statements against the United States, France and Great Britain.
>
> At the same time, Great Britain's efforts to set up a Middle East Treaty Organization (METO) continue to be blocked not only by the intransigent Arab attitude and Egypt's blustering hostility but also by difficulty in resolving Turkey's key position in the plan. Under the defense plans, Turkey would be the link between METO and NATO, and a member of both. The Turkish admission to NATO will come up at the Ottawa conference this month.

In November, Israel formally signalled that it was abandoning its "non-identification" policy and shifting to the West when the Knesset, by a vote of 63 to 16, defeated a motion of no confidence introduced by the pro-Russian Mapam party. At the same time, in order to

placate   fearful   Knesset   members,   Prime   Minister
Ben-Gurion assured them that the "state of Israel is not
for sale and not for rent" even to the United States. He
also avoided a question on Israel's attitude toward the
Allied Middle East Command proposal and warned that any
arms furnished to Egypt under this scheme would be used
only to fight Israel and no one else.

Meanwhile, Foreign Minister Sharett disclosed that
Israel had asked the United States for a new grant in
the 1952 foreign aid program and had strongly urged
"close relations with those countries whose Jewish communities support us in our historic mission and whose
governments give practical assistance." His comment
indicated that at this early stage in its existence as
an independent state, Israel was already finding itself
in a difficult foreign policy position. Fearful of the
Soviet Union's thrust toward the Arab states, and dis-
trustful of the American State Department's obvious policy of appeasing Egypt and the Arab states, Israel could
find comfort only in the knowledge that the American
Congress was sympathetic and supportive. In an analysis
of the Middle East situation when it became apparent
that the British policy had suffered a severe defeat,
the Newsletter offered the following observations:

> The bark of British machine-guns firing on
> Egyptian rioters in the Suez area emphasized
> the stunning setback suffered by the U.S. State
> Department when Egypt rejected a Big Three of-
> fer to become a "founding member" of the pro-
> posed Allied Middle East Command (AMEC). The
> State Department's policy of appeasing the Arab
> states has been formulated by a clique of Amer-
> ican friends of Beirut University and developed
> by Assistant Secretary of State George C.
> McGhee. Israel was **not** invited to join AMEC,
> which consists at present of the United States,
> the United Kingdom, France, Turkey, Australia
> and the Union of South Africa. Big Three
> ministers, however, hastened to assure Israel
> that her interests would be protected, but did
> not elaborate. Acceptance by Egypt would have
> meant her development as a first-class military
> power.
>
> By playing hard-to-get, Egypt is taking
> full advantage of the British decline and
> United States appeasement. She will not get
> Suez, but informed observers believe she stands
> a good chance of getting a much larger slice of

the profits of trade-rich Anglo-Egyptian Sudan
at British expense. Israel fears the United
States may also force her to make concessions,
such as a land bridge across the Negev joining
Jordan with Egypt, which the latter has been
demanding, and a slice of Huleh territory to
Syria.

The full plan for the AMEC was studied very
cautiously by Israel. It called for a unified command,
based in Turkey or Cyprus, with troops assigned by the
member states. This command would plan and execute strategy for the overall military defense of the Middle
East, provide arms and economic aid for needy member
states. It safeguarded member states against any
infringement of their sovereignty and specifically
excluded interference "in problems and disputes arising
within the area," a loophole directed at Egypt's hoped-
for eventual entry into AMEC.

Israel was justifiably concerned that AMEC would
result in rearming the hostile Arab states on her
borders. These states had from the very beginning
refused to implement the 1948 armistice agreements which
called for them to negotiate a peace treaty with Israel,
and they had just as consistently threatened to engage
Israel in a "second-round" war. Following on the collapse of the PCC's efforts, Prime Minister Ben-Gurion
warned the Knesset that there were no prospects for
peace with the Arab states in the foreseeable future.

In this circumstance, I found Israel's failure to
provide the world with adequate information to explain
her policy and her actions to be inexcusable. Something
of my impatience with the Israeli authorities for
failing to recognize the importance of propaganda in the
world of 1951 was expressed in the following letter to
Leftwich:

"The pro-Arab and the State Department boys are
getting their anti-Israel drive under full swing--
there's another editorial in the **New York Times** today
blaming Truman for having 'forced through the swift
creation of the State of Israel regardless of its
effects on the feelings or the rights of the Arabs.'

"I'm pretty sure I know who is running the propaganda drive for the pro-Arabs--George Britt, of the old
World--and he is an extremely capable and dangerous man;
but who am I going to talk to among the Zionists or
Israelis if they won't listen to Lipsky? It's enough to
make one throw up his hands in despair. When they
finally wake up, it will probably be too late and the

poor devils in the wind-ripped tents of the **ma'arbarot** will have to pay for the waste and stupidity here. Apparently the same kind of thinking motivates Ben-Gurion the Great, who has the entire crowd here as bitter as they can be. Whatever he may think of American Zionists, they are in the final analysis far better friends of his and of Israel than anyone else he can find here, and the way they've poured millions into Israel is beyond precedent. Surely the responsible head of a government ought to conduct himself in a somewhat wiser fashion. Even Truman eventually learned when to keep his mouth shut."

On the basis of my wartime experience with the Office of War Information, I had drawn up an elaborate outline of the way Israel should establish an office to direct and implement a positive propaganda campaign. Louis Lipsky, who encouraged me to do it, then sent it to Israel for consideration and possible action. Apparently, his effort got short shrift because he never mentioned it to me again. From other sources, however, I learned that Ben-Gurion had decided against any unified government information service to answer Israel's critics, a policy decision which Israel continues to observe. Therefore, while Israel remained silent, the propaganda war declared against her by the Arab states and most of all by the Soviet Union was intensified. They were not alone. At Christmas 1951, the Vatican radio bitterly denounced Israel allegedly for confiscating two Catholic churches. By the time the Israel radio and press got around to denying the charge as "fantastic," considerable damage to Israel had been done. The Israel radio, which is not government controlled, eventually carried a lengthy report explaining that the two churches had once been the property of the German archbishopric of Cologne and had been seized as alien property by the British during the war, and that when the Mandate ended, they were turned over to the Israel government. But by that time, no one was listening. There is no record of a retraction of the charge by the Vatican.

At the same time, **Life** magazine, with a circulation of about six million readers, chose its Christmas issue to present a viciously biased article by Evelyn Waugh, the noted British novelist and Catholic apologist, entitled "The Plight of the Holy Places." In appealing for measures to implement the Vatican plan for the internationalization of the city of Jerusalem, Waugh misrepresented and distorted the facts not only about Judaism and the Israel government but also about Mohammedanism and Eastern Orthodoxy. Among many allegations, he denied

that Judaism was one of the three great world religions
and relegated it to the status of a national cult.

Waugh further went on to revive what was even then
an old canard about Israel to the effect that "the Jews
were able to stampede the inhabitants (who now live in
destitution, some half million in the wastes of Jordan
alone) and hastily fill their homes with Jewish immigrants." The fact that thousands of Jewish immigrants
were living in the tented misery of the **ma'arbarot** instead of the homes abandoned by their Arab owners, as
Waugh contended, apparently was a situation he preferred
to ignore. Undeterred by the absence of any facts to
support his charges, Waugh in a demonstration of in-
credible bias accused the Israel government of prohibit-
ing travel in or out of Nazareth without a special
police pass and then irresponsibly called for a crusade
against the Jewish state because its government allegedly maintained a "fictitious rate of exchange" in
order to increase the cost of traveling to Israel. This,
he maintained, was "a trick by which a modern government
exacts the dues which were considered intolerably op-
pressive in the Middle Ages."

As far as the Newsletter could determine, there was
no response to the Waugh allegations in **Life** magazine by
any of the Jewish defense or Zionist organizations. The
sole published Zionist response to the **New York Times**
editorial blaming President Truman for recognizing
Israel was what the Newsletter described as a "dish-
water" letter by Carl Alpert, then the education director of the ZOA, which mildly reproved the newspaper for
deliberately misreading history. And immediately below
Alpert's letter, the **New York Times,** in its customary
balancing practice, placed a letter praising its editorial signed by Hans Kohn, professor of history at the
City College of New York. Ignored was the fact that in
1948, the same newspaper had enthusiastically approved
the action of the United Nations in voting for a Jewish
state. Obviously reflecting the pro-Arab position of the
State Department, whose unofficial voice the **New York
Times** frequently tried to be, its 1951 editorial not
only condemned the Truman administration for ignoring
the rights and feelings of the Arabs but it went on to
say that the way in which the U.N. resolution recognizing Israel "was done was so well calculated to shock and
incense the Arab world that a continuing resentment" is
today one of the major causes of unrest in the Middle
East."

To a large extent my concern and indignation at the
failure of Israel and the American Zionists to respond

to all this hostile propaganda was a reflection also of
Louis Lipsky's feelings, although he was careful not to
say anything critical in my presence that that could be
quoted. But he did call my attention to a dispatch by
Stewart Alsop in the **New York Herald Tribune**, which I
summarized in the Newsletter as follows:

"Throw the Jews to the wolves and kick the
British in the teeth!"
This in sum is the Middle East policy which
would prove "highly profitable" for the United
States and one it would adopt if it were as
realistic as the Kremlin, said noted foreign
correspondent Stewart Alsop in the **New York
Herald Tribune**, December 14. Alsop adds: "There
is equally not the slightest doubt that if the
United States backed the Arab states against
Israel, arming and supporting the Arabs to this
end, we could gain a decisive measure of internal power in every Arab state." The only bar
to this policy is that we are "still, fortunately, influenced by moral principles."
In his dispatch from London on Sunday, Alsop dropped the moral cloak and made an all-out
appeal for a new U.S. policy which would establish "reasonably enlightened" dictatorships in
Arab states, arm them "beyond the strength of
Israel," and block an Arab-Iraeli war by an
"unequivocal Anglo-American guaranty against
expansion in either direction." Unless this is
done promptly, the Middle East will fall into
communist hands just as China did, Alsop
warned.
Alsop is read carefully by Washington
legislators and the pro-Arab propaganda he ex-
pounds so skilfully marks the official beginning of an all-out drive against a second U.S.
grant-in-aid to Israel, as the immediate objective. The drive was previously trial-bal-
looned in other papers, notably the **New York
Times** editorial of November 15, and by the **New
York Post** correspondent, William Attwood; increasingly vigorous efforts to turn American
public opinion against aid to Israel should be
expected in coming months.
Some Zionist leaders here are alert to the
danger, but the apathy of others and the diversion of funds into unproductive channels
threaten to block counter measures. More than

occasional "Letters to the Editor," however
authoritative, will be needed to beat back this
pro-Arab drive.
Meanwhile, former Beirut University trustee
Edwin A. Locke Jr., coordinator of the U.S.
grant-in-aid funds to Israel and the Arab
states, arrived in Lebanon. This week it was
learned that the successor to George McGhee as
head of the State Department's Middle East
division is Henry Byroade, who is getting the
job not because he is an expert on the critical
Middle East region but because his current responsibilities as head of the German Affairs
Section are coming to an end.

It is interesting to note how little American Middle East policy has deviated from its formulation more
than thirty years ago. Today, as then, American policy
is directed almost exclusively against Soviet Russian
penetration of the Middle East and North Africa, and unlike the British strategy in 1951, it is based on naval
power in the Mediterranean as the gateway to the industrial heart of the Soviet Union with Egypt, Syria,
Greece and Turkey as allies to protect the flanks of the
navy. This strategy continues to minimize the importance
of Israel in any defense posture even in the face of a
Soviet threat to the oil-rich Arab gulf states and without regard to the demonstrated strength of the Israel
Defense Force. At the same time, the policy followed by
Secretary of State Dean Acheson may very well be held
responsible for planting the seeds of the 1956 war when
he chose not to pressure Egypt to lift the blockade of
the Suez, which the British, French and Israelis insisted was vital for their existence. Acheson, and after
him John Foster Dulles, stubbornly believed they could
keep Egypt allied to the West or at least neutral in any
conflict with the Soviet Union. Neither statesmen, apparently, was aware of the extent of Russian penetration
of the Nasser regime.
Lipsky and the AZC were literally the only American
Jewish organization intimately involved in all these
developments. But as his health began to fail, Lipsky
found himself physically unable to make the numerous
trips to Washington that were necessary to defend the
grant-in-aid program for Israel, and he began to rely
more and more on I.L. Kenen to do the necessary lobby-
ing. Eventually, in 1953, with Lipsky gone, the AZC
decided to establish the American Zionist Committee for
Public Affairs and locate it permanently in Washington,

D.C., with Kenen as its head and registered lobbyist, to carry on the task of safeguarding Israel's place in the foreign aid program.

17

GOALS FOR NON-ZIONISTS

While American Zionists were painfully proceeding to carve out a role for themselves in the post-Israel Zionist movement, the non-Zionist defense agencies were occupied with a similar search for an ideological basis that would justify their continued existence. The American Jewish Committee heard president Jacob Blaustein deliver a keynote address at its annual conference in January which rejected the arguments of those members who believed in confining their activities to purely Jewish matters and appealed for a much broader philosophy. He insisted that the work of the American Jewish Committee should encompass American as well as Jewish interests, and defended the policy in which the American Jewish Committee would be a leader in the fight for "American unity" in all areas. The American interest he defined as the fight against discrimination affecting Negroes, Puerto Ricans, Mexicans and other minority peoples as well as Jews; specific Jewish areas of interest included combating anti-Semitism and restrictive immigration legislation, and fighting for human rights. "We and all other American institutions must mobilize all our resources for the achievement of that American unity and promoting human relations programs directed to bridging the gap between the American promise and the American reality," Blaustein said.

Part of that program included the fight against communism and communist infiltration. The Jewish Labor Committee stressed these objectives even more vehemently than the American Jewish Committee did. At its national executive conference early in February, the decline and liquidation of Jewish life in the Soviet Union as well as in the Soviet satellite countries were described in considerable detail. Delegates also heard that the JLC had rescued more than one thousand Jews from the Soviet satellite countries by its underground network. Benjamin Tabachinsky, the JLC campaign director, reaffirmed the traditional anti-Zionist position of the organization but at the same time pointed to the special projects

297

that the JLC sponsored in Israel. However, "this does
not mean and never will mean that we believe in the
liquidation of Jewish life in other sections of the
world," he asserted.

Israeli sources insisted that the JLC exaggerated
its rescue claims. The Israel government, they said,
maintains friendly relations with all the Soviet
satellite countries and thereby was able to assure the
continuation of Jewish emigration without resorting to
underground methods. In recent weeks, they claimed, 800
Jews had been allowed to leave Poland, 1,100 had left
Rumania, and 400 were the vanguard of 3,000 Jews scheduled to leave Hungary. Further evidence about the decline of Jewish life in Poland was disclosed by Azriel
Ukhmani, a former counsellor at the Israel legation in
Warsaw and a member of the left-wing Mapam. Interviewed
by the London **Jewish Chronicle** as he was about to leave
for Israel, Ukhmani described current Polish Jewish life
as "diminutive," its cultural expression being limited
by the communists to a Yiddish State Theater in Lodz and
one in Wroclaw. There was also one Yiddish newspaper,
called the **Volkstimme,** which appeared three times a
week, and one Yiddish periodical which appeared irregu-
larly called **Literarische Shriften.**

The American Jewish Committee emphasized its non-
Zionist position by publishing in **Commentary** an article
calculated to show its devotion to human rights and its
freedom from Zionist influence. The article, entitled
"Israel's Zealots in Gabardine," was by Alfred Werner,
and it set the tone for the critical approach to life in
Israel that the American Jewish Committee is continuing
to this day in another of its publications, called **Present Tense.** Werner described the Neturei Karta, an anti-
state Orthodox group living in Israel, and warned:
"Neturei Karta may be a very small group, but its very
existence should be a warning to the other Orthodox
groups that until they concede more freedom to their
fellow Israelis, the threat of fratricidal religious
struggle will continue to hang over Israel."

Werner, a German refugee who was primarily an art
critic, had no compunction about leaping to an exaggerated conclusion on the basis of an admittedly insig-
nificant Israeli religious sect. In effect, also, his
article gave notice that Elliot Cohen, the editor of
Commentary, had no intention of allowing his critics to
influence his editorial policy. Efforts to counter the
stinging criticism of men like Rabbi Milton Steinberg
led the American Jewish Committee to arrange a feature
in **Time** magazine on January 29, which sang the praises

of **Commentary** and its editor. **Time** observed that the magazine had lost $104,000 in 1950, but then went on to explain that "the Committee, which foots **Commentary's** bills, wanted a magazine that would exemplify the intellectual dignity of Judaism, and it picked Editor Cohen as the man for the job."

Some months later, when Rabbi Steinberg's book, entitled **A Believing Jew**, was published posthumously, the Newsletter called attention to his observations about **Commentary** magazine and its role in Jewish life. The Newsletter reported:

> In the high praise which reviewers are heaping on **A Believing Jew**, by the late Rabbi Milton Steinberg, one should not overlook the nine pages of his hitherto unpublished "Recommendations" to **Commentary** magazine, which follow directly on his now famous analysis of that American Jewish Committee monthly. It is not widely known that **in the last weeks of his life, Rabbi Steinberg had several meetings with** Commentary's **editor Elliot Cohen in a fruitless effort to persuade him to adopt the following suggestions:**
>
> Pointing out that the writer resources of American Jewry "are much richer than may have been recognized by the Editorial Board; certainly far richer than the columns of the magazine suggest," Rabbi Steinberg urges the adoption of a recommendation by Dr. Louis Finkelstein that writers be assigned to aid scholars and laymen "who have something of Jewish consequence to say but lack either the energy or the skill."
>
> The Editors must overcome the antagonism they have aroused in important Jewish fields by a "repeated, visible demonstration of respect...for the life-interests and sanctities of these groups."
>
> Rabbi Steinberg rejects the publication committee's reason for failing to publish papers by rabbis, and lists a number of demonstrated ability whom the Editor never invited to write, then adds bluntly: "This much is certain: the rabbinate as a whole is convinced, and with warrant, of hostility toward itself on the part of **Commentary's** editors."
>
> Rabbi Steinberg then lists a dozen basic themes "of positive Jewish import" which the

magazine should cover fully, among them: **Kash-ruth**, the Jewish Day School, the worth of de-fense agency programs and the National Confer-ence of Christians and Jews, and the crisis in Conservative Judaism over ritual.

"To persist in neglecting themes of this order is not only to commit a disservice to Jewish life, it is to be guilty of unresource-ful journalism," Rabbi Steinberg said. Either the "editors" of **Commentary** have been ignorant of these subjects, or "have out of bias denied them a hearing," he went on. Rabbi Steinberg concluded: "If the second alternative prevail, they have no business acting as editors of a publication of Jewish reference nor has the American Jewish Committee, as a custodian of communal interests and funds, the right to re-tain them in their posts."

Rabbi Steinberg was very gentle in his criticism. He might have pointed out that **Com-mentary** actually has only one editor who makes policy: $18,000-a-year Elliot Cohen. He might have inquired into Mr. Cohen's background in Jewish life and into his published views. He could have gone into such matters as **Commen-tary's** insulting practice of buying manuscripts and never publishing them. Instead, there was more than enough kindness in the man to subdue his righteous indignation.

I alerted Leftwich to Rabbi Steinberg's criticism of **Commentary** since he, too, had been a victim of its bad manners. I then offered my own analysis of Rabbi Stein-berg as I knew him in the following observations:

"I've spent a lot of time--for me, that is--reading Milton Steinberg's posthumous book, and it is really a brilliant expression of an intelligent Jew's relation with God and his own community. Steinberg was never too positive in his belief in God; he had to arrive at one, and he was never too sure about the accuracy of his rea-soning. In the days before his first heart attack, he was extremely ambitious and vain. The women of his syna-gogue adored him--literally--the men as well as his fellow rabbis all respected him, and since he was only about 40 at this point in his career, the adulation began to go to his head. I know, because I was there as a member of his congregation.

"Also, I shall always feel good about asking him for and publishing in the **Contemporary Jewish Record** one of his Yom Kippur night sermons--in 1940, I think--on American Jews and anti-Semitism. His opinions went quite contrary to prevailing American Jewish Committee 'line' but the front office never said a word in protest. So that was one saved for posterity. It isn't in the current book, which his wife and Maurice Samuel put together.

"After his illness struck, he became an infinitely more lovable person. He knew his days were numbered, and he sincerely wanted to make every day of his life count for some achievement. He wrote with great care and devoted more and more of his interest to philosophy. Withal, I don't think he was a very profound thinker--I don't mean to be critical--he was too much the artist and the actor for his public to be profound, yet his ability to see and express with great clarity the religious problems of himself and his generation made his contemporaries look up to him as the 'rabbis rabbi.' Even after reading his essays on how to find God and believe in Him, I wonder whether he ever really did.

"I have the feeling--and it is only that--that Steinberg was enamoured of the intellectual search, the challenge, because it is certain that he never had much use for traditional observance and ritual. His home was not kosher; neither were the functions at the synagogue until Simon Noveck became his assistant. Steinberg had little use for 'pots and pans' religion, as he disparagingly referred to **kashruth**, and his own trend was more in the direction of the Reform non-observance than the Conservative semi-observance and the Seminary Orthodoxy. But a great man because of his faults, one of the great Jews of our generation, and it is a pity that he went so early."

In the same letter I called Leftwich's attention to a review in the **New York Times** of a book entitled **History of Syria**, by Professor Philip K. Hitti, of Princeton University. Although Hitti's book was an undisguised piece of Arab propaganda, it was uncritically praised by the reviewer, one Morroe Berger, described as the Near East analyst of the American Jewish Committee. The Newsletter pointed out that Berger had failed to criticize the Arab historian's attempt to establish Syria's claim to all of modern Palestine, including the state of Israel, or to take exception to Hitti's erroneous reference to Zionism as "an intruding nationalist movement of Central and Western European Jews," and as a "disruptive, expansive force." Instead, the American Jewish Committee's expert concluded: "This dramatic story of ebb and flow of civilization in Syria...is admirably told by Philip K. Hitti."

The anti-nationalist, anti-Zionist approach of the American Jewish Committee was brought more sharply into focus at its Chicago policy meeting in October, when it adopted a resolution against the educational policies and the request for status of the Jewish Agency, although it did not specifically name the Jewish Agency in its resolution. The same resolution made no reference to the assurances extended five days before the meeting by Prime Minister Ben-Gurion, who had said: "The Knesset may be asked to confer a special status on the Jewish Agency inside Israel.... However, the Knesset cannot and does not wish to affect by its legislation any activity outside Israel's borders. With reference to American Jewry, the position will thus remain as before, namely, that Israel will cooperate directly on matters affecting itself with all Jewish organizations desirous of such cooperation."

In thus limiting the status that the Jewish Agency had sought, the Prime Minister was at the same time giving the American Jewish Committee the kind of assurance of even-handedness that Jacob Blaustein had sought from Israel. The delegates at the policy meeting placed much more emphasis, however, on the question of what the Committee's response should be in its brief on the MacIver Report, and what position it should take on the question of German restitution. A conference of Jewish organizations was scheduled for the following week to resolve matters concerning restitution. All organizations had agreed in advance that German restitution funds should go to Israel, but no decision had been taken on which organization was to be the spokesman for the Jews who would remain in Germany, a prerogative which the American Jewish Committee claimed for itself, and which it feared would be contested by the Jewish Agency.

The American Jewish Committee's insistence on its prerogatives not only where Zionist organizations were concerned but also in regard to **Commentary** prompted me to question why Jewish intellectuals like Elliot Cohen and some of his associates when he was an editor of **The Menorah Journal** found it necessary in their writings to demonstrate their alienation from Judaism. I suggested the following reasons in a letter to Leftwich:

"Cohen has been going his own undisturbed way. You ask what is wrong with his generation? I think they were the bright young men--the Cohens, the Solows, the Irwin Edmans, the Lionel Trillings, etc.--who started as Jews and wanted to be Jews but found no audience for their efforts, no place for them to go once they had landed on

the **Menorah Journal**. The basic fault there was Henry
Hurwitz' and the Zionists'. The one was sterile, the
other too dogmatic for any creative spirit. So they fell
into the Communist trap and eventually emerged spirit-
ually bruised or broken.

"Or else, like Trilling and Edman and Walter Lipp-
man--he was in that group, too--they cast off the ties
altogether though not necessarily in formal conversion.
Even George Sokolsky was once an ardent young Zionist.
Henry Hurwitz and all his group--Horace Kallen--were
rebels against Judaism. They are even to this day. They
thought they could survive on the humanist elements
without subscribing to the religion, on the stalk without the flowers--or vice versa, depending on your point
of view, and in the end they found themselves naked and
barefoot, as the saying goes.

"Now Kallen and Henry argue over the latter's adherence to the Council for Judaism--both of them are completely unprincipled opportunists. In a sense they are
also like the Bundists and the Yiddishists, and all
others who try to live on part of a Jew because they
can't swallow the whole. It all comes down to some form
or other of **selbsthass**, of resentment against being born
a Jew. We've always had that variety of individual, but
in a free environment they have become far more numerous
and influential than ever before in modern history."

In response, my English friend sent me a clipping
from the magazine **Zion**, the English language monthly of
the World Zionist Organization, published in Jerusalem.
It contained another example of a self-hating Jew, this
time a Russian communist writer named Nathan Riback. He
had written a novel which heaped extravagant praise upon
a historical character, a murderous bigot whose name had
become a byword among Jews everywhere. The hero of Riback's novel was Bogdan Chmelniecki, a Ukrainian chief-
tain who lived in infamy as the pogromist who massacred
300,000 Jews in the year 1684. This was the character
hailed by Riback as a "national hero," a tribute about
which **Zion** observed: "If the author, as his name suggests, is a Jew, this will be the first time that a Jew
is immortalizing an historic murderer of his people."

The same impulse to run away from Judaism, or at
least from being Jewish, led many young American Jews to
look for a life-satisfying philosophy in the dogmas of
communism. America in 1951 was caught up in the anti-
communist hysteria of the hearings conducted by Senator
Joseph McCarthy, an excess of reaction against radicalism, in which many Jews were victimized. McCarthyism had
its extremist counterpart in the American Jewish League

Against Communism (AJLAC), an organization sponsored by Alfred Kohlberg, a wealthy importer who had suffered substantial losses when the communists took over China. The executive director of AJLAC was Rabbi Benjamin Schultz, and together in their zeal to cleanse the ranks of Jewish organizations, they managed to offend and out- rage most Jews.

At the beginning of the year, a joint statement was issued by the American Jewish Congress, the American Jewish Committee and the ADL condemning the activities of "any organization employing the name 'Jewish' in its title, which resorts to smear tactics and character as- sassination" in the fight against communism. It espec- ially deplored "such activity on the part of a rabbi." Although the statement avoided mentioning names, it was clearly directed against AJLAC and its executive direc- tor, Rabbi Schultz, and denounced them for their "ir- responsible vigilantism" and for participating in "re- cent slanderous attacks against personalities in the political arena and the entertainment world."

The statement was not released to the newspapers but instead was privately distributed by the three agencies because, as the Newsletter disclosed, two other Jewish organizations had refused to go along with it. The News- letter reported:

> The refusal of the Jewish Labor Committee and the Jewish War Veterans to go along with the other agencies prevented the statement from being issued by the NCRAC, the coordinating body for the defense groups. Originally a much more "militant" statement specifically naming the American Jewish League and Rabbi Schultz was submitted by the American Jewish Congress but, at the insistence of the American Jewish Committee, it was amended to read as a declara- tion of general principles rather than a denun- ciation of a particular organization. It was also planned to publish the statement in the Congress Weekly and other defense agency publi- cations, but a spokesman for the American Jew- ish Congress said they would not publish it be- cause it was not "militant" enough, nor would they release it to the English Jewish press. The American Jewish Committee also had no plans for publication of the statement, but the ADL said it would appear in the next issue of The Facts.

The defense agencies' reluctance to publicize their disavowal and condemnation of AJLAC was shortlived. The Newsletter's report that two Jewish organizations held back from supporting the statement apparently forced their hands and resulted in more open and direct action. At a special meeting on January 30, the NCRAC formulated and issued a scathing denunciation by name of Rabbi Benjamin Schultz for his criticism of Secretary of Defense George C. Marshall and Fleet Admiral Chester W. Nimitz. The statement was signed by John Slawson, executive director of the American Jewish Committee; David W. Petegorsky, executive director of the American Jewish Congress; Benjamin Epstein, executive director of the ADL; Jacob Pat, executive director of the Jewish Labor Committee; Ben Kaufman, executive director of the Jewish War Veterans; Rabbi Maurice N. Eisendrath, president of the UAHC; and Isaiah Minkoff, executive director of NCRAC. It was an action unprecedented in the history of the American Jewish community! The very next day, the New York Board of Rabbis also unanimously passed a resolution denouncing Rabbi Schultz for "unrabbinical behavior" in assuming the prerogative of sitting in judgment upon other persons. For reasons of policy, however, the resolution was not made public.

The Newsletter reprinted the NCRAC statement as a special supplement to its regular weekly edition in order that its readers might have the full text before it appeared elsewhere. Some part of my own sense of accomplishment in reporting the entire episode, whose historical importance I fully appreciated, crept into my letter to Leftwich containing the following description of events:

"The Newsletter is going great guns since the first of the year--every issue so far has been sold out--and I'm holding my breath and praying that it will pay off. Its power was graphically demonstrated yesterday when I learned of the NCRAC condemnation of Rabbi Schultz and his anti-Communist League. Rabbis, the defense agencies and other groups have been wanting to shut him up for some time, and last year decided on an NCRAC condemnation. The Jewish War Veterans and the JLC wouldn't go along, and the Committee was all for soft-pedaling the condemnation--as I wrote in my January story. That report, however, put the JLC, the JWV and the American Jewish Committee on the spot, and the JLC particularly was subjected to a great deal of behind-the-scenes pressure during January as a result of my disclosures. The results you can see in the current Newsletter supplement, my first.

"The story was fed to me on Thursday noon, just as the NCRAC released it and before it was in the mails for the papers. My Newsletter had already been run off, so this was the next best thing I could do. That gives me a first-class scoop on everybody. The story was given me all along by a leak in one of the defense agencies, who was deliberately using me to force just such a result, which his agency wanted but for their own reasons did not want the credit for."

I did not name my informant nor did I keep a record of his identity. The text of the NCRAC statement, issued on Tuesday morning, January 30, just three days after Rabbi Schultz had criticized Secretary of Defense George C. Marshall and Fleet Admiral Chester W. Nimitz in a speech delivered in Washington, D.C., is as follows:

"The undersigned Jewish organizations, representing through their affiliates the overwhelming majority of the organized Jewish community of the United States, regard as infamous the attack by Rabbi Benjamin Schultz, Director of the American Jewish League Against Communism, on the patriotism and moral character of two great Americans, Secretary of Defense George C. Marshall and Fleet Admiral Chester W. Nimitz.

"Rabbi Schultz has been reported in the newspapers as having referred to Secretary Marshall as a 'fall guy' in a plot to shield pro-Red activities; and to Admiral Nimitz, recently named chairman of the President's Commission on Internal Security and Individual Rights, as having a 'bad' record 'on tolerance of pro-Communists' and as a foil 'in a deliberate attempt to whitewash an evil pro-Communist situation.'

"Such irresponsible attacks impair the fight against Communism by creating confusion and distrust at home and by undermining overseas the high confidence earned by Nimitz and Marshall, two of the chief architects in the world-wide fight against totalitarianism.

"These tactics are particularly reprehensible at a time when the preservation of American democracy requires the highest regard for civil rights and liberties as fully as it needs opposition to Communism.

"Rabbi Schultz in no way represents any section of the American Jewish community and the major Jewish organizations repudiate and condemn his repeated resort to vilification and slander of reputable Americans on the pretext of combatting Communism."

The NCRAC denunciation was followed by the resignations from AJLAC of a number of its members. It was probably this as much as the NCRAC action which prompted Alfred Kohlberg, the chairman of AJLAC, to send a letter to all of the organization's members, saying: "I fully support not only Rabbi Schultz's right to say what he did, I support what he said, and I think he put it courteously." Kohlberg attacked the NCRAC for failing to act "when sermons of Rabbi Abba Hillel Silver, scoffing at our bloody defense in Korea, and advocating appeasement of Communism, were printed in the Communist press, including the front page of the **Daily Worker**." He further charged that "NCRAC rushes to denounce anti-Communist statements--never pro-Communist statements." The "Directorates" of the American Jewish Committee, the American Jewish Congress and the ADL, Kohlberg went on to charge, permitted "pinko staffs to lead them around by the nose."

It was a bruising experience for all concerned. But eventually a quiet and peaceful solution to the controversy was arranged by the Jewish Labor Committee when it met with Schultz and Kohlberg and agreed to set up meetings with individual members of the NCRAC in a peace-making effort. The NCRAC thus effectively scotched the excesses of AJLAC and the fulminations of Alfred Kohlberg, but the controversy itself compelled the defense agencies to reevaluate their methods for combatting communism without at the same time trampling on the civil rights of communists and fellow travelers. The American Jewish Congress and its liberal lawyers who made policy for the organization found themselves in an especially difficult position when they continued their attempt to purge their own ranks. Thus, when David Petegorsky, Shad Polier, the chairman of the executive committee, and other Congress leaders issued a statement calling on President Truman's Commission on Internal Security and Individual Rights to investigate the alleged abuses of Congressional immunity and the blacklisting of liberals, other Jewish organizational officials termed the action ill-advised and prejudicial to Jewish welfare. They were also quick to point out that it was less than a year since the American Jewish Congress itself had purged its staff and its West Coast chapters of communists and such communist affiliates as the Jewish Peoples Fraternal Order.

The whole issue flared up again when 27 active members and officers of the Manhattan Division of the American Jewish Congress were dismissed on April 30 after a series of hearings. Pro-communist charges had been made officially against the Manhattan Division after Metropolitan Council president Ben London demanded the resignation of executive director David Petegorsky. London and other division officers refused to attend the hearings and insisted that they would ignore the action of the parent organization and its demand that they re-sign. Petegorsky declined to release details of the hearings or the names of the 27 who were dismissed.

An editorial in the **Jewish Examiner**, of Brooklyn, N.Y., entitled, "Decline of the American Jewish Con-gress," sharply criticized the action against the Man-hattan Division and the dismissal of its officers and members. The editorial went on to charge that the Con-gress duplicated the work of the American Jewish Com-mittee and misused its funds to purchase "its elephan-tine new half-million dollar headquarters." Other critics noted the expansion of the staff and program of the American Jewish Congress under Petegorsky's capable direction and queried where the funds to pay for these enlarged activities were to come from. The purge of the communist elements helped to clear the atmosphere and made possible the return of the Poale-Zion organization and the Jewish National Workers Alliance to the ranks of the groups which were affiliated with the American Jew-ish Congress. There had been a time when the American Jewish Congress was able to list about 24 national and central agencies on its letterhead as affiliates, among them the ZOA and several Zionist fraternal orders, but these had been absent from its councils for many years. At its national convention later that year, however, the pressure from Zionist delegates was strong enough to cause a switch in the election of a president from Shad Polier to Dr. Israel Goldstein, a former president of the ZOA and the World Confederation of General Zionists as well as the rabbi of the prestigious Congregation B'nai Jeshurun in Manhattan.

The communist issue continued to plague Jewish or-ganizations throughout the year. Staff unions were in-filtrated, and in several instances dominated, by com-munists. This led to such embarrassing situations as that experienced by HIAS and USNA, who were ordered in April to sever relations with the Social Service Em-ploye Union, Local 19, which together with its national union had been expelled by the CIO because it was commu-nist dominated. The whole problem was thrashed out again by the Jewish social workers when their organizations met in convention. The Newsletter published the follow-ing exclusive report of the sessions:

Communism and civil liberties formed the big issue at the joint annual convention of the National Conference of Jewish Social Welfare and the National Conference of Jewish Center

Workers in Atlantic City, N.J., on May 18-23.
No hint of the struggle between pro- and anti-
communist forces at the convention was allowed
to reach the general press.

Attempting to forestall trouble, Dr. Maurice B. Hexter, executive head of the New York
Federation of Jewish Philanthropies, chaired a
special meeting on Sunday, May 20 (allegedly
called by him), at which 500 social worker
delegates heard Dr. Simon Segal, American Jewish Committee foreign affairs chief, and Harry
Schwartz, **New York Times** anti-Soviet expert,
urge the anti-communist, anti-Social Service
Employe Union view. And on Monday afternoon,
following a liberal address by Congressman
Jacob Javits (Rep., N.Y.), a strong anti-communist speech was delivered by Julian Cohen,
NCRAC spokesman.

Despite these attacks, the pro-communist
wing had enough voting strength Monday night to
push through a rule barring presentation to the
convention of any social action resolution unless it had the unanimous approval of the resolutions committee. The resolution was adopted
at a business meeting of the Center Workers
after two hours of talk and parliamentary
maneuvering. Communists and their sympathizers
command about half of the Center Workers voting
strength, the report said.

Both sides feared the consequences if a
resolution condemning totalitarianism--commu-
nist and fascist--were presented; and the pro-
communists seemed pleased to have blocked the
possibility of such a resolution. The others
felt that they had averted a possible break-up
of the Center Workers association. And practically all agreed that it was good so few laymen
were present to observe the extent of communist
infiltration among the Center Workers.

Another unpleasant controversy involving charges of
communist affiliation cropped up once more in the B'nai
B'rith Hillel Foundation. This time it was over an issue
which many believed had been settled the previous year.
It involved Rabbi Herman Pollack, the Hillel director at
Brooklyn College, who had been cleared of any suspicion
of disloyalty in December 1950 by an investigating committee headed by Rabbi Joseph Lookstein. The old charges
were revived in June when Judge David Benjamin, of the

City Court, a prominent Brooklyn, N.Y., civic and political leader, was asked to help raise funds for the Hillel building at Brooklyn College. Judge Benjamin refused, insisting that Rabbi Pollack be removed before he
would undertake to help.

The controversy reached a critical stage when B'nai
B'rith president Frank Goldman, without advising national Hillel officials of his plan, invited Brooklyn
College president Harry Gideons to tell a B'nai B'rith
meeting how he felt about Rabbi Pollack, in whom he had
frequently expressed full confidence. Indignant Hillel
leaders threatened to resign in protest over what they
regarded as Goldman's high-handed action, but injured
feelings were apparently soothed by the reassuring words
of the National Hillel director, Rabbi Arthur Lelyveld.

Contributing to the anti-communist climate of the
times was a Sunday sensation report, which appeared in
the **New York Journal American,** of an alleged secret
document involving a Young Israel leader, President
Franklin D. Roosevelt and Soviet Premier Josef Stalin.
The Newsletter described the alleged secret document as
a "clumsily patched forgery" of a letter supposedly sent
by President Roosevelt to Jacob O. Zabronsky asking him
to act as an intermediary with Soviet Premier Stalin.
Zabronsky, who was no longer alive when the alleged
letter was published by the Hearst newspaper, was identified as a president of the Young Israel organization
from 1936 to 1939. Young Israel as well as the State
Department promptly denounced the letter as a forgery
and offered detailed proof of its falsity. The State
Department disclosed that the forged letter had originally appeared in the memoirs of Jose Doussinague,
Spain's wartime propaganda chief and later Spanish
ambassador to Chile.

The Newsletter's observation on the report and its
prediction about the action that would be taken by the
Hearst newspaper editors proved to be only too true. The
Newsletter said:

> Like the **Chicago Tribune** editors, Hearst
> editors will no doubt disclaim anti-Semitic in-
> tent or awareness of anti-Jewish implications.
> Hearst columnist Westbrook Pegler also dis-
> claims bias despite his Coughlin-like tactics
> in recent weeks in attacks on Jewish organiza-
> tions and on prominent individuals who just
> happen to have distinctive Jewish names.

Later that year, the **New York Journal American** at-

tributed to AJLAC a charge that Harold Glasser, the director of the CJFWF Institute on Overseas Studies, was
under investigation. The charge was promptly denied by
Harry L. Lurie, the CJFWF director. Glasser had been
accused by the notorious Elizabeth Bently, a self-con-
fessed Soviet spy courier, of having been a member of
her group, but he was vigorously defended by the Secretary of the Treasury John W. Snyder, for whom he had
once worked. Nevertheless, Alfred Kohlberg, president of
AJLAC, insisted, when he brought his charges, on a retraction. Kohlberg said: "Glasser has never denied the
charges before the committee although he was given an
opportunity to do so." To which Harry Lurie retorted
that in view of "Secretary Snyder's defense of Glasser
we did not take any action. We thought his references
were excellent."

And there the matter was dropped.

18

THE RELIGIOUS AND CULTURAL EXCHANGE

At this early date, barely three years after the independence of the state of Israel, it was not possible to gauge the depth of the impact made by Israel on American Jewish cultural developments. No one can say, for example, that certain American trends in art, music or literature--or in religious thought--would not have developed even if there had not been a state of Israel, although it is most probable that they would have been different, and to that extent, at least, there was some measure of Israel's impact.

There were, of course, some specific signs of the influence that Israel was having on American Jewish thought. Initially, it was the controversy over the question of religious freedom in Israel, brought to public attention in December 1950--as we have noted--by a letter in the **New York Times** that was signed by Harold Riegelman, a vice president of the American Jewish Committee, by Judge Samuel Hofstadter and by Jacob Dinnes. Attention continued to be drawn in the new year to the subject by another letter, signed this time by Lessing J. Rosenwald, president of the American Council for Judaism, which was given a full column in the **New York Times** on January 7.

Interest in the controversy was heightened by the arrival in New York of the Israeli Minister for Religious Affairs, Rabbi Judah L. Maimon, on January 23. He had planned a four weeks speaking tour, but almost immediately faced opposition. He had been scheduled to speak in Cincinnati on February 4, but local sponsors of his visit ran into trouble when leaders of Reform Judaism, which had its headquarters in that city, promptly raised the question of religious freedom in Israel. They refused to join the group that was to welcome Rabbi Maimon because Reform Judaism and its rabbis were not recognized in Israel. Among them were some of Cincinnati's most prominent citizens, including Dr. Nelson Glueck, the president of Hebrew Union College; Lester A. Jaffe, chairman of the board of the Hebrew Union College;

Philip Myers, a vice president of the UAHC; and Rabbi Stanley R. Brav, spiritual leader of the Rockdale Avenue Temple. It was not an auspicious beginning.

The same problem, but this time affecting the recognition of Conservative rabbis in Israel, came under discussion at the conference of the United Synagogue of America in New York on February 18. About 400 Conservative rabbis met and formulated a ten-point program for the "reinforcement of Jewish spiritual values." One of the proposals called for the establishment of a national magazine with an initial circulation of 30,000 which would reflect Conservative opinion and present "discussion material as well as coverage of organizational developments." But of more immediate concern was the urgent appeal by Rabbi Solomon Goldman, of Chicago, for the strengthening of American Judaism now that there was a state of Israel. His comments were summarized by the Newsletter in the following report:

> At the United Synagogue convention last month, Rabbi Solomon Goldman of Chicago strongly urged the establishment of a commission of experts to investigate the reasons why American Jews are not religiously observant and to recommend steps to remedy the situation. In an abridged version of his address, currently appearing in the **Reconstructionist**, Rabbi Goldman points out that for most Jews here, America is not a "boarding-house. It is a home." He asks how long we will accept lip-service to Judaism and look the other way when its tenets are violated; he questions: "Why does Mr. X make such an ado about his boy's becoming Bar Mitzvah, and why, when the happy event occurs, does he start off the Bar Mitzvah feast with a shrimp cocktail? Shall we say he is ignorant and confused?"
>
> The sharpest strictures of the noted Conservative rabbi are for the rabbinate itself. He says: "If it is our considered opinion that American Jews are confused and ignorant, and their rabbis are incompetent and derelict in their duties, then we are duty-bound to say so. The fact is that that is exactly what we have been saying for nearly half a century. We have shouted at Mr. X without abatement, with anger and indignation. But we have never stopped taking his money or doing him honor.... How long shall we play at make-believe?"

An increased consciousness of the need to strengthen religious observance and belief, which was reflected in Rabbi Goldman's stirring appeal, and which obviously was stimulated by the state of Israel, found expression in a number of different areas. Early in April, Columbia University in a special ceremony, honored the memory of Rabbi Gershom Seixas, the American Revolutionary War chaplain who had been a trustee of Columbia from 1784 to 1814. In Israel, a room in memory of Rabbi Stephen S. Wise was set aside in the projected Jewish National and University Library building in Jerusalem, and a grant of $11,000 for equipment for the room was made by the Esco Foundation, the sponsors of which were Mr. and Mrs. Frank Cohen. Famed violinist Yehudi Menuhin and his sister Hepzibah, an equally famed pianist, donated IL 1,500 (about $4200) from the proceeds of their concerts in Israel to be used for the encouragement of composers and performing artists in Israel. The noted American composer Aaron Copland was scheduled to conduct a seminar on music in America at Zichron Yaacov, and his a capella work for choir, entitled "In the Beginning," was to be featured at the Ein Gev festival.

In New London, Connecticut, where the Central Conference of American Rabbis held its convention in June, what the Newsletter described as "probably the most exciting debate in American Judaism since the rise of the Reform movement" took place when Reform Rabbis James G. Heller and Leon I. Feuer debated the question of merging Reform and Conservative Judaism with Conservative Rabbi Robert Gordis and Reconstructionist leader Rabbi Ira Eisenstein. The convention left that question open but it did include among its resolutions support for Israel as well as a demand that Israel recognize the legitimacy of Reform rabbis. An invitation was extended to the Conservative Rabbinical Assembly to join in cooperative action and in the clearance of specific events.

At the Rabbinical Assembly convention, Rabbi Max Davidson, its president, and also chairman of the chaplaincy board of the Jewish Welfare Board, issued a call for a more vigorous Synagogue Council and "a new American Jewish Conference which will be composed exclusively of congregational and religious groups." Dr. Davidson described the existing Synagogue Council as "comparatively impotent and unproductive." At the same convention, a jarring note came from James Marshall, a prominent attorney and the son of the famed Louis Marshall, who urged the rabbis to adopt a more universalist approach to Jewish philanthropy and to Israel. "We must not permit the state of Israel to be a barrier between

Jews and mankind by overemphasizing one segment of mankind," Marshall declared.

The New York attorney's views found similar expression later that year in a symposium published in **American Judaism**, a new Reform bi-monthly, on the subject of "Living a full Jewish Life in the Diaspora." A number of American Jewish communal leaders participated, including Judge Joseph M. Proskauer, Jacob Blaustein, Edward A. Norman, Dr. Joshua Bloch, Rabbi Israel Goldstein and many others. The consensus was, as Dr. Bloch expressed it: "The ability of Jews to live a full Jewish life depends in no way upon any particular land."

Two strikingly contrasting views stand out. One came from Rabbi Goldstein, who said: "The more predominant the Jewish environment, the more fully can Jewish life be lived." A much gloomier prediction came from the ardently pro-Israel philanthropist Edward Norman, who warned: "The indications appear to be that after the next few generations, few people outside of Israel will care to lead a Jewish life." Fortunately, Norman's pessimism does not seem to be justified.

My own views on the future of the Jewish community in the United States were critical but more optimistic than Norman's. Writing to Leftwich early in the year, I focussed on the Jewish reading public for my analysis, and said:

"I will remind you again of my letter of some weeks ago in which I referred to our declining civilization, with the Dark Ages looming up ahead. There is the reason for the death of Jewish culture here; our entire community is infected with the materialistic disease. Professor Ginzberg's sharp analysis of our American Jewry—its Jews who live among Jews, work with Jews and socialize with Jews, yet 'have no vital relation to Judaism'; its rabbis who 'judge their own strength and success by the numbers who attend their lectures...not by their ability to provide...spiritual leadership'; its 'negatively oriented' leadership who 'aware of its limitations will instinctively manipulate the situation to remain in control rather than to work towards a larger and better informed participating group'—is it any wonder that his analysis leads only to the darkest pessimism?

"My own experience, not only with **Cross-Section, U.S.A.** but before that with **The Menorah Journal** and my series of exposes, shows how little the public cares about its institutions. As one man said to me the other day, the only place you will find some Jewish interest is at the top because they make a living—and a darn

good one--out of the 'Jew business.' The circulation
figures of our periodicals are another indication of the
decadence here: the **National Jewish Post**, less than
15,000 weekly; **Commentary**, 20,000 claimed but the actual
is closer to 14,000; **The Menorah Journal**, about 1800.
Need I go on?

"The only large circulation publications are those
given to organization memberships: **Jewish Frontier,
National Jewish Monthly, Congress Weekly, Hadassah**. But
their circulation figures mean nothing. People rarely
read carefully what they do not pay for. And now we're
getting set for another onslaught of house organs--even
the American Jewish Congress is preparing a quarterly
for 'learned' dicussions of its special slant on Jewish
affairs. But a truly literary magazine?--no organization
is that altruistic, I was told.

"They wouldn't even buy **The Menorah Journal** because
it is too high-brow for their purposes--I know because I
actually did ask around whether that would be possible.
In spite of my own feelings and because I recognize the
force of your arguments, I have been sending out feelers
to see if anything can be done about saving **The Menorah
Journal**--without Henry's knowledge, of course. The
answer everywhere is 'no.'

"Yet, I still maintain that there is a hunger among
the people for the values, the certainties, the identification of their religion. But they are so ignorant, so
distracted by the competition of our scientific paradise
that one would have to start very much like the writers
of eastern Europe in the last century, with stories and
plays and folk tales that would make a beginning all
over again of Jewish culture. Our rabbis don't reach the
people--even those few who sincerely try; and our organizations are mostly rackets."

In this climate of reexamination, Rabbi Louis Levitsky, of Temple Oheb Shalom, in Newark, N.J., called for
a reappraisal of the role of the rabbi in the American
Jewish community. In his congregational bulletin, he
pointed out that rabbis devoted to teaching rather than
preaching were needed more than ever. He went on to say:
"In spite of its urgency, fund raising is only a passing
phase, and even at its most critical stage, it is only
peripheral to Jewish life. The rabbi stands for the
eternal and the permanent in Jewish life. Our communities for their own good and for their dignity must begin
to make different demands upon the rabbi. We must recognize the fact that some rabbis are too timid to assert
their true place in the community, and some have so far
forgotten their unique function that they have joined

the 'me too' chorus. It therefore behooves each community to reexamine its needs and its program, and to
reassign functions to those best qualified to perform
them. In this readjustment, the function of the rabbi is
clear and precise: he is a teacher and preacher in
Israel, a unique Jewish historic function. He is not a
counterpart of a Protestant minister. He is heir to
Akiba, Maimonides, Elijah Gaon...."

Another aspect of the religious ferment in this period can be found in the discussions of American Jewish
scholars, who felt that there should be a new translation of the Bible. An announcement that a Protestant
version of the Old Testament on the basis of the King
James translation was to be published drew from Dr.
Joshua Bloch the observation that American Jews had produced only two Jewish translations of the Bible, one by
Issac Leeser more than a century earlier, and the other
by the Jewish Publication Society in 1915. There was a
need, he insisted, for a modern English version by
Jewish scholars.

His recommendation was echoed at the annual meeting
of the Jewish Publication Society by Dr. Jacob R. Marcus, chairman of the publications committee, who voiced
the opinions also of a number of the members when he
said: "Though the present version of the Jewish Publication Society Bible is recognized as the authorized
English version throughout the English-speaking world,
there are still those who feel that it is somewhat archaic in style and language. A number of members were of
the opinion that a revised modern version in more modern
English would be much more widely read and more appreciated. A subcommittee of the Publication Committee will
study this problem."

The Newsletter applauded this interest and went on
to note that in addition, much more attention should be
paid to the translations in Jewish prayer books. It
said:

A survey by your editor reveals that a far
worse situation prevails in prayer-book translations used by Conservative and Orthodox synagogues, complete with distortions of Hebrew
prayers made apparently under "good-will" influence and in the belief that anti-Semites
can't get someone to read Hebrew for them.
Among the distortions spotted were: the psalms
of David for the Hebrew David the Messiah;
elimination of the Chosen People concept. With
few exceptions, the English was either pseudo-

archaic or atrociously bad. Strong American prose to match the Hebrew strength is required.

From overseas Jewish leaders, there also came appeals for more religious content in the Zionist movement. At the silver jubilee of the World Union for Progressive Judaism, held in London, the almost legendary Rabbi Leo Baeck, who had survived the Holocaust, charged that American Zionism was ceasing to be a movement and warned that fundraising alone was not enough to justify its character. At the same meeting, the great philosopher, Professor Martin Buber, emphasized how necessary it was to preserve spiritual values in a "disintegrating" civilization. The Israelis, he said, knew that they had realized the goals of Zionism only in a geographic sense but not in a prophetic one. And on another occasion, the veteran English Zionist leader, Sir Leon Simon, at a dinner celebrating his 70th birthday, called for a revival of the teachings of Ahad Ha'am, and charged the Zionist organizations with the duty and responsibility to spread the spiritual values of Judaism.

Criticism of Israeli and other Jewish scholars and writers for failing to reflect adequately the enormous significance of the independence of the state of Israel came from the pen of Professor Raphael Patai, of Dropsie College, himself one of the first scholars to be granted a degree of Doctor of Philosophy by the Hebrew University. In the **Jewish Quarterly Review** for April, he reviewed sixty books about Israel in the English language, published since 1948, and arrived at the following conclusion: "Most of the books are popular.... Serious studies are few.... Not a single book has been published since the establishment of the Jewish State which deals with any of the numerous social aspects of the great events taking place at present in the country."

A letter from Leftwich raised the question of the cultural development in Israel and the failure of its writers to reflect the great events that were taking place. Drawing a comparison with the way the American Jewish community regarded cultural growth, I defended Israelis in the following reply:

"I say again that I am not as shocked as you and your friends are at the lack of any genuine Jewish spirit in Israel simply because I never could see how a pioneer country like Israel could demonstrate even as much culture as it has. I have been out West in places like Oklahoma, for example, when an oil boom will hit a town and everybody under the sun will come rushing into the place. Until the shock of building, of absorption

and readjustment is over--and it takes years--even your
most cultured individuals lose the elements of civilization which we take for granted so easily. What then
could we expect of a desert like Israel, peopled by con-
centration camp inmates, the dregs of North Africa's
poorhouses, and the primitive tribes of the Arabian
peninsula.

"What makes you assume, even for a moment, that the
elder brothers and sisters of the former Europeans in
Israel--those who emigrated to this country in 1910-
1915--are any better as individuals or as Jews? And
their sons and daughters who are my neighbors in Forest
Hills and Rego Park and other new Long Island communi-
ties--don't you think they exhibit the worst character-
istics of the nouveau riche with **none** of the softening
influence of our religion? They build great million
dollar synagogues, the better to play canasta in, or to
hold fashion shows, or to run gambling wheels and crap
games at building fund bazaars!

"You were the one who pointed out to me--and quite
rightly--when I complained of the character of our Jewish periodicals that at least they are being published,
whatever the quality might be. Israel publishing undoubtedly produces a vast amount of trash, but at least
there is publishing activity and somewhere along the
line a few good books will see the light. In no literary
period in England or America were there ever more than a
handful of works that were deemed worthy of survival,
even in such prolific periods as the late nineteenth
century.

"No, your original argument has convinced me--
activity even for activity's sake alone is far far better for the writer than a literary desert such as our
community here is rapidly becoming. **Commentary's** practice of buying and burying--is there anything more
frustrating to the writer?--may just be an expression of
Elliot Cohen's vanity, but it isn't very different from
the practice of the community itself in hiring ability
and burying it in organizational pigeonholes. In Israel,
where everybody is pushing and shoving to get things
done, or to get settled and make some money, there is at
least the saving grace of a consciousness of a cultural
heritage; here we use the words but they are utterly
meaningless to nine and a half out of ten of our allegedly five million synagogue members. (That figure is
nonsense, of course, and is based on an old **Year Book**
estimate which was a wishful guess to begin with. Actually no one knows how many Jews there are in the
United States, much less how many synagogue members--

even current figures in the **American Jewish Year Book**
are 'guesstimates.' What's worse, no one among the communal organizations is prepared after last year's effort
even to sponsor a statistical bureau.)"

News from Israel supported my contention that there
was considerable cultural activity in Israel though much
of it was of questionable value. In July, the fiftieth
anniversary of the publication of the first poems of
Zalman Schneour became the occasion for a literary celebration. Schneour, who was best known in the United
States as a Yiddish novelist, was eulogized in the
Israel press and a jubilee edition of his poems was sold
out on the day of publication. Writing about Schneour in
Haboker, Baruch Karu observed: "Schneour's Hebrew poems
fill four volumes and his narrative prose in Hebrew
several more. In Yiddish, he wrote more than this, and
he is at present engaged in translating his own works
into Hebrew.... His romances are sung to this day, and
in their time were considered the finest poetry of their
generation." Schneour later rounded out this extraordinary career by serving one term as the president of
Israel.

Also in line with my comments to Leftwich was the
fact, reported in the Newsletter, that the Jewish Publication Society was in a serious financial bind caused by
a sharp rise in publication costs and declining public
interest and support. Another publisher of Jewish books,
Schocken Books, also curtailed its production sharply
for the remainder of 1951, limiting its activity for the
most part to the promotion of the works of Franz Kafka.
The editor of Schocken, Dr. Nathan Glazer, who was
responsible for many of its notable productions, continued in that post but also accepted an appointment as
professor of history at Brandeis University.

In September, the American Jewish Historical Society
became embroiled in a controversy entirely out of keeping with its customary staid character. In an earlier
issue of the **Publications of the American Jewish Historical Society**, it had published a historical study by
Naomi Winter, entitled "The Reaction of Reform Judaism
in America to Political Zionism (1897-1922)." The content of the study apparently had a special appeal for
the anti-Zionist American Council for Judaism because it
presented in scholarly fashion the record of Reform
Judaism in its opposition to Zionism. That anti-Zionist
organization promptly requested a large number of reprints of the study and agreed to pay for them. Behind
the scenes of the hitherto placid historical society
there broke out at once a bitter controversy over this

request. After some hours of discussion, the executive
council of the historical society came up with an acceptable compromise. The issue would be put to a vote of
the membership and barring a negative vote, which no one
expected, the reprints would be sold to the Council for
Judaism on the principle that the fruits of scholarship
must not be repressed. The sole condition of the sale
and distribution of the reprints was that they should
not be used for propaganda purposes. What constituted
"propaganda purposes" was not spelled out, thereby
allowing the historical society to avoid further embarrassment with a clear conscience.

A much more significant literary controversy, reported by the Newsletter, was stirred up by the noted
Yiddish novelist Sholem Asch with the publication of his
novel, entitled **Moses**. It had been translated into
English by my friend Leftwich and rapidly climbed to the
top of the best-seller list in New York. The Yiddish
press, however, sharply criticized it along with other
Asch novels for what the critics considered to be Asch's
"Christianizing." Asch himself was very sensitive to the
criticism and on several occasions tried to make his intentions clear. When he was questioned on this issue
during an interview on his arrival in London in July, he
replied: "One cannot write literature in accordance with
a codex of religion. I cannot write my books in agreement with what is written in the **Schulchan Aruch** [the
code for ritual questions]. I am not a rabbi; I am a
writer. My books, **The Apostle** and **Mary**, have been translated into 21 languages and were standard reading for
theological students in America. When has a thing like
that happened to a Yiddish writer?"

Leftwich, of course, praised Asch and defended his
treatment of Christian and Jewish personalities. He also
strongly denied that Asch had any intention of trying to
convert Jews to Christianity, as the Yiddish press had
charged. While the Newsletter took no editorial position
on the controversy over the novelist, I offered Leftwich
my own opinion of Asch in the following letter:

"I cannot go along with you in your praise of Asch.
True, I do not know him as you do--few people do, I
guess--nor have I read him as intensively and exhaust-
ively. But what I have read--and I have not been influenced by the Yiddish press controversy, the **shmad**
charges, etc.--simply on the basis of what I have read,
I would describe the writer as amazingly ignorant of
what Jews really are, as a man with certain preconceived
notions about Jews that have no relation to reality.

"I reviewed his **Tales of My People**, a selection of
short stories, in **The Menorah Journal**, Winter 1949, pages

144-45. I can't speak of his style because I never read the Yiddish original, but while I would not attack Asch for his notions on Christianity and Judaism as viciously as the Yiddish journalists, I don't think he has the place in Yiddish literature that you would give him. Again, I do not attempt to argue your great authority in this field--I have none--but for my money he was never in a class with Peretz or Schneour, neither in style nor in ideas or philosophy.

"Asch's attitude toward Jews reminds me of that of less literate men of his generation who came to America rebelling against and hating the very thorough Jewish education they received. Only Asch shows no signs of understanding why anyone should voluntarily **choose** to be a Jew. His argument that he is trying to create greater understanding between Christian and Jew is a poor cover-up for his own misgivings about Judaism based, in my opinion, on ignorance of what Judaism really is. The quote I extracted from the **Jewish Chronicle** interview was pathetically revealing--a curious mixture of arrogance, vanity, ignorance and unction. I'm sorry I must disagree with you, but that's what makes literary criticism historical."

Under Leftwich's prodding, I pursued the question of Asch's beliefs and intentions when the great writer arrived in New York at the end of the year. In response to my request, Asch gave me exclusive permission to quote in the Newsletter from his formal statement of religious beliefs and aims. The statement, which had never been published, was part of an address that Asch had delivered in London and would be included in the address he was scheduled to give to the Jewish student group at Columbia University before the end of the year.

In this statement, Asch says that he has "no affinity and no relationship with the Church." However, he affirms his belief in the "messianic ideal" of Judaism which, he says, "gave birth to the world-destiny of Christianity." The basis of his belief, his credo, is expressed in the following sentences from his statement: "My soul's yearning and thirst always for the living fountain of the Jewish spirit had to lead me to this discovery of Jewish Christianity, to its destined part in shaping our civilization. Who can deny that pure primitive Christianity flowers in the garden of the Jewish spirit, and that one who wanders in that garden must discover it sooner or later?"

The Yiddish novelist goes on to call for "brotherly understanding between Jew and Christian" especially since the establishment of the state of Israel has removed much of the "fear of ideological assimilation." He regrets that his books have aroused "embitterment and protest" in Orthodox Jewish circles, and concludes:

"As for the atheistic critics who have not refrained from slandering me, saying that I have changed my religion, I regard this as beneath contempt and I will not humiliate myself to answer them. Whether my books are doing good or bringing harm to the cause of the Jews or of humanity, the present generation of critics cannot judge. They need time and perspective to judge them. And this judgement I leave to Jewish history. I believe I am fulfilling my mission, which God gave me."

19

THE LANDAU LEGACY

In the unwritten guidelines that dictated the selective coverage that the JTA gave Jewish affairs, controversy was a dirty word to be avoided at all costs. Hence, almost nothing of the furious vendetta waged by the Yiddish press against Sholem Asch for his alleged Christianizing ever got into the bland pages of the **JTA Bulletin**. Issued daily, the **JTA Bulletin** was a letter-size four-page typewritten compilation of news stories, and it was distributed by mail to the weekly newspapers that subscribed to the service as well as to individual subscribers in most Jewish organizations. It was much more than a news sheet, however: it proved to be the immediate salvation of the JTA at a time of its most critical financial plight.

We have previously described how the owner of the JTA, Jacob Landau, had selected the New York UJA as the target for his efforts to save the beleaguered news service. Early in the new year, he led a delegation of prominent New York contributors to the offices of the New York UJA to support his urgent appeal that JTA be included as a beneficiary of the 1951 campaign. It had been dropped the previous year when its claim to be a communal agency was rejected. In desperation, Landau resorted to a device that had proved successful in other communities: if New York UJA could not include JTA as a beneficiary of the campaign, it could at the very least purchase a number of subscriptions to the **JTA Bulletin** at $100 a year for each. It was legitimate and a number of welfare funds throughout the country had been buying a number of subscriptions as a way to provide JTA with some support ever since the news agency had been declared ineligible by the CJFWF to receive community funds. Chicago, for example, annually allocated $6,000 for JTA in payment of 60 subscriptions to the **Bulletin**. The New York UJA, however, was in no hurry to subscribe, and Landau in desperate need for money to pay salaries and operating expenses, was able once more to tap the Jewish Agency for a "loan."

At the same time, Landau again undertook to reorganize his board of directors, and in January he announced the appointment of several new men to the JTA board. Among those who accepted the appointment were Benjamin G. Browdy, who insisted that he had agreed to serve only as an individual and not in his capacity as president of the ZOA, adding that his action was not to be understood as a ZOA endorsement of the JTA; Mordecai Danzis, editor of the **Tog**, and Dr. Samuel Margoshes, its English language columnist; David L. Meckler, editor of the **Jewish Morning Journal**; Louis Segal, secretary of the Jewish National Workers Alliance; Rabbi Herbert S. Goldstein, spiritual leader of the West Side Institutional Synagogue; and Isidore Lipschutz and Leon Pines, New York businessmen. The first action of the new board was to pass a resolution describing the JTA as a communal agency, a character that JTA had been trying to assume--but without changing its corporate structure--in order to become eligible for welfare fund allocations.

I informed Leftwich of this latest change in the JTA directorship but noted that Landau still remained in complete control. The change was meaningless as far as I could see. "I confess I am mystified by all these movements," I told Leftwich. "BGR [Bernard G. Richards] insists that Landau adds prestige to JTA every time he finds new names for his board. Maybe. But as long as the welfare funds keep turning him down, not even the Jewish Agency can rescue him."

Early the next month, Landau was forced to close the Paris bureau of the JTA because of a lack of funds. According to E. Davidson, director of the office, staff members had been working without salary since September. Nevertheless, despite this and other setbacks, Landau somehow managed to keep the JTA in operation. The decline in the quality of its news coverage, however, did not go unnoticed, at least by the **Congress Weekly**. A discussion of the English Jewish press had been initiated in the issue of October 30, 1950, by Philip Rubin, and it was continued at the end of the year in an article by Gerhardt Neumann, editor of the **Jewish Chronicle**, of Detroit. Both men agreed that an alert press was essential, but Neumann then went on to blame the Jewish organizations, the Jewish public and the editors of the weeklies themselves for the "sorry state" of the press. Neither critic, however, recalled that an alert press and an informed public had existed in the United States during the first quarter century and that the decline in quality paralleled the rise of the JTA and the increasing dependence of the English Jewish weeklies upon it for their news coverage. Nor did they indicate any connection between the two factors.

In reporting on the discussion, the Newsletter reminded its readers that the JTA had been critically analysed in **The Menorah Journal** for Spring 1949, then went on to observe that there was little point in blaming the public and the organizations, as Neumann had done, for a situation in which they were the victims rather than the instigators. Only a new communal news service, the Newsletter insisted, could extricate the English Jewish weeklies from the difficulties they were in and could help them develop an alert, informed reading public. In my letter to Leftwich of February 17, I commented on the JTA and the apathetic Jewish public for which I held it responsible in the following paragraphs:

"The **American Jewish Year Book** has just arrived--almost two months late as usual--and I have spent a good part of today going through it with my usual fine tooth comb. It falls into your category of 'the best we have,' but I cannot agree with your argument that even bad magazines serve a useful purpose. Bad magazines like **Commentary** and the current **Menorah** corrupt. They destroy standards and rarely have room for the freshness of new talent. Better none, I say, than the insidious rot of a **Commentary**.

"It was the tolerance you defend which allowed JTA to corrupt our press and alienate our reading public to the point where practically no public exists now. I was startled last week when Louis Lipsky, with whom Richards and I were having lunch, expressed himself very definitely along exactly those lines, blaming Landau and the JTA for destroying utterly journalistic standards in the community. When his son, Eleazar, who was there, attempted to defend Landau, Lipsky said he hadn't the slightest hesitation in characterizing Landau as a crook and he didn't care who quoted him!

"Now, poor Henry [Hurwitz] is catching it for his article, 'Mid-Century Inventory'; and the hell of it is that he didn't even get any money for the foolish praise he lavished on the Council for Judaism. Now he regrets what he has done, but it is highly questionable whether the damage that's been done can be repaired. He is planning his next issue and has asked me to do an article-review on [Prof. Eli] Ginzberg's book--which I would have done for somebody sooner or later. I'm working on it now for him, but who knows when the next issue of **The Menorah Journal** will appear? Ginzberg's book is a must for anyone who wants a clear concise picture of American Jewry today. I have rarely found myself in such complete agreement with another man's findings on the community here. But where Ginzberg is pretty much writing his **l'envoi** to the community--he's young, ambitious and the United States government thinks he's terrific and has practically made him comptroller-behind-the-scenes of our manpower--I'm still foolish enough to hope that something can be salvaged from the mess we're in despite the overwhelming mass of evidence to the contrary.

"Were such exposures as I have presented in the Newsletter made about groups affecting the general public instead of the Jewish community, I would by this time either be a hero or a dead villain. But such is the apathy of our public that my reports are met with indignation only from the public relations directors of the organizations attacked. No one else--well, not very many more--give a damn! So that after a time you begin to ask yourself what you are knocking yourself out for, who is your reading public and wouldn't you be a lot smarter to stop acting like Peck's bad boy and be a good little boy from now on at a living salary?

"Incidentally, your optimism about the Newsletter is a little premature. It's the renewals, not the sellouts, that really count and so far they have not been coming in as fast as I would like them to. A few have subscribed in advance, Benjamin Browdy by six months. But the others for the most part are very slow--and that is not a sign to get optimistic about. It's still touch and go."

Several news developments permitted the Newsletter to continue its attacks on the credibility of the JTA, and to emphasize the need for a reliable Jewish news service. In April, a report by M. Beytan, the European director of the Jewish Agency, disclosed that Jews in Tunisia, Algeria, Morocco and Tangiers had contributed over 40 million francs to the Israel campaign and that they were expected to oversubscribe the goal of 100 million francs (about $280,000). This sum was raised at a time when the JDC with the cooperation of the JTA was trying to persuade American Jews to contribute to the welfare of the allegedly poverty stricken Jews of North Africa. As part of the same campaign, the **UPA Report**, in an article on the Jews of Libya, declared: "These Jews of Libya...are now faced by a deadline for emigration which can only be met by the full-fledged support of the United Jewish Appeal." The truth about the situation of the Jews of Libya was something quite different, as the Newsletter pointed out.

At the time the **UPA Report** appeared, the Jewish community of Libya, with the cooperation of the American Jewish Committee, had requested the United Nations to insure their legal rights as a religious minority in the new Libyan constitution. The occasion was the establishment of Libya as an independent state under the auspices of the United Nations. Not only was there no "deadline for emigration" but two months earlier, in January, the Jewish Agency had announced the suspension of virtually all emigration from North Africa. No effort had been made by JTA to reconcile or draw attention to these conflicting reports.

Another, perhaps more damaging, situation affecting the credibility of the JTA occurred at about the same time, when the Associated Press, crediting a JTA dispatch from Tel Aviv, reported that looting mobs in Iraq were endangering the lives of the 54,000 Jews living in that country. The next day, an Associated Press cable from Baghdad, the capital of Iraq, quoting Iraqi officials, asserted that reports of mob violence and looting of Jewish property were "entirely untrue." Despite these denials, however, Moshe Sharett, the Foreign Minister of Israel, notified the American and British Ambassadors in Tel Aviv that the Jews in Iraq were in very grave danger. Israel accompanied the notification by increasing its monthly immigration goal of Jews from Iraq to 20,000, while in New York and other American cities, speakers for the UJA emphasized the importance of providing emergency funds to help speed the emigration of Iraqi Jews. Who was responsible for the report that set off this chain of events was never made clear, but it is noteworthy that as a consequence of the JTA report, the Associated Press dropped the JTA as one of its sources of information and never again used its dispatches.

Undeterred by these happenings, Landau proceeded to launch a new campaign for funds for JTA. I sent Leftwich the following report about it:

"...The second story has to do with our old friend, the JTA, and isn't quite so simple. As a matter of fact, I haven't got all the pieces together yet, and on Monday, I'll have to do some more telephoning for clarification. What happened is this: Landau has reorganized for the -nth time, as you know, and has been pressuring organizations to give him money. He has obtained the approval and support of national UJA, for example, to the extent of a grant of $25,000--$12,500 for 1950, and $12,500 for 1951--allegedly for services rendered.

"So I was informed by Mike Nisselson, treasurer of the UJA, who staunchly defended the JTA as a 'public communal agency,' claiming that Landau had handed over one share of JTA stock to each of 13 directors, retaining only one for himself. At the same time, I learned that the New York UJA had given Landau $2,500 and a promise of $10,000 if other organizations also gave him money. Landau also applied to the UPA for money and its finance committee has his request under advisement, so [Ellis] Radinsky, the executive director, told me. I don't believe him. I think they've already voted to give Landau money, and I'm calling Sonneborn on Monday to find out. I'll probably have a two-page JTA story, and I expect to send copies out to every welfare fund in the country.

"Incidentally, the CJFWF still claims that the JTA is to be treated as a private agency, and apparently a knock-down-drag-out fight is going on between the Zionists and the CJFWF over the question of support for the JTA. A number of the welfare funds have bought 'subscriptions' from JTA for the usual $100 per--Chicago, for example, has taken 60--but that's the subterfuge they use. Talk of corrupting public morals and misappropriating public funds!

"Anyway, my distribution effort next week is being paid for by--and this must be strictly confidential--Blaustein, whom I called and asked for help for this purpose."

I was never able to learn what were the roots of the break between Landau and Jacob Blaustein, who had once been his chief supporter, but when I approached the American Jewish Committee president with the information I had gathered about the scope of Landau's campaign, he offered to pay for enough copies of the Newsletter containing its report of the JTA campaign to reach every welfare fund in the country. The Newsletter's report, which went out on March 29, in addition to the information I had sent Leftwich also included information about contributions to Landau that several Zionist organizations had made as well as the one by UPA. The JNF, for example, itself a beneficiary of the UPA, admitted that it had taken a number of subscriptions for the **JTA Bulletin** at the usual rate but refused to say how many. The AZC admitted making a grant to JTA of $2,500 in 1950 but vigorously denied that it had given or promised JTA any funds at all for 1951. Landau had sent the AZC a letter requesting a grant of $10,000, but apparently Lipsky had something to say about it. Hadassah is also believed to have made a grant to JTA but a spokesman for that organization refused to confirm or deny the grant, or to answer any questions unless they were submitted in writing. Lipsky and Richards both pointed out to me that the Israel government itself was supporting the JTA and that Labor Zionist groups were able to bring pressure to bear on American Zionist organizations to help the JTA. No part of the loan of $110,000 which the Jewish Agency had made to Landau in 1950 had been repaid, they admitted.

The Newsletter continued to report that there had been no change in the position of the CJFWF toward the JTA since the release of the report on the JTA by the Large City Budgeting Conference in November 1950. The LCBC, which had investigated the JTA and its several reorganizations for more than two years, had recommended in its report that welfare funds purchase the JTA service as they would any other service, only as needed. It advised them that the JTA was not to be considered a communal organization eligible for fund allocations, and it disavowed any responsibility for the reorganizations of the JTA. The LCBC added that further study of the JTA was "undesirable and unlikely to yield useful results," and warned its affiliated welfare funds that the JTA was "encumbered with heavy obligations." Not expressed but implied throughout the report was the warning that tax-exempt funds could be endangered by contributions to a private stock company like the JTA.

The conclusion of the Newletter's report on the LCBC condemnation of the JTA contained the following admonition:

> The current crop of JTA supporters would do well to take a lesson from the sad--and frequently costly--experience of their predecessors in Mr. Landau's "reorganizations." They ought to learn, too, from the editors of America's great newspapers and wire services that because of repeated demonstrations of the unreliability of JTA's news coverage, no one will touch a JTA dispatch--thus leaving the Jewish community without an avenue to the general press, with only a few exceptions.
>
> These supporters of the JTA ought to know also that it is possible to put into operation within a matter of weeks a new Jewish press agency that will provide more complete coverage and strict adherence to the standards of modern journalism at a fraction of the $250,000-$500,000 "budget" of JTA--and without its mountain of debt. The Jewish community needs a new

agency and deserves one--without all the
fights, subterfuges and demoralizing influence
of which the JTA has been guilty.

The issue of the Newsletter that carried the JTA expose was sent as a marked copy to about 500 welfare
funds throughout the country as well as to more than
twenty English Jewish weeklies and the two Yiddish
dailies. To my friend Leftwich, I explained that I had
"fired an explosive shell" into the Jewish community and
was waiting to see "what, if anything" the reaction
would be. Three weeks later the Newsletter reported that
"not one weekly paper, including the independent
National Jewish Post, felt that its readers should know"
how their communal funds were being used, not a whisper
of "this scandalous situation" appeared in their pages.
It was even more disheartening to note that with one exception no one even bothered to write to the Newsletter
about this situation. The one exception was an abusive
letter, denouncing the Newsletter for publishing the
facts about the JTA. It was signed by Maurice Taylor,
executive secretary of the United Jewish Fund of
Pittsburgh.
Privately there had been some guarded comments
though, as I told Leftwich, they were not what I had
anticipated, as the following comments make clear:
"So far the thing that some people have commented
upon particularly in the story is the fact, apparently
unsuspected so far, that none of the general newspaper
editors will touch JTA. You must hand it to Landau for
keeping this and other JTA faults away from the notice
of his potential contributors. It is also a reflection
upon our so-called leaders that some of them at least
believe that we'd be completely lost for news without
JTA. The whole situation illustrates with considerable
emphasis how often one must hammer and hammer away at
one point if one hopes to make any impression at all
upon the minds of your readers, no matter how intelligent they presumably are. It is over two years since I
wrote my JTA expose, and I am still sending it to people
who heard about it but never took the trouble to read
it.
"...I'm still hopeful that some sentiment may be
stirred up here for a decent community news agency--
which is why I have been talking with the Blaustein's
and the Sonneborn's. It's an outside chance, of course,
but I think that's the only way to get anything started
in that direction. The communal leaders, such as they

are, must be the ones to inaugurate a communal news agency. Otherwise, it would be impossible to lick Landau. The way in which he plays both sides of the street, applies pressure, frequently on bluff, has everyone scared to death to take him on in a showdown fight--except Lesser--is very little tribute to the moral integrity or standards of our community. We are perhaps worse than the general community, which Senator Kefauver's investigation has aroused, not only because we are Jews but because we refuse to be aroused or disturbed by even greater crimes from a moral point of view. Landau and the USNA are only two instances of the way in which community trust is betrayed."

In the face of community apathy, Landau was able to stave off bankruptcy and keep operating. In May, the Newsletter learned that an organization calling itself the Israel News Agency (INA) and describing itself as the "Eyes and Ears of the Jewish Nation," was conducting fundraising drives in several Jewish communities in different parts of the world. In the **Hebrew Standard,** of Sydney, Australia, a promotion piece implied that INA was a semi-official agency of the Israel government and went on to boast that through INA "Israel must be her own spokesman, just as England is through Reuter, Australia through AAP, and America through AP, France and Russia through their own agencies."

In reporting this development, the Newsletter denounced as false the implication that the Associated Press was subsidized by the United States government and charged that to equate the AP with TASS, the Soviet news agency, was a libel. The INA was nothing more than a subsidiary of the JTA, the Newsletter added, and was formerly known as the Palestine Telegraphic Agency. The name was changed in another of the JTA "reorganizations" during which it acquired jurisdiction over what was left of the European offices of the JTA. In New York, a spokesman for the Israel consulate told the Newsletter that INA was not an arm of Israel's information service and that it was not subsidized by the Israel government.

Another JTA subsidiary, the Overseas News Agency, which Landau founded and supported in part with communal funds, was sold by him in June for an undisclosed sum. The buyer was Julius Stulman, about whom little was known except that he was a millionaire lumberman with headquarters in Brooklyn, N.Y. He said that he planned to continue the service. ONA had been separated from the JTA, its parent organization, and turned over to Landau as part of the JTA reorganization in 1950; it was heavily in debt when it was sold. One of the most important of ONA's subsidiary services was the Trans-World Press, which provided Latin-American newspapers with ONA's news service. When Stulman purchased ONA, he agreed as part of the deal to retain the manager of the Trans-World Press, none other than Mrs. Jacob Landau! Her salary was said to be nominal, and Jacob Landau was reported to be "entirely" out of the ONA organization.

The Landau charade continued in July when still another JTA "reorganization" was announced, this time with Louis P. Rocker, a New York stockbroker and a veteran Zionist, as president; and George S. Wise, a wealthy business executive and also an active Zionist, as chairman of the JTA board. As the same time, JTA announced that Jacob Landau was retiring as managing director but would remain on the JTA board as a "consultant." The family connection, however, was continued unbroken with the appointment of Victor Bienstock, Landau's son-in-law and an able journalist, to succeed him as managing director. No details were revealed about the pension Landau asked for and was granted as a condition of his "retirement."

In my letter to Leftwich about these latest developments, I wrote:

"Lipsky told me this week that Nahum Goldmann is going to have a tough time accounting to the Zionist Congress for giving Landau and JTA $110,000 of the Agency's money and getting nothing for it. I think Landau's 'retirement' is phoney. Now he's got Louis Rocker as his latest sucker--and Rocker was warned strongly by BGR, among others, against going into the JTA. But there's one born every minute for Landau! I'm told that there's a rumor that Landau is planning a new kind of agency, but I've no details. He's always planning something."

In spite of the Newsletter's disclosures and the LCBC's cautions, the welfare funds continued to provide JTA with funds. The Allied Jewish Campaign of Detroit, where Philip Slomovitz, a JTA board member, was the publisher of the Detroit **Jewish News**; and the United Jewish Welfare Fund of Rochester, N.Y., both included the JTA as one of their beneficiaries for 1951. The South African Board of Jewish Deputies, where Eleazar Lipsky had appealed for funds, rejected the request on the grounds that the JTA was not an institution of official standing to be supported by the community. By the end of the year, however, Landau's retirement was confirmed to me as definite, although his wife, Ida, continued to work for ONA. What I did not know at the time was that Landau was a sick man with only a few more months to live. He died in January 1952.

In succeeding years, JTA underwent more changes in management until it achieved a degree of stability and support from the welfare funds. The English Jewish press and the Yiddish press, however, maintained their self-censorship where developments affecting the JTA were concerned. They also carried very little about another communal development, the year-long effort by the Hebrew University, the Technion and the Weizmann Institute to salvage whatever they could from the failure of the U.I.T., their combined fundraising effort. The campaign in 1950 had been a disaster, little more than a million dollars having been raised. After subtracting expenses and dividing the remainder by three, very little was left for each of the Israeli institutions. By the beginning of the year, most of the U.I.T. staff had been dismissed and the Hebrew University had given formal notice that it would no longer participate in the combined effort, thus in effect spelling the end of U.I.T. A last-ditch effort was made, however, to save the U.I.T. with a compromise proposal. Under its conditions, the three Israeli schools would have a free hand to raise funds in the New York area but would work through U.I.T. as a united drive for the rest of the country and overseas, especially South Africa.

A spate of rumors about the U.I.T. alleging that there was dissatisfaction over the size of the staff, the high cost of fundraising and the percentage division of the campaign proceeds was denied by High Salpeter, the executive director of U.I.T., in a telephone call by the Newsletter. He also insisted that U.I.T. had not been dissolved, the U.I.T. board had not met, and there was no change in his own position. Salpeter also claimed that the 1950 campaign had been successful and offered the new, exclusive information that U.I.T. had accepted an agreement which would make it a beneficiary of the New York UJA in lieu of a separate campaign. Although he would not quote the dollar amount on the U.I.T. share of the New York UJA, the Newsletter later learned from other sources that the arrangement would provide U.I.T. with about $600,000.

I sent the Newsletter with this account to my friend in London at about the same time that he was writing to me about the U.I.T. On March 1, I wrote him about the following additional details of the deal:

"Your letter about the U.I.T. and my Newsletter crossed probably in mid-ocean. I got the story origi-

nally from Bill Cohen at the Technion here, then filled
in by calling High Salpeter, U.I.T.'s $20,000 a year
fund raiser. It is dead, as you suspected, and the staff
has been dismissed. Sam Jaffe went to Miami for a vacation (he had been doing their publicity) and since his
return I have tried several times to reach him but without success. Salpeter told me his contract has until
1952 to run and he is sitting pat. Cohen told me that
Salpeter had been offered $15,000 for his contract and
had refused. They all seem to dislike him intensely.
Wechsler (president of the American Friends of Hebrew
University), who originally hired Salpeter for the University, passed him on to U.I.T.

"The campaign raised almost $1.25 million, but after
expenses (which were huge), there was comparatively
little left for the three beneficiaries. U.I.T. will be
retained only as an instrument, a convenience for the
welfare funds who can make one lump sum grant instead of
three individual ones. As I indicated, it will also
probably become a beneficiary of the New York UJA."

The new arrangement impelled changes in the Israeli
institutions. The Haifa Technion, which had been without
a president since the demise of Dr. Shlomo Kaplansky the
previous year, now had to choose a new head, and as the
Newsletter predicted early in January, finally selected
General Yaacov Dori from a field of candidates. General
Dori was a former chief of staff of the Israel army and
at the time of his appointment was serving as scientific
adviser and coordinator to Prime Minister Ben-Gurion.
Dr. Sydney Goldstein, a British authority on airplanes,
was elected vice president of the Technion. The high
caliber of this institution was reflected in its Ameri-
can publication, the **Technion Yearbook**. In 1951, it con-
tained articles by such noted Americans as Harold C.
Urey and William L. Laurence, the science writer for the
New York Times. There were also Professor Robert A.
Millikan, a Nobel Prize physicist and at 83, the dean of
American scientists.

At the Hebrew University, its president Dr. Selig
Brodetsky appealed for help to the Israel government in
covering its budget. In a Jerusalem address, Dr. Brodetsky described the difficulty of holding classes in
twenty buildings scattered around Jerusalem. It was a
makeshift arrangement caused by the loss of the University's home on Mt. Scopus in the 1948 war. The University had to provide for about 2,000 students and 300
teachers on a budget of $3 million. Dr. Brodetsky also
pointed out that the University would like to assist its

students, many of whom had to take outside jobs for their living while studying, but could not because it was itself in a precarious financial position. The government grant in 1950 had been less than $200,000, although it insisted that the University open a school of law and a school of education in order to meet the country's need for lawyers and teachers.

By the middle of the year, Dr. Brodetsky had to return to London for treatment of a heart condition. It was hoped that he would be well enough to return to Jerusalem in time for the opening of the fall term, but on October 18, Dr. Brodetsky sent in his resignation because his health had not improved. He had been appointed president of the University in 1949, succeeding Dr. Judah Magnes. At the same time it was learned that Professor Martin Buber, the famed religious philosopher, was also retiring after reaching the age of 73. And in New York, Dr. Israel Wechsler, the president of the American Friends of Hebrew University, announced his retirement. His successor was Dr. George S. Wise, the wealthy business man who had been a member of the JTA board.

To Leftwich, who was a close friend of Dr. Brodetsky, I described the reaction here to the news of his resignation in the following letter:

"There is still no official news here on Brodetsky's resignation, and I was too ill last week to bother about calling [Bernard] Cherrick. There was a hint of Brodetsky's possible resignation in the **National Jewish Post** this week over a letter he had written making certain demands presumably of the government. But even the **Jewish Chronicle** of November 2 had no word on it. Probably some time next month we will get official news.

"Meanwhile, the **Post** has launched Israel Goldstein's candidacy for the job. Goldstein has been a disappointed man ever since he was forced out of Brandeis U. by Einstein. I'm told that the Einstein threat was used recently by Cherrick in order to oust Dr. Israel Wechsler as head of the American Friends. I wonder if they'll do any better now that they've completed the kind of reorganization they wanted. It seems to me that as long as I have known the American Friends, they have been limping along from one reorganization to another, none of which achieves the purpose for which all the shifting and energy was devoted. They still can't raise enough to cover all their expenses here--which are not inconsiderable--and send enough to Jerusalem to matter."

By December, however, it was learned that Dr. Brodetsky had been persuaded by the Israel government to

delay his resignation until early the following year
when the University's board of governors would meet to
hear his suggestions and recommendations. From Leftwich,
the Newsletter learned that Dr. Brodetsky had been
deeply disappointed by his inability to settle the
rivalries and disputes within the teaching and administrative staffs of the University. He was planning to
tell the board of governors that the University's standards are far too low, that it must attract young men of
reputation as teachers, and finally, that these and
other problems can be solved only by giving the president the executive authority he lacked because of the
European type of administration under which the University had been organized.

In order to flesh out Leftwich's report on Brodetsky, I called Bernard Cherrick, the executive head of
the American Friends, and in a very frank conversation,
obtained from him the following information, which I
relayed to Leftwich in my weekly letter:

"I want to tell you first of all about how I managed
to handle the information you sent me on Brodetsky.
Without betraying any sources, or even hinting that I
had any, I pumped Cherrick for as much of the story as
he would give--and as you will see, I think he gave a
lot for a man in his position. It is true that thanks to
you I knew the right questions to ask--all fairly inno-
cent, of course--but he did answer enough to give me a
first-rate story.

"He confirmed the resignation and the meeting of the
board, although he thought they might more likely meet
late in January or February rather than December; also
what you said about the exchange of foreign funds for
Israeli pounds. He gave me what he thought was an ap-
proximation of Brodetsky's ideas, strictly avoided personalities and blamed all the trouble on the mixture of
'systems' under which the university is organized. I believe that there is a good deal of truth in that argument, but I still think personalities and politics lie
at the bottom of the school's plight. At any rate I had
a story that I could rightly lay at Cherrick's door if
any question came up even though I couldn't quote him
and at the same time use some of the dynamite you sent
me."

Thus in the situation that both the JTA and the
U.I.T. found themselves, the year ended in failure and
frustration. In each instance, the Israel government was
a critical factor in shaping the way the American Jewish
public would respond to their appeals and their efforts

to survive. And in both cases, the JTA and the U.I.T.
somehow managed to overcome almost insurmountable difficulties in order to survive primarily because the community recognized that they filled a need and that there
was no other less costly way to replace them.

20

THE FINAL NEWSLETTER

From the beginning of 1951, it became increasingly clear that the Newsletter was in trouble financially. Landau's success in persuading the community to keep the JTA alive also meant that there would not be room for any other news service. The Newsletter's appeal remained limited in spite of its distinctive news coverage and sharp focus on events affecting the community and its organizations. Its circulation had not increased to any considerable extent and renewals were slow in coming despite repeated and expensive promotional efforts. From the very beginning, for fear of compromising my independence I had decided against making any fundraising appeals or seeking sponsors. I believed and continued to believe almost until the closing months of the year that the Newsletter's disclosures and crusading spirit would attract enough subscribers interested in the welfare of the American Jewish community to keep the publication afloat.

On April 1, in the following letter to Leftwich, I spelled out my discouragement: "I'm still trying to keep going--a little more desperately now than a year ago because the Newsletter is still a very small operation and free-lance work has not been too plentiful so far this year. Living costs are very high, and the result is that my time is growing quite short. If I weren't such a stubborn cuss, I would have given up a long time ago. But every time I get ready to hit bottom, a few checks come in, or something equally encouraging happens to make me want to keep on a while longer. And so we come into April, with our finances and our subscription list worse off than they were in January, and the summer's expenses are coming up. Now I know what the old Jews meant when they would say, 'God will provide.' These days I find myself saying it too--only not with as much faith as they."

My spirits were raised from this low point by the MacIver Report expose, and the controversy which followed attracted so much national attention that I had to

341

keep going. But even more important at this time was the encouragement and help I received from Louis Lipsky. Like my English friend Leftwich, he fully appreciated what I was trying to do and he was also helpful in a practical way. It was his recommendation that led the Progressive Zionists to employ me on a part-time basis as their press officer and as the editor of their newsletter, which incidentally is still being published. That help enabled me to keep the Newsletter going over the summer months.

For the long term, there was the prospect--also made possible by Lipsky--of an appointment as the editor of the English page in the reorganized Yiddish daily, the **Morning Journal**. This newspaper, long respected as the voice of Jewish Republicans and conservatives, had been forced into bankruptcy early in the year, and a group of interested citizens had turned to Louis Lipsky for help in reorganizing the daily. By the middle of the summer, he had helped them raise $140,000. Among his plans for the paper was a page of news features in English which, it was anticipated, would attract a younger generation of new readers.

I had also discussed with Lipsky the need for a Jewish news service to replace the JTA as well as other arrangements for providing the community with responsible information. One of the proposals concerned the **American Hebrew**, an old English Jewish weekly, which was in straitened circumstances. I told Leftwich about it in the following letter:

"I once asked Lipsky about buying the **American Hebrew**--he worked on it in his youth, you know, and regards it very affectionately. He described a grandiose scheme of what he would do with the paper as a nucleus, then concluded by saying that no one would contribute to such a scheme. People just are not interested. Yet he did spur the raising of funds for the **Morning Journal**. They got up $140,000.... Lipsky claims the appeal for the **Morning Journal** was more compelling--where would the Yiddish staff writers earn a livelihood, etc.? BGR [Bernard G. Richards] tried to spur him on the **American Hebrew** proposal, but he wouldn't change his opinion."

Later in the year, Leftwich informed me that he had received a report that William Zukerman, a Yiddish journalist who was also the editor of an English language newsletter in New York, was in line for the proposed English language page of the **Morning Journal**. A thin wisp of a man, Zukerman was an able writer and journalist, fluent in both languages. He had strong ties to the

Bund, a militant Jewish workers union whose orientation was socialist and anti-Zionist, and he reflected those views. Born in Russia, he was brought to the United States as a child, but apparently also spent some of his later years in England, for in an article for **The Menorah Journal** he was sharply critical of the English Jewish community. Entitled "Outpost of Decay: A Note on Jewish Life in England," the article appeared in the issue of April 1929, when Zukerman was about 40. Characteristic of his pen was this sentence from the article: "The Anglo-Yiddish community is probably the largest morass of moral weakness European Jewry can show."

At the time Leftwich wrote me about the rumor, Zukerman was writing letters to the **New York Herald Tribune** critical of Israel and these letters were getting under the skin of the Israel consul in New York as well as a number of Zionists, including Lipsky. When I asked him about the **Morning Journal** and the Zukerman rumor, he said that there was no truth in it, and that in his opinion Zukerman himself was spreading the report. He further pointed out that no changes could be made in the newspaper without permission of the court, which had jurisdiction over the bankruptcy proceedings, and he had checked the story before reporting to me. He hinted quite broadly that I ought to do something drastic about exposing Zukerman, but, as I wrote to Leftwich, "I felt that I couldn't do anything in view of our competitive positions--that is, with my name attached to it. Why does everybody want me to liquidate W.Z.? I'm no hatchet man."

Nevertheless, despite Lipsky's denial, I continued to probe the Zukerman rumor on the basis of the tip from Leftwich, and eventually found that there was something to the story. I told Leftwich about it in the following letter: "You were not altogether wrong when you wrote me about Zukerman and the **Morning Journal**, but somewhere along the line the facts got twisted a bit. Zukerman, it is true, will not handle the English page, but negotiations are under way for the **Morning Journal** to bring out an American edition of London **Jewish Chronicle** foreign news. Schneiderman, of the **Morning Journal**, stopped off in London on his way back from the U.N. General Assembly meetings, had a talk with Kessler, and came back with at least a tentative arrangement in his pocket.

"Part of the agreement calls for Kessler to put up some money--this is what Schneiderman himself told me on Monday, when he joined Lipsky and myself for lunch. I'm skeptical, and so is Lipsky, about Kessler putting up money, but it may be. At any rate, no final arrangements can be concluded without permission of the court. Nothing has been said yet about who was to run the English section—at least not to me or in my presence."

By the end of November, however, it was clear that neither the English section nor the proposal by Kessler was going to be realized. The publisher of the London **Jewish Chronicle** had not changed his mind about the value of his news service or his money, and in the absence of any American purchase of the service, the trustees of the **Morning Journal** had no choice but to do without it and any plan they had for an English page. With this prospect gone, I made a last desperate effort to keep my Newsletter going. I tried to persuade Lipsky to sponsor my idea for an intelligence service and propose it to the Israelis. I pointed out that apart from a clipping service and the local newspapers, the Israel Embassy had no organized news service to inform them about what the American domestic radio and the Voice of America shortwave radio were saying about Israel. The VOA was particularly important not only because of what it said in 24 languages each day, but also because it reflected official American policy toward Israel and the Middle East. Regrettably, my plea and Lipsky's effort fell on deaf ears; to this day the state of Israel does not know what the Voice of America is saying about it in its daily broadcasts.

By the end of November, I told Lipsky that barring a small miracle, I was prepared to give up the struggle and suspend publication of the Newsletter by the end of the year simply because I could no longer afford to keep it going. I told Leftwich about our conversation in the following letter of December 6:

"Lipsky is concerned about my leaving the field, but apparently cannot do anything to place me here. He hasn't said so, and I haven't asked him for anything directly, but I made my situation quite clear on Tuesday. It may be, of course, that I am **persona non grata** with the organization and Agency people because of the things I have said in the Newsletter from time to time. I have not been a conformist, you know; not even a regular Zionist organization member, and while Lipsky may think highly of me, I doubt whether he'd really go to bat for me if it were necessary. There is no reason why he should.

"Tuesday night I went to the Zionist Council party for Lipsky; met everybody who was anybody. Lipsky gave

ZOA hell, and they all took it as nicely as they could. Nobody will carry my version, I promise you."

My shrinking bank account made it very clear to me that without some employment outside of the Newsletter, I could not continue publication, and the failure of my several efforts to promote some outside income made the decision final. On December 20, the Newsletter formally announced that after the next issue, it would suspend publication. On that day I also sent Leftwich the following letter:

"I find myself taking it a lot harder than I really should. After all, I have been turning the matter over in my mind for months now, and the final decision should have come a lot easier. Next issue, December 27, is to be my last. It completes two full years of publication; they have been wonderfully exciting and rewarding—at least in the sense of achievement—but it has been very hard, exacting work, with no time out for a breathing spell. I've got feelers out in Washington, and I rather expect that in a month or so, a job will turn up for me there.

"As for the Jewish field, you have to appreciate the fact that here the power is largely in the hands of the professionals—and they can never forget or forgive anyone who might break up their particular personal racket—whereas in England there is much more lay participation in Jewish life—at least I think so. Jacob Blaustein might give me a job at the American Jewish Committee, but only over John Slawson's dead body—so you can see what I'm up against. Lipsky can and does try, but he too must come to the professionals and they are not giving up one of their boys for me. He has had my memorandum on press and radio intelligence, is impressed with it, yet he tells me he must talk to the 'money boys' but is not too hopeful. He points out that the Jewish Agency will throw away $20,000 a year on Schwadron and his Middle East magazine, which is utterly worthless, but cannot stop or use the money for something else because, what jobs would they be able to give the boys who put out the magazine? And that's the way it is down the line."

On December 20, the readers of the Newsletter were told in a notice of final publication that "in two years of regular weekly publication, **Cross-Section, U.S.A.** has adhered to its initial promise to 'focus its spotlight on hitherto hidden or neglected areas of organizational or communal activities.' By its highly successful efforts in this direction, we believe it has created an awareness of the need for such reporting to the community."

The Newsletter had established the realization that there was much more information about communal activities vital to the welfare of the Jewish community to which the Jewish public was entitled than it was getting from the JTA. Apparently no one was more aware of that need than the publishers of the English Jewish weeklies themselves, for within a week after the notice of the Newsletter's suspension appeared, I was approached by Philip Slomovitz, of the Detroit **Jewish News**. Acting on behalf of the American Association of English Jewish Newspapers, Slomovitz made me an offer to continue the Newsletter as a syndicated column for the weeklies. After some negotiation, I accepted the invitation and for the next year and a half the Newsletter, in much subdued form, appeared regularly in many of the English Jewish weeklies. It contained no news scoops of the sensational nature of the MacIver Report, and I stopped writing it when a Washington job finally did come through, though in a manner I had not anticipated.

The Washington offer was a direct consequence of the publication of the Newsletter. I had been trying for more than a year to locate a federal government job in Washington, D.C., but without success. When my prospects seemed to reach their lowest ebb, Nathan Belth, the ADL public relations director, casually invited me one day to attend an informal press luncheon called to introduce the newly elected president of the B'nai B'rith.

Philip M. Klutznick, born in Omaha, was a mid-Western lawyer about my own age, who had made a huge fortune as the builder and developer of Park Forest, Illinois. During World War II, Klutznick had been President Truman's Housing Administrator; afterward he formulated his plan to build housing in Illinois for returning war veterans. It was a daring and highly imaginative undertaking for a man with relatively little money and a large family to support, for the future Park Forest housing development was only a stretch of barren prairie land some 40 miles south of Chicago. But Klutznick was a persistent and convincing salesman, and managed not only to acquire a partner who was a builder but also to raise the necessary financing. The venture proved successful beyond everyone's expectations.

Park Forest gave Klutznick the financial security he needed, but election to the presidency of the B'nai B'rith was the fulfilment of a lifelong ambition, one that he had nurtured from his earliest years when he was an active member of the B'nai B'rith Youth Organization. At the press luncheon, I introduced myself to him and quite unselfconsciously began to talk about the Newsletter and the kind of Jewish community I believed we should have. I liked the man and apparently he also thought well of me, for about ten days later I was asked to come to Washington and become the public relations director of the B'nai B'rith, which was headquartered there.

My appointment in June 1953 brought me into closer contact with Jewish communities in the United States and Canada than I had thought possible. Phil Klutznick was a fine speaker and he loved to make speeches. I provided the substance: ideas about strengthening the Jewish community and suggestions for joint action to increase its impact and influence. In that first year, we traveled extensively, through much of Canada on one occasion and through Mississippi to gauge the influence of the White Citizens Council upon the small Jewish communities on another. What I saw and heard in that Southern state about the treatment of Negroes left its imprint on my mind in a way I can never forget.

B'nai B'rith is organized into seven regional districts, and in the spring and summer months of 1954, I attended all seven regional conferences, flying more than 7,000 miles from coast to coast in the process. Meeting the leadership of Jewish communities across the country in this way gave me an understanding and a perspective--among other matters--on the failure of the Newsletter to attract a larger readership, and why the issues I had regarded as critical did not meet with the public response I had anticipated. The men and women I talked to at these conventions had a different attitude; to them American concerns were paramount, Jewish matters were parochial. In the vastness of America, Omaha was much further away from New York in its interests and priorities than the geographical distance between the two cities.

Something in the Washington atmosphere helped to impress this realization upon me as, I am sure, it has for many mid-America Congressmen. It was emphasized even stronger for me two years later, when I left B'nai B'rith to join the newly organized American Zionist Committee for Public Affairs (AZCPA). This body was set up by I.L. Kenen at the recommendation of Louis Lipsky in order to carry on the political work of the American Zionist Council without risking the tax-exempt status of the AZC. The Washington organization appealed for funds which were not tax-exempt, and Kenen registered as its lobbyist. We had met in New York when I was publishing the Newsletter, and we became good friends after he moved to Washington.

In 1956, following Israel's smashing victory over Egypt and the Arab states in the Six Day War, Kenen and his small staff were inundated with requests for information and speech materials about the Middle East, mostly from members of Congress. He asked me to become his information officer and made the offer tempting by suggesting that we publish a newsletter on the Middle East. The opportunity to combine my interest in Israel and in a newsletter was one I could not turn down. It was made even more exciting by my very first assignment, which was to formulate the questions Senator Hubert H. Humphrey was going to ask Secretary of State John Foster Dulles the next day at the Foreign Relations Committee hearing on Middle East policy. I delivered the questions personally to the Senator at his modest home in Silver Spring. It was the beginning of a friendship which was to last throughout the Senator's life.

Many months of planning and preparation went into the development of the proposed newsletter and it was not until June 1957 that Kenen and I, as editors, were able to publish the first number of the **Near East Report, A Washington Letter on American Policy in the Near East**. It was issued every two weeks, and despite the support of the Zionist organizations, especially Hadassah, growth was slow. By the third year of publication, however, it was firmly established as an authoritative voice. Now, more than 25 years later, it is still being published every week by the American Israel Public Affairs Committee, the successor to AZCPA.

In 1957, I made my first visit to Israel and had a chance to talk with many of its leading citizens. The experience was very valuable because I was able to write with conviction and sincerity about Israel in the innumerable speechs I drafted, primarily for members of Congress. In particular, they attracted the attention of Senator Jacob K. Javits, of New York, who was known for his advocacy of American friendship for Israel. I met the Senator for the first time in the spring of 1959, when he asked me to prepare a draft of a book on civil rights, which he intended to use during the 1960 campaign for reelection. That summer I took a month's leave and with the help, for research, of several authorities on different aspects of the civil rights problem, I wrote the basic draft of the book which I entitled **Dis-**

crimination--**U.S.A.**, a title I obviously derived from my
Newsletter. The Senator edited the manuscript and it was
published under his name by Harcourt, Brace, in 1960.

I left AZCPA and the **Near East Report** in December
1959 when the Senator asked me to become his executive
assistant. It was a step I took with great reluctance
and considerable hesitation because I doubted whether I
could measure up to the challenge it presented. I was no
longer a young man, and Javits' reputation as an inde-
fatigable legislator was well deserved. My fears were
well founded. For example, I usually required four to
five days to draft a formal speech; the first day I
reported for work, the Senator asked me at nine in the
morning to provide him with a Floor speech on the Middle East by noon of that day, when the Congress recon-
vened! Somehow, I managed an acceptable draft to meet
his deadline; eventually I became so proficient under
this kind of pressure that I could write a speech on the
Floor of the Senate and feed it to the Senator page by
page even as he was delivering it.

Flexibility was a key requirement for work in the
Congress, and in the five years I served the Senator, I
became not only his chief speech writer and Middle East
expert but also his assistant in the fields of health,
education, the arts, and New York State ethnic community matters. In addition to handling much of his private correspondence, I also helped to fashion such
important legislation as medicare--the Social Security
version of which was introduced in 1960 by then Senator
John F. Kennedy--the arts foundation, education aid for
elementary schools and colleges, and help for professional schools. The achievement I was especially proud
of was the rescue of a provision in an omnibus education
bill sent down by the White House authorizing the expenditure of $15 million for a program to train teachers
of handicapped children. It would have been discarded if
the Senator, at my suggestion, had not introduced it
during the mark-up session of the education bill, which
was later passed and signed into law. The program continues to this day in a much more expanded form.

My interest in community development was renewed and
broadened in 1964, when the Civil Rights Act was finally
signed into law after years of exhausting debate in the
Congress. Lyndon Baines Johnson was President of the
Unite States and Hubert H. Humphrey, the Vice President,
both of whom I had known and worked with in the Senate.
Late that year, I was invited through one of the Vice
President's aides, to become the first director of the

Civil Rights office in the U.S. Office of Education, charged with the responsibility of desegregating the nation's schools. I accepted with understandable enthusiasm, but it was not a decision to be taken lightly. I had made many good friends in the Congress on both sides of the aisle and through them I was able to influence constructive legislation, especially where Israel was concerned. As long as I spoke with the Senator's approval and in his name, I could exert a degree of power far beyond anything I had experienced when I was editor of the Newsletter.

Despite these considerations, the new prospect overrode all my doubts. It proved to be a disastrous decision almost from the start. I came to the office with numerous ideas for community development based on my experience in the South in 1953, and with strong convictions on how best to carry out the intent of the law. But Congress had made no provision for funds or staff; they had to be borrowed from other sections of the Office of Education, leaving me with no choice in their selection. The Justice Department lawyers wrote the regulations for enforcement of the law based on their interpretation of a Civil Rights Act that was often ambiguous and sometimes contradictory, a condition that resulted from the numerous compromises and revisions made to secure its passage. Civil rights organizations which had had years of experience were never consulted, and the end result was chaos. Southern school authorities promptly devised numerous schemes to evade the law while Southern Senators pressured a Southern President to tolerate these evasions and in effect undermine the desegregation effort.

The Vice President had been placed in charge of the civil rights enforcement in all government agencies and my fate was tied up with him. As a Senator he had fought along with Senator Javits for a strong civil rights law, and perhaps in his new responsibility he, as well as all of us, probably tried to do too much too quickly. Without the development of community support, which I had advocated, resistance to the strict measures of enforcement insisted upon by the Justice Department lawyers reached a point within six months which President Johnson regarded as politically damaging. He had made a great speech at Howard University on June 4, 1965, a speech which had been written by Presidential assistant Daniel Patrick Moynihan with material supplied by my office. But almost overnight, it seemed, the climate changed, and the President without warning discharged

the Vice President and his civil rights staff and transferred their responsibilities to the Justice Department.
Within days, I was also superseded--the first in a long
line of civil rights administrators to be given such
short shrift--and by the end of the year my unit was
transferred out of the Office of Education. The consequences of this mismanagement and reliance on the courts
to enforce desegregation rather than establishing the
slower community process have continued to plague the
nation to this day.

I remained in the Office of Education for the next
ten years, serving in various capacities including the
direction of one brief but successful program aimed at
training Vietnam veterans to assist teachers in slum
area schools. It died when the American Legion and the
Veterans Administration opposed it. In 1974 I retired
from government service, but early the next year the ZOA
called me out of retirement to direct their newly established Washington office. My friend, Beinesh Epstein,
who had worked for the Republican National Committee
when I was in the Senate, persuaded me to accept. It was
to provide Congressional offices with the information
about Israel and the Middle East that I began once more
to write a newsletter. This time, I called it **Perspective,** and with ZOA sponsorship the newsletter, issued
monthly, quickly found enthusiastic readers not only on
Capitol Hill but also in a number of Zionist districts
throughout the country. Within six months, its circulation reached 5,000 copies. Funding continued to be a
problem, however, and after fifteen months it ceased
publication.

At the present time, although I am fully retired, I
still find time to write and edit the **Brandeis Report,** a
newsletter for the Brandeis Zionist District of the ZOA,
bringing to my Washington, D.C. readers information
about Israel and the Middle East that they are not
likely to find in their daily newspapers. Federal agencies are constantly generating news about their activities, and I have repeatedly pointed out that numerous
reports of Jewish interest are released in Washington
each week that never reach a Jewish public. The JTA, for
example, has undergone many beneficial changes since the
Landau days, but one thing has not changed. Thirty-five
years ago JTA had only one correspondent in Washington
to cover the activities of the Federal government;
today, after the establishment of the state of Israel
and the huge expansion of Jewish interest in the government, JTA still has only one correspondent in Washington
to do the job!

The American Jewish community has grown with the nation in wealth and influence. Its philanthropy has increased correspondingly, and the annual amount of money raised for all Jewish causes is astronomical compared with the amounts raised in 1950. The Jewish Agency is still the active disburser of funds raised for Israel, and its comptrollers are still protesting waste and inefficiency. It has apparently given up completely on its efforts for exclusive UJA fundraising, and today almost all of the UJA beneficiaries, locally as well as nationally, also conduct their own independent campaigns. Appeals from various Israeli institutions and charities have multiplied, while Israel bonds are still being sold in higher multiples and larger quantities than ever. UJA drives continue to have the active support of thousands of ZOA members but the annual reports it mails on request include only selected categories and are not audited.

The defense agencies likewise have expanded their interests and their staffs into ever wider social and political areas, but like UJA, will not release audited reports of their collections and expenditures. Only the ZOA continues to do so. The most important change in the defense picture is the phenomenal increase in Jewish influence and political activity to the point where it has become a factor of growing importance in Presidential campaigns, and good relations with Israel a critical issue.

New agencies have made their appearance, among them several that deal with the problem of Soviet Jewish emigration. There is some reason to believe that in the resettlement of Soviet Jews in the United States, we are repeating the same over-generous mistakes as those made by USNA/NYANA in resettling the European DPs more than 30 years ago. While many new Jewish periodicals are being published, none, as far as I can learn, is planning to undertake the kind of investigative reporting on this issue as the Newsletter did.

Identification with a synagogue has become a social necessity, and synagogue membership has risen accordingly. Membership fees, like the salaries of rabbis and cantors, have likewise risen astronomically, often beyond the capacity of young couples; relatively few congregations, however, are granted the privilege of receiving an audited report of the synagogue's finances. There seems to be a greater degree of observance of ritual practices even in Reform congregations, but the rate of intermarriage and assimilation has risen to levels that are now regarded as dangerous to the life of the community. The one bright spot in the religious picture is the return to Orthodoxy of increasing numbers of young people, a consequence in part of the increase in numbers and proficiency of the Hebrew day school. They are well trained and far more knowledgeable about Torah and Talmud than their parents and immigrant grandparents. Theirs is a genuine Jewishness in the entire complex meaning of the term, a Jewishness that they practice in the home as well as in the synagogue; in them, in my opinion, lies the hope of the future of the Jewish community in the United States.

BIBLIOGRAPHY

FINE, MORRIS, editor. **American Jewish Year Book.** Vol. 53, New York, 1952.

GINZBERG, ELI. **Agenda For American Jews.** New York, 1950.

GOLDMANN, NAHUM. **The Autobiography of Nahum Goldmann: Sixty Years of Jewish Life.** New York, 1969.

LESSER, ALLEN. "On Anti-Defamation Hysteria," **The Menorah Journal,** XXXIV, 144 (1946).
"The Red Kiss," **The Menorah Journal,** XXXVI, 157 (1948).
"The Jewish Telegraphic Agency," **The Menorah Journal,** XXXVIII (1949).

LIPSKY, LOUIS. **Tales of the Yiddish Rialto.** New York, 1962.

MEIR, GOLDA. **My Life.** Jerusalem, 1975.

NEUMANN, EMANUEL. **In the Arena: An Autobiographical Memoir.** New York, 1976.

POSTAL, BERNARD and LEVY, HENRY W. **And the Hills Shouted for Joy: The Day Israel Was Born.** New York, 1973.

SACHAR, HOWARD M. **A History of Israel: From the Rise of Zionism to Our Time.** New York, 1976.

SCHMORAK, DR. E. **Report (Part 2) of the Director of the Comptroller's Office.** Jerusalem, 1951.
The Reply of the Executive of the World Zionist Organization and Jewish Agency. (In the same volume.)

SHANKMAN, SAM. **Mortimer May: Foot Soldier in Zion.** New York, 1963.

STEINBERG, MILTON. **A Believing Jew.** New York, 1951.

INDEX

159,161,178,179,186-188,
197,208,210-212,214,221,
226,255,267,282,311,325,
330
Cranston, Alan,xii
Crossman, Richard,273,274
Crum, Bartley,242
Curtis, Jerome N.,76

Daily Worker,307
Danzis, Mordecai,125,135,
229,326
Davar (Jerusalem),204
Davidson, E.,326
Davidson, G.S.,229
Davidson, Max,253,254,315
Detroit Allied Jewish Campaign,334
Detroit Jewish Community
Council,115
Dewey, Thomas E.,197,280
Diaspora,77,255
Digest,205
Dingol, S.,195
Dinnes, Jacob M.,76,313
Discrimination--U.S.A.,349
Dobkin, Eliahu,212,228,254
**Documentary History of the
Jews of the United States,**
120
Doeblin, Alfred,107
Dori, Ya'acov,7,336
Douglas, Paul,238,276
Doussinague, Jose,310
Dropsie College,282
Duker, Abraham G.,189
Dulles, John Foster, viii,
294,348

Eastern Life Insurance
Company,258
Eban, Abba,28,63,202,206,
214,215,264,265,273,281
Eden, Anthony,284,285
Edman, Irwin,302,303
Ehrmann, Herbert S.,81,82
Einstein, Albert,127,337
Eisendrath, Maurice N.,305
Eisenhower, Dwight David,
vii,viii
Eisenstein, Ira,315

Elath, Eliahu,280
Enchanting Rebel,257
Engel, Irving M.,75,118
Epstein, Beinesh,351
Epstein, Benjamin R.,148,305
Esco Foundation, 315
Essex County (N.J.) Jewish
Community Council,xii,18,
156,164,185,193
European Intelligence Digest,xii
Export-Import Bank,39,63

Facts, The,304
Falk, Louis A.,33,34
54,64,268
Farber, Maxwell M.,104
Federation of Jewish Philanthropies of New York,
39,142,200,210,223,227,309
Federation of Jewish Relief
Organizations,143
Feinberg, Abraham,ix
FEPC (Fair Employment Practices Council),112
Feuer, Leon I.,315
Finkelstein, Louis,82-85,
147,172,173,175,176,184,
190,191,299
Fisher, Mendel N.,208
Foreign Broadcast Information Service,xii
Forrestal Diaries,279
Forrestal, James,280
Forward, The (N.Y.),67,160,
199
Franco, Francisco,118
Frankfurter, Felix,114
Frazer, William,68
Freeman, Julian,41,45,135,
208
Freund, Hirsch E.L.,159,183
Fried, Joseph Harrison,136
Friedenwald, Harry,8,107
Friedman, Herbert,101
Friends of Israel,39,44
Frisch, Daniel,51,53,67
Fulbright, William,119
Fuld, Stanley,120

Gach, Samuel B.,116

Menorah Journal, The,xi-
  xiii,13,80,81,102,116,124,
  148,150,157,172,173,257,
  302,303,316,317,322,327,
  343
Menuhin, Hepzibah,315
Menuhin, Yehudi,125,315
Mesirov, Leon,185
Miami Jewish Federation,115
Middle East Treaty Organi-
  zation (METO),288
Miller, Irving,235
Millikan, Robert A.,336
Minkoff, Isaiah,111,112,
  148,158,305
Mizrachi Organization,8,12,
  66,199,202,253,254,266
Mizrachi Women's Organiza-
  tion,2
Monheimer, Melville,10,11
Monosson, Fred,64,263
Montor, Henry,ix,2,5-11,16,
  17,19,20,21,23,27-29,31-
  33,36-38,40-48,59,65,129,
  131,143-145,193-198,201-
  203,207,213,228,260
Morais, Sabato,108
More Perfect Union, The,147
Morgenthau, Henry, Jr.,8,
  23,28,46,48,114,198,207,
  213,260
Morrison, Herbert,252
Moses,322
Moynihan, Patrick Daniel,
  350
Myers, Philip,314
Myers, Stanley C.,35,36,46,
  98
My Life,6

Nathan, Robert,277
Nathanson, N.L.,113
National Community Rela-
  tions Advisory Council
  (NCRAC),75,76,102,111-115,
  118,120,148-150,152-155,
  157,158,160,161,165-167,
  169-171,174,176-179,181,
  183-191,304-307,309
NCRAC Special Committee on
  Evaluative Studies,147-

150,153,156-158,164,165,
  174,175,177,178,185,187,
  189
National Conference of
  Christians and Jews,174
National Conference on Jew-
  ish Education,36
National Council of Jewish
  Women,2,3,61,72,111,143-
  145,222,227
National Jewish Monthly,
  317
National Jewish Post (In-
  dianapolis),32,33,45,133,
  156,158,161,167,171-173,
  176,186,212,228,229,317,
  332,337
National Jewish Welfare
  Board (JWB),4,30,79,80,
  158,171,174,315
NATO (North American
  Treaty Organization),277,
  278,288
Nazism,xi,99,112
Near East Report,348,349
Neturei Karta,298
Neumann, Abraham,84
Neumann, Emanuel,6,8,49,53-
  56,65,66,233,234,249,250,
  262,266
Neumann, Gerhardt,326
Neustadt, Meilech,50
Newark (N.J.) News,229
New Neighbors,95
New Palestine,6,9,57,258
New School for Social Re-
  search,128
New York Association for
  New Americans (NYANA),13,
  15,16,17,96,97,212,217,
  219-224,226,227,229,352
New York Board of Rabbis,
  13,183,305
New York Catholic Chari-
  ties,200
New York Daily Compass,124
New York Herald Tribune,42,
  44,65,76,95,167,172,209,
  279,280,293,343
New York Journal American,
  229,310

New York Post,167,172,293
New York Public Library,
160,217
New York Sunday Telegraph,
257
New York Times,11,28,32,37,
42,44,64,76,88,115,118,
167,193,223,264-266,269,
273,274,279,287,290,292,
293,301,309,313,336
New York UJA,13,14,19,29,
30,78,90,96,124-126,136,
198,200,210,211,224,325,
330,335,336
New York University,xi,61
New York World-Telegram,199
Nimitz, Chester W.,305,306
Nisselson, Mike,329
Noah, Mordecai Manuel,251
Norman, Edward A.,316
Norwegian Labor Party,91
Noveck, Simon,301
Nussbaum, Max,263

Office of Jewish Population
Research (OJPR),79,80
Office of War Information
(OWI),xii,39,291
Oheb Shalom, Congregation,
52,317
On Anti-Defamation Hys-
teria,150
Opinion,117,119,170
Organization for Rehabili-
tation Through Training
(ORT),4,50,96,98
Otzar Haposkim,217
Overseas News Agency (ONA),
123,124,127,129,133,136,
333,334

Palestine Economic Corpora-
tion,20
Palestine Foundation Fund
(Keren Hayesod),2,11,16,
50,53,56,231,232,238-242,
254
Palestine Light House,13
Palestine Symphonic Choir,2
Palestine Telegraphic
Agency (PTA),129,133

Palmer,Ely,286
Park Avenue Synagogue,81,
140
Partisan Review,83
Passman, Charles,219
Pat, Jacob,305
Patai, Raphael,319
"Patria, SS,"105
Pegler, Westbrook,310
Pekarsky, Herman,156,164,
185
Penrose, Stephen,276
Perry, Burton Y.,273
Persitz, Shoshanah,143
Perspective,351
Petegorsky, David,ix,148,
159,305,307,308
Philadelphia Jewish Com-
munity Relations Council,
168
Pierce, Richard,229
Pilch, Judah,36,37
Pines, Leon,326
Pioneer Women's Organiza-
tion,2,3,13,142
Pittsburg Platform,99,100
Pittsburg United Jewish
Fund,332
Poale Agudath Israel,5,13,
15
Poale-Zion Organization,3,
50,91,308
Polier, Shad,112,113,307,
308
Pollack, Herman,309,310
Pravda,277
Present Tense,298
Preston, Dixon,229
Princeton University,301
Progressive General Zionist
Party,65,254,255,261,264,
266
Progressive Zionist,167,
258,260-263,266,342
Proskauer, Joseph M.,316
Protocols of the Elders of
Zion,114,115
Rabbinical Assembly,183,
190,253,315
Rabbinical Council (Ortho-
dox),19,82,103,183

366